A Publication Sponsored by the
Society for Industrial and Organizational Psychology, Inc.,
A Division of the American Psychological Association,
and Published by Jossey-Bass Publishers

**Other books in the SIOP/Jossey-Bass
Professional Practice Series**

Employees, Careers, and Job Creation
Manuel London, Editor

Organizational Surveys
Allen I. Kraut, Editor

Performance Appraisal
James W. Smither, Editor

Individual Psychological Assessment
Richard P. Jeanneret and Robert F. Silzer, Editors

Evolving Practices in Human Resource Management
Allen I. Kraut and Abraham K. Korman, Editors

Managing Selection in Changing Organizations

Human Resource Strategies

Jerard F. Kehoe

Editor

Foreword by Eduardo Salas

Jossey-Bass Publishers • San Francisco

Substantial discounts on bulk quantities of Jossey-Bass books are available to corporations, professional associations, and other organizations. For details and discount information, contact the special sales department at Jossey-Bass Inc., Publishers (415) 433–1740; Fax (800) 605–2665.

Jossey-Bass Web address: http://www.josseybass.com

 Manufactured in the United States of America on Lyons Falls Turin Book. This paper is acid-free and 100 percent totally chlorine-free.

Library of Congress Cataloging-in-Publication Data

Managing selection in changing organizations : human resource strategies / Jerard F. Kehoe editor ; foreword by Eduardo Salas.
      p. cm.—(Jossey-Bass business & management series) (Jossey-Bass social and behavioral science series)
      Includes bibliographical references and index.
      ISBN 0-7879-4474-2
      1. Personnel management. 2. Organizational change. I. Kehoe, Jerard F. II. Series. III. Series: Jossey-Bass social and behavioral science series

HF5549.M31385 1999
658.3'112—dc21

99-052731

FIRST EDITION
HB Printing   10 9 8 7 6 5 4 3 2 1

A joint publication in
The Jossey-Bass
Business & Management Series
and
The Jossey-Bass
Social & Behavioral Science Series

Society for Industrial and Organizational Psychology
Professional Practice Series

Contents

Foreword

This is the tenth volume of the Professional Practice Series, sponsored by the Society for Industrial and Organizational Psychology, and with this volume there is a new beginning. There is a new series editor and a new editorial board.

However, the aim of the Professional Practice Series remains the same—influencing organizational practice. That is, the volumes in this series are aimed at showcasing how the theories, ideas, concepts, tools, methods, techniques, and technologies developed in the field of industrial/organizational psychology can shape and guide organizational practice.

These volumes should serve as translation mechanisms for our science, transforming our scientific findings into practical information and tools. Not an easy task. A challenging goal, but realistic and reachable. We will accomplish this, I believe, by providing human resource specialists, managers, executives, and those interested in managing behavior at work with proven principles, guidelines, specifications, tools, and strategies that work, help their practice, and ultimately increase organizational effectiveness. Each volume in this series contributes to this goal. This book is no exception.

This volume is about the practice of selection strategies in rapidly changing organizations. A timely topic for both practitioners and scientists alike. Jerard F. Kehoe was able to assemble an excellent group of industrial/organizational psychologists to write about how selection interfaces with individual, social, and organizational factors. The chapters describe how demographic changes, a union-represented workforce, team membership, cultural differences, legislation, and social policy influence the selection strategy process. The chapters offer many useful and practical insights about the practice of selection strategies in an ever-changing organizational world. This volume is invaluable to those concerned with applying selection processes in organizations and to those who research selecting systems.

A personal note in closing. I would like to thank Kevin Murphy for giving me the opportunity to continue my passion for following the scientist-practitioner model and to help translate what we do as industrial/organizational psychologists into useful applications for organizations. I am honored, as I take over as series editor, to follow in the footsteps of Douglas W. Bray and Manuel London. I would add that Manny made this transition easy and seamless. He is a true professional, and the volumes he edited are indeed a significant contribution to our field. In fact, this volume was developed under his tenure. Manny and his editorial board deserve all the credit for this volume.

I would also like to thank the professional staff at Jossey-Bass—Byron Schneider, Cedric Crocker, and Julianna Gustafson—for their help and support throughout the transition. I look forward to working with them on future volumes.

Finally, I would like to thank my editorial board—Jerry, Scott, Wayne, Tim, Ken, Cathy, Jim, and Ken—for their support, energy, enthusiasm, and commitment to making this series a success.

October 1999   EDUARDO SALAS
University of Central Florida   *Series Editor*

Preface

The purpose of this Professional Practice Series volume on selection is to inform and influence the research about and the practice of selection in organizations, particularly in light of today's rapidly changing context. Significantly, eight of its eleven chapters are authored by industrial/organizational (I/O) psychologists whose primary function is to manage selection programs or consult in their development and management. The remaining three chapters are written by I/O psychologists with considerable professional experience in the application of I/O psychology to selection. So this volume is not so much directed at the practice of selection psychology as it is a forum for selection practitioners to address our scientific profession about the most important issues we face today.

Perhaps the most common thread throughout the chapters is that they place selection strategy management squarely in an organizational and social context. As a whole, this volume portrays the management of selection strategies as business decisions made by scientific professionals who are informed by research and influenced by a wide variety of organizational, individual, and social conditions. While acknowledging the primacy of research as the foundation of our practice, the authors challenge our research and profession to continue to expand beyond a central focus on selection procedures in order to address organizational, social, and individual factors that affect the usefulness, appropriateness, and likely success of specific strategies.

Most chapters are not intended to be a primary source or summary of research evidence on selection procedures themselves; other sources have served that purpose well. (Although some chapters do serve that purpose where there is a unique contribution to make, such as the chapter on accommodations by Campbell and Reilly, the chapter on selection in team settings by Jones, Stevens, and Fischer, and the chapter on "customers" of selection strategies by Gilliland and Cherry.) Most chapters describe, analyze, and evaluate the relationships between selection and other organizational, social, and individual factors.

Overview of the Contents

The chapters are organized into three parts: Organizational Context, Regulatory Context, and Professional Context. Because organizational context is the primary focus of this volume, seven of the eleven chapters are in Part One; there are two chapters in each of the other parts.

Part One begins with Pearlman and Barney in Chapter One, who provide a comprehensive overview of business process changes and demographic changes. They develop models of work components and worker skills and use these models to help evaluate the likely impact of work and worker changes on the management of selection strategies. This chapter provides a disciplined summary of the changes that are likely to have significant implications for selection and establishes the context for this part of the book. In Chapter Two, Higgs, Papper, and Carr review the linkages between selection and other organizational processes and systems, particularly focusing on those relating to human resource management. These within-organization linkages are becoming increasingly critical to the success of selection strategies as organizations demand more integrated and efficient business practices. Also, the prospects for such linkages are becoming more apparent to business managers as worker attribute models (for example, competency models) are being associated with other organizational processes.

In Chapter Three, Jayne and Rauschenberger describe, analyze, and evaluate selection in terms of organizational metrics and values that reflect the linkages discussed in Chapter Two. This is not a matter simply of translating quantitative utility assessments into managerial terminology but also of identifying and distinguishing the values of the different stakeholders who influence the success of selection strategies. In Chapter Four, Gilliland and Bennett provide a comprehensive summary and analysis of the ways in which people are affected by and respond to their experience with selection processes. The theme of this chapter is that selection programs are increasingly subject to the same types of business analysis as are such other programs as compensation, benefits, and the like.

Whereas Chapters One through Four address issues common to virtually all large organizations today, Chapters Five through Seven treat selection topics that may be more relevant to some organizations than others. In Chapter Five, Bownas comments on the management of selection programs in organizations whose workforces are unionized. This chapter offers insights into union and management perspectives relating to organizations' selection practices. In Chapter Six, Jones, Stevens, and Fischer address the complex issue of selection for teams, summarizing a wide range of research and offering guiding principles for selection program managers who must make decisions about team-oriented selection strategies. This chapter also has value for readers who are responsible for the development and management of work in team contexts. Finally, in Chapter Seven, Nyfield and Baron describe and evaluate cultural differences that influence the appropriateness and success of selection strategies across borders. The authors identify key underlying differences between cultures that are important to consider when developing single cross-cultural applications or multiple within-culture applications.

The two chapters in Part Two advance our understanding of the regulatory environment that influences most important selection program decisions. Chapter Eight by Sharf and Jones presents a comprehensive analysis of case law relating to employment discrimination in order to assess relative degrees of legal risk for employers. In Chapter Nine, Campbell and Reilly focus on the issues associated with accommodating selection procedures under the Americans with Disabilities Act (ADA). This chapter provides a structured reference tool that summarizes relevant research and analyzes types of accommodations in a variety of circumstances that selection program managers frequently face. Like Chapter Eight, the chapter provides a comprehensive summary of the relevant legislation and case law that selection managers must consider in this area where there is so little research to inform good decisions.

The chapters in Part Three address the professional context that shapes and governs most research and decisions about selection practices. The purpose of this part of the book is to enhance our profession's support of selection practice in organizations. In Chapter Ten, Zedeck and Goldstein comment on the relationship between research and social policy. Our field of selection psychology has strongly influenced and been strongly influenced by equal employment opportunity policies. Our professional debates frequently pivot on social policy values as well as scientific values. From their considerable experience, particularly in public sector selection work, Zedeck and Goldstein offer a point of view about the involvement of selection science and selection scientists in the development, evaluation, and advocacy of social policies. This chapter provides a framework for further professional discussion about the social value of our science and the manner in which it remains neutral while also advancing individual and organizational well-being. In Chapter Eleven, Kehoe addresses the somewhat narrower topics of professional governance and research direction. This chapter calls attention to the types of research that will advance the practice of selection and evaluates current professional governance by comparing it with the current demands of selection practice.

As a whole, this volume attempts to serve the interests of professionally applied selection practices by informing not only practitioners but also researchers and our scientific professional community about the key organizational, regulatory, and professional issues that our applied field faces today.

Acknowledgments

The authors of the chapters that follow provided an invaluable learning experience for me as they transformed broad notions about their chapters into focused and valuable contributions beyond what I imagined. Each of these authors donated their time out of sincere dedication to our profession and its contribution to the well-being of organizations and the individuals in them. The value of this volume stems directly from their collective experience and insight. I am grateful to them.

I would also like to thank the Professional Practice Series editorial board of the Society for Industrial and Organizational Psychology for their insight and enthusiasm in shaping the direction of this volume. In particular, both Manny London and Ed Salas, as earlier and later series editors, provided valuable encouragement and support. Also, I would like to thank Ken Pearlman and Jim Smither for their unerring advice and counsel whenever I asked for it.

Finally, I would like to thank Byron Schneider and Julianna Gustafson at Jossey-Bass for their unflagging support. They kept a very steady hand on the rudder and were always enthusiastically positive about the success of this book.

October 1999   JERARD F. KEHOE
Morristown, New Jersey

The Authors

JERARD F. KEHOE received his doctorate in quantitative psychology from the University of Southern California in 1975. After serving on Virginia Tech's psychology faculty in the applied behavior sciences program, he joined AT&T in 1982, where he has been responsible for selection programs in manufacturing, customer sales and service, and management jobs. Currently the sourcing and selection director, he is responsible for AT&T's selection policies, strategies, and practices. Kehoe has been active professionally, with several publications and conference presentations on selection topics including computerized testing, fairness, and test validity. He has served on several professional committees including the American Psychological Association's Division 5 (as program chair in 1987), Society for Industrial and Organizational Psychology (SIOP) subcommittees, a National Skills Standards Board advisory committee, and the Equal Employment Advisory Council's subcommittee on testing standards.

Matthew F. Barney is responsible for technology program management in the Learning and Performance Center of Lucent Technologies Inc. He earned his Ph.D. in industrial/organizational psychology from the University of Tulsa in 1996. Prior to his current role, he was responsible for worldwide HR strategy for Lucent's Microelectronics Business Unit. Barney's research and practice interests focus on linking worldwide human resource interventions to strategic business problems and using technology to solve I/O and HR problems. He is principal author of several U.S. patents that are pending and has presented papers on strategic integrated HR systems. He is a member of the Society for Industrial and Organizational Psychology and the American Psychological Association.

Helen Baron is deputy director for research and development at SHL Group plc, an international consultancy and test publisher. Baron received her master's in psychology from the Hebrew University of Jerusalem in 1988 and worked in both clinical and educational spheres before moving to the occupational field. Her work with SHL includes psychometric test development, selection and equal opportunities consultancy, and advising on the adaptation of materials for use around the world. In addition to her work on published psychometric instruments, she has authored and coauthored articles and chapters on fairness in selection, testing people with disabilities and motivation, and technical psychometric topics.

David A. Bownas is deputy director of personnel systems at Metro-North Railroad in New York City. He earned his Ph.D. in industrial psychology at the University of Minnesota in 1982. He managed test development research projects at Personnel Decisions Research Institute for six years, then worked in the psychology department at Virginia Polytechnic Institute and State University for four years. He currently directs the selection test development function at Metro-North, a company with fifty-four hundred employees represented by nineteen different union organizations.

Wanda J. Campbell is the director of employment testing at Edison Electric Institute. She earned her Ph.D. in industrial/organizational psychology from Old Dominion University in Norfolk, Virginia, in 1990. She worked as an equal opportunity specialist with the Equal Employment Opportunity Commission for five years and as a compliance officer for the wage-hour division of the Department of Labor for a year. Currently chair of the SIOP public affairs subcommittee in charge of the development of a membership referral system, Campbell has been actively involved in the Personnel Testing Council of Metropolitan Washington. She was the senior author on "Employment Testing in Private Industry," a chapter in *The Handbook on Testing* (1997), which was written with David Kleinke. Campbell is particularly interested in employment law and the practical application of I/O psychology to the workplace.

Linda S. Carr is a senior staff research analyst in workforce research at the Allstate Research and Planning Center, Allstate Insurance

Company. Previously, she was a consultant with HRSrategies (now Aon Corporation). She has designed several tests and selection programs for Allstate and other organizations. Her research has focused on a wide range of topics, including diversity, employee benefits, survey design, linking management behavior to customer satisfaction and organizational performance, and compensation systems. Carr's particular interest is in legal issues in HR processes and the use of information processing theory in the design of selection tools. A 1992 graduate of the University of Akron with a Ph.D. in industrial and organizational psychology, she is a member of the Society for Industrial and Organizational Psychology, the SIOP Job Analysis and Competency Modeling Task Force, and the Upward Feedback Forum.

Bennett Cherry, a doctoral student in the Department of Management and Policy at the University of Arizona, plans to receive his Ph.D. in May 2000. Before he obtained his master's degree at the university in 1997, he worked for SENTRE Partners, a commercial real estate firm, where he developed strategic real estate plans for multimillion dollar commercial properties in southern California. His primary research focuses on the notion of dyadic trust, and he has looked into individuals' justice and fairness considerations and how these relate to their expectations. Cherry is an active member of the Academy of Management, the Society for Industrial and Organizational Psychology, the Society for Human Resource Management, and the Society for Judgment and Decision Making.

Donald L. Fischer received his Ph.D. from The Ohio State University in 1980. He is a licensed psychologist and associate professor in the psychology department at Southwest Missouri State University in Springfield, where he has been employed since obtaining his Ph.D. Fischer teaches both graduate and undergraduate courses in psychology, in addition to supervising student field experiences and conducting training workshops for area employers through the university's Management Development Institute. He has worked as a substance abuse counselor and developed the "Curriculum Guide for Weekend Intervention Programs" for the Missouri Department of Mental Health. He has been active in the American Psychological Association, the Society for Personality Assessment, and the Society for Industrial and Organizational Psychology, and has held elected office in the Missouri Psychological Association and the Ozarks Area Psychological Association.

Stephen W. Gilliland is an associate professor and the FINOVA Fellow of Management and Policy in the College of Business and Public Administration at the University of Arizona. He received his Ph.D. in 1992 from Michigan State University and was previously on the faculty at Louisiana State University. He serves on the editorial boards of the *Academy of Management Journal, Journal of Applied Psychology,* and *Personnel Psychology.* He is the 1997 recipient of the Society for Industrial and Organizational Psychology's Ernest J. McCormick Award for distinguished early career contributions. With primary research interests in the justice and fairness of human resource practices and policies, he has authored or coauthored over fifty published papers and conference presentations. His consulting and executive education work has addressed issues involving managerial communication and goal setting, team development, strategic planning, and designing and implementing effective performance management systems.

Irwin L. Goldstein served as professor and chair of the psychology department of the University of Maryland at College Park from 1981 to 1991, when he became professor and dean of the College of Behavioral and Social Sciences. Goldstein's research career as an industrial/organizational psychologist has focused on issues facing individuals entering work organizations, including understanding and resolving race and gender discrimination. The third edition of his book *Training in Organizations* was published in 1993. He is also author of the training chapter in the *Handbook of Industrial and Organizational Psychology* and editor of the 1989 Frontiers Series volume *Training and Development in Organizations.* In 1992, he received the Society for Industrial and Organizational Psychology's Distinguished Service Award; in 1995, he received the American Society for Training and Development's Swanson Award for research excellence. Goldstein has been president of the Society for Industrial and Organizational Psychology and is a fellow of the American Psychological Association, the American Psychological Society, and the Human Factors Society.

A. Catherine Higgs is executive research director for strategic business research at the Allstate Research and Planning Center, Allstate Insurance Company. For over a decade she has directed research staff on a wide range of topics, including economic effects of human resource decisions, management policy and practices, workforce strategy and forecasting, organizational design and effectiveness, measurement of organizational performance and productivity, management and employee selection and performance, and communication programs. She is a member of the Professional Practice Series editorial board for the Society for Industrial and Organizational Psychology, is secretary-treasurer of the SIOP Foundation, and has chaired the SIOP professional practice committee and the continuing education and workshop committee. She received her Ph.D. in social and quantitative psychology from the University of Maryland in 1974.

Michele E. A. Jayne is personnel research services manager for Ford Motor Company, where she is responsible for managing Ford's Global Salaried Employee Selection Project. Her work focuses on developing competency-based selection systems for entry-level salaried positions globally. Previously, she assisted in the launch of Ford's first intranet-based global employee opinion survey. Jayne is a member of the Society for Industrial and Organizational Psychology and the American Psychological Association, is currently the secretary-treasurer elect for the Michigan Association of Industrial and Organizational Psychology, and is a member of the International Selection and Assessment Council, a consortium of fifteen major companies dedicated to sharing current practices in employee selection and placement. She received her Ph.D. in I/O psychology from Tulane University in 1994.

David P. Jones is president of The Human Resources Consulting Group, Aon Consulting. Under his leadership, the company is recognized as one of the nation's preeminent employee assessment and development organizations. Employing over five hundred people at offices across the country, it assists corporations in reengineering and organizational transition, employee selection, performance measurement, skills assessment, and litigation support, and it specializes in the introduction of high-performance systems and empowered leadership systems. Jones, who holds a Ph.D. in industrial/organizational psychology, has served as a consultant to major organizations for twenty years. He is a member of the American Psychological Association, the Society for Industrial and Organizational Psychology, the American Compensation Association, and the Society for Human Resource Management. He has written articles on employee skills assessments, the Americans with Disabilities Act, workforce diversity, corporate transitions, and related subjects, and he has appeared on television and radio programs to discuss human resource issues.

Robert G. Jones is associate professor of psychology at Southwest Missouri State University in Springfield. Previously he served as internal consultant to a large insurance company during its conversion to team structures. Before receiving his Ph.D. in industrial/organizational psychology from Ohio State in 1992, Jones had dual careers as banker (by day) and musician (by night). His interest in team functioning dates back to his involvement in musical ensembles; his work with Richard Klimoski on team selection (for the Jossey-Bass SIOP Frontiers Series) solidified this interest. He has published in *Personnel Psychology, Human Resource Management Review,* and *Journal of Business and Psychology,* and is active in the SIOP and the Academy of Management.

Gill Nyfield is a director of SHL Group plc, where for over five years she has been responsible for the research and development program. She obtained her degree in psychology at the University of Newcastle-upon-Tyne, United Kingdom, in 1974, before joining the test department of the National Foundation for Educational Research in England and Wales. Nyfield has been with SHL for nearly twenty years, from its start as a small U.K.–based company. Her work has involved considerable psychometric test development of both cognitive and behavioral tests, including adaptations to different countries and cultures. As a consultant, she has worked with major organizations in the public and private sectors, designing and implementing selection and assessment procedures, and she has written articles and papers on related topics.

Ellen M. Papper is a senior research manager in workforce research at the Allstate Research and Planning Center, Allstate Insurance

Company. She conducts research on topics including personnel selection, employee attitude and behavioral measurement, program effectiveness evaluation, employee communications, and external stakeholders' perceptions of the organization. Before joining Allstate, she was manager of human resource planning at Baxter Healthcare Corporation, with responsibility for selection, surveys, and performance management. Papper is a member of the Society for Industrial and Organizational Psychology. She received her Ph.D. in industrial/organizational psychology from Bowling Green State University in 1983.

Kenneth Pearlman directs the measurement and selection systems group at Lucent Technologies Inc. (formerly AT&T), where he has been responsible for personnel selection research and development since 1983. He also has a courtesy appointment as professor of industrial/organizational psychology at the University of South Florida. He has written extensively on job family development, cumulative analysis of research results, and the productivity implications of person-job matching procedures and systems, and was senior editor of the 1983 readings text *Contemporary Problems in Personnel*. Pearlman is a fellow of the American Psychological Association, the American Psychological Society, and the Society for Industrial and Organizational Psychology. He received his Ph.D. in industrial and organizational psychology in 1982 from the George Washington University.

John M. Rauschenberger is manager of personnel research at Ford Motor Company's Personnel Research & Development Office, where he is responsible for salaried selection practices, employee opinion assessment, and external education relations. He was an active participant on the Michigan Employability Skills Task Force of the Governor's Commission on Jobs and Economic Development and more recently in the school-to-work efforts of the National Employer Leadership Council. He is the chair of the Manufacturing Skills Standards Council's steering committee. A charter member of the American Psychological Society, he also is a past president of the Michigan Association of Industrial and Organizational Psychologists, and holds active memberships in the Society for Industrial and Organizational Psychology and the Academy of Management. He is the author and coauthor of research articles and has been an editorial board member on *Personnel Psychology*. Rauschenberger earned his Ph.D. degree in industrial psychology from Michigan State University in 1978.

Maureen E. Reilly practices law as an associate in the labor and employment section of the Philadelphia office of Morgan, Lewis & Bockius LLP, where she counsels and represents employers on labor relations, employment discrimination, wrongful discharge, and employment policies. Her law degree is from the University of Virginia School of Law, where she received an award from the Bureau of National Affairs for excellence in the study of labor and employment law. She received her Ph.D. in industrial/organizational psychology from George Mason University in 1994. Reilly has spoken and written articles on a variety of labor and employment issues, with an emphasis on employment testing and the Americans with Disabilities Act. She is the coauthor with E. A. Fleishman of *Human Abilities: Their Structure, Measurement, and Job Task Requirements* (1991).

James C. Sharf is president of Sharf & Associates, employment risk advisers. He has taught on the graduate faculties of the American University and the George Washington University. In the mid-1970s, he served as chief psychologist at EEOC, for which he negotiated the 1978 *Uniform Guidelines on Employee Selection Procedures*. Later, he was special assistant to the chairman of EEOC and drafted the race norming prohibition in the Civil Rights Act of 1991. He has testified as an expert for both EEOC and the civil rights division at the U.S. Department of Justice and provided risk management advice, expert testimony, and litigation support to employment attorneys nationwide. He was a contributing editor of *The Industrial-Organizational Psychologist* for over twenty years, has published articles and book chapters, and has been guest editor of several journals. His research specialty in biodata culminated in the chapter on legal and EEO issues and personal history inquiries in *The Biodata Handbook: Theory, Research, and Application* (1992). A fellow of both the Society for Industrial and Organizational Psychology and the American Psychological Association, Scharf obtained his Ph.D. in organizational psychology from the University of Tennessee in 1970.

Michael J. Stevens is director of consulting at Psychological Associates, a consulting firm based in St. Louis. His primary areas of expertise include improving organizational performance through empowerment and teamwork systems, individual assessment and selection (especially for teams), leadership development, and employee motivation and reward systems. He received his Ph.D. from the Krannert School of Management at Purdue University and won the Ralph G. Alexander Best Dissertation Award from the human resources division of the National Academy of Management. He has published articles in respected management journals and regularly gives presentations at professional conferences. He is also principal author of the Teamwork-KSA Test, an employment test widely used in industry to measure aptitude for working successfully in a self-directed team environment. Stevens is active in several professional societies and has held management positions in industry, government, and nonprofit organizations.

Sheldon Zedeck has been at the University of California at Berkeley since 1969, after completing his Ph.D. in industrial and organizational psychology at Bowling Green State University in Ohio. He has served as chair of the Psychology Department and as director of the Institute of Industrial Relations. He has coauthored four books relating to research in organizations, edited the book *Work, Family, and Organizations,* which appeared in the Society for Industrial and Organizational Psychology's Frontiers Series, and served as series editor on the Frontiers Series. Zedeck has written journal articles, book chapters, and conference presentations on topics ranging from research methodology, validity, selection strategies, test fairness, performance assessment, and stress, to work and family issues. He has served on the editorial boards of journals including the *Journal of Applied Psychology, Contemporary Psychology,* and *Industrial Relations,* and as associate editor for *Human Performance.* A past president and fellow of SIOP, he has had extensive applied experience in both public and private sector applications of selection strategies.

PART 1

Organizational Context

CHAPTER 1

Selection for a Changing Workplace

Kenneth Pearlman
Matthew F. Barney

The twenty-first-century workplace has arrived—a few years early. Sweeping economic, demographic, and technological changes have, seemingly overnight, reshaped the U.S. workplace in such fundamental ways as to be considered by many to constitute a new industrial revolution—with one important difference: it is happening about ten times faster than the transition from an agrarian to an industrial society did (Maney, 1998). In just the last ten years organizations have been almost literally turned upside down, with customers now placed at the top of many organization charts and CEOs at the bottom. In between, instead of a well-ordered, hierarchically arranged series of functional boxes and job titles, we now often find a bewildering array of overlapping circles, dotted lines, process flows, and interacting roles performed by people with job titles like "associate," "team member," and "coach"—and by people who are not even company employees. As dramatic as these developments have been, the pace of change appears, if anything, to be accelerating, and the unrelenting demands and stresses that changes inevitably bring are clearly taking their toll on both employers and employees. As one commentator at a recent conference symposium on planning for work in the twenty-first century noted: "Business strategies are changing faster than workers can respond. Technology is changing faster than the workers who can use it.

Work environments are changing faster than the workers who work in them. Organizational cultures and climates are changing faster than the workers can adapt. And management structures and systems are changing faster than workers can accommodate" (Jeanneret, 1998).

This state of affairs has created unprecedented challenges for the field of personnel selection, which refers to the various procedures, tools, and methods used to screen people for jobs or evaluate applicants' job qualifications. Selection procedures encompass such things as aptitude or ability tests; performance or skill tests; physical ability tests; assessment centers, job simulations, and work samples; structured or unstructured interviews; personality, interest, or background data inventories; and systematic or structured evaluations of education, training, or work experience. Although we most often think of selection procedures as applying to the screening of applicants for initial employment in an organization, they can also apply to the evaluation of people already in an organization for transfers, promotions, international assignments, job or skill certification, demotions, or outplacement.

The basic proposition underlying personnel selection is so simple as to be almost a truism: if you want effective job performance and high productivity, pick good people. By itself, this statement is about as helpful as stock market advice to buy low and sell high. The devil, as they say, is in the details. How do we define effective job performance? What do we mean by "good" people, and how do we measure this quality? Nevertheless, a wide array of tools and methods has evolved in personnel selection research and practice over many decades—dating back to the early twentieth century—with which such problems have been effectively addressed. This area is clearly one of the most well-established and well-researched in human resource (HR) practice in modern industrial society.

The procedures through which selection tools traditionally have been developed are conceptually straightforward. First, the job to be selected for is systematically analyzed using any of a variety of task- or behavior-based job analysis methods. Second, the job analysis results are used to develop job performance criterion measures. Third, the knowledge, skills, abilities, and other worker characteristics (KSAOs) likely to underlie performance of the important tasks and behaviors found in the job analysis are identified or derived. Fourth, measures (tests or assessments) of these KSAOs are identified or developed. And fifth, these measures are validated either by judgment-based linkages to important tasks or behaviors (as in a content validity strategy, or as part of a construct validity strategy, along with elements of the fourth step) or by gathering empirical data demonstrating that people who score higher on the KSAO measures actually perform better on the job (as measured on the performance criteria developed in the second step) than people who score lower on these measures (as in criterion-related validity strategies).

Selection tools developed through such methods have served organizations well for a very long time. In fact, during the last twenty years or so, personnel selection researchers have demonstrated empirically through selection process *utility analyses* what astute managers and leaders have intuitively known for centuries: good selection pays off big-time. This research has shown that valid selection procedures usually produce dollar benefits (or productivity gains that translate into dollar benefits) that are often tens or hundreds of times greater than their costs (Schmidt, Hunter, McKenzie, & Muldrow, 1979). For example, we have found that high-level salespeople selected through a combination of aptitude testing and an assessment center generate, on average, over $100,000 more new revenue annually than salespeople selected through a less valid process (informal resume review and unstructured hiring manager interview). Compared with the cost ($3,000 on average) of getting one qualified candidate (by testing and assessing an average of five applicants at a cost of $600 each), this represents a return on investment of over 3,300 percent—and this benefit continues to accrue over each year of an employee's tenure. For large organizations that select perhaps hundreds of such salespeople each year, the utility (dollar benefits minus costs) of valid selection can amount to tens of millions of dollars annually.

Another way to look at the benefits of the traditional selection model is in terms of the time and costs involved in each of the four typical stages or processes by which prospective job applicants are "transmuted" into productive employees, as displayed in Table 1.1.

It can be seen from this table that the standardized selection process is by far the quickest and least expensive means of creating employee value.

**Table 1.1. Typical Time and
Costs of Different Stages of Employment.**

Employment Stage	Time Required	Cost per Applicant
Recruitment	1 to 16 weeks	$80 to $10,000
Standardized selection process	1 to 16 hours	$25 to $1,000
Formal training	1 to 12 months	$10,000 to $100,000
Job tryout/probationary period	3 to 24 months	$25,000 to $200,000

At an even simpler level of analysis, in our own work we often speak about the hiring of an employee as "the $5 million decision" in discussions and presentations about selection to other HR staff and line managers. We make the point that, putting aside all the sophisticated utility models and cost-benefit analyses, on average across all jobs every person hired represents an investment of a whole lot of money, usually between $2 million and $8 million, factoring in the salary, overhead, training, and benefits paid on behalf of an employee over the length of a career. Our conclusion is that this makes it well worth the modest amount of an organization's time, cost, and resources required to do it well. Formal standardized selection programs rarely cost more than $1,000 per applicant or add more than two days to the length of the hiring process. This means that the time and cost spent on good selection is truly minuscule relative to the investment it represents and the dollar benefits that can accrue.

Although the basic selection proposition—pick good people to get good performance—is not much different now than it has always been, the changing workplace is dramatically redefining what lies just beneath this truism. The purpose of this chapter is to create a better understanding of the changing workplace and the challenges it presents for personnel selection. We draw heavily on our own experience as personnel-industrial psychology practitioners who have witnessed firsthand the process of large organizations reshaping themselves in response to a rapidly changing world and who at one time or another have had to grapple with most of the issues and challenges described. Wherever possible, we try to present various facets of these issues and alternative ways to approach them from a practitioner's perspective.

The first section of the chapter describes the main antecedents of the workplace changes and discusses the nature of their effects on organizations. The second section of the chapter deals with possible means for conceptualizing and analyzing the nature of work from both theoretical and applied standpoints. This section begins by presenting a general model of work performance as an integrative framework for better understanding the relationship between the various elements of the changed workplace and the worker attributes we measure in selection programs. It goes on to discuss several recent trends in the practical analysis of work, including an innovative software tool we developed at Lucent Technologies Inc. that provides a technology-based means of leveraging facets of the work performance model into selection program design.

The discussion of the third section of the chapter is based on our belief that recent and emerging workplace changes necessitate rethinking virtually every facet of personnel selection systems: selection system strategy (what we want selection programs to predict), selection system content (what we want selection programs to measure), and selection system design and operation (how we design, integrate, and implement the components of operational selection systems). We consider a variety of specific issues related to each of these new challenges.

Finally, the appendix presents a case study from our own experience that illustrates at least one way to address a complex selection problem that is fairly representative of the selection issues and challenges faced in modern high-technology workplaces.

The Changed Workplace

The massive reshaping of the modern workplace that has taken place in just the last ten to fifteen years has been chronicled in numerous sources and analyzed and described in various ways (Cascio, 1995; Coates, Jarratt, & Mahaffie, 1990; Johnston & Packer, 1987; Offerman & Gowing, 1993; Reich, 1991).

Three Influences

It is generally agreed that these workplace changes are most immediately the result of three developments or influences: *economic, demographic,* and *technological.*

Economic Influences

The emergence within the last decade or two of a truly global economy has created business competition—and interdependence—the likes of which has never before been seen. The effect of global competition for products, markets, supplies, and labor has been pervasive, affecting small and large companies alike, and is undoubtedly the single most influential factor affecting changes in the workplace. Spurred on by a combination of new international trade and licensing agreements, democratic reforms in formerly totalitarian countries, the increasingly unobstructed movement of capital, products, and resources across the globe, and virtually instantaneous worldwide access to data and information over the Internet, U.S. companies' exposure to international competition has increased at least tenfold between the 1960s and the 1980s (Cascio, 1995). Consequently, the effectiveness and profitability of many organizations have become increasingly dependent on their ability to penetrate and compete in global markets that are being continuously redefined.

The global economy has also given rise to a new level of global economic interdependence—among producers, suppliers, and business and trading partners across the world. Problems in the Asian economy are affecting job growth in the United States. Digital Signal Processing (DSP) chip designs from Bangalore, India, compete with those in Silicon Valley, Ireland, and Israel. Companies that were formerly exclusively U.S.–based are reaching out to form alliances or partnerships with non–U.S. companies to strengthen their competitive position at home and enter new markets abroad.

In addition, domestic competition has increased dramatically as a result of deregulation in such industries as telecommunications, banking, and airlines. Taken together, these factors have created unrelenting competitive pressure on companies, boards of directors, and CEOs to innovate, build new kinds of strategic partnerships, shorten product and service development and delivery cycles, cut costs, and maintain quality—in other words, to build and maintain "high-performance" companies that create shareholder value and produce consistently strong bottom-line results.

Demographic Influences

Changes in the character and makeup of the labor market have seemed less dramatic than the economic influences because they have occurred a bit more gradually, but they are no less profound in their impact on organizations. Perhaps most salient has been the changing composition of the U.S. workforce in gender, ethnicity, and culture, a consequence of slowing U.S. population and workforce growth coupled with rapid world workforce growth. As a result, more women, minorities, and immigrants are in the available labor force, with white males representing only 15 percent of the projected net increase in the workforce over the next ten years (Coates et. al, 1990). Of particular relevance for emerging technology-related businesses and industries is increasing diversity in the culture and gender of the scientific, engineering, and technical workforce. Another important trend is the changing age distribution of the workforce. Slower U.S. population growth has meant that significantly fewer young people are entering the job market than ever before, leading to a shrinking pool of entry-level talent and greater competition among organizations for their services.

As a result of these trends, there have been severe skill and knowledge shortages in many critical work areas and industries— the much-written-about *skills gap*. That is, the demand for an increasing array and level of skills, particularly in a technology-driven global economy, has begun to outstrip the supply in the labor market. In the United States, these problems have been exacerbated by the continued shift from a manufacturing to a service economy, a concomitant decline in hands-on production-oriented work, and an increase in technology-driven service-oriented work for which many new entrants into the labor market are ill-equipped (Offerman & Gowing, 1993).

Other demographic trends include shifts in worker lifestyles and attitudes. The last two decades have witnessed dramatic increases in single-parent households, dual-income families, dual-career couples, and unfortunately, an underclass of disadvantaged, disaffected people. In addition, today's workers have increasingly high expectations of work, which are reflected in their desire for greater autonomy and personal opportunities, career development, and a better balance between work and family life (Hall & Richter, 1990).

Technological Influences

Advancements in technology continue to reshape virtually all aspects of work, at all levels and in all types of industries. The last few years have witnessed one major technology explosion after another: Internet- and Web-based information dissemination, communication over wireless networks, intelligent voice and data communication systems, fully automated production processes based on robotics and artificial intelligence that have vastly sped up product and service development and delivery cycles, and of course, continued advances in personal computer and software applications, which are turning formerly lengthy, complex projects into relatively simple, routine tasks. In particular, the widespread availability and use of personal computers, electronic mail, facsimile machines, wireless communications, and the Internet have massively increased the speed with which large amounts of information can be accessed and shared; it has also fundamentally changed the way in which services are provided and business is conducted in many industries. For example, consider how the use of interactive-voice-response (IVR) telephone technology has reshaped the delivery of customer services in virtually every industry. Or even more dramatically, consider how the Internet is revolutionizing both business- and consumer-oriented commerce. It is rapidly creating an entirely new "networked economy" made up of an evolving system of what have been dubbed "e-business communities": electronic networks of suppliers, distributors, commerce providers, customers, and even competitors who produce products and services by exchanging information on-line. These communities are projected to generate more than $526 billion in revenue by the year 2002 (Maney, 1998; Tapscott, 1998). They are "reshaping entire industries, and in many sectors of the economy, destroying the concept of the company as we know it" (Tapscott, 1998, p. 1E).

Technological developments are radically altering how work gets done, by whom it gets done, and the skills and knowledge required to get it done. For example, consider how easily programmable software has begun to enable nontechnologists to have tasks performed around-the-clock on a worldwide basis, whether or not they are present to pay attention to them. Some computer experts expect this easy-to-program "reusable" software to be one of the great advances in productivity improvement in the next few years (Seltzer, 1998). One potential use of such technology is to perform traditional wage and salary surveys with little effort. Compensation analysts can use their Web browsers to specify the types of data they would like to share with others and create a variety of software "robots" that use their rules to exchange information ("Don't exchange salary data with company X unless it has data set Z"). Many mundane and laborious tasks, such as wage and salary surveying, can simply be embodied in software, with the human worker supervising and interpreting the meaning of results. Under such a scenario, the compensation analyst is, in effect, performing simplified computer programming that formerly was the province of computer scientists and software engineers. In a similar vein, Lucent Technologies Inc. has a patent pending on a system that would allow automated benchmarking by "intelligent agents" that work perpetually over the Internet (Barney, 1998).

In sum, advances in technology are overturning traditional concepts of work, location, space, and time, while enabling people almost instantaneously to access, create, or exchange vast amounts of information and work together in real time from virtually anywhere in the world.

Effects of Changes on Organizations

The economic, demographic, and technological developments described have in one way or another affected virtually all types of organizations (not just large or high-tech organizations) and virtually every aspect of organizational functioning, often in fundamental ways. Unrelenting global and domestic competition causes organizations to continue to reshape and reinvent themselves in order to keep their costs down while maintaining quality products and services. They seem to be constantly breaking up, downsizing, rightsizing, and restructuring, as well as participating in mergers, acquisitions, buyouts, and newer forms of strategic partnerships and alliances with vendors, suppliers, agents, and even competitors. In the past, organizational efficiencies were usually achieved through vertical integration, mass production, economies of scale, and long production runs. However, such strategies are no longer sufficiently flexible to meet the rapidly changing—and rapidly escalating—demands of a global marketplace in which customers don't care about their suppliers' problems but only about results. Many products are nearly obsolete by the time they hit the market. As we heard one manufacturing executive recently state (paraphrasing Vince Lombardi's well-known football philosophy), "Time to market isn't everything—it's the only thing. It's what matters." In this unforgiving economic environment, a missed opportunity (for example, because of a slow or bureaucratic decision or "permission" process or an inefficient product or service delivery system) can mean a failed business. Furthermore, the costs and consequences of human errors or equipment failures are often extremely high. In one recent example, a communications satellite failure shut down most U.S. wireless pager communications for almost a day.

Changes in Organizational Strategy, Structure, and Culture

Organizations have developed a variety of new strategies, structures, and internal "cultures" in response to these new challenges. Strategically, organizations are shifting to a production model based on flexible automation, real-time and on-line quality control, and the deployment of horizontally integrated networks of specialists and professionals. Such strategies enable more rapid integration of new technology (usually termed *reengineering*) into product and service development and delivery processes. In addition, organizations are focusing on their "core competencies" and relying to ever-greater degrees on purchased components and outsourced services for many staff and support functions. They are making greater use of contingent workers—temporary and part-time workers, contractors, consultants, "life-of-project" workers, and leased employees—rather than maintaining a large (and costly) internal force of employees. This strategy gives organizations greater structural flexibility, enabling them more easily (and more cheaply) to expand and contract the size and composition of their workforce as needed to adapt to unpredictable market conditions. Organizations are focusing on speed, quality, and customer service in all their processes and products, not merely as organization values but as genuine business strategies. And they are adopting new and innovative HR strategies (such as pay for skills, flexible work schedules, nontraditional work arrangements like telecommuting and job sharing, and "family-friendly" policies like on-site child care) that reflect adaptation to changing demographics and competitive pressures.

Competitive pressures have also made it increasingly necessary for organizations to adopt new structures that better enable them to capitalize on ever-smaller windows of opportunity to respond to changing market conditions and demands. Traditional organizational boundaries are shrinking, both vertically (with fewer layers of management) and horizontally (across departments and work groups), promoting greater responsiveness to customers as well as decision making that is quicker and closer to the points of production or service. This trend has been abetted enormously by high-speed information and communications technologies that have further reduced the temporal, geographic, and task boundaries by which organizations and work have been defined for centuries. At the same time, organizational structures and boundaries have become more fluid, a trend perhaps best exemplified by the steadily increasing use of different types of work teams (such as autonomous or semiautonomous teams, process teams, cross-functional teams, quality teams, task forces, self-managing work teams, and so forth) that vary in permanence and composition. Driven primarily by the growing interdependence of increasingly specialized work activities that require a combination of skills and knowledge rarely found in a single individual, the practice of bringing specialists from different departments together for particular work initiatives also serves as a mechanism by which organizations can maintain flexibility and fluidity of structure.

Organizations' cultures—that is, the complex of shared values and operating styles that shape and define the social and psychological environment in which people work—have also been undergoing profound change. Because most fields of work depend on new and constantly changing technology and because of competitive pressures in the marketplace, organizations place ever-greater value on their *intellectual capital*—the aggregate knowledge and skill base of their workforce—as a key competitive advantage. As a result, more and more organizations have embraced the need for continuous learning on the part of all employees and have sought ways to create "learning cultures" and "learning organizations" to nurture this expanding class of knowledge workers (Senge, 1990). Organizations are also paying more attention to the contextual aspects of work performance that facilitate the performance of others and of the organization as a whole (this is described further in the next section) in order to enhance quality of work life and maintain competitiveness and service quality in today's results-oriented climate. They are adopting a "tools, not rules" philosophy, doing away with hard-and-fast one-size-fits-all corporate policies and replacing them with more flexibility and choice; as an example, many organizations' benefit packages now offer a dizzying array of options and alternative structures for retirement, health and medical, vacation, and insurance plans. Organizations are creating cultures that champion speed, quality, continuous process improvement, and customer service. They are encouraging ever-greater worker participation and empowerment (along with accountability) to exercise judgment and make decisions affecting work and customers. At the same time, they are grappling with the reality (and irony) that some of the same external trends that are creating new types of corporate cultures are also placing these cultures in jeopardy. For example, flexible work arrangements, remote supervision, use of contingent workers, and the often heterogeneous subcultures that result from mergers, acquisitions, and other types of partnerships all make it more difficult to establish, communicate, and sustain a shared, compelling organizational vision and a strong, meaningful organizational culture or to foster employee loyalty and commitment to the organization's values (Lowisch, 1998).

Changing Nature of Work and Jobs

The economic, demographic, and technological changes have also had enormous impact on the design, execution, and character of work itself. From the earliest days of the industrial revolution, an organization's competitive advantage derived from its access to the means of production—raw materials and the capital and equipment or technology to produce goods and products cheaply and efficiently via mass production. Fueled by the scientific management philosophy of Frederick Taylor, workers in such systems were viewed and treated almost literally as cogs in the machine, a concept epitomized by manufacturing assembly-line workers. Workers were, by design, given minimal discretion and responsibility to stray beyond the assigned and relatively fixed bundle of tasks, duties, and expectations of their jobs as institutionalized in detailed written job descriptions. Plans, decisions, and supervision came from a rigidly bureaucratic, hierarchical management structure.

In contrast, in today's economy the traditional means of production have become commodities available to even small players in the global marketplace, the provision of data- and information-related products and services has overtaken the market for manufactured products, and competitive advantage is increasingly derived from an organization's knowledge base, its ability to innovate and create value from ideas rather than things. As the conditions that created "jobs" have changed, the concept itself has become increasingly less useful in many organizations. It is often seen to undermine many of the adaptive strategic initiatives mentioned in the previous section (empowerment, reengineering, automation, use of self-managed teams, organizational flattening, alternative work arrangements, and so forth) that organizations are now deploying to stay competitive. This is because most such strategies are rooted in the need for flexibility and rapid response to constantly changing business conditions. Under such circumstances the conventional concept of jobs may discourage rather than promote real accountability and value-added performance because it rewards people for satisfying their (job description–prescribed) roles and responsibilities rather than for doing whatever is needed at a particular point in time to fulfill, further, or promote their organization's mission, vision, or values.

As a result of these developments, the definition of work itself continues to evolve—from a relatively fixed and stable bundle of hierarchically managed, independently performed, prescribed tasks and activities to a broader set of self-managed responsibilities and work requirements, highly interdependent tasks and activities, and constantly changing roles to meet the demands of changing markets, customer needs, and technology. Even the physical, temporal, and geographic structures of work have evolved, as seen in the increasing frequency of alternative work arrangements such as flexible hours and work schedules, telecommuting, "virtual offices," job sharing, and the like. Such arrangements are seen by many employers as a way to address worker shortages through a form of job redesign while simultaneously avoiding expensive relocation and real estate costs. These arrangements are being facilitated by the widespread availability of relatively inexpensive communications and information management and movement technologies (fax, e-mail, wireless communications, teleconferencing, video and multimedia computer applications, and the like). They are causing the fixed person–fixed task–fixed location–fixed schedule model of work to become an anachronism in the increasingly fluid and boundaryless 24-hour global business day. As one CIO of a large software company recently put it, "Work is not a physical place anymore" (Dannhauser, 1998, p. 38).

Many recent articles, books, and conference presentations have characterized this state of affairs as signaling the death of the concept of a job (Bridges, 1994; Pearlman, 1995). To paraphrase Mark

Twain, such reports may be greatly exaggerated—or at least misleading (Lenz, 1996). Recent studies suggest that most employed people still work at what can be meaningfully conceived of as a job (U.S. Department of Labor, 1995). But there is little doubt that the changing workplace conditions described here have made many jobs more complex and difficult than they used to be, primarily because of the accelerating knowledge and technology base underlying much modern-day work. The scope of responsibility, breadth of activities, and variety of roles demanded by many jobs is expanding. Multispecialists—people with in-depth knowledge of multiple specialties or aspects of a business or organization—are becoming increasingly valued over both narrow specialists and broad generalists. Jobs are more demanding cognitively (because of the need for almost continual integration of new knowledge and technology), socially (because of the increasing interdependence of work tasks and activities, teams and groups constantly forming and ending, and frequent changes in people's roles and relationships), perceptually (because of the decline in hands-on work and the increase in work involving controlling, monitoring, and responding to signals and information generated by new technology), and emotionally (because of the stress of continual organizational change and uncertainty, less routine work, and fewer prescribed rules and roles).

Understanding and Analyzing Work and Work Performance

Not surprisingly, the trends in organizational strategy, structure, culture, and the nature of work itself have potentially profound implications for organizations' concepts of work performance and how they go about selecting people who will perform effectively and contribute to important outcomes. As we will discuss in more detail later, these developments call for a rethinking of the strategies, substance, and processes by which organizations select their people. Such a rethinking process is greatly facilitated by having a conceptual framework or model of work performance, as well as appropriate methods and tools for analyzing work. In the next section we propose such a work performance model, and in the subsection following we describe several work analysis methods and tools that can facilitate the design of selection systems based on this performance model.

A Model of Work Performance

Various theories and models of work performance have developed and evolved in recent years. Figure 1.1 presents a general model of work performance (adapted from Pearlman, 1994, 1997) that integrates and updates much of this work. The theoretical underpinnings of the model and additional details about the interactions among its major components are described by Pearlman (1994). We believe this model can be helpful in understanding how today's workplace changes affect performance and the worker attributes we try to measure in selection programs.

In brief, the model proposes the following:

1. Performance has two distinguishable aspects or components: *task performance,* or performance of formally prescribed and recognized tasks and activities required by a specific job, and *contextual performance* (Borman & Motowidlo, 1993), or performance of activities that are not specific to a particular job but rather support the organizational, social, and psychological environment in which task performance occurs.

2. Results (that is, the effectiveness or evaluation of the outcomes of performance) are distinct from performance and are jointly determined by a worker's task and contextual performances and certain characteristics of the work context. In other words, final results can be subject in part to factors beyond a worker's own performance or control. For example, good sales performance may not result in a high proportion of closed sales in a depressed market or in high profits if selling prices have been temporarily lowered as part of a strategy to increase market share. In this model, the overall work context is viewed as consisting of three important levels of analysis—the *external context* (including economic, cultural, social, demographic, and technological influences and trends, labor market conditions, legal and regulatory factors, and so forth), the *organizational context* (including organizational structure and culture and the terms and conditions of employment), and the *immediate work or job context* (including specific work or job design characteristics; physical working conditions; machines, equipment, or technology used; specific work performance standards; and so forth).

Figure 1.1. General Work Performance Model.

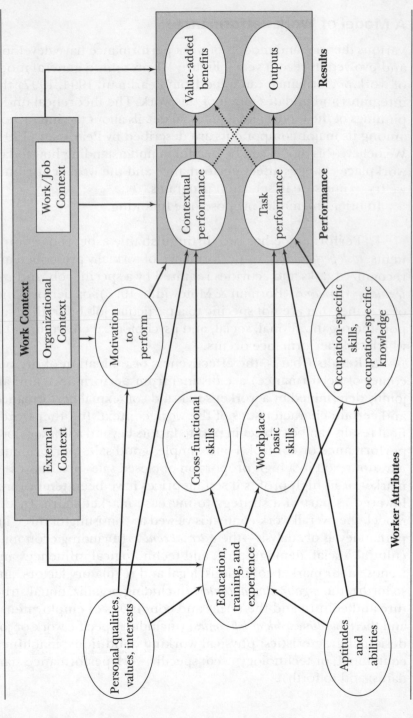

3. Results have two distinguishable aspects or components: *outputs*—which are related to the more formally recognized, objectively measured, and more or less concrete deliverables for which a worker is held accountable—tend to have immediate, short-term consequences, whereas *value-added benefits*—which are related to less formally recognized, more subjectively measured, and less concrete outcomes—tend to have more indirect and longer-term consequences (for example, customer and employee satisfaction, enthusiasm, loyalty). It is further proposed that task performance effectiveness is a direct determinant of outputs and an indirect determinant of value-added benefits, whereas contextual performance is a direct determinant of value-added benefits and an indirect determinant of outputs.

4. Task performance is primarily determined by a combination of an individual's occupation-specific skills, occupation-specific knowledge, workplace basic skills, aptitudes and abilities, and (through its effect on performance as a whole) motivation to perform. Contextual performance is most directly determined by a combination of an individual's (work-related) cross-functional skills, personal qualities, values, and interests, and (through its effect on performance as a whole) motivation to perform. (Definitions and examples of each of these worker attribute categories are provided in Exhibit 1.1, which appears later in this chapter.)

5. An individual's motivation to perform is jointly determined by certain specific characteristics of the work environment (for example, recognition and reward systems, presence of goals or performance standards) and certain work-related personal qualities, values, and interests (for example, high achievement orientation and entrepreneurial interests for sales jobs). Motivation to perform can be thought of as the combined effects of the choice to expend effort, the level of effort to expend, and persistence in this chosen level of effort (Campbell, McCloy, Oppler, & Sager, 1993).

6. Cross-functional skills, workplace basic skills, and occupation-specific skills and knowledge are attributes that are acquired during an individual's education, training, and experience, that is, through an individual's opportunities to learn and practice.

7. The opportunities for and effectiveness of education, training, and experience vary as a function of the individual's aptitudes and abilities and possession of particular skill- or knowledge-related, and learning-motivation-related, personal qualities, values, and

interests. Education, training, and experience opportunities vary also as a result of the external context. These linkages are based on the notion that an individual's opportunities for experience (as well as education and training) are created in part by the options made available and encouraged in a given economic and socio-cultural context and in part by the recognition of his or her general abilities by others, such as parents, teachers, professors, and mentors, who are in a position to influence these opportunities. They are also based on the notion that people's skill- or knowledge-related, and learning-motivation-related, personal qualities, values, and interests determine the type of development (that is, the types of skills or work) an individual chooses to invest these attributes in. For example, a person who values altruism and has an interest in working closely with others is more likely to seek education, training, and experience in social work than in sales.

Although the figure does not depict it, this work performance model also holds that the *quality* or *level* of worker performance (distinct from the content of such performance, as described in the first item in the preceding list) is a function of (1) the congruence between the specific characteristics or demands of the work environment (such as skill/knowledge, role, and results requirements) and an individual's occupation-specific skills and knowledge, cross-functional skills, workplace basic skills, and personal qualities, values, and interests; and (2) the individual's degree of proficiency or possession of those work-related attributes. In other words, an individual's performance is a function of the degree to which he or she is proficient in the attributes required by the work.

Two features of this performance model are of particular relevance to this chapter. The first is the model's delineation of two components for both performance and results. This stems from mounting research evidence that the two components have somewhat different antecedents. Contextual performance appears to be more influenced by personal qualities and cross-functional skills, whereas task performance appears to be more influenced by general cognitive abilities and specific skills and knowledge (Borman & Motowidlo, 1993). Thus, contextual and task performance are likely to require somewhat different selection strategies, and they may have a different value to an organization. In particular, there is growing evidence of the increasing strategic importance of contextual performance and value-added benefits because of the various emerging demographic and workplace trends described earlier. For example, the skills gap problem noted earlier has substantially increased the strategic value of maintaining high job satisfaction among employees in order to retain highly skilled workers, who have become increasingly critical as a competitive advantage. This implies that HR strategies and programs need to emphasize the contextual aspects of job performance and the value-added benefits of results. Unitary definitions of performance and results mask these differences, whereas recognizing, identifying, and highlighting these distinctions enable them to be capitalized on in employee selection programs, as well as by other HR strategies and programs.

The other important feature of the model has to do with its delineation of multiple categories of worker attributes, skills, or what are nowadays often called *competencies*. Building on the work underlying the development of a new national occupational information system (Advisory Panel for the Dictionary of Occupational Titles [APDOT], 1993; American Institutes for Research [AIR], 1995), the model embraces the notion that *skill* (or competency) is not a unitary concept. With no single, generally accepted definition in the professional or scientific literature, such terms have been used to refer to a wide range of worker attributes, variously described as personal characteristics, traits, temperaments, dispositions, attitudes, values, work preferences, aptitudes, abilities, basic skills, competencies, proficiencies, functional skills, specialized skills, technical skills, and specialized or technical knowledge. The fact that these different classes of attributes can have very different implications for selection and training (for example, traits are much less malleable, and hence much less trainable, than specialized knowledge), treating them in a unitary manner can lead to poorly targeted HR programs. Recognizing this problem, APDOT (1993), as part of its broader content model of work- and worker-oriented occupational information taxonomies, articulated a more or less hierarchical set of skills-related information categories as a provisional framework for defining and understanding the full range of worker attributes commonly referred to as skills or competencies. These are incorporated in the present work performance model as the worker attribute ovals. Definitions and examples of these categories, adapted for this performance model from the APDOT work, are presented in Exhibit 1.1.

Exhibit 1.1. Definitions and Examples of Work Performance Model Worker Attribute Categories.

Attribute Category	Definition	Examples
Aptitude and abilities	Capacity to perform particular classes or categories of mental and physical functions	Cognitive, spatial/perceptual, psychomotor, sensory, and physical abilities
Workplace basic skills[1]	Fundamental developed abilities that are required to at least some degree in virtually all jobs	Reading, writing, and arithmetic or computational skills
Cross-functional skills	Various types of developed generic skills that are related to the performance of broad categories of work activity and tend to occur across relatively wide ranges of jobs	Oral communication, problem analysis, interpersonal skills, negotiating, information gathering, organizing and planning, teamwork skills
Occupation-specific skills	Developed ability to perform work activities that occur across relatively narrow ranges of jobs or are defined in relatively job- or activity-specific terms; includes the ability to use or operate specific machines, tools, or equipment	Ability to read blueprints, to repair electrical appliances, to operate a milling machine, to operate a forklift, to do word processing
Occupation-specific knowledge	Understanding or familiarity with the facts, principles, processes, methods, or techniques related to a particular subject area, discipline, trade, science, or art; includes language proficiency	Knowledge of financial planning and analysis, fire protection systems, computer graphics, data communication networks, patent law, Spanish, COBOL, spreadsheet software

Personal qualities (also known as personality traits, temperaments, or dispositions)	An individual's characteristic, habitual, or typical manner of thinking, feeling, behaving, or responding with respect to self and others, situations or events	Adaptability, empathy, conscientiousness, self-esteem, autonomy, sociability, service orientation, emotional stability, integrity, honesty
Values	Goals, beliefs, or ideals an individual holds as important and that function as the standards or criteria by which one evaluates things	Empowerment, cooperation, achievement, initiative, work ethic
Interests	An individual's characteristic work-related preferences or likes and dislikes regarding specific (or classes of) work activities	Realistic, investigative, artistic, social, enterprising, and conventional

Workplace basic skills are differentiated from aptitudes and abilities because of their significant knowledge and learning components.

Work and Job Analysis

Some form of work or job analysis underlies just about all work on employee selection. Because the nature of work is changing faster than ever before, traditional methods of job analysis—particularly those limited to analyzing the specific task components of static and narrowly defined jobs—may be less than optimal bases for meeting some of today's selection challenges. These challenges include the need for methods that (1) are sufficiently process-oriented to reflect the dynamic nature of work, (2) capture the contextual aspects of job performance, (3) lend themselves to the analysis of team or group performance, and (4) provide common language and metrics that allow for the analysis of multiple levels of work and worker characteristics, which, in turn, facilitates such increasingly important applications as job family development, cross-job skill and knowledge comparisons (for skill transferability analysis), and analysis of skill or knowledge gaps (for example, between current applicants or workers and either current or anticipated work requirements). This section briefly describes developments in the analysis of work that we think are particularly relevant to selection tool development for a changing workplace.

Strategic Job Analysis

Various forms of *strategic job analysis* (Schneider & Konz, 1989) have come into practice in recent years. Strategic job analysis seeks to identify the worker KSAOs likely to be needed in the future, usually in order to identify current or potential workforce skill gaps and develop strategies for filling these gaps through new selection or development programs. An approach that we have taken, which is fairly typical of what we have seen of practice in this area, builds on the results of a traditional task, work behavior, or worker attribute–oriented (KSAO-based) job analysis. We bring together business "visionaries" (business leaders, organizational strategists, business development planners, and so forth) to talk about their expectations of how work will be changing in the future in light of planned business strategies. Using the business strategy to understand operational objectives and the key work activities required to realize the objectives gives these people a new framework for thinking about current and future task, work function, and KSAO importance. We collect judgments, usually in the form of ratings, which contrast the present versus expected future importance of previously identified tasks, work behaviors, and KSAOs. Work behaviors that are critical to accomplishing the organization's strategic goals should demonstrate greater importance for future selection system design than other dimensions, even when traditional indicators (such as average task importance ratings) suggest otherwise. We also collect information on work behaviors and KSAOs that are not currently important but are judged to be essential for the future based on the organization's business strategy.

To ground the thinking, we suggest asking participants to think first about how each major element of work (activity or task) is expected to change, and then later determine which worker-oriented constructs are most important to accomplishing that work. It can be tempting simply to brainstorm or derive a list of seemingly important "new" KSAOs, but such results are not very sound (nor will be the selection or training programs developed from them) if they have not been linked to important work of the future to ensure alignment with the organization's strategy.

Competency Modeling

Competency modeling is a form of job analysis that has come into widespread use in recent years. The results of competency modeling work have been increasingly used as the basis for a variety of HR systems, including training and development, performance appraisal, upward or multisource feedback, compensation, and selection. Discussions of competency modeling are often complicated by the fact that neither *competency* nor *competency modeling* has a commonly accepted single meaning. There are almost as many definitions of these terms as there are practitioners and users of them. What are called competencies can range from traditional, well-defined KSAOs to complex, multifaceted, ill-defined (or undefined) concepts or ad hoc constructs, such as visioning, value selling, systems thinking, personal maturity, customer focus, and diversity orientation. Such labels are often embraced by managers and business leaders because they capture the spirit of an organization's culture or strategic direction. But they also create huge dilemmas for the people who have to operationalize them in the form of measures and HR programs.

Depending on the practitioner, competency modeling can employ a variety of processes and methods ranging from the fairly rigorous, systematic, and quantitative methods used in most traditional job analysis practice to ad hoc, idiosyncratic, and qualitative methods. For example, some competency modeling practitioners do little more than facilitate a group discussion among whichever managers are available at a given time, with the end result of producing a hodgepodge of a "wish list" of desired employee characteristics. In our experience, competency modeling work usually results in the development of a set of worker characteristics (which may be skills, knowledge, abilities, and a variety of personal qualities that encompasses dispositions, values, attitudes, and motivation-related traits) related to performance in a given job, functional work area, or organization. Each characteristic is briefly defined and is often accompanied by several behavioral indicators that serve to exemplify what good performance of the competency would look like in behavioral terms. The combined set of characteristic labels, definitions, and behavioral indicators is the competency model.

Despite its understandable appeal to line managers and business leaders, the practice of competency modeling is often of limited value for selection system development for two reasons: First, competencies are often derived with little or no reference to, and rarely any systematic—much less quantitative—linkage to, the work requirements they are intended to be related to, and second, there is usually little or no focus on the ultimate measurability of the derived competencies, a situation partly rooted in the frequent absence of meaningful operational definitions. Such issues create big problems for the use of competencies in selection programs. For example, as already noted, *diversity orientation* is frequently identified as an important competency because of the increasingly heterogeneous workforce and global focus of many organizations. The term is generally defined along the lines of "willingness and ability to work with diverse individuals" or "ability to embrace and capitalize on individuals' diversity in order to accomplish goals." But such definitions are nearly useless for measurement purposes without much more detail regarding both their derivation (in terms of related theory, constructs, skills, or knowledge) and their manifestation (preferably in performance or behavioral terms, but of a far more comprehensive nature than presentation of a few sample behavioral indicators). If the competencies have not been rigor-ously derived and clearly defined, these deficiencies will carry over into any selection tools (or other measures or programs) developed from them.

Automated Person-Job Matching Systems

An increasingly common application of competency modeling, especially in larger organizations, is its incorporation into automated systems for job and worker profiling and person-job matching. Such systems are usually deployed as part of broader HR information systems aimed at improving the logistics of staffing and selection, as well as many other HR functions. Some matching systems use keywords gleaned from resumes as a source of possible matches among competency-based keywords in the organization's job requirements database. This can speed up an organization's ability to determine likely candidates for a more thorough assessment (for example, through a structured interview). Another system uses archived data about internal job candidates' competencies and compares them with the job requirements to uncover possible candidates for a new position.

Such systems are appealing at first glance because they appear to provide instant staffing solutions for new or open positions. The important point about all such systems, however, is that they are only as good as the data they manage. If competency-based assessments are suspect or deficient (which is likely when based exclusively on self-ratings) or if the competency-based job profile used does not capture the essential job characteristics, then such systems will not lead to accurate staffing or selection decisions. Unfortunately, system vendors often position their systems primarily as repositories for personnel data and provide little or no guidance about how best to ensure the integrity of these data. For example, the knowledge and skill requirements of work change over time. Employees develop new skills while their unused skills degrade over time. But few such systems have an elegant way to capture this information in a reasonably comprehensive database. As a result, if an organization wants to maximize measurement fidelity to ensure accurate staffing decisions, alternative (for example, paper-based) methods must be used. Further, if the data in such a system are based on less-than-rigorous competency analysis and derivation methods, the automated system is simply making these suspect data more readily and widely available—in effect, making it easier to make poor personnel decisions that undermine the strategic value of the system and increase the risk of successful legal challenges.

In contrast, when built on a foundation of rigorously developed information about both work and workers, such systems can be extremely powerful HR levers capable of enhancing both the speed and accuracy of selection and staffing processes. Perhaps the best current example of such a system is the U.S. Labor Department–sponsored O*NET (for Occupational Information Network) system (AIR, 1995), a still-evolving automated database of national occupational information based on the APDOT framework. Premised on the need for a comprehensive, theoretically based, and empirically validated common language for describing the characteristics of both work and workers at multiple levels of analysis, O*NET information and tools are being incorporated into an increasing number of state employment service job referral, vocational guidance, and career planning systems. Significantly, O*NET includes a great deal of content specifically designed to capture information related to key aspects of our work performance model—such as contextual performance, the broader organizational context and immediate work-job context, and personal qualities, values, and interests—that has been previously absent from most major work- and person-analysis systems. It thus provides a means for addressing many of the challenges described at the beginning of this section.

Job Analysis Wizard

Technology is dramatically changing the way work is done in nearly all professions, and selection work is no different. A technology we recently developed at Lucent provides a good illustration of the improvements possible in the speed, coordination, and capabilities of work or job analysis. The tool, the Job Analysis Wizard (JAW; Barney, Pearlman, & Harkey, 1997) was designed to reduce a number of limitations of traditional survey- and task-based job analysis methods, such as their labor-intensiveness and dependence on the skills of a job analyst for their validity and defensibility. Although generalized PC-based job analysis tools had been developed previously to remedy some of these problems, their utility was often constrained by such factors as limited work- or worker-oriented content and inability to aggregate data flexibly. Furthermore, such programs are limited to functioning on personal computers or mainframes on local- or wide-area networks and are thus inaccessible across wide geographical spans and multiple types of computer platforms simultaneously. Before our project, no existing approach allowed the job analyst to quickly identify, review, and manipulate preexisting information and materials (such as tests and training courses) derived from prior job analyses.

Lucent (as part of AT&T) has had a long history of job analytic work, but few analyses were available to inform and accelerate future work. The paper-based storage of job analytic data and the turnover of analysts had caused valuable information to be unavailable. In addition, no system existed that could automate the job analysis process and provide information on the products created in the past to support business imperatives. This caused redundant job analyses, training curricula, selection tests, realistic job previews, and performance appraisals to be created for the very same purposes. The problem had been exacerbated as our business had expanded globally. For example, Singaporean trainers had no straightforward way of knowing about statistical process control courses developed in Orlando, Florida, and consequently redesigned a new class. Because these key HR data were not accessible, it was not possible with existing systems to simulate the effects of business cases (such as new joint ventures) on the resulting HR systems, plans, budgets, and practices.

The Job Analysis Wizard was designed to be based on the World Wide Web to systematize and partially automate the acquisition of job requirements information, provide information about the products constructed from this information (such as tests and training courses), and allow for strategic queries. The system uses what is known as *fuzzy logic* (see following example) as a decision aid to assist in the appropriate placement of new dimensions (such as knowledge of new or emerging technologies) into preexisting dictionaries (taxonomies) modeled in part on the APDOT and O*NET work described earlier, as well as prior AT&T–Lucent research. The system contains thousands of different elements organized in broader work- and worker-related dimensions. A partial list of these elements is shown (as the second level) in Exhibit 1.2.

**Exhibit 1.2. First Two Levels
of the Job Analysis Wizard Taxonomy.**

First Level	Second Level
Work requirements	Work context
	Generalized work behaviors
	Tools and equipment
Worker requirements	Abilities
	Knowledge
	Skills
	Education
	Certifications
	Languages
	Work styles

The process used by the JAW is similar to the one we describe in our case study (Goldstein, Zedeck, & Schneider, 1993; see appendix). After completing job observations, critical incident meetings, or structured interviews, job analysts use a program that helps them find relevant dimensions in the corporate dictionary. Rather than sorting through thousands of papers, they can use a graphical interface, showing or hiding a tree of hierarchical dimensions and using a search engine. Before e-mailing an electronic survey to subject matter experts (SMEs), the system requires them to estimate how long an average item will take to complete, so that the survey can be adjusted if it will be unreasonably long. One way a job analyst can shorten a survey is by selecting a higher-order category instead of asking many questions about lower-order dimensions. For example, the JAW allows the analyst to treat the category of verbal ability (a subcategory of cognitive abilities in the worker requirements dimension of abilities) as a single item on the survey instead of asking separate questions about oral comprehension, oral expression, written comprehension, and written expression. The final time estimate is passed to the SMEs so they can allocate time to the survey in the constraints of their other responsibilities. SMEs are then notified via e-mail that an electronic survey is available on a particular Web site. After downloading and completing it, they are asked to report any dimensions that are critical to the job but were not included on the survey. All responses are ultimately uploaded onto the central Web site, where the job analyst can periodically access and study the results. The data can be filtered using such statistics as item means and standard deviations in the JAW software or studied using the analyst's preferred statistical software. The job analyst filters out unimportant dimensions and the system automatically creates a series of linkage matrix surveys designed to link the key work (tasks, tools, or equipment) and worker (knowledge, skills) dimensions. In paper format, these often become unreasonably long for subject matter experts to complete. The JAW allows the analyst to parcel out portions of the linkage matrix to different SMEs via e-mail and then later recombine them. When complete, the JAW allows the analyst to record information required for legal purposes (such as SME background and qualifications), upload the results to the common Web site for others to use, and immediately identify preexisting materials (such as tests or interviews) that are relevant to their job of interest.

The Job Analysis Wizard overcomes numerous problems associated with other systems. Because the system is Web-based, job requirements can be studied by Lucent staff anywhere in the world as long as they have access to the internal Lucent Web site. It provides instant demographic information about the products constructed from previous job analyses, as well as the materials themselves (such as test items) in the form of downloadable files. This is a significant improvement over alternative approaches because it directly reduces costs by improving cross-geographic coordination and eliminating redundant development efforts. The JAW system is more viable in the long term than any other previously designed system because it employs a fuzzy logic–based approach that reduces the human labor required for maintenance by suggesting the appropriate placement of new components. Because the system uses a hierarchical taxonomy–based, dictionary-style approach to studying job requirements, it allows for strategic queries and multiple levels of work analysis. Users can select a job or task and examine all the specific knowledge elements required for each. This dramatically improves the speed and scope with which HR managers can do such things as estimate budgets, evaluate job accommodation needs in connection with Americans with Disabilities Act requirements, or target HR system development efforts anywhere Lucent does business.

Early on in JAW development, we recognized that, to be useful in the long term, the system needed a process by which the common language dictionary used to describe work and workers could be quickly and efficiently updated. Without a sound process for adding elements to our taxonomies, they would eventually lose their utility. After considering a number of options, we ultimately devised a fuzzy logic–based protocol that capitalizes on previously collected data to help analysts decide for themselves the optimal placement of new elements. One of the key data sets the JAW produces is a matrix that shows a quantitative relationship between each work requirement element (such as a task or a tool) and the important worker attributes (KSAOs). Tasks that are similar are more likely to require the similar worker attributes than are dissimilar tasks. For example, analytic tasks such as computer programming are more likely to require knowledge of C++, Basic, or Java than are physical tasks. Because the JAW studies diverse jobs using the same common language, the system exploits these similarities. It creates a sort of fingerprint by comparing ratings on a new knowledge (gathered from a confirmatory survey) with the pattern of data for all knowledge elements in the dictionary across every task and tool. Table 1.2 shows an example of the types of patterns the fuzzy-logic system uses to make recommendations about the preexisting worker attributes (in this case, knowledge elements) most similar to the new attribute that must be added to the common language dictionary. If a new programming language, such as Java, is discovered to be important in the confirmatory survey stage, the system would calculate similarity indices with all other knowledge elements in the database. Then it would recommend a placement near the other programming languages (such as C++) because of the similarity of the patterns they share with similar tasks and tools.

As we built the JAW system, we were concerned about the possible impact of current limitations of Internet-intranet capacity (bandwidth) and features (Java). We knew that some system users would have slow network connections, especially our colleagues in other countries. Also, we recognized the differences in functionality among various Web browsers that would challenge our ability to have a dynamic system that would work on all computers. To

Table 1.2. Example of Knowledge Requirements Across Tasks.

Task	Knowledge of C++	Knowledge of Visual Basic	Knowledge of Cost Accounting Rules
Debugs programs	High	High	Low
Designs pseudocode	High	High	Low
Generates ledger reports	Low	Low	High

accommodate these concerns we chose to compartmentalize the different features of the Wizard into separate programs, so users could select just those features they needed. Users can thus select a program to pick job dimensions, administer confirmatory or linkage surveys, analyze data, find products, or upload products only when they need to perform that particular activity. If they have a slow connection, they can simply work on other activities while the application is downloading. Because all data are managed by the Web server, however, all work is still available to others and based on the same common language.

The JAW system can be very powerful in the hands of expert job analysts and others needing to build selection systems quickly, but in the wrong hands it can, of course, be misused. Without security features such as passwords and appropriate encryption protocols, such technologies can compromise the security of test and interview questions. Access to the various system features and information needs to be restricted to individuals with the capability to use them appropriately, so as not to jeopardize the integrity of work analysis results or other system products, lessen their value to the organization, or make the organization legally vulnerable, especially when used for selection or staffing. It is therefore crucial to establish clear policies regarding user qualifications and build in appropriate controls before deploying such technology.

Rethinking Personnel Selection

To the degree that organizations are being affected by and are changing in response to the workplace trends described—and few organizations are not—it will be difficult for them to become or

remain successful without reevaluating how they go about selecting their people. Organizations are increasingly recognizing that
their only long-term, sustainable competitive advantage lies in the
capabilities of their workforce, the knowledge, skills, abilities, and
other important characteristics of their people. As a result, the premium on highly competent workers—and on figuring out how to
identify and select them—has become greater than ever. In this
section we consider some of the key issues, challenges, and options
related to this needed rethinking of selection system strategy, content, and design and implementation.

Rethinking Selection System Strategy

The changing workplace has created different kinds of strategic
choices when conceiving selection systems and has raised the stakes
surrounding conventional choices. In this section we consider
some of the strategic selection system decisions and questions
many organizations are now facing.

Issues of General Selection Strategy

What does the organization want its selection systems to predict?
Traditionally, the simple answer was "job performance," which
more or less equates to what our work performance model describes as task performance—that is, selecting people predicted to
be effective in fairly prescribed and well-defined jobs. Now the prediction of contextual performance is often as crucial or more crucial, given the increasing importance to many organizations of the
"value-added benefits" aspect of organizational results, such as
maintaining customer and employee loyalty, displayed in our work
performance model. In addition, selecting for retention—that is,
hiring people likely to stay with the organization for a considerable
time—is becoming particularly important strategically because of
the growing competition for scarce critical skills and knowledge in
the labor market. Thus, incorporating measures of applicant interests and values into selection systems is desirable. (So, for example,
an organization might design a selection program that identifies
people with strong entrepreneurial interests and high need for
achievement for face-to-face sales jobs that have highly leveraged
incentive compensation plans.) It also implies the need to integrate

selection programs with other organizational strategies and interventions designed to minimize turnover by improving employees' job satisfaction and commitment to the organization.

Organizations now face a host of strategic selection system decisions and choices that did not even present themselves or were of little consequence in the past. Should they favor the selection of generalists (who may more readily and effectively navigate the "churn" of changing roles, responsibilities, and relationships) or specialists (to improve task performance in increasingly specialized knowledge-based workplaces)—or attempt to get the best of both worlds through selection of multispecialists? If the answer lies in some combination of these alternatives—the likely case—on what basis should organizations determine the optimal proportions of each, and should these be different for different types and levels of work? Organizations also must decide whether to hire for specific jobs or for broader work roles, longer-term careers, and organizational "fit" (Schneider, Kristoff, Goldstein, & Smith, 1997). The decision also often comes down to evaluating the tradeoffs between selecting primarily for task performance (and associated basic skills and occupation-specific skills and knowledge) or for contextual performance (and associated cross-functional skills, which create greater potential for lateral movement, as well as personal qualities that are compatible with an organization's culture and values). To the degree that organizations hire for careers and person-organization fit, they are hiring to predict retention.

A critical strategic selection issue that virtually all organizations face concerns whether to select for people's immediate contribution to the organization (that is, people with sufficient current skill, knowledge, or experience to "hit the ground running" immediately upon hiring) or for their potential to make contributions after sufficient training or experience. Often stated as the experienced-versus-inexperienced-hire question, it is analogous to the classic make-or-buy business decision. This decision has a significant impact on selection program components in terms of the degree to which they are based on measures of current skill versus the potential to acquire such skill.

There has been a clear trend in recent years for many employers faced with mounting competitive pressures and looking for quick results to favor hiring workers who can be immediately productive and require minimal investment in training (Rynes, Orlitzky, & Bretz, 1997). At the same time, however, this strategy is frequently difficult to implement because of the shortage of experienced applicants, particularly in technological fields. The strategy rarely boils down to an either-or decision but rather is a question of determining the appropriate mix of experienced and inexperienced workers. This in turn is usually based on such factors as the nature of the labor market at any given point in time (that is, what sort of experienced talent is available), the organization's market position or overall competitive situation (that is, balancing the need for short-term results with the time needed for people to grow and develop on the job), and the availability of the necessary resources to support entry-level employee training and development. Another consideration is the evolving or desired state of an organization's culture: organizations with very strong, well-defined cultures may prefer to hire inexperienced workers who will be more easily trained, socialized, and assimilated than experienced workers who may be "tainted" with well-embedded work styles and views and thus will have difficulty adapting to a particular organizational style.

More recently, the traditional make-or-buy selection strategy decision has expanded to include a third possibility: leasing employees. Leasing refers to the use of various forms of contingent workers—that is, contract, term, temporary, or life-of-project workers—who can be more readily brought into, and shed from, an organization to meet expanding, contracting, or cyclical work and project needs. When considering such an option, organizations must pay attention to the types of work, functions, and roles that are most suitable for contingent workers. They also need to determine the optimal balance between a contingent and permanent workforce. There is usually a point at which too small a regular employed workforce will compromise the "critical mass" needed for an organization to maintain and nurture its intellectual capital. Organizations also need to consider how their selection systems may be modified, adapted, or applied to contingent workers. When such workers are drawn from temporary agencies or other third-party sources, there is a further issue of the desired and appropriate interaction between the agency's selection process and the organization's own selection process. Finally, a number of important legal and labor relations issues related to the status of such workers often come into play when evaluating this option (Lenz, 1996).

Another strategic choice concerns whether to make or buy selection programs or tools themselves. That is, should organizations build or maintain internal staff capability for this function or acquire it by outsourcing or purchasing commercially available selection products? This is a complex business decision involving many factors and tradeoffs, and one having potential legal ramifications as well, because under the Federal Uniform Guidelines on Employee Selection Procedures ("Uniform Guidelines," 1978) employers are ultimately responsible for the validity of the selection procedures they use, regardless of their source. Our own experience with this issue at Lucent has been mixed, with purchased or outsourced selection program components (including outsourced administration of selection tools) producing substantial cost savings and administrative efficiencies under some circumstances but at times proving more costly and difficult than anticipated because of complexities in monitoring contracts and integrating vendor products, services, and methods with in-house policies and business requirements. As for test administration, we have recently adopted a model involving the development of a network of part-time, strategically located independent contractors (such as company retirees) to administer tests on an as-needed basis in locations remote from our employment centers. They have proven to be a flexible, timely, and cost-effective supplement to regular in-house test administration staff.

The changing nature of work and jobs, along with several of the strategic decisions described earlier, also has important implications—and can create significant dilemmas—for an organization's strategy regarding the legal defensibility of its selection programs. Under the Uniform Guidelines, organizations must be able to demonstrate the job-relatedness (validity) of their selection practices in order to defend themselves against discrimination charges. Charges can be brought based on a finding that the selection practices in question produce an "adverse impact" (significantly disproportionate hiring rates) on groups protected by federal civil rights law (such as racial or ethnic minorities and women). In the past, organizations willing to invest in sound job analysis and rigorous selection tool development and validation work were in effect able to accomplish two strategic objectives for the price of one because they helped to ensure legal defensibility while also leading to the use of good selection programs that yielded high-quality employees. Current difficulties, however, arise because the concepts of validation and job analysis embedded in the Uniform Guidelines are rooted in the concept of a job as a relatively fixed and stable set of tasks. That is, under the Guidelines the job being selected for is the basic unit of analysis for calculating adverse impact, conducting job analysis, and developing criterion measures against which to validate selection procedures, whereas the emerging reality for many organizations is that conventional job boundaries are shifting or disappearing and the prediction of non-job-specific criteria (such as contextual performance, performance of anticipated future activities, and "fit" with organizational culture and values) is taking on increasing importance.

This creates a number of potential dilemmas for organizations that, from the standpoint of their business and HR strategy, would like to design selection tools and programs, for example, to select people for projects or roles that may change over time, select people for an internal contingent workforce whose "job" will vary from assignment to assignment, or select people on skills or knowledge that have no immediate application to their work but are expected to become important in the future. For example, we know of organizations that wished to select only computer-literate applicants based on the general principle that "everyone in a high-tech business should be computer-literate," even though computers were not currently being used in the specific jobs being selected for. We have also seen cases where particular selection system components for broad classes of jobs have been "mandated" by upper management based on aspirational (and often ill-defined) organization-wide values that would be difficult to document as requirements for the performance of specific jobs and hence difficult to defend legally using conventional methods of job analysis and criterion development (such as those required by the Uniform Guidelines). Because the defensibility of such practices under the Uniform Guidelines has yet to be tested in the courts, employers now often find themselves having to evaluate the tradeoffs and choose between two strategic goals—a selection system's legal defensibility and its value to the organization—that may no longer overlap to the degree they once did.

Finally, it is also important for organizations to recognize when selection strategy is *not* the answer to a business problem. We have seen organizations attempt to address what are fundamentally non-selection issues, such as training, compensation, job design, or performance management, by adding, deleting, or modifying selection tools, often with disastrous results. For example, an organization might change or drop an effective sales selection program because of unacceptably high turnover; yet that turns out to be the result of a poorly designed incentive compensation program. Or it might wish to add selection process components—thereby increasing both the time and cost of the hiring process—to measure skills or knowledge that are peripheral to effective performance, can be learned in a short time, or would not be necessary if the job were better designed. We know of organizations that have added performance tests of basic computer literacy to the selection process for professional jobs requiring a level of computer skill (such as basic Windows navigation, simple word processing) that could be readily learned on the job or in a brief training session. The tests were not only logistically difficult and expensive to deploy and administer but also ended up screening out otherwise desirable candidates (that is, people with strong skills and experience in the specialty) for these jobs.

One conclusion we can draw from this discussion is that the answers to these kinds of selection strategy questions depend heavily on the organization's broader business plans and strategies. In other words, it is crucial to view and understand selection systems as part of broader HR systems, and they should be consciously designed for integration with these other HR systems, which themselves should be linked to and aligned with the organization's broader goals.

Linking Selection and Training

We believe the link between selection and training to be of particular strategic importance for the changing workplace. As the Cirent case study illustrates (see the appendix), employers often cannot find candidates who possess all desired knowledge and skills prior to employment. This is particularly true for jobs in technological fields, for which it has been estimated that 20 percent of the skills and knowledge possessed by workers becomes obsolete every twelve to eighteen months. As Microsoft CEO Bill Gates (as cited in Matloff, 1998) put it, summing up the key attributes for success in computer programming: "We're not looking for any specific knowledge because things change so fast, and it's easy to learn stuff. You've got to have an excitement about software, a certain intelligence. . . . It's not the specific knowledge that counts." The greater the scarcity of needed knowledge and skills, the more important it is for organizations to integrate their selection and training systems strategically—focusing on measures of broad ability and interest and then providing new hires with developmental opportunities to acquire more specialized knowledge and skills, for example. As described in our case study, we helped to create a new degree program to ensure a long-term supply of talent with the required technical skills, but in the short term we emphasized the difficult-to-teach attributes of cognitive ability and interpersonal skills in our selection process and provided in-house training so that new hires would have a good chance of acquiring the more job-specific skills they lacked. If internal job candidates do not qualify on the more trainable components of the selection system (such as knowledge tests), then specific developmental experiences (training classes or on-line tutorials) can be recommended to close such skill gaps. This strategy is enhanced to the degree that specific selection process feedback (that is, indicating which specific skills or knowledge need improvement) is provided to job candidates and training curricula are designed to correspond to these selection "modules." One of the keys to making such a strategy effective is to use the same work or job-analytic information as the common foundation for both selection and training, as discussed earlier. Another key is to create a strong partnership between selection system and training course developers.

Skill Certification Programs as a Selection Strategy

Organizations are increasingly making use of various certification programs, particularly for technology and knowledge-intensive jobs. Such programs seek to ensure, generally through testing or other structured evaluation processes, that workers acquire and maintain the knowledge and skills they need for continuing performance effectiveness. These programs may be external (for example, through an accredited entity, such as a vocational-technical institute or community college) or internal (such as when a group or "review board" of relevant subject matter experts within the organization are assembled to evaluate individuals' levels of critical skills and knowledge). When certification is required as a condition of continued employment, it is in effect functioning as a selection program, and the decision to use it can really be seen as an extension of an organization's overall selection strategy.

Certification programs generally are most appropriate and useful to organizations in circumstances such as the following:

- There are high-stakes consequences of performance (in terms of public safety or potential harm to people, property, equipment) or crucial organizational interests (as when an organization might require certification on relevant language proficiency and cross-cultural skills and knowledge as a condition of assigning people to negotiate critical transactions in other countries).
- The requisite skills or knowledge are relatively concrete and observable and hence reliably measurable (for example, the occupation-specific skill and knowledge worker attribute categories in our work performance model rather than the broader categories of aptitudes and abilities and personal qualities).
- There is a high obsolescence rate of the requisite skills or knowledge (as is typical, for example, of technological skills) and a mechanism is needed to ensure ongoing currency.
- It is not practical to assess the requisite skills and knowledge as part of the initial selection procedure (for example, if the supply of applicants with these skills in the available labor market is inadequate, and hence too many candidates would be screened out if such an assessment were built into the initial selection process).
- It is unnecessary to assess the requisite skills and knowledge as part of the initial selection procedure (for example, if they are not needed immediately upon job entry because they will be acquired in the course of normal work or career progression).
- The organization has the capacity (that is, the resources, budget, and support structure) to provide or sponsor the necessary training and development for people to acquire the skills and knowledge on which they eventually need to certify.
- There is a well-developed career path that structures and reinforces the acquisition of requisite skills and knowledge for various types and levels of related work.

A number of important practical, strategic, and policy questions and issues arise in the development and use of certification programs. For example, should certification apply to a whole job or just to particular skill or knowledge components of it? Should an organization develop its own program or use existing outside programs (developed by professional associations, trade or industry groups, or government-sponsored agencies)? (Greater customization can obviously be achieved in the former approach but often at higher cost; the latter approach offers the possibility of lower costs, but organizations must establish the program's appropriateness and job-relatedness for its own application.) Should a length of time be specified within which employees must certify after hire, and if so, what should be the consequences of not meeting this time line? (Consequences might range from time line extension for further training, to job transfer, to termination.) What role will certification play in an employee's movement along a career path? That is, will certification be a condition for promotion? If so, will it be the only condition? If not, what other factors will be considered? What (if any) forms of reward or recognition (monetary or otherwise) will be associated with certification? Will there be provisions for "testing out" of the certification process (if skills or knowledge were acquired previously) or for retesting or reexamination (if an individual fails to satisfy particular components of the assessment)? If so, should the whole process or just the failed components be reevaluated? Will there be any appeal or dispute resolution process? If so, how will this be structured? Will there be any provision for program monitoring and quality control? (Many organizations have found it useful to institute a neutral "certification manager" role for this purpose.)

In addition, a number of measurement-related questions and issues must be addressed in certification program design. For example, what will be the content of the certification program? (Possibilities range from formal training delivered via classroom instruction or self-paced electronic media to on-the-job training, structured work experience, or a combination of these.) How will skill or knowledge acquisition be assessed? (Possibilities include written or computer-delivered tests, live or computer-based simulations, structured interviews, structured roundtable, panel, review board processes, or a combination.) At what level will cut scores, or the criteria for passing or failing the certification program, be set? Here organizations must strike the appropriate balance between setting too high a standard that few people can attain and too low a standard that could inadvertently promote a minimum competency mindset that does not achieve the purpose for which the program was developed.

There is no uniformly right or wrong way to resolve such questions. Organizations must make such decisions based on what is useful in the context of their business strategy, structure, and culture. However, when appropriately developed and deployed, certification programs can be extremely valuable in promoting, reinforcing, and rewarding the workforce skill and knowledge development and maintenance that has become such a competitive necessity for today's organizations.

Rethinking Selection System Content

The changing nature of work and jobs has also created new challenges when it comes to the content of selection systems—that is, what we want selection systems to measure. In this section we discuss current thinking about the worker attributes needed in the changing workplace, thoughts about the conceptualization and measurement of skills, and some ideas on the specific (and increasingly important) issue of selecting those people who have come to be known as knowledge workers.

What Attributes to Measure?

The work performance model presented earlier in this chapter identified a number of categories of worker attributes that influence aspects of work performance in different ways. Changes in the nature of work and organizations are giving new importance to attributes spanning many of these categories and creating a challenging array of KSAOs for organizations to consider measuring in their selection systems. Exhibit 1.3 provides examples of these, along with the rationales for measuring them.

We are not suggesting that organizations can or should attempt to measure all the attributes listed in the exhibit; furthermore, they are only examples and not intended to represent exhaustive lists. Even if justified by appropriate job or work analysis results, there

Exhibit 1.3. Worker Attributes Needed for a Changing Workplace.

Attributes	Examples	Rationale
Learning, knowledge, and skill acquisition	• General cognitive ability • Motivation to learn • Openness to input	Employees' need for frequent training/retraining for new work roles and for assimilating and applying new knowledge and information within their own specialties
Problem solving	• Higher-order and critical thinking skills • Abstract reasoning • Creativity/resourcefulness • Information-processing, evaluation, and analysis skills	The increasing complexity of work and increasing knowledge- and information-intensiveness of many jobs
Effective team performance and effectiveness in working collaboratively with people of heterogeneous backgrounds	• Interpersonal and communication skills • Negotiating skills • Resource management skills • Conflict management skills • Empathy • Extroversion • Social sensitivity • Adaptability • Multiple language skills • Knowledge of specific countries and cultures	The increasingly networked, decentralized, and often global structure of organizations, growing interdependence of work activities, and various demographic trends that are increasing workforce diversity
Effective contextual performance	• Such cross-functional skills as interpersonal, leadership, teamwork, communication, and conflict management skills • Such personal qualities as service orientation, adaptability, social sensitivity, responsibility, empathy, conscientiousness, honesty, and integrity	The role of contextual performance in important organizational outcomes (e.g., employee retention and customer loyalty) and the increasing importance of customer service as the service sector of the economy continues to expand

Handling uncertainty, ambiguity, stress	• Emotional stability • Resilience • Adaptability • Time and resource management skills • Stamina/energy	The impact of change and churn in organizational structures, cultures, and work itself due to broader technological, economic, and demographic changes
Ability and willingness to work outside of traditional temporal, geographic, and organizational boundaries	• Adaptability • Time, resource, and self-management skills • Organizing and planning skills • Communication skills • Conscientiousness	The shrinking of traditional boundaries due to technology and changing organizational structures
Employee retention	• Work-related interests, preferences, and personal qualities	Skill/knowledge shortages in labor market and consequent need for organizations to retain their intellectual capital
Ability to act quickly and capitalize on opportunities for business growth or process improvements	• Decisiveness • Risk taking • Initiative/proactivity	The speed and pace of marketplace changes and increased global competition
Prediction of counterproductive behavior (e.g., tardiness, absenteeism, malingering, vandalism, drug or alcohol abuse, theft, disciplinary problems, white-collar crime, workplace violence)	• Conscientiousness • Honesty • Integrity • Self-management skills	Undermines effective contextual performance and its associated organizational outcomes (value-added benefits such as customer loyalty and satisfaction)

are both practical and technical constraints on the number of attribute measures that would be desirable to include in a selection system. At some point the costs of additional measures inevitably outweigh their benefits in terms of incremental validity, that is, increased predictive value. Nevertheless, Exhibit 1.3 does imply a contrast from past practice, when simple selection processes measuring relatively few attributes were adequate for most jobs. Organizations that can develop innovative and practical ways to measure as many of these attributes in their selection practices as appropriate for their work stand to gain significant advantage in the performance of their workforce.

Skills: New Thoughts About Old Ideas

There has been a great deal of discussion recently in government, business, and economic circles on the subject of skills and related issues, catalyzed by the publication of such widely cited reports as "A Nation at Risk" (National Commission on Excellence in Education, 1983) and "America's Choice: High Skills or Low Wages" (National Center on Education and the Economy, 1990). Concerns range from existing or predicted skill gaps in the American workforce, to the lack of transferable skills that would enable workers more readily to shift their career directions as organizational needs change, to the failure of our educational system to equip young people with the skills they need to enter the workforce. As noted earlier, a problem with much of this sort of discussion is that the term *skill* has no single, generally accepted definition but instead is used to refer to a wide range of human attributes, such as personal characteristics, traits, attitudes, values, work preferences, aptitudes, abilities, generic skills, specialized skills, and specialized knowledge. This has created a sort of contemporary Tower of Babel, wherein the same terms are often used to mean different classes of skills and different terms are used to mean the same classes of skills. The term *skill gaps* itself refers at times to problems at the level of fundamental aptitudes or abilities (in discussions about workforce literacy and numeracy deficiencies, for example), at times to problems at the level of relatively generic or cross-functional skills (in discussions of the need for greater interpersonal, teamwork, and decision-making skills among production workers who have been reorganized into semiautonomous teams), and at times to problems at the level of very specialized skills or knowledge (in discussions of the need for workers to become proficient in the use of new technology). More recently it has become apparent that one of the gaps of greatest concern to many employers is not about skills at all but about attitudes and personal qualities, such as integrity, reliability, and dependability (Cappelli, 1992b; National Center for Educational Quality of the Workforce, 1994).

The lack of clarity and specificity in the type of gap referred to has its origins in the absence of an appropriate vocabulary concerning skills, which greatly impedes the development of appropriate strategies and interventions for remediation. The work performance model and the Job Analysis Wizard, discussed earlier, both address this problem by explicitly including and differentiating among many categories of skills-related information delineated in ongoing work to develop a national system of occupational information (APDOT, 1993; AIR, 1995). The value of such differentiation lies in the fact that different attribute categories vary in a number of ways—such as how broadly or narrowly their components are defined (level of analysis), the degree of attribute relevance (transferability) across different jobs, ability to modify or train for an attribute, the methods by which attributes can be meaured, and the reliability and validity with which they can be measured. Each of these variables can have important implications for selection program content and measurement.

What are termed cross-functional skills in our work performance model (skills such as decision making, organizing and planning, information gathering, oral communication, problem solving, as well as interpersonal skills, such as leadership, teamwork, social sensitivity, behavior flexibility, and negotiating skill) have been a particular focus of discussion about skills and are of increasing interest to organizations (Pearlman, 1997). Because they represent a kind of middle ground on the attribute generality-specificity continuum (with personal qualities and aptitudes at the most general end and occupation-specific skills and knowledge at the other end), they have potentially great strategic value for selection system content: they are sufficiently generic as to be applicable to relatively wide ranges of jobs (thus enhancing skill transferability and worker mobility), they are relatively trainable, and they appear to be key contributors to effective contextual performance. Yet they present formidable challenges for measurement and incorporation in employee selection programs. Such skills are most commonly measured through assessment centers, work or job simulations, structured behavioral interviews, situational interviews, accomplishment records, and "low-fidelity simulations" (essentially multiple-choice situational judgment tests). Although the predictive validity of overall performance on such measures has been fairly well established, less evidence is available regarding the predictive validity of their component dimensions (that is, for particular cross-functional skills). Moreover, virtually no evidence supports the construct validity of the component dimensions of any of these approaches, that is, evidence that the procedures are actually measuring the intended skills. As a result, developers and users of such measures commonly rely on content validity as the basis for establishing their job-relatedness and ultimate legal defensibility.

Unfortunately, the content validity of nonsimulation-based measures of cross-functional skills is often suspect. This is particularly true for the increasingly widespread practice of measuring such skills in the context of automated staffing systems, as described earlier, through supervisory or self-ratings, or in the context of multisource feedback programs (Dalessio, 1998), where they are also measured in ratings from peers, colleagues, subordinates, or customers. In the more traditional selection context, many commercially available tools and instruments now claim to measure such cross-functional skills as teamwork, customer service, decision making, and the like in video form (wherein a scene presenting, say, a customer service problem is acted out), in oral form (as in situational interviews), and in written form (as in situational judgment tests). In each case applicants indicate how they would handle the presented situation, either by selecting among multiple given alternatives, responding orally, or providing a written response. Despite the labels ascribed to these measures and the claims of some of their developers, there is no evidence that they tap the target skill content domains to any significant degree. Particularly for interpersonal or performance skills (teamwork, leadership, customer service, communication, and so forth), responding cognitively (multiple-choice judgment tests), orally (situational interviews), or in writing (free-response tests) to hypothetical situations, however realistic and appropriate these situations might be, is not the same as performance on the target skills. The often legitimate, empirically based claims of predictive validity for such instruments should not be confused with attributions of content (or construct) validity; such conclusions are not appropriate until relationships between responses to such instruments and "true" performance on the target skills are established through the appropriate research. Thus, in our view, live simulation-based methods such as assessment centers, job simulations, and work samples remain the preferred means for assessing such skills.

New Skills for High-Performance Organizations: Myth or Reality?

Closely related to the skills issues discussed previously is the premise, fostered by a number of government studies and economic reports (Bailey, 1990; Carnevale, Gainer, & Meltzer, 1988; National Center on Education and the Economy, 1990; National Governors' Association, 1992; Secretary's Commission on Achieving Necessary Skills [SCANS], 1991, 1992) as well as federal legislation (such as the Goals 2000: Educate America Act, which promotes a system of voluntary national skill standards), that U.S. businesses must evolve into what have come to be called *high-performance organizations* (HPOs) in order to establish and maintain their own, and the country's, global competitiveness. The assumption is that the structure, culture, and nature of work in HPOs is significantly different from that of traditional organizations. But there is no singular definition, much less any definitive measure or index, of precisely what constitutes an HPO; it is clearly a popular rather than a scientific concept. The term is generally used to describe organizations in which there is explicit commitment to the principles of operational excellence, continuous learning for employees, high product quality, and a strong customer service ethic (SCANS, 1991, 1992). In organizations that are described (or describe themselves) as HPOs, work tends to be problem-oriented, flexible, and organized in teams of multiskilled workers; production is customized and production control is decentralized; labor is viewed not as a cost but as an investment; and quality is designed into the product development process through, for example, process reengineering and quality management principles, which usually implies high employee participation and decentralized decision making close to the point of production or of service delivery.

The HPO movement seems simultaneously to have driven many leaders to move their organizations in genuinely progressive directions and fueled concerns that it will take new kinds of workers with new skills to flourish in such organizations. It has also spawned an ever-growing number of studies and surveys (Bailey, 1990; Cappelli, 1992a; Carnevale et al., 1988; Grubb & Associates, 1992; Michigan Department of Education, 1989; National Center for Educational Quality of the Workforce, 1994; National Governors' Association, 1992; Secretary's Commission on Achieving Necessary Skills, 1991, 1992; Olsten Forum on Human Resource Issues and Trends, 1994; Van Horn, 1995) designed to identify the skills that employers and other stakeholders deem most needed in HPOs. Most of these lists include such worker attributes as reading and writing; applied mathematics; interpersonal skills (such as teamwork, leadership, customer service, negotiation); oral communication; information gathering and analysis; problem solving; critical and creative thinking; organizing, planning, and decision making; technical or functional skills specific to an occupational area; and personal attributes such as motivation, integrity, dependability, self-management.

Although these attribute lists were not in most cases developed directly or systematically from work or job analysis, they nevertheless appear plausible, at least for jobs in general. They tend to reinforce points we made earlier in this section about the attributes likely to be important in the changing workplace and the strategic importance with which cross-functional skills (which make up the majority of those identified by these studies) are viewed by employers. Yet little on such lists reflects skills that are new or different from those that have been long recognized (and demonstrated empirically) to be important for most areas of work. What might be "new" is that many of them reflect skills that formerly characterized higher-level occupations but are now becoming relevant to a wider range of jobs because of workplace changes.

The important lesson in all this is that selection practitioners must be able to look beyond skill or competency labels to develop relevant and accurate attribute definitions that lead to meaningful and valid measurement. The newly deemed importance of certain skills may be more myth than reality upon analysis of their identifiable and measurable components. For example, recent research on teamwork (Klimoski & Jones, 1995) identifies four clusters of KSAOs (not necessarily obvious from the mere label *teamwork*) needed to be an effective team member: performance skills, team process skills, team task skills, and team boundary management skills. Similarly, *practical intelligence* (Sternberg & Wagner, 1993), despite its claims as a new construct representing something akin to practical problem-solving ability and organizational "savvy," arguably represents little more than a combination of general cognitive ability and occupation-specific and organization-specific knowledge (Schmidt & Hunter, 1993).

In other words, the notion that new skills are needed for organizations to transform themselves into HPOs is part reality and part myth. The *reality* is that the importance of some skills for some jobs and settings is undoubtedly increasing. In some areas of work, skills that are now very important rarely came into play in the past—for example, interpersonal and communication skills for technical specialists who formerly worked in relative isolation but now are teamed with, and must work and coordinate closely with, product developers and marketing staff. The *myth* comes into the equation when one realizes that few such skills are really new, despite what their names or labels might suggest; rather they just represent a different configuration, weighting, or rank ordering, within given jobs or areas of work, of well-established, previously identified KSAOs.

Selection Issues for Knowledge Workers

We have noted throughout this chapter that technology is a major driver of change throughout the global economy, affecting both the context and content of selection work. Many economists have attributed the strength of the U.S. economy in the late 1990s to its leadership in technological innovation. These trends have led to dramatic shifts in the U.S. job structure, creating over 340,000 white-collar and "gold-collar" (that is, high-tech knowledge-worker) jobs that cannot be filled by information technology workers alone (Duff, 1997; Peterson & Forcier, 1998). Even the sometimes-maligned service sector is growing because of high-skilled technology jobs and not just "hamburger-flipping" jobs (Sanger, 1996). Thus, technology is creating new high-skilled jobs while simultaneously eliminating lower-skilled jobs through automation and computerization of routine tasks. This creates almost constant churn in the task structure of many jobs and the consequent need to reassign or retrain existing employees or hire new ones (Coopers & Lybrand, 1998). The combination of rapid growth in demand for technology-intensive jobs, decreasing numbers of engineering and computer-science graduates, and a tightening of U.S. immigration is creating a shortage of skilled technical employees that the U.S. Commerce Department projects will inhibit productivity across all U.S. industries both now and in the near future (Murray, 1998; Vesely, 1997).

This environment has affected the selection of knowledge workers, who are enjoying unprecedented bargaining power thanks to their scarcity. Even inexperienced graduates receive multiple offers from employers. Increasing numbers of technically sophisticated high school graduates are foregoing college to accept well-paying technology-related jobs. Employers are offering high salaries, signing bonuses, and unique benefits and "perks" (from flexible hours and work schedules to permitting pets at work) to attract people with valued expertise (Munk, 1998), some of whom earn more than their bosses. In this context, traditional selection practices are increasingly challenged. It is more critical than ever for organizations to ensure that their selection programs are not overly burdensome and are perceived as job-relevant. Otherwise, employers may either fail to attract sufficient numbers of applicants or have their job offers turned down, because applicants with valued skills and knowledge who are "turned off" by an organization can in most cases choose to work for others with simpler or more palatable selection and hiring processes. Some of the key concerns related to knowledge worker selection include the following:

Applicant Attraction Issues. Organizations that can redesign jobs to be technically interesting may gain a competitive advantage in attracting knowledge workers. For example, interesting work and a start-up atmosphere is a key reason why Vinod Dham, the designer of the Pentium and K6 computer chips, quit both Intel and AMD for an unknown start-up called Silicon Spice ("Chip Wizard," 1997; LaPedus, 1998). Many knowledge workers are not particularly motivated by pay and opportunity for advancement (they may have already made a fortune at a previous start-up) but are highly motivated by interesting work. In addition, it is generally to an employer's advantage to disclose fully both the positive and negative aspects of the work to applicants in order to minimize the loss of costly new employees when they ultimately discover that the work is not a good fit with their interests and values. This situation is becoming increasingly commonplace as employees are less loyal to organizations and less willing to perform unfulfilling work in a traditional environment (Munk, 1998). Using realistic job previews (RJPs) can be an extremely useful tool in this regard (Wanous, 1989). RJPs can be as simple as a written list or brochure describing the work setting and major activities (greatly facilitated these days by Web-based recruiting and job posting) or a hiring manager mentioning key aspects of the job in an interview, or as elaborate as a multimedia work simulation.

Face Validity of Selection Tools.   Face validity (that is, the appearance or perception of job-relatedness), often scoffed at as an unscientific concept by personnel psychologists, has taken on increasing importance in today's (job) buyer's market (Smither, Reilly, Millsap, Pearlman, & Stoffey, 1993). This is likely to be especially true for knowledge workers. For example, use of paper-and-pencil tests may give applicants the impression that the organization lacks technical savvy. This in turn could cause them to be concerned about the support they might expect as an employee (antiquated computers, for example) and lead them to choose a competitor that uses procedures that appear more contemporary and relevant.

Similarly, "generic" job interviews conducted by nonspecialists (HR employment staff) can also create credibility gaps for technically sophisticated applicants. Organizations can often effectively address such issues by using alternative measures of the same skills or knowledge (such as computer-based tests or knowledge-based structured interviews instead of written tests) that may be more palatable to such applicants. Face validity is likely to be less of a problem for selection tools that measure occupation-specific skills and knowledge (such as a word processing performance test for clerical work or a programming knowledge test for information technology work); however, organizations must also be prepared to invest in the updating, revision, and replacement of such measures, which can quickly become outdated as their related technology and knowledge bases evolve.

Lengthy Selection Procedures. Long tests, work samples, or multiple interviews are frequently time consuming and uncomfortable, and they may be a turnoff to applicants who have multiple job options that do not involve such burdens. Furthermore, experienced professionals are often not accustomed to being required to go through some types of selection procedures (such as paper-and-pencil tests) and view such preemployment activities as more appropriate for inexperienced applicants than those with a proven track record. It is generally to an organization's advantage to do everything possible to streamline the selection process and its components (by combining all selection procedures in one company visit or using computer-adaptive tests rather than conventional tests, for example). Doing this can often be a substantial challenge to organizations that wish their selection process to measure a combination of cognitive abilities (to predict continuous learning ability), softer interpersonal and teamwork skills (to predict contextual performance), and particular specialized skills and knowledge (to predict task performance).

Rethinking Selection System Design and Implementation

In this final section we consider how workplace changes necessitate new ways of designing and deploying operational selection systems. Most selection systems have multiple components, both implicit and explicit. For example, implicit selection factors such as how and by whom resumes get screened before a candidate is even invited into the more formal parts of the selection system (such as testing or interviewing), or how managers choose an individual to fill a specific position from among a pool of candidates who successfully qualified on the formal selection process, can significantly affect the overall effectiveness of a selection system. This section addresses a number of issues relevant to the overall design, integration, and application of selection systems in the changing workplace.

Selection System Design

As competition for increasingly scarce talent intensifies, HR departments have been under growing pressure to design their selection systems to be more efficient and cost-effective than ever.

Borrowing a concept from the inventory management field, many organizations are aspiring to a just-in-time selection model, that is, a process wherein sufficient numbers of people with the necessary KSAOs are available to fill vacant positions just when they are needed. However, because selection costs and efficiencies must be balanced with the need for high-quality hires, the real challenge for organizations is in optimizing these often conflicting factors in operational selection processes. An overemphasis on either of these factors (cost-efficiency and quality of hires) at the expense of the other can lead to very undesirable consequences. For example, if an organization deploys a valid selection system that requires applicants to go through multiple steps (such as a written test, a simulation, and an interview) and takes several weeks to complete, many desirable job candidates may be lost to competitors who can evaluate and hire more quickly. In contrast, organizations that focus almost exclusively on speedily filling vacant positions stand to compromise the quality and productivity of their hires, which ultimately will hurt their operations.

There are various selection system design strategies through which organizations can attempt to maximize (or at least optimize) selection process cost-effectiveness and quality. When a selection system consists of multiple components, a basic design decision concerns whether applicants will be required to "pass" or "qualify" above some established level or cut score on each component (traditionally called a *multiple hurdles approach*), or whether applicants' performance on all the components will somehow be integrated into an overall composite score on which qualification or selection decisions will be made (called a *compensatory approach,* in that stronger performance on one component can compensate for weaker performance on another). In the case of the multiple hurdles approach, organizations need to pay attention to the optimal sequencing of selection process components. Other things being equal, it is generally advantageous to sequence the selection process components that applicants will go through from the least to the most expensive, from the least to the most time consuming, and from the most to the least valid. Such a strategy enhances cost-effectiveness, efficiency, and quality of hires because the largest numbers of applicants are screened (at the first step) using the least expensive, fastest, and most valid component, whereas relatively smaller numbers of candidates—only those who have qualified on the early components—are screened (at the last step) on the relatively costlier, lengthier, and less valid components.

However, the flexibility of the compensatory approach can offer advantages both to the organization and to applicants in that applicants cannot be disqualified based on their performance on just one of multiple components. But these advantages must be weighed against the disadvantage of relatively higher cost and less efficiency. Such design decisions are not trivial for organizations because they have a direct effect on both the number and quality of applicants available for hiring consideration. Ultimately, the choice involves evaluating a set of relatively complex trade-offs among both technical factors (such as the validity and intercorrelation among components, and the cut scores and associated qualification rates of both components and the composite) and nontechnical considerations (such as administration costs, resource requirements, size of the relevant applicant labor market, and the urgency of the need to fill positions) (Boudreau, 1991).

Another set of selection system design strategies involves the use of various forms of preselection or self-deselection mechanisms, which facilitate unqualified applicants removing themselves from the applicant pool. Such strategies can lower the cost or improve the efficiency of selection process administration by increasing the yield (qualification rate) of the more formal selection process because prescreening or self-selection has produced a higher-quality applicant pool, thereby reducing the number of applicants going through the process. In turn, administration costs are reduced. Possible methods include:

- The use of carefully constructed applicant self-rating or supplemental application forms (for self-assessment of occupation-specific skills and knowledge).
- The use of other forms of structured applicant-provided information (such as work experience questionnaires).
- The use of college or high school transcripts.
- The use of required prehire training as a prescreening procedure.
- The use of realistic job previews (via paper, video, Web, telephone, or other media).

- The use of telephone- or interactive voice response–based pre-screening on basic job qualifications and work preferences. This can also usefully incorporate realistic job preview information on both work content (major tasks, responsibilities, and outputs) and work context (the work setting and facility, pay, hours, special work requirements, and other conditions of employment).
- The use of self-administered on-line practice tests or simulations providing diagnostic feedback regarding probability of success on the operational selection process and providing linkages to related training.

Attempts to optimize selection system efficiency and effectiveness are often challenged by real-world conditions—resource, budget, geographic, and labor market constraints, as well as business needs—that can jeopardize the deployment of what an organization knows to be its preferred selection strategy. The "reality factor" often intrudes into the best laid selection system plans, calling for creative solutions. There may be insufficient time or resources available for rigorous selection tool development, so that selection tools or services that develop them need to be outsourced or purchased. There may be budget or resource constraints on selection process administration or delivery, so that more up-front prescreening using information generated by applicants rather than gathered by the organization is needed. (For example, structured work experience questionnaires or "accomplishment record"–type approaches [Hough, 1984] may be taken, which can reduce the number of applicants to be processed.) There may be geographic constraints on selection process administration, suggesting the possibility of technological solutions—such as telephone-based or live video–based interviewing or assessment, or assessments that are delivered and videotaped remotely but scored centrally—or logistical solutions, such as the use of contracted third-party administrators. Business conditions may create a very narrow hiring window and great urgency to fill many positions quickly. Such circumstances may also be addressable through technological solutions, as well as by finding ways simply to shorten existing selection tools—through computer-adaptive rather than conventional testing or by creating mini-assessment centers or more limited simulations as an alternative to full-length assessment centers—which can enable the processing of larger numbers of applicants in a given time frame. There may be labor market issues, such as a shortage of qualified applicants or particular skill or knowledge gaps. Possible solutions here might include building in prehire training or certification as a prerequisite to job application; temporarily lowering qualification requirements while providing posthire mechanisms such as training or certification programs to address potential resulting skill or knowledge gaps; excluding from selection programs measures of skills or knowledge that are in relatively short supply in the labor market and establishing internal development mechanisms that ensure their acquisition; or developing strategies, processes, and selection tools that facilitate hiring from wider geographic areas, including globally.

Selection System Stakeholder and Policy Issues

We have emphasized the importance of viewing selection as part of broader HR, and organizational, systems. Thus, selection systems can never be fully optimized unless they are coordinated with other key HR and business processes, such as recruiting, training, performance management, business planning, strategy development, and so forth. This in turn implies the need for selection professionals to be attuned to the needs of the direct and indirect stakeholders in an organization's selection processes, as well as those who contribute to or participate in the end-to-end operation of a selection system. Participants may include recruiters, selection process administrators, selection system database administrators, interviewers, employment process managers, hiring managers, legal and labor relations staff, the top leadership of both HR and the units into which people are hired, as well as job candidates themselves.

In today's changing workplace, selection practitioners, who historically associated their work predominantly with the industrial side of industrial/organizational psychology, must increasingly appreciate the social and organizational psychology aspects of personnel selection. For example, on the social psychology side, we previously noted the importance of applicant attraction issues in designing selection systems for knowledge workers and the potentially negative effects that selection tools lacking face validity can have on attracting desirable candidates, as well as on such candidates' subsequent perceptions of the organization. Similarly, selection systems that provide meaningful diagnostic feedback to candidates about their strengths and areas for improvement (and better yet, appropriate training and development information and resources linked to identified improvement needs) stand to create favorable perceptions of the organization among applicants. On the organizational psychology side, it is not hard to recognize selection programs as a type of organizational intervention that is subject to most of the conventional wisdom on the factors that contribute to the success of virtually any intervention: the need for buy-in and support from top levels of the organization, good communication about implementation and ongoing operations that includes all stakeholders in the process, and mechanisms and systems for ongoing feedback among all stakeholders.

From this perspective one can appreciate the importance for selection practitioners of educating—by any and all means possible—stakeholders on the strategic value to the organization (and hence to themselves) of good selection and the opportunity costs of poor selection. Doing so can greatly facilitate all players buying in to a common goal—high-quality hires—and understanding their role or contribution to the goal, thereby forming the basis for developing the types of partnerships among all stakeholders that will promote a truly effective selection system.

The absence of stakeholder understanding and partnerships can lead to a variety of systemic problems that too often plague and can ultimately undermine the value of selection programs. One such phenomenon is when developers and the deliverers or administrators of selection programs work at cross-purposes or under different implicit or explicit incentives or accountabilities. For example, selection program delivery staff, such as employment office recruiters or interviewers who screen resumes and conduct initial qualification interviews, are sometimes measured on keeping hiring costs down and producing as many qualified applicants as quickly as possible. Thus they have the incentive to produce high selection ratios (that is, to generate high proportions of qualified job applicants) and short time-to-fill-position results. Selection program developers, in contrast, are often accountable primarily for the validity and utility of their selection tools (that is, for maximizing quality of hires and optimizing person-job fit regardless of time and cost factors) and thus have the incentive to produce moderate to low selection ratios. An appropriate analogy is of two oars in the same boat pulling in opposite directions—with the organization and its stakeholders, as well as new hires themselves, the potential losers (if such conflicting accountabilities compromise the achievement of an optimal balance among selection program time, cost, and validity considerations).

Another systemic problem derives from perceived or actual control or "ownership" of the selection process, what it should consist of, or how it should be used. For example, hiring managers who are unaware of the potential value of systematic and rigorous selection tools may wish to "default" to the use of an expedient, ad hoc, and often low-validity selection process, such as a brief resume review and informal interview. Or top leadership may mandate that the organization's values and culture be reflected in all its HR programs, including selection programs, possibly creating tension between such requests and what is possible to operationalize in a technically sound and legally defensible way.

One approach to take when faced with such dilemmas that we have found useful is to use high-validity, standardized, systematic selection procedures such as standardized ability, skill, and knowledge testing for initial applicant screening to produce a pool of well-qualified applicants for a given job or job family. Then hiring managers are given wide latitude to make final selection decisions from among the qualified applicants but are provided with appropriate tools to assist them, such as a well-designed structured interview on which they are trained and other relevant information, such as a summary of applicant performance on the standardized selection tools. This approach allows selection program staff to bring the best available technology (the most valid selection tools) to the initial, larger-scale selection task, while allowing hiring managers to select for the "fit" of (already qualified) applicants for specific positions based on more specific factors (specialized knowledge or experience, affinity for the organization's culture and values, and so forth) that are not measured in the formal selection process. Thus, hiring managers have their desired (and we believe, rightful) role of making the final decisions about people they have to "live with" rather than have new hires "forced" upon them by HR, while the potential liability of managers using idiosyncratic or ad hoc criteria for hiring is minimized, since all applicants seen by hiring managers would be qualified.

As these examples highlight, the policies under which selection programs are administered can have a significant impact on selection system effectiveness, and it is important to think through them and attend to them carefully. Poorly conceived or less than optimal selection policies can seriously undermine the utility of even high-validity selection procedures or components. However, all formal or highly structured policies—whether well or poorly conceived—are becoming increasingly challenged and problematic to enforce in many organizations that embody or aspire to a decentralized, empowerment-oriented culture. Centrally developed, inflexible policies are now often viewed as irrelevant, if not harmful, to both the spirit and the operation of fast-moving, fast-changing (especially high-technology) organizations for whom "tools, not rules" is becoming the operative philosophy of line management's desired relationship with HR. This can create a serious tension for selection practitioners in view of the legal and regulatory context in which they must operate.

Many of the examples we described earlier in this section, such as using compensatory selection models and clearly differentiating among the roles and responsibilities for which different selection program participants are accountable, can provide the means for successfully working through such tensions. They also illustrate the benefits of selection practitioners recognizing and addressing the social and organizational context in which selection programs operate. Although it is much more easily said than done, we have found that many if not most of the conflicts, tensions, and control issues that frequently surface around personnel selection design, implementation, and use can be lessened through appropriate education, partnering, communication, and feedback among stakeholders.

Conclusion

This chapter has described some of the broad economic, demographic, and technological changes reshaping organizations and the nature of work itself. Through a case study from our own company (see appendix) as well as other examples, we illustrated the profound implications of such changes on the practice of personnel selection. We presented a model of work performance and strategies for the analysis of work that we believe provide useful frameworks and approaches for conceptualizing and developing selection programs that will be effective and appropriate for today's global workplace and workforce.

As stated at the beginning of this chapter, the basic selection proposition—that is, if you want effective job performance, select good people—belies a much greater complexity in personnel selection practice than may be apparent to nonspecialists. And although selection practice in reality was never as cut-and-dried as it may have seemed to some, today's workplace changes have created new challenges in virtually every facet of selection—from how organizations think about their overall selection strategy, to the content of selection tools and programs, to selection program design and implementation. As many organization leaders like to say, "Every challenge is an opportunity." From our vantage point on the edge of the twenty-first century, it seems that the opportunities—for creativity, innovation, and expansion of thought about the practice of personnel selection—have never been greater.

Appendix: Lucent Technologies Inc. Joint Venture Chip Factory Case Study

We have had to address many facets of the changing nature of work in developing our own selection systems at Lucent Technologies Inc. An example of a successful integration of selection and other HR systems can be drawn from our experience at Cirent, a computer chip manufacturing facility that was originally a joint venture between Lucent Technologies Inc. and Cirrus Logic. In 1995 Cirent was planning to build a new $600 million clean room in Orlando, Florida, and needed to hire many types of personnel, starting with technicians. Our competitors in other regions were able to secure technicians with skills in domains as diverse as robotics and interpersonal communication, both from competitors and from specialized degree programs (Barton, 1996). Cirent had neither type of resource in Orlando. In addition, Cirent's HR processes were slow and out of date. Originally designed when the existing AT&T (now Lucent) factory was first opened in 1984, they could not easily accommodate a massive influx of new, inexperienced personnel.

Job Analysis

We based all of our HR systems on a solid understanding of current and future technician work and worker requirements, using a combination of conventional job analysis methods and adaptations of "future-oriented" job analysis methods (Goldstein, Zedeck, & Schneider, 1993; Schneider & Konz, 1989). First, we compiled a list of required tasks and KSAOs from our observations of incumbents and critical incident–like interviews with managers that elicited examples of exceptionally good and poor performance. Next, we administered two surveys designed to identify the key dimensions and understand which KSAOs were essential to performing each task. Finally, we asked a set of managers responsible for planning future business strategy to review our results and ensure that our tentative model would serve the needs of the business for the next three years. We asked them to tell us how the jobs and tasks would change in the future and how those changes would likely affect each required KSAO. This provided us with a competency model that showed which key KSAOs were needed to perform important current and future job tasks. The entire job analysis process flow is shown in Figure 1.2.

Selection

The job analysis results clearly indicated that the existing selection process was too narrowly focused. For example, in addition to the electronics knowledge it assessed, our technicians needed to have expertise in robotics, pneumatics, vacuum technology, electromechanical systems, silicon processing, statistical process control, interpersonal communications, writing, and teaching (Prince, Barney, & Artman, 1995). They also needed to adapt effectively to constant change, learn quickly, and perform their job tasks conscientiously. We ultimately decided that some constructs (such as knowledge and cognitive ability) would be best assessed through paper-and-pencil tests and others (such as interpersonal and communications skills)

Figure 1.2. Job Analysis Process Flow.

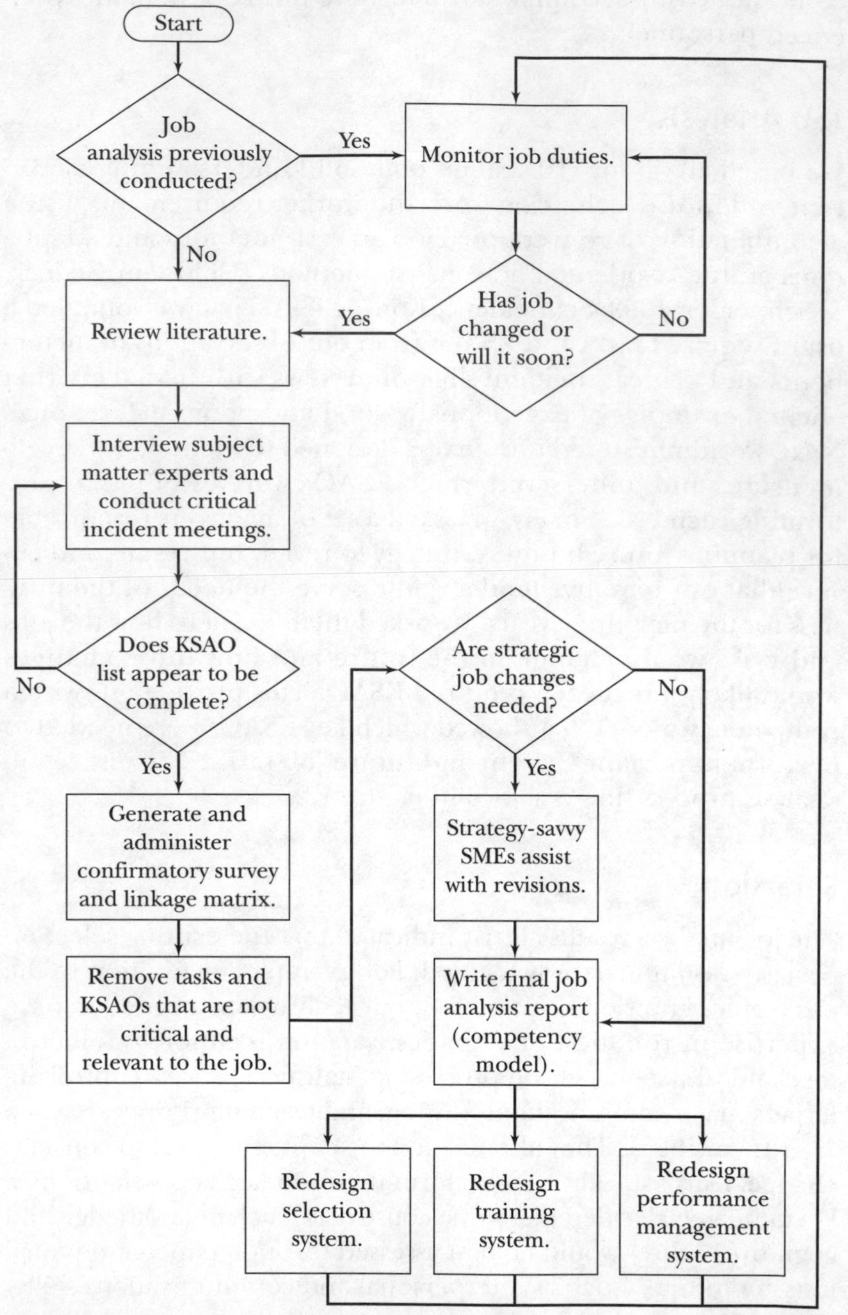

through a structured behavioral interview based on past experience. We made final modifications to the selection system components after pilot testing and criterion-related validation studies based on a sample of current employees.

Process Redesign

Before we implemented this new selection system, however, we needed to address the slow cycle time of the former selection process. The original process took fourteen weeks to complete from the time a decision was made to hire new personnel to the time the individuals actually started work. We interviewed recruiting specialists and asked them to verbally flowchart the entire process so we could analyze the reasons for the lengthy time frame. Through various process improvements, such as queuing all job advertisements, automating the test scoring process, combining process steps, creating multiple sources for drug screens, and restructuring the orientation training, we were able to shorten the process to eight weeks—a 43 percent improvement.

Training

Training curricula were also derived from the job analysis to ensure job relevance. We grouped trainable knowledge and skills into courses and created behavioral objectives for each based on its links to key job tasks. We then selected vendor courses through a systematic ranking process in which relevant staff assigned weights to the various course characteristics that were important to us, such as scope, flexibility, teaching methods, ability to evaluate trainees, cost, duration, and upgradability. Next, pre- and posttests were created for each course based on the behavioral objectives and instructional materials, enabling us to measure change in students' knowledge, skills, or abilities. (Later, once sufficient numbers of students had taken the courses, standardized difference scores were calculated for each set of pre- and posttests, demonstrating an average trainee improvement of one-half a standard deviation across all courses.) Although this training plan was necessary and effective in the short run, our longer-term strategy was to have a local labor pool from which to select people with the required knowledge and skills rather than continue to do extensive (and expensive) training at Cirent.

Toward that end, we worked with a local community college to build a new associate degree program that directly met our needs.

Performance Management

Finally, a performance management program was created and included the development of a performance appraisal rating form. The tasks and dimensions derived from the job analysis were used to create this performance appraisal form. The results from the performance appraisal had an impact on pay, with low ratings resulting in no pay increase and high ratings resulting in a pay progression. Because supervisors had never rated their employees' performance and because such ratings are prone to subjectivity, we developed a training course to ensure reliable and valid ratings and responsible reporting of behavior. This course included segments on frame-of-reference training and performance management training. For the frame-of-reference segment we developed videotaped examples of behaviors for each dimension at each level of performance (high, average, low). These simulations were used as an aid in calibrating participants' ratings. Supervisors were then taught performance management concepts and trained in effectively communicating job performance information to their subordinates. The training was well received by supervisors in the factory.

Challenges and Obstacles

One-hundred-year-old companies such as ours experience unique challenges in the face of large-scale organizational changes, which are, at best, complex and difficult. Because of this we took a number of steps to facilitate the implementation of these various HR systems and to gain support for them—from both senior management and the affected workers. We had begun the project during negotiations with the local labor union representing most of the factory's workers. The new labor contract, which was negotiated by senior plant management, required performance measurement systems and training curricula linked to pay. We were able to show how our approach—based on integrated HR systems founded on common job analysis data—would both fulfill the requirements of the labor contract and support factory goals, in contrast to the pre-existing selection, training, and performance appraisal systems. Although this argument was effective at gaining plant management's initial buy-in, we continued to keep them updated on the project's progress to ensure continued support.

We also experienced challenges with our training curriculum. Six months into the program, we discovered that some factory operations managers felt that employees were spending too much time off their jobs taking training courses. Also, because the initial course of the curriculum was targeted to basic foundation skills, one influential manager was skeptical of its job-relatedness ("Writing skills aren't getting chips out the door"). In response to these concerns we reviewed the job analysis data with the concerned managers, showing them how and why the selected courses were related to effective performance of critical job tasks, and we were able to ameliorate their concerns.

Case Study Conclusion

Cirent succeeded at overhauling several business-critical HR systems. Two features of this HR process redesign effort are especially noteworthy. First, the job-relatedness and future focus helped to ensure that Lucent would receive a return on its investment over the long term. Second, all of the HR systems—selection, training, and performance management—were completely integrated. (Figure 1.3 provides a graphical representation of the links between these systems.) If internal candidates seeking promotions failed a trainable portion of the selection system (such as technical knowledge), they were provided specific feedback and directed to appropriate training courses. At the same time, incumbents whose job performance was less than satisfactory were directed to courses that addressed specific job-related deficiencies. The close integration between the processes gave the company a competitive advantage because the various systems served as backups to one another if errors occurred in one part of the process. This case also illustrates how integral a selection program can be to a broader HR intervention, and it demonstrates the importance of building close linkages between the selection program and the HR process components that precede and follow it.

Figure 1.3.   HR Systems Integration.

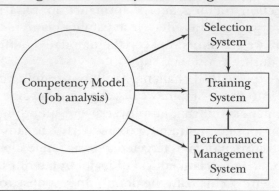

References

Advisory Panel for the Dictionary of Occupational Titles. (1993, May). *The new DOT: A database of occupational titles for the twenty-first century.* Washington, DC: U.S. Department of Labor.

American Institutes for Research. (1995). *Development of prototype occupational information network (O*NET) content model.* Salt Lake City: Utah Department of Employment Security.

Bailey, T. (1990, Spring). Jobs of the future and skills they will require: New thinking on an old debate. *American Educator, 14,* 10–15, 40–44.

Barney, M. F. (1998). Automated benchmarking Internet agent. Patent Pending, Assignee: Lucent Technologies Inc.

Barney, M. F., Pearlman, K., & Harkey, S. T. (1997). System and method for analyzing work requirements and linking human resource products to jobs. Patent Pending, Assignee: Lucent Technologies Inc.

Barton, C. (1996, October). *Sematech workforce development report.* Presentation to the Sematech Training Council biannual meeting, Burlington, VT.

Borman, W. C., & Motowidlo, S. J. (1993). Expanding the criterion domain to include elements of contextual performance. In N. Schmitt, W. C. Borman, & Associates (Eds.), *Personnel selection in organizations* (pp. 71–98). San Francisco: Jossey-Bass.

Boudreau, J. W. (1991). Utility analysis for decisions in human resource management. In M. D. Dunnette & L. M. Hough (Eds.), *Handbook of industrial and organizational psychology* (2nd ed., Vol. 2, pp. 621–745). Palo Alto, CA: Consulting Psychologists Press.

Bridges, W. (1994). *Job shift: How to prosper in a world without jobs.* Reading, MA: Addison-Wesley.

Campbell, J. P., McCloy, R. A., Oppler, S. H., & Sager, C. E. (1993). A theory of job performance. In N. Schmitt, W. C. Borman, & Associates (Eds.), *Personnel selection in organizations* (pp. 35–70). San Francisco: Jossey-Bass.

Cappelli, P. (1992a). *College and the workplace: How should we assess student performance?* (National Center on the Educational Quality of the Workforce report). Philadelphia: University of Pennsylvania.

Cappelli, P. (1992b). *Is the "skills gap" really about attitudes?* Philadelphia: National Center for Educational Quality in the Workplace, University of Pennsylvania.

Carnevale, A. P., Gainer, L. J., and Meltzer, A. S. (1988). *Workplace basics: The skills employers want.* Washington, DC: American Society for Training and Development.

Cascio, W. F. (1995). Whither industrial and organizational psychology in a changing world of work? *American Psychologist, 50,* 928–939.

Chip wizard Vinod Dham quits AMD. (1997, November 13). *Indolink NRI News.* [http://www.indolink.com/NRINews/vinDham.html].

Coates, J. F., Jarratt, J., & Mahaffie, J. B. (1990). *Future work: Seven critical forces reshaping work and the workforce in North America.* San Francisco: Jossey-Bass.

Coopers & Lybrand. (1998, February 19). Fast-growth firms demand well-educated workers with advanced skills for the information age, finds Coopers & Lybrand L.L.P. *Business Wire.*

Dalessio, A. T. (1998). Using multisource feedback for employee development and personnel decisions. In J. W. Smither (Ed.), *Performance appraisal: State of the art in practice* (pp. 278–330). San Francisco: Jossey-Bass.

Dannhauser, C.A.L. (1998, November). The invisible worker. *Working Woman,* p. 38.

Duff, C. (1997, March 13). Economy still rolls with mild inflation. *Wall Street Journal,* p. A2.

Goldstein, I. L., Zedeck, S., & Schneider, B. (1993). An exploration of the job analysis-content validity process. In N. Schmitt, W. C. Borman, & Associates (Eds.), *Personnel selection in organizations* (pp. 3–34). San Francisco: Jossey-Bass.

Grubb, N. W., & Associates. (1992, December). *Betwixt and between: Education, skills, and employment in sub-baccalaureate labor markets* (National Center for Research in Vocational Education report). Berkeley: University of California.

Hall, D. T., & Richter, J. (1990). Career gridlock: Baby boomers hit the wall. *Academy of Management Executive, 4,* 7–22.

Hough, L. M. (1984). Development and evaluation of the "accomplishment record" method of selecting and promoting professionals. *Journal of Applied Psychology, 69,* 135–146.

Jeanneret, P. R. (1998, April). Discussant comments. In R. J. Klimoski (Chair), *Planning for work in the 21st century: What does it mean for I/O psychologists?* Symposium conducted at the 13th annual conference of the Society for Industrial and Organizational Psychology, Dallas.

Johnston, W. B., & Packer, A. E. (1987). *Workforce 2000.* Indianapolis: Hudson Institute.

Klimoski, R., & Jones, R. G. (1995). Staffing for effective group decision making: Key issues in matching people and teams. In R. A. Guzzo, E. Salas, & Associates (Eds.), *Team effectiveness and decision making in organizations* (pp. 291–332). San Francisco: Jossey-Bass.

LaPedus, M. (1998, April 3). Former Intel, AMD exec joins Silicon Spice. [http://www.techweb.com/investor/story/INV19980403S0007].

Lenz, E. A. (1996). Flexible employment: Positive work strategies for the 21st century. *Journal of Labor Research, 17,* 555–566.

Lowisch, H. (1998, May 9). Cultural differences pose challenge to Daimler-Chrysler merger. *Agence France Presse, NewsEdge Corporation.*

Maney, K. (1998, November 16). The networked economy changes everything. *USA Today,* pp. 1E–2E.

Matloff, N. (1998). Debunking the myth of a desperate software labor shortage. [http://heather.cs.ucdavis.edu/itaa.html]. November 8, 1998.

Michigan Department of Education. (1989). *Michigan Employability Survey.* Ann Arbor: Author.

Munk, N. (1998, March 16). The new organization man. *Fortune,* pp. 63–74.

Murray, B. (1998, June). Dipping math scores heat up debate over math teaching: Psychologists differ over the merits of teaching children "whole math." *APA Monitor, 29*(6), 34–35.

National Center for Educational Quality of the Workforce. (1994, March). *First findings: The EQW national employer survey.* Philadelphia: University of Pennsylvania.

National Center on Education and the Economy. (1990, June). *America's choice: High skills or low wages.* Rochester, NY: Author.

National Commission on Excellence in Education. (1983). *A nation at risk: The imperative for educational reform.* Washington, DC: U.S. Government Printing Office.

National Governors' Association. (1992). *Enhancing skills for a competitive world.* Washington, DC: Author.

Offerman, L. R., & Gowing, M. K. (1993). Personnel selection in the future: The impact of changing demographics and the nature of work.

In N. Schmitt, W. C. Borman, & Associates (Eds.), *Personnel selection in organizations* (pp. 385–417). San Francisco: Jossey-Bass.

Olsten Forum on Human Resource Issues and Trends. (1994). *Skills for success.* Westbury, NY: Olsten Corporation.

Pearlman, K. (1994, March). Job families in the United States Employment Service: Review, analysis, and recommendations (Technical report prepared for the U.S. Department of Labor; Contract No. 92–442). Salt Lake City: Western Test Development Center, Utah Department of Employment Security.

Pearlman, K. (Chair) (1995, May). *Is "job" dead? Implications of changing concepts of work for I/O science and practice.* Panel discussion conducted at the tenth annual conference of the Society for Industrial and Organizational Psychology, Orlando.

Pearlman, K. (1997). Twenty-first century measures for twenty-first century work. In A. Lesgold, M. J. Feuer, & A. Black (Eds.), *Transitions in work and learning: Implications for assessment* (pp. 136–179). Washington, DC: National Academy Press.

Peterson, R., & Forcier, J. (1998, April 25). *The economics of the information technology worker shortage.* Information Technology Association of America [http://www.itaa.org/workforce/resources/a19980425.htm].

Prince, A., Barney, M., & Artman, D. (1995, December). *Job analysis report: Process analysts.* Unpublished technical report, Microelectronics International University, AT&T Microelectronics, Orlando.

Reich, R. B. (1991). *The work of nations: Preparing ourselves for 21st century capitalism.* New York: Knopf.

Rynes, S. L., Orlitzky, M. O., & Bretz, R. D., Jr. (1997). Experienced hiring versus college recruiting: Practices and emerging trends. *Personnel Psychology, 50,* 309–339.

Sanger, D. E. (1996, April 24). Workplace fears disputed in politically delicate study. *New York Times,* p. C3.

Schmidt, F. L., & Hunter, J. E. (1993). Tacit knowledge, practical intelligence, general mental ability, and job knowledge. *Current Directions in Psychological Science, 2,* 8–9.

Schmidt, F. L., Hunter, J. E., McKenzie, R. C., & Muldrow, T. W. (1979). Impact of valid selection procedures on workforce productivity. *Journal of Applied Psychology, 64,* 609–626.

Schmidt, F. L., Mack, M. J., & Hunter, J. E. (1984). Selection utility in the occupation of U.S. park ranger for three modes of test use. *Journal of Applied Psychology, 69,* 490–497.

Schneider, B., & Konz, A. M. (1989). Strategic job analysis. *Human Resource Management, 28,* 51–63.

Schneider, B., Kristoff, A. L., Goldstein, H. W., & Smith, D. B. (1997). What is this thing called fit? In N. Anderson & P. Herriot (Eds.), *Handbook of selection and appraisal* (2nd ed., pp. 393–412). New York: Wiley.

Secretary's Commission on Achieving Necessary Skills. (1991, June). *What work requires of schools: A SCANS report for America 2000.* Washington, DC: U.S. Department of Labor.

Secretary's Commission on Achieving Necessary Skills. (1992, April). *Learning a living: A blueprint for high performance: A SCANS report for America 2000.* Washington, DC: U.S. Department of Labor.

Seltzer, L. (1998, June 9). PC 2001 software in the new millennium: Component software. *PC Magazine, 17*(11), 184.

Senge, P. M. (1990). *The fifth discipline: The art and practice of the learning organization.* New York: Doubleday.

Smither, J. W., Reilly, R. R., Millsap, R. E., Pearlman, K., & Stoffey, R. W. (1993). Applicant reactions to selection procedures. *Personnel Psychology, 46,* 49–76.

Sternberg, R. J., & Wagner, R. K. (1993). The g-ocentric view of intelligence and job performance is wrong. *Current Directions in Psychological Science, 2,* 1–4.

Tapscott, D. (1998, November 16). New universe forming as business between businesses explodes. *USA Today,* pp. 1E–2E.

Uniform guidelines on employee selection procedures. (1978). *Federal Register, 43,* 38290–38315.

U.S. Department of Labor. (1995). *Report on the American workforce.* Washington, DC: Author.

Van Horn, C. (1995, October). *Enhancing the connection between higher education and the workplace: A survey of employers.* Denver: State Higher Education Executive Officers and the Education Commission of the States.

Vesely, R. (1997, September 29). Study: Glut of IT openings, few candidates. *Wired News.*

Wanous, J. P. (1989). Installing realistic job previews: Ten tough choices. *Personnel Psychology, 42,* 117–134.

CHAPTER 2

Integrating Selection with Other Organizational Processes and Systems

A. Catherine Higgs
Ellen M. Papper
Linda S. Carr

It may seem a strange question to ask in a book that is entirely devoted to selection, but precisely what *is* selection? The general definition of *to select* is "choose from a number or group by fitness or preference." For industrial/organizational (I/O) psychologists who do research on selection and develop assessment procedures used in employment settings, selection generally means those assessment procedures used in hiring decisions as well as in other employment situations where people are chosen. For human resource managers, selection generally means the process of hiring people, from the decision to hire someone to actually having a new employee onboard working. Thus, though different professional groups have large common content in the term *selection,* there are also some differences in connotation. All these views are appropriate. The point

Note: We would like to acknowledge the efforts of our colleagues at Allstate Insurance Company and at the Allstate Research and Planning Center. It is a pleasure to work with many talented people who have assisted and advised us with our research, consulting, and management assignments. Sincere thanks also to colleagues in other organizations: Candy Albertsson, Steve Ashworth, Bruce Erenkrantz, Sally Hartmann, John Callender, Jeff McHenry, Eric Monier, John Rauschenberger, Nancy Tippins, and Anna Marie Valerio.

of this chapter is to suggest that selection concepts are central to many human resource processes and that how an organization thinks about and handles selection can be a key element in achieving its goals and strategy. We also address practical issues that can make selection processes succeed or fail.

Though the profession of I/O psychology is characterized by research about work issues using scientific methods, this chapter is largely not about research. Our goal is to address the relationship or integration of selection procedures and concepts with other systems and operations of organizations. Also, although there is much research on individual issues in selection, there is relatively little about these organizational relationships or integration concerns. We found only three published studies to date that address the issue of the integration of HR into broader organizational processes, and none of these studies specifically addresses the issue of selection (Bennett, Ketchen, & Schultz, 1998). To write this chapter, we drew on the base of our own knowledge and experience in managing selection research (broadly defined), our experience consulting with organizations and training managers in how to hire and manage employees, and our experience in directly managing staff in several organizations. We also used a series of informal and formal interviews with I/O psychologists and HR managers in different organizations. We offer thanks to all who spoke with us, both those who are cited in this chapter and those who are not.

In the following discussion, our assumption is that established professional practice in the development and use of selection assessment procedures is followed, and that relevant legal guidelines and precedents are honored. Because these issues are addressed in other chapters of this book, we will not devote further space to them here.

It strikes us that the nature of the organization and the nature of the work are two key concerns that could thread through this chapter. How an organization sees its own mission, what it considers to be the legitimate tools to accomplish its goals, how the organization values people, and how it defines work and rewards are the factors that define the range of daily organizational decisions including selection decisions. We will return to this idea later.

This chapter is organized into eight sections. The first looks at the "temporal aspects" of selection defined as hiring. In other words, we combine the I/O psychologist and human resource manager viewpoints and address where "selection assessment procedures" fit into the full sequence of organizational systems and processes as a decision is made to hire an employee. The second section addresses the organizational decisions made about the job, work, and structure that influence the specific details of the hiring sequence. Section three addresses employee selection assessments in settings other than hiring. Our tenet is that many other HR processes also involve selection; nearly everyone knows this, and we all often seem to forget. The fourth section addresses practical details about how and why selection processes may or may not work when faced with daily work details. A selection process with high validity and excellent technical design can be a complete failure in an organization—why does this happen? Section five addresses the relationship of selection to other HR domains and to integrated HR systems and workforce planning. Section six relates selection to business systems and strategy. The final two sections identify some areas for potential research counterbalanced by a list of practical tips for those who manage HR departments, manage HR planning and business strategy, or develop selection processes.

Figure 2.1 illustrates the different components that will be addressed in this chapter, starting with the hiring process itself, which appears at the bottom of the figure. The next level illustrates the different HR processes that will be discussed, within the framework of the KSAOs or competencies, which may integrate these processes. Finally, the top of the figure depicts that both HR processes and other functions in the organization must develop from overarching organizational goals and strategies.

Because words associated with selection can have different connotations, it is helpful to define how we will use them in this chapter. By *hiring* we mean the entire process of adding a new employee to an organization. In most organizations, both external and internal candidates may respond to these position openings and go through the same qualification process. When formal assessment processes are used, either in the hiring process or other HR processes using selection, we have called them *selection assessment processes.* When we use the word *selection,* our meaning is very simple: one or a subset of people is picked from the many. This fits with one of our main points, which is that selection occurs in many organizational

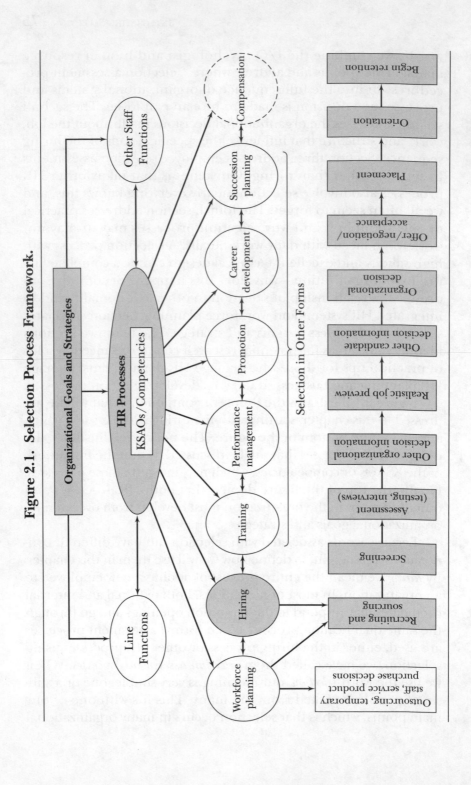

Figure 2.1. Selection Process Framework.

situations and that similar approaches and tools are helpful in these diverse situations.

The End-to-End Hiring Process

When line managers or HR staff think of employee selection, they think of the sequence of processes and decisions that result in having a new employee in their organization. Depending on the scope and nature of the job, the hiring sequence can begin with a decision as simple as "Hire another equipment operator because our new piece of equipment has arrived" or the more complex "Find out what data mining is, hire someone who knows how to do it, and produce a 1 percent sales increment because of these new marketing leads." The hiring sequence can end with the job offer–acceptance–showing up for work, or it can continue into paid pre-job training (and evaluation), placement into the "best fit" opening, orientation to the organization, and initial retention efforts. Exhibit 2.1 outlines the different components of the hiring process that will be addressed.

In addition to this sequence of processes, other key decisions are made implicitly or explicitly when there is a new hire. These are decisions related to the design of the job, work and organization, the setting in which the work will be done, where in the organizational structure the person fits and why, the people who participate in various aspects of the hiring decision, and how much will be paid for the job. The organizational factors that influence the broader design and implementation of a hiring sequence are addressed in the second section of this chapter.

The requirements of any actual assessment process used in hiring can be defined by other aspects of the hiring process. For example, the scope of recruiting efforts may limit the population that can be considered, the organization's image may deter some applicants and attract others, the pay offered will include or exclude applicants with certain experience levels. In turn, the decisions made about the selection assessment process can determine other aspects of hiring. If the selection assessment process does not screen for skills or orientation to working in teams, or for skills or orientation to serving customers, then more time and effort may be needed in training and motivation to meet these job performance requirements.

Exhibit 2.1. Role of Each Component in the End-to-End Hiring Process.

Component	Role
Recruiting and sourcing	Draw people to the organization.
Initial screening	Identify the minimally qualified pool.
Selection assessment	Sort the candidates from most to least qualified.
Other organizational decision information	Review other information the organization considers important; may be go–no go hurdles.
Realistic job preview	Ensure that the candidate understands the job and its context.
Other candidate decision information	Review other information the candidate considers important; also may be go–no go hurdles.
Organizational decision	Combine information from all sources and techniques for selection decision.
Offer, negotiation, acceptance	Extend offer to candidate for candidate selection decision.
Placement	Match the new hire to the best job or situational choice.
Orientation	Integrate the new hire into the organization.
Begin retention	Ensure that selection decision results in performance for adequate time period for organizational payoff from selection investment.

Marketing the "Product": Recruiting and Sourcing

Finding the right people to do the organization's work on an on-going basis is a process parallel to selling a product or service. But with hiring, one is selling a job rather than a car, a tube of toothpaste, or an insurance policy. Once the organization has decided how to define the job it is filling, it then has a product to sell. Recruiting is marketing the job and the organization, and it can have both *push* and *pull* components (to use two marketing terms). The push components are the various outreach aspects that publicize the job opening and try to attract interest and response. The pull components are the image and information about the firm that draw people to it who are likely to want what the organization has to offer.

How do the dimensions used in the marketing campaign relate to the dimensions used to screen candidates? Clearly, publicizing the knowledge, skill, abilities, and other factors required for the job makes sense. It helps the candidate do the first screening by self-matching his or her own qualifications to the job requirements.

Recruitment or marketing is the point when the organization should realize there is another side to hiring: selection of the organization by the job candidate. Hiring is a two-way process. The organization may be deciding, but so is the individual. And the way in which the organization conducts its hiring process, starting with recruiting, may result in the candidate not choosing the organization.

Most organizations do not want to select the person who wants the highest salary but rather one who wants to do the work and supports the organization's goals. How can such people be attracted? The recruiting approach can stress what the organization has to offer as well as its climate and culture. Similarly, the selection assessment process could actually assess what the individual wants to do, so the organization can choose those people.

It is important to know what aspects of the job elicit interest and to determine how these factors fit into the selection assessment process. Can one recruit "innovative staff" if the subsequent selection process assesses only ability to follow direction? Can one recruit high-tech candidates using only recruiting and selection assessment processes that assess low-tech skills? How does the total picture fit together in terms of what an organization has to offer and who applies for the job? For example, in our organization we are working on a selection assessment process that will be Internet-based. We want the process to be valid and efficient, but we also want it to convey the image of an innovative company that is an attractive employer. Our industrial engineer who tested the user-friendliness of the software told us the assessment was user-friendly, but nearly all participants in our usability study were struck by the impact of the screen design (font and background colors) in creating an impression of the job and the company as much more conservative than was true.

Nearly all organizations make some effort to sell themselves and their jobs to potential employees. Of course, people form all types of impressions about the organization during the recruitment and hiring process, impressions the organization may or may not intend. Research by Rynes (1993) and Rynes, Bretz, and Gerhart (1991) clearly show that companies can gain reputations based on how they treat people during the hiring process. From the organization's viewpoint, at the one end of this continuum would be potential assurance that the job applicant the company wants also wants the company. At the other end would be the assurance that the company will suffer no undesirable actions from its hiring processes. Examples of undesirable action range from poor word-of-mouth among job applicants to formal complaints or even lawsuits by dissatisfied job applicants. As discussed elsewhere in this book and established in research by Gilliland (1993), the manner in which hiring processes are handled affects applicants' perceptions of fairness and justice.

Selection is somewhat a moot issue unless there are multiple applicants for each job, and the chance of finding the best applicant is a function of the number of applicants. How does one produce multiple applicants? Traditional recruiting sources have stressed advertisements in print and broadcast media, and the use of recruiting or "headhunter" firms. In the last few years, technology such as the Internet has changed the recruiting industry dramatically. Companies advertise general and specific job openings on their Web sites. There are multiple Internet master job listing sites (such as "Hot Jobs") where employers can list jobs. Applicants can respond with simple e-mails indicating interest or fill out formal job applications on the Internet. Some companies actually score these on-line applications in the same way other selection assessment procedures are scored. Employers are also distributing CD-ROMs to potential candidates to try to sell their company or the position. In addition, there are Web sites where candidates can post their resumes for potential employers to find.

The consequence of this shift to increased technology, including national and international databanks of job openings, is actually to make selection from the job candidate side easier and more efficient and give the job candidate more power in the labor market. These growing job databanks convey systematic information about employment opportunities, enabling applicants to compare and evaluate the positions. There are even Internet-based calculators that allow candidates to equate job offers across geographic areas by considering cost-of-living factors—information that strengthens the candidate's negotiation position.

News media write of job applicants who configure intelligent search agents to do daily searches for jobs that match their requirements in terms of content, geographic location, industry sector, or even range of company names (Weingarten, 1998). In fact, some business analysts have forecast dramatic restructuring of the employment recruiting industry, or even its demise (Weingarten, 1998). For example, Texas Instruments (TI) has established an Internet recruiting page in which job seekers can complete self-assessments and tap into resources useful for job searches and career development beyond TI. TI's assumption is that the more prepared candidates are for job hunting, the easier the process will be for its recruiters (Flynn, 1998).

In a tight labor market, such as that in Silicon Valley in 1999, a variety of innovative recruiting techniques are seen, from advertisements as the lead-in to feature movies in movie theaters to highway billboards, booths at arts and crafts fairs and sporting events, supermarket bag-stuffers, and so on.

Knowing which recruiting sources yield a reasonable volume of qualified responses is the sourcing component of recruiting. For example, nearly every organization uses its own employee force as recruiters, or even as "bounty hunters," paying a hiring bonus to a referring employee. Rynes et al. (1991), in a review of interview transcripts, found that friends and acquaintances inside an organization were an important source of information for a large portion of recruits. The selection assumption built into this approach is that existing employees will know their work situation and make some evaluation of the likely success of potential job applicants before referring them. Research on the relative value of recruiting sources generally supports the strength of employee referral in predicting job applicant success, particularly when one of the success criteria is turnover (Gannon, 1971; Taylor, 1994). Several small internal studies we have done at Allstate have supported this finding. But it is important to note that a variety of recruiting sources may be necessary in order to ensure the diversity of applicants. Caldwell and Spivey (1983) found that more formal sources such as employment agencies were more effective in minority recruiting.

Which recruiting sources will be most successful depends on the job, geographic location, and industry. But individual organizations can examine recruiting sources and work histories of their applicants and identify patterns with respect to how workers reach or do not reach the organization (Watson & Garbin, 1981).

One issue that is not addressed anywhere we know of is this: If you have only limited funds to spend, where should you invest them—in improving recruiting or in selection assessment processes? Like all such questions, the answer is, "It depends." But that is precisely the point—it does depend. And we would guess the first answer many I/O psychologists would give is to invest their funds in selection assessment. This may not be the best decision. Microsoft's strategy, for example, is to recruit heavily and from many different sources. With close to two hundred full-time recruiters reviewing more than two hundred thousand resumes a year, the company's large number of applicants for a job allows it more choice, and in management's opinion, makes it easier to select only top candidates. For other organizations, two hundred recruiters would be regarded as a very large cadre for an organization with approximately twenty-seven thousand employees. But it depends on the organization's view of where it wants to concentrate its efforts. More effective recruiting may not only produce more applicants to consider but also produce a wider choice among applicants with desirable features that are not part of the formal screening. Such features may range from job-relevant skills, to candidates with easier commutes and thus higher preference for the job being offered, to more affordable employees.

Initial Screening and Timing for Selection Assessment

Nearly all organizations use some initial screening process before beginning their more formal selection assessment procedures. Although informal and variable, these initial screening processes are also selection. The simplest version of these processes is some screening of applications or resumes for prior work experience or training. In this type of resume screening, a selection process is being used. Although valid scoring keys can be developed for resumes and applications (for example, Ash, 1983), they are seldom used. Terpstra (1997) found in a survey of human resource managers that they do not use several value-added recruiting and selection practices because they are unfamiliar with them, make assumptions about the usefulness of certain techniques, or have legal concerns or resource constraints.

Commercial software is available for employers to review a large number of resumes and sort them into their defined acceptable and unacceptable categories using criteria such as particular educational degree, former job title, appearance of given words or phrases in the resume, specific prior employers, years of work experience, and so on. Any of these example criteria are selection criteria. Partially automating this task saves the HR department time and staffing, but the automation does not ensure that the screening criteria are the best ones to use, though they may be most feasible for the software.

A key question for any hiring process is "Where in the sequence does the formal assessment occur?" Most formal noninterview selection processes are designed with the idea that they will occur early in the screening so only the more qualified applicants are interviewed. This decision is driven by economic factors that acknowledge the cost of the interviewers' or managers' time. Large organizations often consider the "cost per candidate" of a hiring process and put selection assessments, such as group-administered tests, early in the process to minimize the total cost of hire. This timing may be followed particularly in organizations with formal selection units. In other organizational settings, however, the selection assessment or test may migrate to the end of the hiring process as the final hurdle if both HR staff and line managers want to talk to job applicants before they decide to do anything else. In this case, image concerns for the company or personal preferences for interpersonal contact by the HR representative influence the hiring sequence more than cost-per-candidate considerations.

Selection assessment processes include a wide range of processes such as scored job applications or resumes, interviews, tests of skills and abilities, job sample and simulation processes, biographical profiles or biodata questionnaires, and so on. The details on the range of choices will not be addressed here because they are discussed well in other chapters of this book.

Other Hiring Decision Information for the Organization

Some organizations collect other information they consider to be important in the hiring decision as assessments of job-relevant skills and abilities. It can include verifying that the candidate has particular academic degrees, certifications, or licenses. It extends to verifying prior employing organizations, dates, salary, job title, and details of duties. Some reference checks go further and try to obtain the prior employer's evaluation of the candidate's job performance or potential for learning. Additional procedures can include tests for drug use, a review of arrest and conviction records, credit checks, and for some occupations, assessment of physical health to meet job demands. Although all these processes are part of the hiring decision and are actually used as selection criteria, we know of little systematic research on how these processes should best be done or on the validity of the criteria used beyond research on physical job requirements. Some research has established validity for preemployment drug testing (Normand, Salyards, & Mahoney, 1990), but there are legal as well as fairness issues that should be carefully considered before implementing such a program (Ravid, 1991; Sujak, Villanova, & Daly, 1995).

Realistic Job Previews

A realistic job preview is simply giving a job applicant an accurate idea of what the job will be like, both tasks and context, to the extent one can within the limited time frame of the hiring process. Research shows that realistic job previews help applicants make better decisions about their own preference for the job, lead to less surprise and disappointment and thus to lower turnover after work begins (Wanous, 1973; Dugoni & Ilgen, 1981).

From the employer side, a candidate's reaction to the various job aspects also can be gauged, and this can contribute to the employer's selection decision. Ford, for example, uses an inventory of typical situations the person might encounter on the job. This not only provides a realistic job preview for candidates but also serves as an assessment tool to evaluate the match between the candidate and effective ways of handling these situations. Assessment center simulations can serve similar purposes.

Some organizations go even further than a job preview and have the candidate perform the job or samples of the job for a half-day to several weeks, perhaps even as a probationary hire or trainee. In these instances, given the organizational resources involved, the purpose of the job preview is likely to be for the assessment of fit and task performance more than for an individual applicant to determine his or her preference.

How do job previews relate to recruiting, hiring, and the organization as a whole? The basic dimensions involved in selling the job and the organization and in determining if the individual is qualified for the job are key factors. Other critical information includes contextual factors such as setting, equipment, schedule, coworkers, and so on. Almost by definition, job previews will reduce the number of job candidates and job acceptances and so must be carefully crafted to provide a balanced picture that will maximize the number of high-quality and desirable candidates (Meglino, Ravlin, & DeNisi, 1997; Bretz & Judge, 1998).Careful communication to managers and recruiters about the value added by realistic job previews is critical, because these groups may be reluctant to use a process with the potential to reduce the number of candidates being considered or change the ratio of employment acceptances.

Other Hiring Decision Information for the Candidate

Recruiting and hiring new employees may be discussed as if the only consideration from the organization side is "Who is the best choice?" and the only consideration from the candidate side is "Will I like this job and this organization?" But hiring is also a labor market relationship, where the individual job candidate offers his or her labor for an economic return from the organization. Even more, a decision by a job applicant to take a particular position with a particular organization is an investment decision. The individual is deciding to invest his or her time and knowledge (or labor) for an anticipated return. In today's complex reward packages of multiple pay formats, signing bonuses, relocation packages, stock and stock options, deferred compensation, profit sharing, organization-sponsored investment vehicles, and benefits alternatives, the "anticipated return" is a multiple element package too. The return is much more than the hourly wage or salary paid for the job. More job candidates than ever are beginning to evaluate job offers from this perspective. Those who do take this view have been driven partially by the downsizing activities of the 1980s, when employees realized their assumptions about long-term payoffs would not be fulfilled (Cascio, 1995).

Thus, parallel to an organization's using information beyond job-specific skills, job candidates themselves may take the same broad views.

Organizational Decision

An organization can garner much information about candidates during the hiring process. In some cases, this selection information is weighed and combined using formal and systematic approaches, in other cases it is not. A typical approach is to have the initial screen operate as a go–no go hurdle. A weighting and combining formula could be used to combine all selection assessment scores (though some may operate as "knockout" scores) and possibly interview results. Then reference checks, background checks, and so on would operate as an additional series of go–no go hurdles. Because the way in which this is done varies widely across companies and within companies, it is difficult to conduct research to determine what might be the optimum way to handle this information combination task.

One danger is that information from one part of the process will dominate so that an unbalanced decision will be made. Another challenge is that although many people may participate in the hiring process, each may participate in only some parts, so summary decisions can be difficult.

When twenty or fewer candidates are being considered, a simple approach could be to build a decision matrix (for example, a spreadsheet) that maps out which decision areas (this works most easily with competency areas, described later) are addressed by each source of information. Then, focus on each matrix cell, rank-order each candidate for that cell, and record the rankings. Sum the candidates' rankings, and examine the patterns that emerge. Is this a valid process? We have no idea, for we have used it in situations where there are too few data for any validation research.

It has helped organize the process, ensured that all information sources were considered, allowed integration of input from persons with different levels of participation in the total process, and been an effective mechanism for group decision and consensus.

Offer, Negotiation, Acceptance

Once the organization decides who to select for its job, the process begins to convert this decision to reality. This is where there may be the greatest contrast between the words *hiring* and *selection*. Hiring implies completion of the process and acknowledges that additional work may have to be done to achieve it. Selection almost assumes that once the organization has decided, the process is complete. In a tight labor market, this is far from true. Although much information is collected about job candidates, we are not aware of any organization that attempts to collect systematic information from candidates that would help it be more successful in "closing the sale." In our own consideration of job candidates, for example, we use various probes, structured listening (where we listen for a predefined list of things we could highlight in offers to candidates), direct questions, reactions to packages of promotional information on the company and geographic area, and so on to try to come to the decision of how to present and structure our offer for acceptance.

As with any sales situation, someone (the organization) is selling and someone else (the candidate) is choosing whether to buy. One organization with which we spoke monitors its "turn down" rates and reasons to understand why job candidates choose not to buy, so that its ratio of selection by candidates can be improved.

Placement

The simplest version of the hiring decision is to hire or not hire. But the selection assessments involved in reaching a hiring decision can also assist with specific job placement. There are three situations where this approach may be useful. The first is when one is hiring in a tight job market and has to hire a "sufficient" candidate rather than a "best" candidate. The selection assessment information can be diagnostic of exactly where the strengths and weaknesses lie, what training is required, and in what order and which particular job performance demands are likely to be met early in the job. If designed to do so, selection assessments can also be used to estimate readiness for training and potential speed of progress through training. When an organization knows it will have to train after hire, potentially extensively, then designing training diagnostics into the hiring process may be wise.

A second situation where selection may apply to specific job placement is when there are many job openings of the same type and there is a choice of whom to put where. Information gained in the selection assessment process may help decide which person best matches which situation, based not only on knowledge and skill profiles but also in terms of job context preferences. Selection assessment information may be especially useful in organizations using cross-functional and self-managing work teams. Often the key to highly effective and innovative teams is a diversity of skills, knowledge, expertise, and personal characteristics. Several companies such as Motorola, 3M, and Du Pont use a form of "skill mix" teams (Gupta & Singhal, 1993).

A third, highly related, situation where selection assessment information may help with placement is when there is a scarcity of training resources and a need to optimize the use of them across individuals. Selection assessment results can help decide who needs which training and in what order.

Orientation

At minimum, orientation includes the procedures and processes to convert an applicant into an employee. It usually involves basic training on the facility and the job, and at least the physical aspects of "how things work around here." In certain occupations, work rules, safety and security procedures, and other points of basic knowledge are imparted. However, many organizations, desiring to capture the dedication and initiative of their employees, have instituted far more extensive orientation programs that cover the history and values of the organization and its goals and business strategies.

In some organizations, an emphasis on goals or motivation match has extended beyond a desire to educate employees about the focus of the organization after they start work. It includes a desire to hire individuals who match the organization's goals prior to hire. Thus, the orientation or enrollment or communication focus has moved into the arena of an employment qualification. This is actually nothing new. Organizations such as the military or the ministry have focused on goals or values for a long time. Recent trends include values such as *quality, customer service, benefit to the community,* or *world-class product.* And at least a few organizations are incorporating measures of "values match" into their formal selection assessment procedures, though this is challenging to do in the short time frame of a hiring sequence. At some organizations, internship programs before formal employment may be viewed as a combination of recruiting, selection assessment, and values matching programs. Procter & Gamble, for example, uses its extensive internship program in this way.

Begin Retention

When an organization hires a new employee, the hope may be that it is a permanent decision, barring market and financial problems or employee performance problems. Some say the first day of employee retention begins on the first day of work. In fact, some aspects of the hiring process, including the selection assessment process, also may be targeted at retention by selecting candidates who have a higher probability of maintaining job stability or even staying with the particular organization. At Procter & Gamble, where there is a clear value to promote from within, there is emphasis on selecting employees who will stay with the company and have long-term potential.

Selection Design

Although the process described in the previous section is broad, it is focused on the tasks involved in hiring. Some organizations may take an even broader view of hiring and think of it as another one of several ways the organization "interfaces" with its customer base and the community or society in which it exists. Thus, a large organization that hires thousands of employees yearly realizes that over several years the thousands of job applicants not hired, each with a network of friends and relatives, have a sizable overlap with the customer or client base the organization wishes to serve. Large organizations, particularly those with strong social values, also may think of the impact of hiring and selection approaches on the communities where they exist. Chapter Ten in this book, which discusses support for social policy, offers an example of this perspective. How hiring affects a community may be of particular concern to organizations operating outside the United States. The point of these organizations, even with for-profit businesses, may be seen as job creation in the community more than profit or enhancement of value for shareholders.

Hiring for the Job, the Work, or the Organization?

In recent years, many organizations have begun to ask themselves if they are recruiting for the job, for a related job family, or for the organization. The pace of organizational change, especially market-driven change, has led to rapid or frequent restructuring, automation, creation of new business areas, sale or closure of long-established organizational groups, and consequent redefinition of work processes and jobs. The job one is hired for may be a different job in a different part of the organization or even a different company a year later. For example, an acquaintance of ours in Silicon Valley sat at the same desk for seven years but worked for five different companies during that same time span. Technical job content stayed largely the same, but organizational performance goals, which had to be met, changed frequently.

With such change in the external organizational setting and resulting internal reaction, organizations realize they need a workforce that can perform in changing situations. Achievement of the organization's goals may be more likely if the individuals who compose the organization can change how they work in response to the organization's needs. Selection assessment procedures that depend on clear definition of stable jobs may not be feasible or useful in situations with changing market demands. Several organizations have been shifting from explicit job definitions to descriptions of families of jobs, sets of roles a position may involve, or groups of skills or competencies desired. This more fluid definition of work requires selection techniques that determine potential for both immediate assignments and a range of long-term assignment options.

The increasing use of *competency models* in organizations as a basis for various HR processes is one response to this organizational view. The traditional view of job analysis and selection, which focuses on performance at one phase in time using a defined set of tasks, does not easily meld with organizations using temporary self-managing teams staffed with groups of individuals in the organization (Cascio, 1995; Lawler, 1994; Stewart & Carson, 1997). Competencies define organization-level skills that enable an employee to move quickly through multiple assignments and responsibilities in an increasingly turbulent environment. If a competency perspective is taken, selection processes can become easier if they are related across HR processes but more difficult as the definition moves away from specific job tasks and skills. Additional discussion of a competency approach appears later in this chapter.

Group and Team Dynamics

The new employee joining any work situation is joining an organization already in place. Both social psychology and sociological research have focused on the impact of changing group composition on group roles and relationships. In some work situations, where there is little task interdependence, this may be less of an issue. But in most organizations, and particularly in service organizations, integration into the group context is a factor to consider.

Ramamoorthy (1998) found that individual differences in emphasis on individual achievement versus group goals is significantly related to employee preference for a number of alternative human resource management practices (for example, individuals with a focus on group goals preferred team-oriented performance management and rewards). Similarly, Bretz and Judge (1994) found that prehire and posthire perceptions of fit were highly congruent. As mentioned earlier, organizations may want to consider the type of employee they wish to attract (for example, engineers with a high need for autonomy and achievement) along with HR practices in place that are communicated to candidates (for example, the need for cooperative behavior and use of team-oriented reward systems). How well this process is managed may determine the successful performance of the new employee as much as any other knowledge or skills the person brings to the job.

In fact, an area largely overlooked in hiring decisions and selection procedures is the group context within which the job will exist and the potential importance of coworkers in the hiring decision and subsequent new hire success. Perhaps one of the most extreme examples of this was work done by the U.S. Army in the early 1980s with its "new manning system." Concerned about the negative impact of group divisiveness on unit combat effectiveness given the constant churn of personnel through infantry units, the army tried recruiting and selecting an entire unit at one time and having them serve thirty-six months of duty as a coherent whole (Funk, 1983). Although the experiment was put in place, comprehensive studies of this innovation were never completed and released. Still, it is a striking example of considering the potential importance of changing group membership on group and individual performance, and the importance of considering the role of the coworker group in the group integration process.

Research on selection for teams has centered on team-based skills, and this is well discussed in Chapter Six of this volume, which focuses on team selection. However, as far as we know, there is no systematic work on various ways one can define work done by a team as a whole and have team-based jobs using a compensatory model. A *compensatory team model* is one in which the total team needs certain skills or abilities but any particular team member need not possess these skills. Of course, as each team member is chosen, there will be fewer options for the skills that must be in the remaining choices. If a team compensatory model approach is used, it can dramatically change the entire hiring process, and the selection specifics may shift as each hiring or assignment choice is made.

Selection as an Expense Management Tool

Various economic forces lead organizations to make hiring decisions—from replacing turnover, to expanding or starting new businesses. The economic reason for a hiring decision will also affect the factors considered in selection and the focus of the recruiting process. Hiring decisions can be driven by employer goals of replacing more expensive talent with less expensive talent, for example, redefining a job at a lower pay level because complex aspects of the job may now be done by software. In this case, the compensation requirement the individual candidate places on his or her qualifications may play as important a role in the selection process as the qualifications themselves.

An organization also may consider other alternatives to hiring as a way to manage expenses. Choices include retaining a temporary staffing agency (for example, secretarial, accounting, or programming staff), purchasing services or products from other organizations rather than building them itself (for example, purchase of twenty delivery cycles of word processing training), or even outsourcing entire company processes (for example, the mail room or the entire information technology department). In this case, the selection decision is to select another organization and its employees rather than to hire one's own.

"Advanced" Human Resource Processes: Selection in Other Forms?

Employee selection is usually thought of as hiring a qualified person for a particular job. In fact, selection can have a far broader meaning: choosing the right people, with the right qualifications, at the right time and place, to achieve the organization's strategies or goals. From this perspective, selection involves all situations where "many are called but few are chosen."

Taking the employee viewpoint of how one moves through a job history or a career with an organization, "advanced HR processes" are those that come later in the employment sequence. Such situations include access to training courses and developmental assignments, superior performance evaluations, promotion, career development processes, inclusion in succession planning processes, participation in task forces and special project teams, representation of the organization in industry or government work groups, and so on. Thus, selection processes and techniques may be at the core of effectively executing other human resource processes. The tools, techniques, and technology used in the hiring process also can be extended readily and economically to these other HR processes. Further, to the extent that one views the assets of an organization as including skilled people in addition to financial capital, concrete physical assets, and goodwill in the marketplace, selection and related human resource processes are the vehicle for ensuring that the organization's goals will be achieved. As mentioned earlier, other HR processes beyond the initial hiring decision depend on selection. Exhibit 2.2 summarizes the role of selection in a range of HR processes beyond hiring.

Most selection techniques are based on a job analysis. More comprehensive selection processes may be based on tools for analyzing multiple jobs or families of jobs. More recently, selection approaches may be based on competency approaches. But regardless of the job specificity of the approach, the selection of one or a few individuals from a larger group is a situation that applies as equally to training, performance evaluation, promotion, special assignments, career development options, and succession planning as to hiring.

Exhibit 2.2. HR Processes Depending on Selection.

Hiring	Multiple-stage process using various techniques and types of information for mutual selection decision by organization and candidate
Training	Selection for participation in particular training programs
Superior performance evaluation	Selection for limited frequency ratings or for distribution controlled rankings
Promotion	Selection for limited promotional opportunities or for job families or job levels with limited population sizes
Special assignments	Selection for assignment to task forces, committees, special projects
Career development	Selection for development processes, programs, or mentors
Succession planning	Selection for inclusion in replacement planning or succession planning databases or management planning sessions

Training

Training that is not a limited resource and that is widely available to any employee needing it does not use a selection process. However, training that has restricted access uses selection techniques to determine who participates and who does not.

Superior Performance Evaluation

In organizations where the number or frequency of higher-level performance ratings is limited, some selection process is in operation. Sometimes these limits are managed by default or by individual manager quotas such that no manager can have more than X percent of his or her group with ratings at the highest level. In other organizations, formal rating or ranking procedures are used that result in forced choices across the organization. The criteria used for these rankings are selection processes.

Promotion

Whether selection applies in a promotional situation is a function of the nature of the promotion. From a human resource planning perspective, promotions are created either by *supply-push* from below or by *demand-pull* from above. In the former situation, selection considerations may not apply; in the later situation, they clearly do.

Supply-push promotions are particularly common in a work setting where there are dual career paths—technical and managerial. In a technical career path, promotional decisions can come largely from the development of additional technical skills that are seen as having greater external value and thus greater economic value to an organization. In the overall scope of financial resources of the organization, or some general guidelines for the size of various job levels, there may not be limits on promotions from one job level to another except the acquisition of more sophisticated skills or higher competency levels. In a unionized work setting, such movement among job levels may be more a function of tenure, assumed to equate to different skill levels, than to the evaluation of specific skill levels themselves. Similar examples are some government agencies' grade or job step systems, where each anniversary year the employee advances a job step until some maximum is reached. Supply-push promotions may be selection processes if defined criteria are used. However, in the case of promotions based on automatic tenure status, it is the passage of time rather than a selection assessment process that results in the promotion outcome.

In contrast, demand-pull promotions come from the creation of a vacancy in a job that an organization determines it must fill, such as an office manager, a regional manager, a legally required corporate officer, a battalion or division commander, and so on. In nearly all cases, these are management jobs with defined spans of control. In most organizations, because of either financial concerns or concerns to "empower" lower-level employees the number of such management positions is limited. Many candidates vie for such appointments, but only a few secure them.

The selection processes used for candidates for demand-pull promotions could be very similar to those used for candidate hiring. But except for public agency employment, such as fire, police, or certain governmental appointments, these promotions are seldom handled as if they were selection situations. The vacancies may not be known, interested and potentially qualified individuals may not be able to apply, candidates may have little choice about position acceptance, and the decision may be based more on reward for performance in the old position than on the requirements to perform in the new position. In some cases, the most important qualification may be the extent to which the senior executive making the decision personally knows the candidate. Of course, an organization that takes these views could probably be characterized as "looking back" rather than "looking forward." An organization focused on strategies for changing markets, industry restructuring, and increased competition is likely to realize that a vacancy is a potential redefinition and that new criteria and a broader search may be required to fill key executive positions—even if an entrenched workforce may not support these views. This is often the situation when executive search firms are retained.

Special Assignments

The Center for Creative Leadership points out that only a small percentage of higher-level employee development comes from formal course work (McCall, Lombardo, & Morrison, 1988). Far and away the majority of advanced employee development comes from on-the-job development and special assignments such as task forces, committees, special projects, and so on. Given this fact, selection for these special assignments is a selection situation as much as for training situations where access is limited.

Career Development

Career development is a person-centered process, and thus distinguished from succession planning, which is organization-centered. The two can work in complementary fashion, and they should for either to be most effective. If there is limited access to career development processes, career development programs, or career development counselors or mentors, then selection processes are operating in each of these situations. In addition to limitations on access, other variations may include limits on the specific options offered to some persons and not others, the resources made available, and the financial investment in various internal or external counseling, seminars, assessment or feedback tools, and so on.

Succession Planning

The simplest version of succession planning that exists in organizations is replacement planning, when one or several individuals may be "listed" to succeed a particular person. True succession planning adds the element of multiple contingencies across individuals, and it allows one to focus not only on potential vacancies to be filled but also on the full range of individuals in the group available for future assignments.

As vacancies become available, of course, individuals chosen for them have gone through some selection process, even if a default one. As individuals are chosen to go into the group for which planning is done, another type of selection process occurs.

The time and effort it takes to collect complex information on individuals, keep it updated, and forecast workforce alternatives means that most organizations operate succession planning systems only for their more senior levels, potentially for their executive levels. Succession planning systems are frequently based on some formal knowledge and skill dimensions, often assessed with multiple source feedback. Some organizations will use information gained from a formal assessment center or other simulation processes to contribute to their succession planning evaluation. For example, BP Amoco uses multiple formal processes—two levels of assessment centers, multilevel feedback, and performance appraisals to contribute to the succession planning decision-making process. These processes are based on an established leadership competency model that captures behavior that differentiates outstanding leadership performance from average.

What Makes Selection Processes Successful in Organizations?

A successful selection process is one that works, but this can mean different things to different people. What makes a selection process successful? Without doubt, the clearest answer is the ability of the process to create either observed or perceived benefit in the organization's performance in meeting its goals. Our goal in this chapter is merely to describe some of the experiences that are common in organizations and why they happen. The results are not always desirable, and in many instances they are not best practices at all. But unless one is aware of these issues, one cannot design and manage selection processes that will work. Exhibit 2.3 outlines eight drivers of selection process success.

Empirical Validity

From the viewpoint of an I/O psychologist, a selection process will be successful in an organization if it is valid. Validity to an I/O psychologist means that the test or other measurement procedure has been determined to measure what it purports to measure, using one of the recognized professional methods for establishing validity. For an I/O psychologist, empirical validity can be expressed in several ways, including the extent to which the selection assessment process represents the content of the job, the extent to which the selection assessment accounts for performance in the job, and the incremental performance or productivity the organization can expect from individuals who score higher on the selection assessment process.

Exhibit 2.3. Drivers of Selection Process Success.

Empirical validity	Concrete information, usually statistical, which associates some screening measure with a favorable organization outcome
Face validity	Meets commonsense criteria of a manager, HR representative, or job candidate
Selection ratio	Ensures sufficient numbers of candidates to make good selection decisions but involves some selectivity
Marketability	People who are supposed to use the tools can do so and want to do so
Management of selection processes	People who have the responsibility to manage the selection process are prepared to do it, and are accepted by the organization
Candidate reaction	Not stressful, offensive, too lengthy; provides a positive image of the organization
Expense	Judged appropriate by the organization for the importance of the job to achieving organizational goals
Timeliness	Ready when needed, and facilitates hiring process rather than delays it

Face Validity

To other groups in an organization, a selection process also is likely to be used and be successful if it is "valid," but the term *validity* can have a far different meaning. Managers or others in the organization often will use a selection process only if they perceive it to make sense, that is, to have what an I/O psychologist would call *face validity*. Thus, processes that "look like the job," such as actual or simulated sales calls for a sales job, presentations or speeches for a public representative of the organization, data entry tests for a computer transaction job, or a programming simulation exercise for a programmer—all appear to make sense. It is much more difficult to get managers in an organization to be comfortable with selection tests such as biodata profiles that are empirically scored (meaning scored according to research results rather than some logic obvious to a layperson) or with a variety of structured interview guides that call for substantial change in manager behavior to use them. Research by Gilliland (1994) and Steiner and Gilliland (1996) has shown that face-valid procedures such as resumes, work sample tests, and interviews are perceived more favorably and are seen to be fairer than other less face-valid procedures.

In addition to the selection process making sense to a manager, there is the issue of what a manager has to learn to use it. Test administration procedures, structured interview guides, job sample or job simulation exercises, the use of complex equipment including computer administration—all may require training in order for the process to be properly implemented. One practitioner noted that the key to success for selection tools in her organization was the development of "incredibly user-friendly processes and clear value for the time invested."

Another practical feature that will affect line manager confidence is the time it takes to get an "answer" from the process. Interestingly, this involves not only the time it takes for the turnaround for any scoring procedure but also how the overall decision process is handled. For example, in a hiring situation a line manager will want a process that can fill the necessary number of positions, respond in the time frame in which the position must be filled, and allow quick action on behalf of attractive candidates in a tight labor market.

Selection Ratio

How many people pass the formal assessment processes? Paradoxically, though one would think that the more stringent a selection process the better for an organization, in the case of hiring new employees recruiters will be opposed to processes that screen out too many applicants. Many recruiters believe that it makes the recruiting job (finding people) too hard, rather than see its value in helping with the subsequent installation and performance of new hires (finding qualified people).

In addition, for the line manager and sometimes for HR staff there may be difficulties with a selection process that screens too severely because it creates too many occasions in which they find it hard to tell candidates "no." Though candidates not selected have to be told no at some point, it can seem easier if they are screened out based on informal processes such as a resume review or a "chat" than one in which a formal assessment procedure has been used.

Finally, it must be acknowledged that a more stringent selection process can seem to be more expensive because perhaps a larger candidate pool must be found. Line managers, of course, might say this is shortsighted because some incremental expense prior to a selection decision can save hours of management time and expense in dealing with performance issues if poor selection decisions are made.

Marketability

Clearly, a selection process is a product to be marketed in the organization. But it is not as simple as just announcing and using a selection process if line managers and HR staff throughout the organization are the routes for implementation. Communication about what is being done and why, and clear evidence of the usefulness and value to the organization are critical. There must be planning not only for initial training in using the tools but also for ongoing training as new persons assume responsibility for the selection processes. As one psychologist told us, a once successful assessment process came close to derailing completely when management of the process was transferred to staff with little background or training in the use of the tool.

Top organizational support can be particularly critical for a selection process that applies to key jobs or large numbers of incumbents. In both cases—one due to scope and the other to size—making the right decisions can have a significant organizational impact, so the organization needs to be focused on and supportive of effective approaches rather than using more casual processes.

Management of Selection Processes

Another factor that accounts for whether certain types of selection procedures will succeed in organizations is how they are managed.

In many government organizations and in large established companies, particularly those with geographic concentration, there will be an organizational unit responsible for the development and administration of the selection processes, though often restricted to use of selection in hiring. Historically, the most formal selection programs using tests and other highly structured assessments have occurred in these settings. In contrast, organizations that are widely dispersed geographically, or new and rapidly growing organizations without formal human resource functions, may use few formal processes because there simply is no organizational infrastructure to support them. In developing any selection process, it is critical to know exactly how the organization will be able to support the process implementation and maintain the procedures. As one I/O psychologist said, "It's not the tools. It's bringing the resources where they need to be." Another colleague emphasized the need to follow through to be sure tests or other assessments are used and used properly if the resources invested in design and development are to have any payoff. To ensure successful implementation of their selection assessment process for entry level managers, for example, Sears has a team of people assigned to manage the process from beginning to end.

Candidate Reaction

Particularly in a hiring situation, candidate reaction to a selection process also can be a determinant of its success. If the process takes too long, appears to be inappropriately difficult for the job, has aspects that offend candidates, or is seen as "worse" than what competing organizations do, people will "vote with their feet" and depart in the middle of the process or even fail to appear. Clearly, the extent to which candidates have economic power will influence their behavior. Candidates are less likely to reject selection procedures when they feel they have less choice.

Of particular note is the extent to which the selection process or any aspect of a hiring process is offensive or perceived as a hassle. Three areas appear to drive this concern. First is the direct impact on candidates. Microsoft, for example, does not use standardized testing in hiring because it could "turn off" the people they are trying to attract. Second, many organizations, particularly large ones, realize that over the course of several years, hundreds or thousands of individuals may be considered for jobs, and whether selected or not, these individuals and their friends and relatives may be customers of the organization. As noted earlier, in a competitive market situation it is foolish for an organization to squander the goodwill of its customers or potential customers. The selection process must not create ill will.

A third, more defensive area of concern for companies is that selection processes that offend or annoy candidates may be more likely to be the object of legal challenges of various types. Target stores (part of Dayton-Hudson Corporation) settled a class action lawsuit for $1.3 million over the use of MMPI items (a psychological test) in the hiring of security guards. The test items were described as "intrusive" and potentially violating gender and religious discrimination laws (*Soroka* v. *Dayton-Hudson Corporation,* 1991). Regardless of whether a complaint, charge, or legal challenge is found to have merit, such situations place a demand on the resources of the organization and divert these resources from other business purposes. If such stories are released to the media, they can affect the company's image as well. Most organizations wish to avoid these costs and publicity. On the positive side, some organizations have developed materials for candidates that explain their process, how it works, and why it is used. Perceptions of the process and the organization have been more positive with this approach (Hamill, 1997).

Expense

A selection process involves a variety of expenses for an organization. To be implemented successfully, there may be expenses related to the following:

- *Development cost:* Cost for the staff or outside organization to develop the selection process
- *Publicity or public relations expense:* Recruiting costs related to hiring, which can include advertisements in multiple media, recruiting staff expense, commissions or incentives or bounties paid to various persons, including external recruiting firms, and so on
- *Licensing or royalties:* Ongoing licensing or royalty costs for any commercial materials or procedures to be used on a continuing basis
- *Operating expense:* Expense for materials production, facilities, and equipment that are needed in the process, including hardware and software expense, and any related fees

- *Training expense:* Cost to train the organization's staff to use the process, including the expense to develop and deliver the training, whether it is done internally or is a purchased service
- *Administration expense:* Time for staff or contracted service to administer the selection assessment process to each candidate and time to manage the process overall
- *Candidate expense:* Fees for candidate time, travel, and so on, if such are paid; for internal organizational staff, the expense related to time away from normal job duties and perhaps time from the candidate's manager to participate in the process also; and in a hiring situation, possibly relocation expenses, signing bonuses, and various ancillary fees
- *Records or database expense:* Expense for building and maintaining a records system
- *Reporting expense:* Preparing and distributing reports per candidate, and overall reports on the selection process
- *Legal and "employee relations" expense:* Expense associated with those who object to decisions made, how the processes are designed, or how the situation is managed

In addition to these expenses, streams of other expenses derive from associated processes.

Organizations that hire more than a few individuals should be concerned about total hiring expense, though few actually take a systematic cost-benefit approach to the full range of expenses such as those listed here. In the topic area of selection assessment process validity, there may be consideration of utility, which usually involves calculating the additional economic return an organization will receive in improved employee performance by individuals who score more highly on a selection assessment process. However, personally, we have rarely encountered organizations that evaluate the full cost of a sophisticated or complex selection process in an organization. Utility analyses done by I/O psychologists may ignore the costs of the management and implementation of the selection tools they themselves develop. Line managers, however, are generally attuned to daily expenses, and they may refuse to use selection processes they perceive as costly, and particularly, as requiring significant time to learn or use.

Timeliness

Product development timing is a final factor that affects successful implementation. Are the tools and processes ready now? Many organizations have a very short time horizon. When they are not growing, not hiring new staff, and not promoting to new upper-level job openings, they may have little interest in the development of techniques to do these things. Paradoxically, given the lead time that it takes to create selection processes, this may be precisely the time to do it. The selection approach that will be used is the one that is ready when needed.

Relationship of Selection to Other Human Resource Domains

In previous sections we have maintained that several different HR processes can all be selection processes, including hiring, training, performance evaluation, promotion, special assignments, career development, and succession planning. Other HR processes also may be closely related to selection, if not conceptually then operationally. Associations among these processes can be seen most closely in organizations that have attempted "integrated human resource systems" (Byham, 1982).

Selection processes are based on assessing the extent to which candidates possess the knowledge, skills, abilities, and other characteristics (usually behaviors), or KSAOs, that match the requirements of the job or job families. The common skeleton of the KSAO structure is used first to define and describe the job. This KSAO skeleton also is the basis for the design of selection assessment techniques, the development of training programs, and the identification of dimensions for performance evaluation, promotion into the job, personal career or professional development, and planning future job assignments. However, moving past selection processes, the KSAO skeleton can also be used to build reward systems and to plan and forecast future personnel needs.

There is an appealing logic to an integrated HR approach, and it is not surprising that several organizations have tried to build HR systems using the common skeleton of a KSAO structure. Sometimes the integrated system is broadly designed, meaning that the broad conceptual structure is there. Less frequently, the design appears at a specific detail level with all related HR processes tightly woven together.

Integration Based on Common KSAOs or Competencies

When such an integrated HR approach has been attempted, it has been built on a common underlying job analysis or competency system. Although this would not seem complicated when one is thinking of just one job or a family of jobs, when extended to a sizable organization with dozens or hundreds of jobs, the system can quickly become overwhelming.

In order to build an integrated HR system, the job analysis has to be designed to supply information to support all the related applications—what we have called a KSAO skeleton. Job analyses for employee hiring often focus on what is needed to begin the job. To have a broader view of hiring for the work or the organization or to incorporate the other definitions of selection—for example, promotion or career development—one needs to place emphasis not only on what is needed to begin a job but also on what is needed to be fully functional in both the job and the broader organization. Many organizational practitioners feel these broader views are supported more effectively by a focus on competencies. A competency (as the term is used in most organizations) is a somewhat higher level of abstraction than the KSAOs included in traditional job analysis (for example, Gael, 1988) and refers to skills or abilities broadly applicable to a diverse group of jobs or employees in an organization.

A system addressing all HR needs must operate simultaneously at micro and macro levels. Figure 2.2 outlines these different levels, which apply to organizational focus, how work components are viewed, and how success will be defined. For the development of selection tools, an executive selection program may require competencies at the organization level for all leaders, specific knowledge, skills and abilities for the specific management job, and tasks, underlying KSAOs, and required behaviors. A performance management program for those same executives also will require expected outcome measurements at multiple levels.

Figure 2.2. Integrated HR Focus.

	Micro			Macro
Level of organizational focus	Individual job	Job family	Unit/team	Division/ organization
Level of work analysis	Job tasks and KSAOs	Job family tasks and KSAOs	Team tasks and KSAOs	Competencies
Level of outcome measurement	Individual behaviors or work products	Job dimensions or outcomes	Unit/team performance	Organizational performance

Even given a complete taxonomy of jobs based on tasks, KSAOs, competencies, and behaviors, some HR processes still would require additional considerations and analyses beyond a selection focus. Compensation or reward processes would require a determination of the scope of factors for which the organization is willing to pay, such as mastery of higher-level job tasks, criticality of knowledge for the organization, management duties if any, extent to which the job incumbent could place the organization at sizable risk, responsibility level of individuals with whom the job incumbent works, and so on. HR planning concerns would also add information beyond a selection focus, such as how long an incumbent needs to be in a job to gain necessary skills, typical job tenure, likely feeder sources for the job (that is, where the new job incumbents come from), rate at which various patterns of job entry and exit occur, and a forecast of demand and adequacy of supply with the requisite KSAOs.

Several ambitious organizations have tried to carry this approach even further and not only built HR systems on a related structure but also tried to classify each and every incumbent employee in terms of his or her status on each of the major dimensions. In order to build this degree of HR process integration, one can have a *skills management system,* a *knowledge management system,* or a *workforce planning system.* These require a variety of interlinked databases, including one that describes the jobs, their requirements, and either the needed numbers of incumbents or the work to be outsourced; one with the financially compensable factors of the jobs; one that profiles individual workers; and other databases including training courses or developmental activities, succession planning, and possibly outsourcing resources. It takes only a few moments of thought to realize how complex such a system can be to design (but some organizations have done large parts of it) and how much work it is to maintain both the currency and accuracy of the information and the underlying software systems. Most systems like this that we know of have held great conceptual promise but most have eventually died of their own administrative weight and expense.

More recently, perhaps to simplify the information complexity, organizations have been building HR systems on the basis of more broadly stated competencies rather than on extensively detailed task, skill, and knowledge areas. As discussed earlier, a competency is defined at a higher level of abstraction than the KSAOs included in traditional job analysis. Most large corporations currently use some form of competency model as a basis for leadership and (in some cases) professional development programs. In many situations, competencies are derived from groups of behaviors that differentiate "superior" from "average" performers in the organization and these behaviors are usually over and above specific technical skills and knowledge required for jobs or tasks. Reilly and McGourty (1998) describe a competency-based approach to performance management in team settings in which a certification process is developed based on competencies linked to critical team behaviors.

Competency as a term and a concept is currently controversial (for example, Barrett & Depinet, 1991; Lawler, 1996), but it provides a common and easily understood language for identifying and communicating critical behaviors expected in order to be most effective in an organization. In our classification, competencies provide important organization-level information and input into the design of multiple HR processes. Sears, for example, has nine leadership competencies that serve as the focus for all HR processes in their organization. Similarly, Ford has twelve leadership behaviors that serve as the integrating or unifying mechanism across their different processes. These competency models can provide management agreement about HR systems and increase understanding of how HR processes work together to affect the organization positively. However, a competency assessment may not provide the detail necessary to serve as the basis for a defensible selection process against any legal challenge. In 1997, the executive committee of the Society for Organizational and Social Psychology (SIOP) requested that its Scientific Affairs and Professional Practice Committees appoint a joint task force to explore the use of competencies as a central construct in designing human resource systems. At press time for this chapter, the task force was completing its report with an anticipated publication in 2000. Interested readers should contact SIOP's administrative office for additional information on this publication.

Although many organizations are trying to use competency models to integrate selection with other HR processes, colleagues we spoke with report having different levels of success. In one company, for example, competencies are used for selection and performance management but reward systems are not linked to these factors. In another company, competencies are used for executive and senior management 360-degree assessments and personal development, but another set of core skills is used as the central point for all hiring interviews. This company's job-compensable factors then include elements from the competency model and the core skills, plus additional factors.

Integration Based on Common Values and Motivation

Other organizations have different reasons for integrating selection with complementary HR and management systems. Among the factors that organizations may attempt to optimize in the selection process are the following: belief in the mission of the organization, common values or attitudes, comfort with or preference for the work environment offered, interpersonal style that is congruent with established workers, and appreciation for the nonfinancial rewards that are offered or create the context for the work.

In such situations, organizations may try to select for these factors and use them as a basis for satisfaction with a worker or associated rewards and career opportunity. Examples of such approaches include religious organizations for which a belief system must be shared, and various high-tech or entrepreneurial companies for which dedication to the company identity and its technology must be dominant. Wright, Smart, and McMahan (1995) found that the strategies of NCAA basketball coaches influenced the characteristics they looked for in recruits and that teams implementing a strategy different from the coaches' preferred strategy performed less well.

Using selection in the context of organizational fit is to some extent using selection as an organizational development (OD) tool. An alternative to extensive use of training and OD techniques to develop and "mold" employees is actually to select employees with the characteristics the organization values. The assessment of organization value and fit dimensions is not currently an exact science and has more in common with tools and techniques used in organizational diagnosis and development. It is often a qualitative integration of information obtained from interviews with key executives, employee communications, and public relations material. Interest in organizational fit has coincided with a resurgence of interest in personality testing (for example, Liedman, 1998). In addition to assessing characteristics associated with specific job skills (for example, extroversion and some sales positions) developers of many new personality measures are promoting the usefulness of these measures for organizational fit (for example, caring, innovation, quality focus, and integrity).

Although quite different from the preceding examples, another type of situation in which HR approaches may be integrated based on values and motivation is at the executive level in organizations. "Vision," expression of common values, and apparent motivation are factors that may be used in defining executive jobs, selecting executive candidates, assessing performance and potential, and planning future assignments. Yes, ultimately, executives may be held accountable for organizational performance in attaining market share, customer retention, sales growth, or profitability. But these are seldom the sole accountable factors. Organizations that make use of executive assessment as a selection process are relying as much on the likely fit of the candidate to the organization and its values as they are on the knowledge and skills needed to do the job.

HR Planning, Workforce Planning

The two integrated HR approaches described earlier work from the bottom up—that is, from the level of looking at jobs (even if several jobs at the same time) to the level of the overall perspective of the organization. The HR planning approach, which moves from the broad to the specific, also can foster an integrated approach to HR including selection processes. A HR planning approach would start with a view of the overall business goals of the organization, and how these translate into HR *demand*. Demand is what kind of people will be needed when to do what. The response to demand is *supply*, or where one will get the people needed. The process of matching the demand and supply and addressing shortfalls either way is *capacity planning*. All the HR processes used to ensure supply can become integrated if they are designed in complementary fashion to match demand. As discussed earlier, many of these processes are selection processes. They are integrated because to the extent that supply does not come from one source, such as current incumbents, it must come from another. Incremental supply can be provided by external hires but it also can be provided through other means such as through temporary staffing agencies, independent contractors, purchase of specific services, or outsourcing an entire organizational process.

Though much has been written about human resource planning, and several professional associations in this area continue to exist, few organizations have made sophisticated human resource planning a reality as part of their strategy design. As with skill or knowledge databases, human resource planning and the necessary databases supporting it can be complex and administratively expensive. It also seems to be difficult conceptually to move from the organization level to the specific job level and vice versa. It is generally not the way that I/O psychologists are trained to work, so relatively few of the selection processes I/O psychologists develop simultaneously have taken a HR planning viewpoint. It is, perhaps, worthy of more extensive consideration.

In the late 1990s, however, there is one area of workforce planning which many HR departments are pursuing. We use the term *workforce planning* rather than *HR planning* to refer to planning for people who will do the organization's work but may not be its employees. A key workforce planning decision is whether to create employee positions for work to be done or create business relationships with other organizational entities to complete work—the essential make-versus-buy decision. Though one reason for vending out part or all of an organization's work may be for expense management, in times of tight labor supply or difficulty in finding particular skill sets, vending out may be a business strategy to ensure that the organization's functioning can continue.

Is this a selection decision also? Yes it is, in two ways. First, a decision is made not to select or hire at all. And second, the organization now faces the challenge of specifying the key performance requirements for the work and selecting an organization to do the work in a way that will meet its performance goals without using the usual HR or line management techniques. We have found that this conceptual and management shift can be difficult, but in fact the same clear specifications of required skills or competencies and performance requirements necessary for an effective selection process are the basis of a clear vendor contract task description. Similarly, understanding where particular work fits into the organization's work flow and structure is as important for contracted work as it is for work done by employees. However, one must also be very cautious not to handle these situations in any way that makes them appear to be employment situations, otherwise the organization will end up with imputed employees, undesirable tax situations, and negative financial outcomes (*Vizcaino* v. *Microsoft*, 1995).

Selection and Business Processes or Systems

The purpose and direction of the organization make a notable difference in the use of selection processes. Youndt, Snell, Dean, and Lepak (1996) and Buller and Napier (1993) found human resource management practices to be related to firm strategy and other factors, such as stage of organizational development. Organizations with HR practices aligned with structure and strategy tend to have stronger performance (Youndt et al., 1996). Regardless of whether an organization defines selection just within the hiring process or across all the related HR domains, four organizational aspects create the direction and focus of the organization and the context for any HR activity:

- *What is the organization's "business?"* What does the organization do? What are the organization's strategies? One may have far different concerns—beyond job content—in recruiting for the military, the ministry, the Internal Revenue Service, an assembly line, a public relations agency, or an insurance sales team.

- *How is the organization structured?* Where does the job fit in a work sequence? Is the work independent, in a flow of other jobs, or team-interdependent? Is the job part of a family of related jobs, and what are the career alternatives open to job incumbents?
- *How does the organization value people?* Does the phrase *value people* have any meaning at all? Are people viewed as workers or intellectual capital, new hires and trainees or a way to expand the organizational skill capacity? What is the organizational climate and culture?
- *What is the job content and corresponding reward structure?* Are these manufacturing or hourly jobs, salaried management or knowledge worker jobs, jobs with direct interaction with customers or clients tied to measures of satisfaction, commission-based sales jobs, or incentive jobs that share in rewards from achievement of organizational goals?

The Organization's Business

What are the specifics of the organization's business operations? Specifics include details such as customers, products or services, distribution systems, pricing strategy, competitive situation, regulatory or political environment, mature or emerging industry sector, and centrality of technology to organizational success. All these factors influence the skills that are needed, both at the time a person is hired and in the future. They also influence the type of environment that a new employee enters. Clearly, the characteristics of a military environment are different from those of an innovative high-tech start-up firm. Organization-person fit will be an important consideration in environments with strong organizational climates.

What are the goals and strategies of the organization? Colleagues at Sears, Ford, and GTE all emphasized the need to start with the company strategy and what needs to be accomplished, then focus on what will be needed to achieve these goals. In the last five to ten years, organizations have been emphasizing both quality and customer-focused service as distinguishing features of their market positioning. A number of organizations have invested sizable resources in providing employee training in these areas but also have begun to use concepts like "customer orientation" in selecting new hires as well as those who receive certain assignments in the organization.

In many organizations, there also is an increasing emphasis on understanding financial aspects as well as business and industry issues. Decisions, therefore, need to be made about whether these skills will be required of people entering the organization or if training will be provided after they have joined. The decision affects not only the selection process that is used but the recruiting strategy as well. If business knowledge is required, then perhaps business education may be a job prerequisite.

Organizational Structure

The structure of the organization has numerous implications. Is the organization fairly flat with relatively few layers of management? Flat organizations may offer more autonomy or empowerment, but they also offer fewer opportunities for advancement. To what degree is the organization organized in "silos" rather than with more opportunities for cross-functional work? To what extent are employees encouraged to rotate through different parts of the organization?

Focusing on the jobs themselves, to what extent is work done in teams? Is "matrix" management used by the organization? Do people report to more than one manager or have reporting relationships that are ambiguous or confusing? Some employees can survive and thrive in such environments and some cannot—how do we know which ones?

Climate and Value for People

How the organization treats employees will influence who wants to work for the organization, what people say about the company, and how long employees stay once hired. Organizations that are known for "chewing people up and spitting them out" attract different candidates than organizations viewed as supportive and concerned about their employees.

Reward Systems

When most people think of rewards, they think in terms of financial rewards including base compensation, bonuses or other incentive rewards, and benefits. Many organizations today have compensation systems that focus on pay for skills, pay at risk, gain sharing, and other rewards that vary depending on the individual and the organization. The specific approach used depends on factors such as type of industry, type of position, and strategy of the company. In some cases, organizations reward people for skills they have; in other situations they reward people based on business results. In terms of selection, in tight labor markets it may be necessary for an organization to pay a premium for specific skills, and these dimensions may dominate selection considerations beyond other dimensions. In the technology field, for example, programmers with the latest skills are in demand. If an organization needs those skills to be competitive in the future, being able to find and hire employees who have them is critical, and compromises may be made to hire people with some potential who could be trained after hire.

Reward systems can also affect selection in a very different way. In many organizations employees receive a financial reward for people they recruit. Some organizations provide incentives to the person who made the referral if the new employee stays with the company at least six months. One company mistakenly paid incentives for anyone who passed the selection test and was hired by a group of managers. As a result, rather than spending extra time looking for the best candidates, many candidates were hired with fairly low test scores. The incentives drove behavior that ultimately worked against achieving the goals and strategies of the company.

Research Opportunities

What we have said in this chapter was based on observations from experience, our own and others, as much as it was a summary of research results. One reason for this is that we simply did not find a volume of research literature with a broad and integrated view on selection. In fact, I/O psychology research in the area of selection has some parallels to research in the area of performance management. There is much emphasis on measurement and development of selection techniques and less emphasis on effective and strategic building of workforce capacity. In performance management, there is much emphasis on measuring and evaluating performance and less on how to guide and motivate staff effectively.

Following are some of the topic areas that could be researched to provide a knowledge base for more effective management of workforce capacity by organizations. The research designs for these topics are not easy.

- *Selection assessment procedures used in hiring explain only part of the variance in subsequent employee performance; what about other factors related to the hiring process?* The usual assumption is that other postemployment factors account for variable job performance. What is the impact of the role of coworkers in the selection decision, in worker orientation, and in team integration, and how do these forces moderate the characteristics in selection that usually predict employee retention?
- *Are particular recruiting sources always more effective, and why?* What is the impact of Internet job databanks on employers and job candidates? How is the Internet affecting selection options and decisions on either side?
- *How does the job candidate side of the selection process operate?* We know the impact of some particular features, but what are the "scoring" processes that candidates use to evaluate various organizations and decide which offer they should accept? Are some decision processes optimal and would they lead candidates, in general, to make better decisions?
- *How does the particular sequence of procedures or tools in a selection process affect candidate reaction, management support, and validity of the process?* Sequence is often built on economic bases, with the most expensive items last. But what if the apparently low-cost sequence is less valid? There could be little economy overall.
- *What is the impact of various selection tools on job candidates?* Are there some types of tools that may be effective and valid but a disadvantage to an organization because candidates perceive them negatively? Is it the use of particular tools that has an impact, various tools in combination, or the overall context and

impression of a selection process, particularly a hiring process? Do certain interpersonal aspects compensate for more formal or structured aspects?

- *Does it matter who makes the position offer, how, and the form in which the details are presented?* What aspects of negotiation work most effectively with candidates in different situations?
- *Is there any specific business benefit to companies who use an integrated HR approach that extends the conceptual basis of selection into other HR areas?* Is there any benefit to their employees, in terms of speed or efficiency of skill development or more diverse career choice?
- *What are the characteristics of organizations that implement and sustain effective selection processes?* Where in the organization does responsibility lie for managing selection? What specific processes, packaging, communication techniques, and training do these organizations use to ensure maximum use of selection tools?

Practical Advice

Research, however, is in the future. What are the practical tips we recommend to HR executives or those responsible for a broader view on the use of selection in any of its manifestations?

Start from the Widest View

First, start from the widest view possible of selection and work down to the specific level. Identify how workforce planning needs support building the future capacity of the firm. Consider that the firm might require a different type of person who could be more flexibly assigned or more readily recruited if there were changes in the organization, the work, and the job.

Ensure That Selection Processes Link with Organizational Goals

Second, ensure that any selection processes tie back to the organization's goals and strategies. How will the specific approach support the achievement of goals and strategies? Try to demonstrate this with results as appropriate for the type of organization. Express these results in the practical daily language of the managers using the selection approach, not in research formulas or jargon. There will be little support for a selection process if managers do not clearly understand the payoff.

Find a Champion for Selection Process Changes

Section processes usually require changes from how things have been done in the past. Be sure someone with respect and influence in the organization is championing the selection work. Get this person's support to drive the implementation of any new processes. We know of examples of great selection processes that were developed for substantial cost and had strong validity but were never implemented because of political factors in the organization.

Involve Key Stakeholders in the Process

Colleagues at several organizations, including Ingram Micro, Inc., cited this as a very important factor. Involve not only the line manager users of the system but also key executives, people from related HR processes, and even people like those who could be assessed. Key stakeholder involvement will build support for the approach actually implemented and increase the likelihood of a practical and acceptable process that will get used. And needed cooperation among different groups will be difficult to achieve if they are not working together on the development.

Be Careful with Technology!

This fifth point is probably our major point of advice. If selection processes are developed using technology, it is important to have the financial backing to ensure sufficient equipment. Technology evolves rapidly, so it is also important to have ready access to the knowledge necessary to support system changes. Be sure the system is designed for easy update anticipating the next several hardware and software generations. We know of one elaborate selection process that was developed using interactive technology. Unfortunately, the technology was extremely expensive (so there were not enough machines from a practical standpoint) and the technology became outdated before implementation was completed.

Think Practically About the Kind of Process

Think in very practical terms about what kind of process the organization will really use. A well-developed, valid, good selection process that the organization does not use has little value. How do any of the possibilities being considered integrate with how people now work? How much of a change is being requested? What kind of training will have to be provided for the new processes? How will users now and in the future be assured they will have the necessary training to use these processes?

Make Sure the Process Fits with the Organizational Culture

At one large electronics firm, for example, consensus building is critical, so the process used by their interviewers includes the need to reach consensus on any candidate decisions.

Work Out a Specific Infrastructure Plan

A plan will be needed for the infrastructure to support the selection process. Who will have to do what and when? Decide if that can be accomplished through a distributed process managed by line managers. Some techniques are possible only with centralized groups who tightly manage various HR processes. If this approach is not acceptable in the organization or if the organization does not have these resources, then the selection approach may need to be revised to what can be managed.

Try to Get the Organization to Use Common Language for Discussions

One cannot have an integrated approach to HR processes if different groups use different terminology, and particularly if different groups in HR use different terminology. Decide if the process is being built on KSAOs, competencies, or whatever, and use that approach and those words consistently. In addition, as more than one colleague suggested, it is important to use language that the company understands.

Go for Broad Integration First

Go for broad, conceptual integration first, rather than a detailed data-based system. Processes with too much data on too many people and too many aspects of organizational operations will collapse in upon themselves. So much time will be spent to build and maintain databases that one will never get to address the business issues that provoked the work in the first place.

Know That Selection Decisions Are Among the Most Important

Finally, be confident in knowing that selection decisions are among the most important decisions that any manager makes. If selection decisions are handled properly, many other HR processes, which may be "fix it" processes, will demand less time and effort. Getting the right people for the organization is one of the most important and lasting contributions anyone can make to accomplishing organizational goals. Many selection tools work, work well, effectively support a wide range of management decisions beyond hiring, and can be simple and affordable to use.

References

Ash, R. (1983). The behavioral consistency method of training and experience evaluation: Content validity issues and completion rate problems. *Public Personnel Management, 12*(1), 115–127.

Barrett, G., & Depinet, R. (1991, October). Reconsideration of testing for competence rather than intelligence. *American Psychologist,* pp. 1012–1023.

Bennett, N., Ketchen, D., & Schultz, E. (1998). An examination of factors associated with the integration of human resource management and strategic decision making. *Human Resource Management, 37*(1), 3–16.

Bretz, R., & Judge, T. (1994). The role of human resource systems in job applicant decision processes. *Journal of Management, 20*(3), 531–551.

Bretz, R., & Judge, T. (1998). Realistic job previews: A test of the adverse self-selection hypothesis. *Journal of Applied Psychology, 83*(2), 330–337.

Buller, P., & Napier, N. (1993). Strategy and human resource management integration in fast growth versus other mid-sized firms. *British Journal of Management, 4*(2), 77–90.

Byham, W. (1982). Applying a systems approach to personnel activities. *Training and Development Journal, 36*(2), 86–90.

Caldwell, D., & Spivey, A. (1983). The relationship between recruiting source and employee success: An analysis by race. *Personnel Psychology, 36*(1), 67–72.

Cascio, W. (1995). Whither industrial and organizational psychology in a changing world of work? *American Psychologist, 50*(11), 928–939.

Dugoni, B., & Ilgen, D. (1981). Realistic job previews and the adjustment of new employees. *Academy of Management Journal, 24*(3), 579–591.

Flynn, G. (1998). Texas Instruments engineers a holistic HR. *Workforce, 77*(2), 30–37.

Funk, S. L. (1983). U.S. Army combat unit effectiveness: The state of the art and a conceptual model. (Tech. Rep. No. 0002AF). Monterey, CA: McFann-Gray & Associates.

Gael, S. (1988). *The job analysis handbook for business, industry, and government.* New York: Wiley.

Gannon, M. (1971). Sources of referral and employee turnover. *Journal of Applied Psychology, 55*(3), 226–228.

Gilliland, S. W. (1993). The perceived fairness of selection systems: An organizational justice perspective. *Academy of Management Review, 18*(4), 694–734.

Gilliland, S. W. (1994). Effects of procedural and distributive justice on reactions to a selection system. *Journal of Applied Psychology, 79*(5), 691–701.

Gupta, A., & Singhal, A. (1993). Managing human resources for innovation and creativity. *Research Technology Management, 36*(3), 41–53.

Hamill, L. S. (1997). *Structural equation modeling of attitudes toward employment testing.* Unpublished doctoral dissertation, Old Dominion University, Norfolk, VA.

Lawler, E. (1994). From job-based to competency-based organizations. *Journal of Organizational Behavior, 15,* 3–15.

Lawler, E. (1996, November-December). Competencies: A poor foundation for the new pay. *Compensation and Benefits Review,* pp. 20–42.

Liedman, J. (1998). Louder than words. *Human Resource Executive, 12*(11), 22–25.

McCall, M., Lombardo, M., & Morrison, A. (1988). *The lessons of experience.* New York: Free Press.

Meglino, B., Ravlin, E., & DeNisi, A. (1997). When does it hurt to tell the truth? The effect of realistic job previews on recruiting. *Public Personnel Management, 26*(3), 413–422.

Normand, J., Salyards, S., & Mahoney, J. (1990). An evaluation of preemployment drug testing. *Journal of Applied Psychology, 75*(6), 629–639.

Ramamoorthy, N. (1998). Individualism/collectivism orientations and reactions toward alternative human resource management practices. *Human Relations, 51*(5), 571–588.

Ravid, R. (1991). Legal and legislative trends in drug testing. *Journal of Psychiatry and Law, 19*(3–4), 281–294.

Reilly, R., & McGourty, J. (1998). Performance appraisal in team settings. In J. Smither (Ed.), *Performance appraisal: State of the art in practice* (pp. 244–277). San Francisco: Jossey-Bass.

Rynes, S. (1993). Who's selecting whom? Effects of selection practices on applicant attitudes and behaviors. In N. Schmitt, W. Borman, & Associates (Eds.), *Personnel selection in organizations* (pp. 240–274). San Francisco: Jossey-Bass.

Rynes, S., Bretz, R., & Gerhart, B. (1991). The importance of recruitment in job choice: A different way of looking. *Personnel Psychology, 44,* 487–520.

Soroka v. *Dayton-Hudson Corp.,* 235 Cal. App. 3d 654 (1991).

Stewart, G., & Carson, K. (1997). Moving beyond the mechanistic model: An alternative approach to staffing for contemporary organizations. *Human Resource Management Review, 7*(2), 157–184.

Steiner, D., & Gilliland, S. W. (1996). Fairness reactions to personnel selection techniques in France and the United States. *Journal of Applied Psychology, 81*(2), 134–141.

Sujak, D., Villanova, P., & Daly, J. (1995). The effects of drug-testing program characteristics on applicants' attitudes toward potential employment. *Journal of Psychology, 129*(4), 401–416.

Taylor, S. (1994). The relationship between sources of new employees and attitudes toward the job. *Journal of Social Psychology, 134*(1), 99–110.

Terpstra, D. (1997). Why some potentially effective staffing practices are seldom used. *Public Personnel Management, 26*(4), 483–495.

Vizcaino v. *Microsoft,* 754 F.2d 1499, 1501 9th Cir. (1995).

Wanous, J. (1973). Effects of a realistic job preview on job acceptance, job attitudes, and job survival. *Journal of Applied Psychology, 58*(3), 327–332.

Watson, C., & Garbin, A. (1981). The job selection process: A conceptual rapprochement of labor turnover and occupational choice. *Human Relations, 34*(11), 1001–1011.

Weingarten, T. (1998, April 6). The all-day, all-night, global, no-trouble job search. *Newsweek,* p. 17.

Wright, P., Smart, D., & McMahan, G. (1995). Matches between human resources and strategy among NCAA basketball teams. *Academy of Management Journal, 38*(4), 1052–1074.

Youndt, M., Snell, S., Dean, J., & Lepak, D. (1996). Human resource management, manufacturing strategy, and firm performance. *Academy of Management Journal, 39*(4), 836–866.

CHAPTER 3

Demonstrating the Value of Selection in Organizations

Michele E. A. Jayne
John M. Rauschenberger

Like any organizational member competing for resources, industrial/ organizational (I/O) psychologists must frequently convince organizational decision makers to invest in structured, scientifically based selection procedures. Substantial research exists demonstrating the technical merits of scientifically based selection processes (Reilly & Chao, 1982; Guion, 1991). The challenge, however, lies in translating the psychological evidence (for example, validity) into terms managers understand and value (Rauschenberger & Schmidt, 1987). To address this challenge, utility analysis has been offered as a promising tool for translating the technical merits of I/O type practices into economic terms (Boudreau, 1991; Brogden, 1949; Cronbach & Gleser, 1965; Schmidt, Hunter, McKenzie, & Muldrow, 1979). Utility analysis is a decision-making tool designed to help managers organize pertinent information to assess the financial impact of human resource interventions (Cascio, 1993).

Utility analysis, however, has achieved only marginal success as a decision-making and communication tool (Latham, 1988; Latham & Whyte, 1994; Macan & Highhouse, 1994). The propensity of utility analysis to produce dollar-based estimates that dwarf the national debt (Ashe, 1990; Cascio, 1993) as well as increasingly complex formulas for calculating utility stretch the credibility of the tool and make it difficult for practitioners to use and explain to managers (Macan & Highhouse, 1994). Furthermore, the emphasis on communicating value in dollar terms overshadows other criteria managers also use to evaluate selection initiatives, many of which have been largely ignored in the I/O psychology literature (Cascio, 1993; Johns, 1993). Although economic considerations are important, factors such as administrative efficiency, benchmarking data, fit with organizational culture, and reactions from applicants and selection process administrators play crucial roles in decisions to adopt a structured selection approach.

The purpose of this chapter is to review various definitions of value from the view of I/O psychologists and members of organizations. First, this chapter will briefly review evidence from the I/O psychology literature on the technical merits of structured selection practices and the value they bring to organizations. Next, it will discuss promises and shortcomings of utility analysis as a mechanism for communicating value in organizations. Drawing primarily from our experience in a large multinational organization, we will review value definitions held by organizational decision makers, many of which have received scant attention in the research literature. In addition, we will review recommended strategies for communicating value in organizations. Finally, this chapter will highlight strategies for balancing competing values associated with structured selection process.

Evidence of Selection Value in the I/O Psychology Literature

Selecting employees with the requisite knowledge, skills, and abilities (KSAs) is critical to organizational success. The quality of the choices an organization makes can affect it for decades. Much research has been devoted to identifying procedures that will optimize the hiring decisions organizations make. The majority of this research has been directed at the validity, fairness, and utility of employee selection procedures (Hunter & Hunter, 1984; Reilly & Chao, 1982). Overall, selection research shows that by following certain basic principles such as conducting a thorough job analysis, systematically identifying relevant job performance measures and KSAs, and developing appropriate assessment devices that differentiate among candidates, an organization greatly enhances its ability to identify and select candidates who will contribute to its success (Gatewood & Field, 1994).

A number of criteria have been used by researchers to demonstrate the value of selection procedures to organizations. The following section reviews the three most common definitions: *validity evidence, legal defensibility,* and *utility analysis.*

Validity Evidence

Perhaps the most enduring measure of selection system value in the I/O psychology literature is the validity coefficient. Although researchers in recent years have expanded the concept of validity to include content and construct validity (Binning & Barrett, 1989; Landy, 1986; Society for Industrial and Organizational Psychology, 1987), the validity coefficient continues to play a central role in personnel selection research (Guion, 1991). Many studies have demonstrated a statistically significant relationship between structured, standardized selection measures and measures of job performance in various job settings. Ability tests, biodata inventories, weighted application blanks, structured interviews, and assessment centers have all been shown to be valid predictors of various indices of job performance (Hunter & Hunter, 1984; Reilly & Chao, 1982).

The advent of validity generalization has provided additional evidence of the value of structured, professionally developed selection methods. Validity generalization challenges the traditional "situational specificity hypothesis," which argues that the validity of a test is specific to the job or situation where the validation study was completed (Ghiselli, 1966, 1973). Although validity generalization research is not without its critics (see Schmidt, Pearlman, Hunter, & Hirsh, 1985, and Sackett, Schmitt, Tenopyr, Kehoe, & Zedeck, 1985, for reviews of the issues surrounding validity generalization), it has produced impressive findings regarding the generalization of employee selection research. Perhaps the most widely quoted and controversial generalization is that "professionally developed cognitive ability tests are valid predictors of performance on the job and in training for all jobs . . . in all settings" (Schmidt & Hunter, 1981, p. 1128). Guion (1991) also cites a number of studies demonstrating the transportability of various mental ability and aptitude tests across a wide variety of jobs. In addition, Gaugler, Rosenthal, Thornton, and Bentson (1987) showed that assessment center performance is a valid predictor of managerial performance and associated criteria across many different situations.

Legal Defensibility

In addition to validity evidence, protection from legal challenge represents another frequently cited advantage of professionally developed selection procedures. It is common knowledge that the process of selecting employees is subject to several legislative acts and governmental directives designed to eliminate discrimination in employment decisions (Ledvinka & Scarpello, 1991). Legal precedents emerging from case law indicate that organizations can take proactive steps to avoid or successfully defend against legal challenge. For example, basic selection principles such as conducting a thorough job analysis, measuring only job-relevant KSAs, and using a consistent process across candidates are recognized strategies for avoiding or protecting against legal challenge (for example, Arvey & Sackett, 1993; "Uniform Guidelines," 1978).

Utility Analysis

Research on personnel selection has produced a wealth of evidence demonstrating that psychologically based selection processes aid decision makers in identifying candidates who are more likely to perform successfully on the job. Psychologists know that, given the robustness of regression methods, the higher the validity coefficient the more likely an organization will identify employees who will perform well. Although the validity coefficient does provide useful information on the predictive efficiency of a selection process, the psychological concept of validity means little to most organizational decision makers. Instead, they want assurance that a selection process will enable them to identify the "best employees"—meaning that the process merely avoids selecting employees who will fail or perform poorly on the job.

Nevertheless, researchers have focused their attention on translating the validity coefficient into terms they believe managers should understand. Utility analysis, in particular, has received much attention from psychologists as a tool for communicating the value of psychologically based selection processes to managers. One question just receiving attention in the research literature, however, is the reaction of the "customer" to utility information. Preliminary evidence suggests utility analysis is not living up to its promises as an effective decision-making and communication tool. This issue will be discussed in depth later in this chapter.

The goal of utility analysis is to help decision makers organize costs, consequences, and anticipated payoffs of all available courses of action in a systematic manner (Cascio, 1993). Utility analysis is also advocated as a tool for translating the outcome of selection systems into dollar metrics, although some researchers have tried to extend the metrics beyond economic terms (for example, Eaton, Wing, & Mitchell, 1985; Vance & Colella, 1990). The technique was born out of a desire to address the inadequacies of traditional measurement and test theory in expressing the usefulness of tests (Cronbach & Gleser, 1965). Although utility analysis can be applied to any HR program, most research has focused on personnel selection initiatives (for example, Cascio, 1991; Cascio & Ramos, 1986; Cascio & Sibley, 1979; Cronshaw, 1986; Cronshaw & Alexander, 1985; Schmidt et. al, 1979).

Brief History of Utility Analysis

The evolution of utility analysis can be traced back to early efforts by I/O psychologists to interpret the validity coefficient. Schmidt et. al (1979) and Boudreau (1991) provide comprehensive reviews of the development of utility models. The following provides a brief overview of the primary events in the development of the utility analysis technique.

The index of forecasting efficiency (Hull, 1928, Kelley, 1923), a nondollar-based metric that shows the percentage improvement in selection by using a valid predictor as opposed to a nonvalid one, represents one of the earliest attempts to interpret the validity coefficient. The index, however, proved to be useless both for organizational decision makers and human resource professionals (Rauschenberger & Schmidt, 1987). Next came the coefficient of determination, or the squared validity coefficient, which reflects the proportion of variance shared by the predictor and criterion. Although the coefficient of determination is still referred to by selection specialists, it has no direct relationship to productivity gains resulting from use of a selection device (Schmidt et. al, 1979).

Later approaches considered the impact of other selection system attributes on a test's usefulness. Taylor and Russell (1939) extended the utility model concept by taking into account two additional properties of the selection problem—the selection ratio measured as the proportion of applicants hired and the base rate measured as the percentage of applicants who would be "successful" if selection was made without the use of a selection process. It too has been criticized for ignoring other important selection system attributes, such as the number of employees affected, the amount of time during which the effect will last, and program costs (Boudreau, 1991).

Brogden (1946, 1949) is credited with the next major advance in utility analysis. Using the principles of linear regression, he demonstrated how test results could be translated into a dollar value of job performance. Cronbach and Gleser (1965) extended this work by including decision theoretic models of test utility involving employee placement and classification issues in addition to selection situations. Today, despite efforts to broaden the model, the Brogden-Cronbach-Gleser formula remains the most popular utility analysis formula. In its simplest terms, the Brogden-Cronbach-Gleser model conceptualizes utility as gains minus costs of a selection system. In the selection context, gains are conceptualized as the product of four parameters: the number of individuals selected (N); the validity coefficient expressed as the relationship between scores on the selection device (for example, test, assessment center) and scores on a measure of job performance for the selected cohort (rxy); the standard deviation of a dollar-valued measure of job performance or outcomes (Sdy); and the average standardized score on the selection device of interest of those selected (mean Zx). Costs are expressed as the product of the number of applicants multiplied by the fully loaded cost of recruiting, processing, and assessing each applicant (Cascio, 1993).

Despite the allure of translating the benefits of HR interventions into economic terms, research on utility analysis languished until a seminal article by Schmidt et. al (1979), which outlined a simple rational approach to Sdy estimation that was much less cumbersome than traditional cost accounting approaches. This prompted numerous applications of utility analysis to HR activities with the greatest attention focused on personnel selection interventions.

Findings Regarding the Utility of Selection Programs

Application of utility analysis to selection practices has produced overwhelming data indicating that selection programs pay off handsomely. Boudreau (1991) cites twenty-one empirical studies with utility values for forty-eight selection interventions for a variety of jobs and job settings. Virtually every study produced dollar-value payoffs that clearly exceeded costs. Furthermore, studies that take into account more employees, multiple-year tenure, and inflation rates produce utility estimates that are always positive and range in the millions. Although an exhaustive review of the literature is beyond the scope of this chapter, the following provides some examples of the findings reported in the utility analysis literature. Arnold, Rauschenberger, Soubel, and Guion (1982) found that use of a physical ability test for selecting entry-level steelworkers could double output among new workers and thereby increase worker output by $5,000 per year. Schmidt et. al (1979) reported that under the most conservative selection conditions, an estimated productivity increase for one year's use of a test for entry-level computer programmers was $5.6 million.

Research has also demonstrated that substituting a more valid, often more costly selection method for a less valid one, usually an interview, produces a greater estimated utility (for example, Burke & Frederick, 1986; Cascio & Ramos, 1986). In each case, the more valid, and usually more costly, assessment method produced greater utility. However, even the interview, despite its high cost and sometimes lower validity, has been shown to produce positive utility. These findings illustrate that even mildly valid selection processes may produce substantial utility estimates.

Efforts to Refine and Extend Utility Models

The utility analysis literature provides ample evidence of the value of valid selection procedures. Surprisingly, given that utility analysis is touted as a decision-making tool, little research exists examining utility analysis as a method for communicating the value of HR activities to organizations. Instead, researchers have concentrated on refining various components of the model, particularly Sdy estimation (for example, Burke & Frederick, 1986; Cascio & Ramos, 1986; Hunter & Schmidt, 1982), to improve the accuracy of the estimates produced. Although several approaches to Sdy estimation have been offered, the three most popular methods are the global method (Schmidt et. al, 1979), which involves averaging supervisor estimates of employee value at the fiftieth (average) and eighty-fifth (one standard deviation above average) percentiles; a method developed by Hunter and Schmidt (1982) that involves multiplying the average salary in a job by some proportion (for example, 40 percent) based on national trends in performance data; and the Cascio-Ramos (1986) estimate of performance in dollars (CREPID), which involves partitioning annual salary among a job's principal activities based on each activity's job analysis importance rating, multiplying performance ratings for each individual on these activities by the proportion of annual salary associated with them, summing the products across all job activities, and using the standard deviation of these values across employees to estimate Sdy.

Other researchers have extended utility models to include additional factors likely to influence payoffs (for example, Cascio, 1993). Efforts such as these have opened the field to yet another criticism that utility models are becoming so complex that most novices to the field, including many I/O psychologists, are reluctant to use the technique (Macan & Highhouse, 1994). Efforts to fine-tune utility equations, however, continue to be a focal point of the research despite evidence suggesting that such refinements do not appear to lead to significant differences in the conclusions regarding the value of interventions (Burke & Frederick, 1986; Schmidt, Ones, & Hunter, 1992) and that the added complexity may further alienate practitioners from using the technique (Macan & Highhouse, 1994).

Effectiveness of Utility Analysis as a Decision-Making Tool

The limited research examining utility analysis as a decision-making tool has provided mixed results. Macan and Highhouse (1994) surveyed members of regional associations of applied psychologists and HR professionals concerning their perceptions of utility analysis. They found that less than half of respondents reported using utility estimates when presenting an HR activity to management. The association members also reported that although managers were interested in the bottom line when it came to HR interventions, they did not respond well to utility analysis information.

Latham and Whyte (1994) presented managers enrolled in an executive training program with information on the effectiveness of a selection initiative. The information provided varied from validity evidence alone to validity evidence combined with utility evidence. The results showed that the managers responded most favorably to the selection intervention when validity evidence alone was presented. Alternatively, inclusion of utility information led to a decrease in support for the selection intervention. In a follow-up study, Whyte and Latham (1997) explored whether their findings would extend to a situation where an expert on the topic of utility analysis explained the value of utility information to managers. They reported not only that the results of a highly positive utility analysis failed to convince managers to adopt a new selection practice but that the presentation of the analysis undercut support for such a change. This study replicated their earlier findings even with the addition of an expert communicating the value of the utility information.

Alternatively, Carson, Becker, and Henderson (1998) were unable to replicate Latham and Whyte's findings even though they used a similar sample and the same stimulus material as in the original study. However, their results showed that managers were not particularly impressed with the proposed new selection system despite the positive utility evidence. This result casts further doubt that utility information is persuasive in convincing managers of the value of structured, scientifically based, selection systems.

Factors Affecting Managerial Reactions to Utility Analysis

In response to marginal findings on the utility of utility analysis, researchers have begun to explore factors that might affect the credibility of the utility message. Simply presenting the final dollar estimate in a utility equation is not likely to provide adequate evidence for the value of a selection intervention (Rauschenberger & Schmidt, 1987). Instead, managers are likely to ask for some explanation of the source of the dollar-based estimate. Boudreau (1991) has pointed to the need for research to determine not only if utility estimates influence managerial decision making but also if reactions to utility estimates are affected by different parameter estimation techniques and whether the models accurately reflect the concerns of decision makers.

Once again, only limited research has focused on this question. For example, much of the research seeking to perfect Sdy estimation has been conducted independently of decision makers' reactions to the various techniques. Lack of research in this area is surprising considering the central role Sdy plays in utility estimates and the fact that any explanation to managers on the source of utility estimates is likely to center on this parameter. Edwards, Frederick, and Burke (1988) represent a rare exception in that they collected reactions from a small sample of managers on the three most popular methods of Sdy estimation: the global method, the 40 percent method, and the CREPID method. Their results showed that managers perceived CREPID as the most credible of the three.

Hazer and Highhouse (1997) offer perhaps the most extensive empirical study to date on the factors influencing managerial reactions to utility information. In addition to exploring the impact of Sdy estimation methods, they also looked at the way utility analysis information is framed and the type of HR activity under consideration. Specifically, they examined whether presenting utility information as a cost of not taking action is more likely to lead to favorable reactions than a utility estimate presented as a gain due to taking action. This hypothesis was based on research on human decision making (for example, Meyerowitz & Chaiken, 1987; Rowe, 1989) showing the greater judgmental effect of negative versus positive information. In addition, hypothesizing that the mixed results regarding managerial reactions to utility analysis may be caused by differences in the specific HR activity under consideration, they tested whether managerial reactions would be more favorable to utility estimates regarding a training program as opposed to a selection program.

Unlike the findings by Edwards, Frederick, and Burke (1988), this study showed that managers reacted more favorably to the 40 percent estimation method than the global or CREPID methods. One explanation offered for this result is that the 40 percent method is the most simple and direct approach of the three and thus likely to be easiest for managers to understand. Their research also offered some evidence that managers' general reactions to utility analysis are influenced by the type of Sdy technique used. Another notable finding is that framing utility estimates as an opportunity cost rather than an opportunity gain had a greater impact on managers with a moderate understanding of utility analysis than managers with a stronger understanding. This finding provides some support that framing may influence receptivity, although level of understanding appears to moderate the relationship. Finally, they found no effects for type of HR intervention on managerial reactions to utility analysis.

The Hazer and Highhouse (1997) study offers some insight into factors that might influence managerial receptivity to utility estimates. Additional research, however, is clearly needed. One factor that has yet to be clearly addressed in the literature is the impact of managers' involvement in utility analysis estimation on their reactions to the dollar estimate derived. The studies by Latham and his colleagues as well as the work by Hazer and Highhouse (1997) involved presenting managers with utility estimates that had been derived with no involvement on their part. Direct involvement in the estimation process should engender both commitment to and understanding of it. Communicating utility information in the language of the organization will also enhance receptivity. Rauschenberger and Schmidt (1987) have suggested following a few clear communication principles, such as getting organizational decision makers involved in the utility analysis process early, tying utility analysis efforts to organizational sources of information that are familiar to decision makers, and talking to accounting and financial people in the organization to determine standard formats for presenting economic information.

Field research offers some support for the positive role of managerial involvement. Morrow, Jarrett, and Rupinski (1997) attributed the acceptance of training program utility estimates in a Fortune 500 pharmaceutical company in part to the fact that company officers and senior strategic planning and human resource managers preapproved the utility model. In another field application, D. Moretti (personal communication, April 1998), attributed successful use of utility analysis in a large electronics organization to steps such as having senior organizational leaders nominate those managers involved in estimating Sdy, working closely with operating and HR management to determine what variables to include in cost estimates, and having the most senior financial manager critically review the utility calculations and assumptions. Implementation of utility analysis in this last case was so successful that it earned the team a corporate achievement award and has led to numerous requests to apply utility analysis techniques to other selection initiatives in the company.

Additional Factors Affecting Credibility of Utility Analysis

Although Sdy estimation method, framing, and managerial involvement appear to influence managerial receptivity to utility estimates, several other features of utility analysis must be addressed before it will be widely accepted. One is the credibility of utility estimates. As Cascio (1993, p. 310) notes, "Astronomical estimates of the economic value of selection methods abound in the literature." Utility calculations tend to produce extremely high estimates, sometimes dwarfing the national debt, and often surpassing more traditional investment opportunities in plant and equipment purchases, marketing, or the financial arena (Boudreau, 1991). Researchers' failure to consider the realities of selection systems in organizations has led to inflated estimates of utility. For example, as Cascio has noted, the assumptions that organizations hire in a top-down fashion and that all applicants who are offered jobs accept them are rarely if ever met in organizational settings. Such simplifying assumptions lead to inflated utility estimates that undermine the credibility of the tool. Faced with the sheer magnitude of these numbers, it is not surprising that practitioners are reluctant to present such estimates to management. Furthermore, because managers usually think of HR activities as costs rather than investments (Cronshaw & Alexander, 1985), they are likely to be skeptical of such extreme estimates and ask for proof that such gains can actually be achieved. To date, however, no studies follow up utility predictions to determine whether the expected gains actually materialize.

Others (for example, Skarlicki, Latham, & Whyte, 1996) have challenged fundamental assumptions underlying the rationale for using utility analysis. For example, researchers have questioned the assumption that managers emphasize and rely heavily on rational analysis and technical merit evidence when making decisions about adopting HR activities. Mintzberg (1975) reported that managers tend to rely heavily on intuition rather than quantitative information for decision making. Research on human judgment has also shown that individuals tend to place greater weight on anecdotal information and underestimate analytical input (Mintzberg, 1989; Kahneman & Tversky, 1973). Similarly, Johns (1993) has argued that managers are likely to view HR initiatives as administrative innovations rather than technical innovations. He concluded that technical merit—precisely what utility analysis attempts to measure—carries little weight with managers when it comes to adopting administrative innovations. Such findings indicate that although utility analysis presents decision makers with information on factors they probably should consider, it is likely that actual decisions will depart from utility prescriptions (Boudreau, 1991).

Utility analysis research has also overlooked the fact that investment in a selection process depends on the availability of funds to support implementation and maintenance of the system. Both economic and political factors can determine whether funds are committed to a project. Periods of economic downturn, aggressive cost-cutting initiatives, or prior commitments to fund other major initiatives may make it economically impossible or politically risky to invest in a new initiative no matter how sound the project. Therefore, even if managers can be convinced of a substantial return on investment in a selection process, such an argument is likely to have little impact on the decision to adopt it. If the dollars aren't available or cost cutting is the latest thing, investment in a selection system is likely to be denied no matter how strong the business case.

Organizational characteristics such as industry and culture can also affect the acceptability of utility estimates. An organization with a large technical workforce or one heavily focused on metrics and data is likely to be more receptive to the application of utility analysis than an organization with a more service-based workforce or one less focused on metrics. Moretti (personal communication, April 1998) attributed the successful implementation of utility analysis in his organization in part to the fact that the organization has a large population of engineers and is used to dealing with numbers. Another factor that must be considered in applying utility analysis is the predisposition of managers to the HR activity in question. Managers who are highly skeptical of the merits of a proposed HR intervention to begin with are likely to be more suspicious of utility analysis estimates than those who are favorably predisposed to the intervention. In these situations, dollar savings estimates may not be enough to persuade managers to accept the intervention.

Another issue that has received minimal attention in the utility literature is whether equal validity implies equal value or utility. Consider a finding showing that a cognitive ability measure and a measure of customer service orientation have equal validity for a customer service position. Despite the equal validities, the organization is likely to value the performance dimensions predicted by the two measures differently: those predicted by customer service orientation may have greater value to the organization than those predicted by the cognitive ability measure. However, utility analysis techniques to date provide no method for taking into account the relative value of various predictors.

In summary, research on the use of and receptivity to utility analysis estimates has yet to produce strong support for utility analysis as a decision-making tool and communication technique. Although field results are more optimistic than laboratory results, the evidence is too preliminary to draw firm conclusions. Practitioners should proceed with caution in building a business case solely on utility analysis estimates. Furthermore, several factors that might affect the use of and receptivity to utility analysis estimates have yet to be investigated. Additional research is needed to determine if utility analysis results affect managerial decisions, if decision makers' reactions to utility analysis results are affected by different parameters, and whether utility models accurately reflect decision makers' concerns.

Finally, research on the value of selection has paid scant attention to the fact that managers use criteria other than dollar return to evaluate the merit of investment in a selection process. The following section discusses alternative dimensions of value in organizations and methods for effectively communicating value to organizational decision makers.

Alternative Definitions of Value

Research on demonstrating the value of selection processes in organizations has concentrated almost exclusively on the dollar criterion. Although a few researchers have proposed alternatives to the dollar criterion, such as percentage improvement in productivity (Burke & Pearlman, 1988; Schmidt, 1993) and annual profits and turnover rates (Vance & Colella, 1990), empirical tests of these variables, particularly as they compare with the dollar criterion as a means of expressing value, have largely been ignored in the literature.

The intense focus on the dollar criterion has overshadowed others important to managers when evaluating HR initiatives. Although few would argue that bottom-line results are unimportant, other dimensions of value exist in organizations that are just as compelling or perhaps even more compelling than cost justifications. Macan and Highhouse (1994), for example, found that 48 percent of practitioners who did not use utility estimates indicated that it was because they were not needed, requested, or supported by management. Instead, practitioners reported using techniques such as logic or selling (for example, anecdotes, face validity, expertise), legal defensibility and compliance arguments, validity evidence, and noneconomic business objectives (for example, employee development, retention) to demonstrate value. These findings support Latham's (1988) assertion that managers are not interested solely in dollar estimates and usually consider other factors when determining the value of a selection intervention.

The key to demonstrating the value of selection in organizations is to identify value definitions of interest and to tailor the value argument to the audience. Practitioners must satisfy several constituents, including senior operating management, senior HR management, hiring managers, and HR administrators when seeking to implement a selection intervention. Each constituency considers various factors when evaluating a selection initiative, some of which are common and others which are unique to a particular group. Table 3.1 outlines key constituents and the value definitions most relevant to each. Key factors senior operating managers consider, for example, include up-front development and maintenance costs, benchmarking data, improvement in the quality of new hires, applicant reactions to the process, and administrative efficiency of the process. Senior HR managers use similar criteria to evaluate a selection system. In addition, diversity and legal defensibility criteria as well as process measures such as cycle time and candidate flow data (for example, selection ratios) are also considered. Alternatively, HR administrators emphasize such factors as time and resources required to administer the process and ease of administration. Finally, hiring managers focus on cycle time for filling a position, ease of using the selection process to make hiring decisions, and the quality of candidates identified by the process.

Table 3.1. Value Definitions Held by Organizational Constituents.

Organizational Constituent	Value Definitions			
	Financial	Business Impact	Process	People/Culture
Senior operating management	• Development costs • Implementation costs • Maintenance costs • Utility analysis	• Benchmarking evidence • Quality of new hires (job performance, testimonials from hiring managers, validity evidence) • Alignment with diversity and affirmative action goals	• Benchmarking evidence • Administrative efficiency (perceptions of ease of use from hiring managers) • Process metrics (candidate flow statistics, selection ratios, cycle time to fill a position, administrative time) • Flexibility (meets various organizational needs)	• Applicant reactions • Fit with organizational culture • Alignment with organizational goals/objectives
Senior HR management	• Development costs • Implementation costs • Maintenance costs • Utility analysis	• Benchmarking evidence • Quality of new hires (job performance, testimonials from hiring managers, validity evidence) • Alignment with diversity and affirmative action goals	• Benchmarking evidence • Administrative efficiency (perceptions of ease of use from hiring managers and HR administrators, resources required to administer the process) • Process metrics (candidate flow statistics, selection ratios, cycle time to fill a position, administrative time)	• Applicant reactions • Reactions from hiring managers and HR administrators

HR administrators	• Administrative efficiency (ease of use) • Process metrics (cycle time to fill a position, administrative time)	• Applicant reactions
Hiring managers	• Administrative efficiency (ease of use) • Process metrics (cycle time to fill a position) • Quality of new hires (job performance, validity evidence)	• Applicant reactions
Applicants	• Administrative efficiency (ease of use) • Relationship with job content • Fairness • Quality of information received about job/company	

A variety of strategies are effective for demonstrating the value of selection processes in organizations. Although validity and utility evidence can play a role (for example, Macan & Highhouse, 1994; Moretti, personal communication, April 1998; Morrow et al., 1997), other criteria can be as or more effective in communicating the value of selection to the organization. Specifically, the criteria that are most effective in demonstrating value to a variety of organizational constituents are *benchmarking evidence, quality of new hires, administrative efficiency, process flexibility, applicant reactions, alignment with diversity and affirmative action goals,* and *process metrics* (for example, pass rates, selection ratios).

Benchmarking Evidence

Evidence that other organizations use similar selection processes is a powerful tool for demonstrating the value of a selection intervention. In recent years, benchmarking has become standard practice among organizations. As Johns (1993) notes, executives are fascinated with comparing the practices of their own firms with those of others. Benchmarking data are effective for two reasons. First, they provide decision makers with specific real-world examples that a proposed initiative works. Second, such data reduce the level of uncertainty of many managers when confronted with arguments for the potential benefits of an HR intervention (Johns, 1993). Often, although organizations don't want to fall behind in the adoption of a process that might add value and provide a competitive advantage, many also don't want to be so far out front that they perceive they are taking an unreasonable risk.

It is important to note that for benchmarking information to be effective, practitioners must name names. Vague references to field research demonstrating that a particular selection process is effective will have limited impact. Furthermore, practitioners should carefully pick the organizations that they benchmark. Using such criteria as key competitors or most admired companies will increase the persuasiveness of the message. Internal benchmarking evidence can also be persuasive. Particularly in large organizations, a variety of selection processes may exist. Piloting a new process in one part of the organization before full implementation is another effective strategy. Evidence that a process is working well for a particular component of the organization, particularly one that is respected, is an effective technique for demonstrating the value of a selection intervention.

Quality of New Hires

When presented with a proposal for a new selection process, managers will ask for evidence that it is more effective in identifying quality candidates than an alternative or existing process. Managers define new hire quality as the ability of the selection process to identify the "best candidates"—meaning that the selection process eliminates those who will fail or perform poorly. Indices of new hire quality include job performance measures such as productivity, accident rates, grievances, absenteeism, and turnover. Changes in these indices following implementation of a selection system can be leveraged effectively to demonstrate the value of that system to the organization.

Validity evidence is another way of demonstrating increased new hire quality. Ideally, validity evidence can be used to demonstrate the increased ability of one system over another to identify qualified candidates. However, using validity evidence as part of the value argument presents several challenges. First, managers usually want organization-specific evidence as opposed to general research findings. Organizational constraints, however, often limit the availability of organization-specific validity evidence. For example, validity evidence is usually unavailable early in the decision-making process. Furthermore, even if organization-specific validity evidence (for example, pilot data) is available, data on a previous or existing process are often unavailable, making an objective comparison of alternative selection processes time consuming and costly, if not impossible. Situations where hiring volume is low also prevent the feasibility of collecting organization-specific validity evidence. Finally, even if organization-specific validity evidence is available, the psychometric concept of validity has little meaning to most managers.

Rarely can validity evidence stand alone in demonstrating increased quality of new hires. Other evidence must also be presented. Qualitative data in the form of anecdotes or testimonials are powerful tools for demonstrating the value of a selection process.

Macan and Highhouse (1994) found that the most popular technique used by practitioners to communicate the value of an HR intervention involved anecdotes. The power of anecdotal evidence has also been acknowledged in research on human judgment and decision making (Kahneman & Tversky, 1973).

A few testimonials from respected managers touting the benefits of the selection process will go a long way toward convincing organizational decision makers of its value. For example, testimonials from hiring managers praising the quality of candidates hired using a structured selection process is an effective way to demonstrate the impact of the process on new hire quality. Such information can be presented either in a few well-crafted quotes or, if more quantitative data are desired, as survey feedback from hiring managers.

Anecdotal evidence can also be used to support other value dimensions held by organizational decision makers. It should be noted, however, that although anecdotal evidence can play a key role in convincing managers of the benefits of a selection system, a few negative testimonials can be just as powerful in undermining support. Often, if not carefully managed, a few negative comments can completely undermine a wealth of positive and even objective data. A recent case in point involves a company attempting to implement a new selection process across a variety of departments. At the last minute one department pulled out of the project—even though it had invested a great deal of time and money to develop and implement the process and despite the fact that the process was being used successfully in other areas of the company, as evidenced by managerial feedback and preliminary validity evidence. The project was put on hold in response to concerns raised by a handful of "significant" managers recently trained in the process, who reported that they did not feel comfortable using it and still had reservations about the new assessment center process being better at identifying qualified candidates than their structured interview process.

Administrative Efficiency

Another factor organizational decision makers consider in evaluating a selection intervention is administrative efficiency. Managers scrutinize the resources required to administer a selection system.

There are several dimensions of administrative efficiency. The first is the amount of time that line managers must devote to the process, including the amount of time required to assess candidates and any training required. Perceptions of ease of use of the selection process is another important dimension of administrative efficiency. A process that is cumbersome or time consuming will be perceived negatively, which will undermine support for the selection process.

A second dimension of administrative efficiency is cycle time for filling a position—that is, the total time it takes to recruit, assess, and hire a new employee. Cycle time is an important metric because organizations often have difficulty accurately forecasting personnel needs and therefore find themselves needing a new employee immediately. In addition, during times when the job market is particularly competitive, managers will demand assurances that any new selection process does not pose a barrier to identifying and securing top candidates quickly. Although other aspects of the recruiting process also affect cycle time, time requirements of the selection process will be closely scrutinized. Demonstrating that a selection process contributes to cycle time efficiency is an important factor in demonstrating its value.

A third aspect of administrative efficiency is the time and people resources HR must devote to administering the process. Usually the HR organization is responsible for coordinating activities related to the selection process. HR managers in particular are interested in the amount of time and number of people required for process administration. HR administrators' perceptions of administrative ease will also affect both successful implementation of the selection process and evaluation of its merits.

The power of administrative efficiency in determining the fate of a selection process should not be underestimated. As any practitioner will relate, a great deal of effort goes into balancing the "ideal" or best way of implementing an initiative with the tolerance level of the organization. Organizations are full of examples of technically meritorious processes that collapsed under their own weight because of unrealistic administrative burdens. For example, several years ago a large company considered implementing a one-day assessment center to evaluate candidates for a senior-level plant position. Despite the technical merits of the assessment center approach and the critical nature of the position, the program collapsed because plant managers were not available to serve as assessors. It was simply unrealistic to pull plant managers away from their jobs for a day to participate.

Several metrics are used in organizations to demonstrate administrative efficiency. Quantitative data regarding time and people to administer a process are common. Testimonials from individuals involved in the process, including HR administrators and hiring managers, are other important sources of information on the administrative efficiency of a selection process.

Process Flexibility

Related to administrative efficiency is flexibility of the process to meet the needs of various organizational units using a selection process. Today's focus on process efficiency leads many organizations to attempt to implement "common" HR practices to streamline costs and capitalize on economies of scale. Organizational units, however, often have different practices, philosophies, and goals for the selection of new employees. Successfully implementing a selection system involves building a process that satisfies these various needs. The extent to which the process is flexible enough to meet organizational differences while maintaining its integrity and strategic goals is important for gaining its widespread support and use.

Process flexibility is particularly important for multinational organizations. Globalization has presented organizations with the challenge of implementing HR practices on a worldwide basis. The few studies examining selection practices globally indicate that there is a great deal of diversity in practices used (for example, Levy-Leboyer, 1994). Ryan, McFarland, Baron, and Page (1998) found that this diversity can be explained both by national and cultural differences. These results demonstrate that attempting to convince units in various countries to adopt a standardized selection battery is a difficult if not unrealistic goal. A more realistic approach is to satisfy both management and local interests by identifying how locally acceptable selection practices fit with the overall strategic goals and principles of the selection process. Such an approach meets the multinational organization's need of using a "common" selection process while accommodating local needs.

Demonstrating process flexibility can be as simple as listing the various organizations and regions that are using the process. For example, the ability of a system to accommodate one or multiple candidates and be modified to meet various cultural needs is powerful evidence of its flexibility. Obtaining testimonials from various process users regarding its flexibility to meet various organizational and regional needs is, once again, another effective method.

Applicant Reactions

Applicant reactions to a selection system are another dimension of value important to organizational decision makers. Often, managers want to ensure that a selection procedure is not "turning off" applicants from pursuing employment with an organization. Such concerns are particularly pronounced in competitive labor markets where organizations find themselves competing for the best candidates. Furthermore, applicants represent potential customers of the organization and managers have a vested interest in making sure that they perceive the organization positively no matter what the selection outcome.

The concerns raised by managers have been echoed in the research literature on applicant reactions to selection procedures. Research shows that applicant reactions vary according to the type of selection process used. For example, applicants favor procedures with a strong relationship to job content particularly when administered in a job simulation or work sample format as opposed to paper-and-pencil format (Rynes, 1993). Research findings also suggest that the information applicants receive about a job and company from the selection procedure may affect their attraction to the organization (Breaugh, 1992; Rynes, 1992) or withdrawal from the selection process (for example, Rynes, Bretz, & Gerhart, 1991). Perceived fairness of the selection process has also been hypothesized to influence job search decisions, including probability of offer acceptance (for example, Cascio, 1991; Murphy, 1986).

Several sources of information can be used to assess candidate reactions. One obvious method is to survey or collect testimonials from applicants about their perceptions of the selection process. Steps to encourage candidates to offer honest reactions—such as using an outside vendor and protecting anonymity—should be taken to preserve the integrity of the data. Benchmarking other companies that use similar processes to pursue similar types of candidates can provide additional evidence of candidate receptivity—that is, if it works for them, it should work for us.

Another avenue to take is to hold focus groups or conduct surveys with prospective applicants. The latter strategy was used by a large company implementing a new entry-level salaried employee selection process. Candidate reactions were among the key concerns expressed by managers in the early phases of the project. Managers were concerned that the caliber of students targeted (students from the best schools with the best GPAs) would be dissuaded from applying if asked to complete anything other than an interview. As a result, the organization spent a great deal of time visiting college campuses to conduct focus groups and surveys of potential applicants on a proposed selection process involving a written test and job simulation. Interestingly, the results of these focus groups and survey showed that the actual selection process accounted for only 4 percent of a candidate's decision about whether to apply to a company. Other factors such as type of work, advancement opportunities, and compensation and benefits carried much more weight than the nature of the selection process. Nevertheless, candidate reactions to the proposed selection process played a powerful role in convincing managers to support it.

Alignment with Diversity and Affirmative Action Goals

In recent years, many organizations have undertaken major diversity initiatives. Many of these initiatives have been in response to workforce demographic projections (for example, Johnston & Packer, 1987) indicating that a small proportion of new labor force entrants will come from "traditional" white male populations (Rynes & Rosen, 1995). High-profile legal cases have also driven interest in diversity initiatives. The extent to which it can be demonstrated that the selection process contributes to the diversity of the workforce is thus an additional factor that can be used to justify investment in it. Metrics to illustrate the link between the selection process and diversity and affirmative action initiatives include the demographic breakdown of new hires as well as traditional adverse impact analyses demonstrating that the process is fair to various groups. In addition, reaction data from applicants of various demographic groups can play a role in demonstrating a positive relationship between the selection process and diversity goals.

Process Metrics

When considering the merits of a selection process, process metrics such as candidate flow statistics, selection ratios, and cycle time to fill a position can also be used to demonstrate the value of selection processes. For example, demonstrating that a multiple hurdle approach with low-cost prescreening tools up front reduces the number of candidates who must be assessed using more expensive tools later in the process is a compelling argument for a selection process. Selection ratios demonstrating that only the "best of the best" in the candidate pool are being hired also speaks to its quality. Finally, timing metrics, such as administration time and cycle time for filling positions can be used to justify the utility of a selection process.

This section has illustrated the various value dimensions organizational decision makers consider when evaluating a selection intervention. Usually, practitioners must present evidence on a variety of criteria as opposed to one or two alone. Economic considerations are often one aspect of the value argument, but other sources of value evidence must also be presented to justify investment in a selection intervention. Furthermore, practitioners must often juggle competing values. The following section reviews some of the most common issues practitioners must balance when demonstrating the value of a selection intervention.

Managing Competing Values

As illustrated, constituents of a selection process hold a variety of value definitions that must be satisfied. Often, these values conflict with one another and with efforts on the part of a practitioner to implement a rigorous selection process. In addition, various scenarios exist under which decisions about selection processes are made. These scenarios vary regarding the key considerations that affect the ultimate decision outcome. Balancing competing values as well as key considerations effectively is critical to demonstrating the value of selection in organizations. Successful implementation of a selection process often involves compromises so that a variety of goals and values can be met.

Some of the most common issues that must be balanced involve cost, quality, and timing. For example, one issue that has been largely overlooked in the literature is that decisions about investment in a selection process usually compete for HR dollars with other processes or systems. Decision makers are often confronted with a variety of choices on how to distribute and spend HR dollars. Reengineering efforts, implementation or revisions of other HR processes such as training or performance management, modification or upgrading of HR computer system infrastructure, and major capital investments in equipment or facilities are just a few examples of opportunities that may compete. Therefore, decisions about selection programs do not merely compare cost to benefit of the selection system but also selection system benefits to benefits that would accrue from other investment opportunities. An effective argument for a selection system, therefore, must include evidence that it will provide a greater value to the organization than another effort. Arguing the value of selection, therefore, will require comparison against other investment opportunities using similar criteria, including up-front development and maintenance costs, expected return on investment, cost savings, and the extent to which a particular initiative supports major organizational goals and objectives.

Similarly, up-front and maintenance costs of a system must be balanced against the availability of funds to support various HR initiatives. As mentioned previously, impressive return-on-investment projections may prove irrelevant if the organization does not have the money to support the project. Economic constraints can prohibit investment in new initiatives regardless of the merit or long-term returns they might provide the organization. This trade-off, although frustrating, represents a real-world dilemma that practitioners and managers often face.

Other common trade-offs involve balancing the quality of the selection process with the amount of time and people resources the organization is able and willing to devote to it. Practitioners frequently encounter immense pressures to reduce the time required for training and for evaluating candidates. Meeting both the resource needs of the organization and the organization's desire to hire quality candidates represents a critical challenge. As already mentioned, many a quality selection program has collapsed under its own weight because the organization simply could not support it. Practitioners must manage this balance carefully by understanding fully the resource limits of the organization as well as principles of quality selection.

Similarly, fit with organizational culture must be balanced against the quality of a selection process. Organizations vary in the extent to which structured evaluation of behavior and performance is conducted. They also vary in the human resource strategy they pursue. As Cascio (1993) notes, companies that pursue human resource strategies that emphasize innovation or quality enhancement are most likely to invest in valid selection programs. An organization that historically has relied on informal methods for evaluating candidates or that pursues conservative human resources strategies, for example, may not be ready to leap immediately into a highly structured, albeit more valid, selection procedure. In this case, rather than expecting the organization to jump immediately into such a process, a more successful strategy might be to introduce a less technically advanced procedure initially (for example, structured interview rather than an assessment center) with the hope of easing it to more advanced processes later. In contrast, an organization that values objective evaluation or one that is striving to promote cultural change that stresses this objective will be more receptive to a highly structured selection process than one that uses more informal methods for assessing performance.

The context in which selection decisions are made also raises unique sets of issues that must be balanced and managed when demonstrating the value of a selection intervention. Russell and his colleagues (Russell, Colella, & Bobko, 1993), for example, have argued that the strategic needs of an organization must be considered when estimating the utility of a selection intervention. They note that the extent to which a selection intervention supports the strategic needs of the organization affects the overall utility of the intervention. To date, utility models have failed to consider compatibility with strategic needs. Because strategic needs change frequently, successful implementation and maintenance of a selection intervention requires practitioners continually to evaluate and demonstrate the extent to which it supports the organization's strategic intent.

Another contextual factor is the scenario in which selection decisions are made in organizations. A variety of decision-making scenarios exist, each one presenting different issues and key considerations for practitioners. Table 3.2 lists some of the most common

decision-making scenarios and the key considerations that influence the decision-making outcome. Take, for example, the professional scenario, an ideal but often elusive situation that occurs
when an I/O psychologist identifies an opportunity to implement
or improve a selection process. In this case, the I/O psychologist
is the initiator and success lies in his or her ability to assess accurately the value definitions of key constituents and build a persuasive business case for the selection system.

Other decision-making scenarios pose other challenges. Consider the disease scenario, where a performance problem occurs
and management has identified selection as the appropriate solution for the problem. In this case, an organization is likely to be

Table 3.2. Common Decision-Making Scenarios.

Scenario	Description	Challenge
Professional	Practitioner identifies opportunity to implement or improve selection process.	Develop business case tailored to value definitions of major constituents.
Disease	Selection is identified as solution to performance problem.	Balance organization's need for a "quick fix" with implementation of effective selection process.
Run amok	Management identifies "latest and greatest" selection process for implementation.	Balance management desire with sound selection practice.
Legal challenge	Defense of a selection practice to regulatory agency is unsuccessful.	Satisfy both organizational needs and regulatory agency requirements.
But we're different	Organizational unit argues it has unique needs that can't be satisfied by corporate selection process.	Balance process flexibility with goal of staying as common as possible to avoid administration burden.

looking for a quick fix. The challenge for the practitioner is to confirm that selection is the appropriate solution. If it is confirmed, the practitioner must then identify a selection intervention that addresses the problem. If selection proves not to be the issue, then the practitioner must build a persuasive business case for an alternative solution. All of this usually must be done under tight time constraints.

Another common scenario is the run-amok scenario, where management becomes enamored with the latest and greatest selection intervention and has either begun developing the selection process or is actively campaigning for a particular selection process to be implemented. Often, practitioners find shortcomings in the intervention of interest. For example, it may represent a current fad with little research supporting its use. In this case, the practitioner must convince management that an alternative intervention meets the same goals as the initial intervention of interest. Still another scenario is the legal-challenge scenario, where an organization is unsuccessfully defending its use of a current selection process to a regulating agency and is considering replacing the offending process. In this case, the practitioner must satisfy both the regulatory agency and the needs of the organization. Finally, the but-we're-different scenario occurs when an organizational unit insists that it is so unique that a corporate selection process must be altered significantly before the unit will agree to use it. In this case, a practitioner must balance the principle of process flexibility with the goal of keeping processes as similar as possible to avoid unnecessary customization or placing an unrealistic administrative burden on the organization.

Conclusions

Demonstrating the value of selection in organizations remains a challenge. Utility analysis, despite its promises, has achieved only marginal success in communicating the value of selection to organizational decision makers. A primary reason for the lack of understanding of how best to demonstrate the value of selection in organizations is the narrow approach researchers have taken in addressing the issue. First, they have concentrated almost exclusively on the dollar criterion. Although Cascio (1993) and others (for example, Johns, 1993; Vance & Colella, 1990) have offered alternatives to the dollar criterion, researchers have been slow to investigate these alternatives. A primary purpose of this chapter was to highlight the wide variety of criteria managers use when evaluating the merit of a selection process. Future research is needed to identify important value dimensions and to determine the relative weight managers place on these alternatives.

Second, a glaring omission from the value research has been customer involvement, namely, organizational decision makers. In the business world, customer involvement is a key principle of product design. The void is especially apparent in the utility analysis literature, which has only just begun to address the issue of how managers react to utility analysis estimates. However, research is also needed upstream to determine the type of information managers use to evaluate the utility of human resource initiatives. Once again, researchers need to go beyond dollar criteria in determining how best to communicate value in organizations.

Third, researchers have put little effort into studying the organizational context in which decisions about selection are made. Several practical realities have been all but ignored, including the complexity of managing competing values, the role that economic and political factors play, and the fact that selection processes usually compete against other organizational initiatives for dollars. It is hoped that the issues raised in this chapter will spark new avenues of research on methods for demonstrating value in organizations.

For the selection practitioner, identifying the value definitions of the important constituents and developing an appropriate business case are key to demonstrating the value of selection in organizations. This chapter has outlined some of the significant value definitions that organizational decision makers hold and highlighted challenges associated with managing the competing values and contextual factors that influence their decisions. The information provided can be used to develop an effective business case tailored to the needs of the organization.

Finally, it should be noted that attitudes toward selection have changed over the years. In the past, greater deference was given to the person making the selection decision than to the selection tools or process used to aid in decision making. For example, an individual's characteristics, such as time with the company and field expertise, played an important role in establishing his or her qualifications to make a hiring decision. Comments by organizational members to the effect of "give me ten minutes with the applicant and I'll tell you if he or she will make a good employee" were common and well accepted. Today, attitudes have changed. Greater deference is given to the role the selection process plays in identifying qualified candidates. This change in attitude provides practitioners and researchers with a unique opportunity to implement scientifically sound selection processes. But the challenge will continue to be to demonstrate successfully the value of selection in terms managers understand and value.

References

Arnold, J. D., Rauschenberger, J. M., Soubel, W., & Guion, R. M. (1982). Validation and utility of a strength test for selecting steelworkers. *Journal of Applied Psychology, 67,* 588–604.

Arvey, R. D., & Sackett, P. R. (1993). Fairness in selection: Current developments and perspectives. In N. Schmitt, W. C. Borman, & Associates (Eds.), *Personnel selection in organizations* (pp. 171–202). San Francisco: Jossey-Bass.

Ashe, R. L., Jr. (1990, April). *The legal defensibility of assessment centers and in-basket exercises.* Paper presented at the meeting of the Society for Industrial and Organizational Psychology, Miami Beach.

Binning, J. F., & Barrett, G. V. (1989). Validity of personnel decisions: A conceptual analysis of the inferential and evidential bases. *Journal of Applied Psychology, 74,* 478–494.

Boudreau, J. W. (1991). Utility analysis for decisions in human resource management. In M. D. Dunnette & L. M. Hough (Eds.), *Handbook of industrial and organizational psychology* (Vol. 2, pp. 621–745). Palo Alto, CA: Consulting Psychologists Press.

Breaugh, J. A. (1992). *Recruitment: Science and practice.* Boston: PWS-Kent.

Brogden, H. E. (1946). On the interpretation of the correlation coefficient as a measure of predictive efficiency. *Journal of Educational Psychology, 37,* 65–76.

Brogden, H. E. (1949). When testing pays off. *Personnel Psychology, 2,* 171–183.

Burke, M. J., & Frederick, J. T. (1986). A comparison of economic utility estimates for alternative Sdy estimation procedures. *Journal of Applied Psychology, 71*(2), 334–339.

Burke, M. J., & Pearlman, K. (1988). Recruiting, selection, and matching people with jobs. In J. P. Campbell & R. J. Campbell (Eds.), *Productivity in organizations* (pp. 97–142). San Francisco: Jossey-Bass.

Carson, K. P., Becker, J. S., & Henderson, J. A. (1998). Is utility really futile? A failure to replicate and an extension. *Journal of Applied Psychology, 83*(1), 84–96.

Cascio, W. F. (1991). *Costing human resources: The financial impact of behavior in organizations* (3rd. ed.). Boston: PWS-Kent.

Cascio, W. F. (1993). Assessing the utility of selection decisions: Theoretical and practical considerations. In N. Schmitt & W. C. Borman (Eds.), *Personnel selection in organizations* (pp. 310–340). San Francisco: Jossey-Bass.

Cascio, W. F., & Ramos, R. A. (1986). Development and application of a new method for assessing job performance in behavioral/economic terms. *Journal of Applied Psychology, 71,* 20–28.

Cascio, W. F., & Sibley, V. (1979). Utility of the assessment center as a selection device. *Journal of Applied Psychology, 64,* 107–118.

Cronbach, L. J., & Gleser, G. C. (1965). *Psychological tests and personnel decisions* (2nd. ed.). Urbana: University of Illinois Press.

Cronshaw, S. F. (1986). The utility of employment testing for clerical/administrative trades in the Canadian military. *Canadian Journal of Administrative Sciences, 3,* 376–385.

Cronshaw, S. F., & Alexander, R. A. (1985). One answer to the demand for accountability: Selection utility as an investment decision. *Organizational Behavior and Human Decision Processes, 35,* 102–118.

Eaton, N. K., Wing, H., & Mitchell, K. J. (1985). Alternative methods of estimating the dollar value of performance. *Personnel Psychology, 38,* 27–40.

Edwards, J. E., Frederick, J. T., & Burke, M. J. (1988). The efficacy of modified CREPID Sdy estimation procedures on the basis of archival organizational data. *Journal of Applied Psychology, 73,* 529–535.

Gatewood, R. D., & Field, H. S. (1994). *Human resource selection.* Orlando: Harcourt Brace.

Gaugler, B. B., Rosenthal, D. B., Thornton, G. C., & Bentson, C. (1987). Meta-analysis of assessment center validity. *Journal of Applied Psychology, 72,* 493–511.

Ghiselli, E. E. (1966). *The validity of occupational aptitude tests.* New York: Wiley.

Ghiselli, E. E. (1973). The validity of aptitude tests in personnel selection. *Personnel Psychology, 26,* 461–477.

Guion, R. (1991). Personnel assessment, selection, and placement. In M. D. Dunnette & L. M. Hough (Eds.), *Handbook of industrial and organizational psychology* (2nd. ed., Vol. 2, pp. 327–399). Palo Alto, CA: Consulting Psychologists Press.

Hazer, J. T., & Highhouse, S. (1997). Factors influencing managers' reactions to utility analysis: Effects of Sdy method, information frame, and focal intervention. *Journal of Applied Psychology, 82*(1), 104–112.

Hull, C. L. (1928). *Aptitude testing.* Yonkers, NY: World Book.

Hunter, J. E., & Hunter, R. E. (1984). Validity and utility of alternative predictors of job performance. *Psychological Bulletin, 96,* 72–98.

Hunter, J. E., & Schmidt, F. L. (1982). Fitting people to jobs: The impact of personnel selection on national productivity. In M. D. Dunnette & E. A. Fleishman (Eds.), *Human performance and productivity.* Hillsdale, NJ: Erlbaum.

Johns, G. (1993). Constraints on the adoption of psychology-based personnel practices: Lessons from organizational innovation. *Personnel Psychology, 46,* 569–592.

Johnston, W. B., & Packer, A. E. (1987). *Workplace 2000: Work and workers for the 21st century.* Indianapolis: Hudson Institute.

Kahneman, D., & Tversky, A. (1973). On the psychology of prediction. *Psychological Review, 80,* 237–251.

Kelley, T. L. (1923). *Statistical method.* Old Tappan, NJ: Macmillan.

Landy, F. J. (1986). Stamp collecting versus science: Validation as hypothesis testing. *American Psychologist, 41,* 1183–1192.

Latham, G. P. (1988). Human resource training and development. *Annual Review of Psychology, 39,* 545–582.

Latham, G. P., & Whyte, G. (1994). The futility of utility analysis. *Personnel Psychology, 47*(1), 31–46.

Levy-Leboyer, C. (1994). Selection and assessment in Europe. In H. C. Triandis, M. D. Dunnette, & L. M. Hough (Eds.), *Handbook of industrial and organizational psychology* (Vol. 4, pp. 173–190). Palo Alto, CA: Consulting Psychologists Press.

Ledvinka, J., & Scarpello, V. (1991). *Federal regulation of personnel and human resource management* (2nd ed.). Boston: PWS-Kent.

Macan, T. H., & Highhouse, S. (1994). Communicating the utility of human resource activities: A survey of I/O and HR professionals. *Journal of Business and Psychology, 8*(4), 425–436.

Meyerowitz, B. E., & Chaiken, S. (1987). The effect of message framing on breast self-examination attitudes, intentions, and behavior. *Journal of Personality and Social Psychology, 52,* 500–510.

Mintzberg, H. (1975, July-August). The manager's job: Folklore and fact. *Harvard Business Review,* pp. 49–61.

Mintzberg, J. (1989). *Mintzberg on management: Inside our strange world of organizations.* New York: Free Press.

Morrow, C. C., Jarrett, M. Q., & Rupinski, M. T. (1997). An investigation of the effect and economic utility of corporate-wide training. *Personnel Psychology, 50,* 91–119.

Murphy, K. M. (1986). When your top choice turns you down: The effect of rejected offers on the utility of selection tests. *Psychological Bulletin, 99,* 133–138.

Rauschenberger, J. M., & Schmidt, F. L. (1987). Measuring the economic impact of human resource programs. *Journal of Business and Psychology, 2*(1), 50–59.

Reilly, R. R., & Chao, G. T. (1982). Validity and fairness of some alternative employee selection procedures. *Personnel Psychology, 35,* 1–62.

Rowe, P. M. (1989). Unfavorable information and interview decisions. In R. W. Eder & G. R. Ferris (Eds.), *The employment interview: Theory, research, and practice.* Thousand Oaks, CA: Sage.

Russell, C. J., Colella, A., & Bobko, P. (1993). Expanding the context of utility: The strategic impact of personnel selection. *Personnel Psychology, 46*(4), 781–801.

Ryan, A. M., McFarland, L., Baron, H., & Page, R. (1998, April). *An international survey of selection practices.* Paper presented at the annual conference of the Society for Industrial and Organizational Psychology, Dallas.

Rynes, S. L. (1992). Recruitment, job choice, and post-hire consequences: A call for new research directions. In M. D. Dunnette & L. M. Hough (Eds.), *Handbook of industrial and organizational psychology* (2nd. ed., Vol. 2, pp. 399–444). Palo Alto, CA: Consulting Psychologists Press.

Rynes, S. L. (1993). Who's selecting whom? Effects of selection practices on applicant attitudes and behavior. In N. Schmitt & W. C. Borman (Eds.), *Personnel selection in organizations* (pp. 240–274). San Francisco: Jossey-Bass.

Rynes, S. L., Bretz, R. D., & Gerhart, B. (1991). The importance of recruitment in job choice: A different way of looking. *Personnel Psychology, 44,* 487–521.

Rynes, S., & Rosen, B. (1995). A field survey of factors affecting the adoption and perceived success of diversity training. *Personnel Psychology, 48*(2), 247–270.

Sackett, P. R., Schmitt, N., Tenopyr, M. L., Kehoe, J., & Zedeck, S. (1985). Commentary on forty questions about validity generalization and meta-analysis. *Personnel Psychology, 38,* 697–798.

Schmidt, F. L. (1993). Personnel psychology at the cutting edge. In N. Schmitt & W. C. Borman (Eds.), *Personnel selection in organizations* (pp. 497–515). San Francisco: Jossey-Bass.

Schmidt, F. L., & Hunter, J. E. (1981). Employment testing: Old theories and new research findings. *American Psychologist, 36,* 1128–1137.

Schmidt, F. L., Hunter, J. E., McKenzie, R., & Muldrow, T. (1979). The impact of valid selection procedures on workforce productivity. *Journal of Applied Psychology, 64,* 609–626.

Schmidt, F. L., Ones, D. S., & Hunter, J. E. (1992). Personnel selection. *Annual Review of Psychology, 43,* 627–670.

Schmidt, F. L., Pearlman, K., Hunter, J. E., & Hirsh, H. R. (1985). Forty questions about validity generalization and meta-analysis. *Personnel Psychology, 38,* 697–798.

Skarlicki, D. P., Latham, G. P., & Whyte, G. (1996). Utility analysis: Its evolution and tenuous role in human resource management decision making. *Canadian Journal of Administrative Sciences, 13*(1), 13–21.

Society for Industrial and Organizational Psychology. (1987). *Principles for the validation and use of personnel selection procedures* (3rd. ed.). College Park, MD: Author.

Taylor, H. C., & Russell, J. T. (1939). The relationship of validity coefficients to the practical effectiveness of tests in selection: Discussion and tables. *Journal of Applied Psychology, 23,* 565–578.

Uniform guidelines on employee selection procedures. Section 3D. (1978). *Federal Register, 43*(166), 38297.

Vance, R. J., & Colella, A. (1990). The utility of utility analysis. *Human Performance, 3*(2), 123–139.

Whyte, G., & Latham, G. (1997). The futility of utility analysis revisited: When even an expert fails. *Personnel Psychology, 50*(3), 601–610.

CHAPTER 4

Managing "Customers" of Selection Processes

Stephen W. Gilliland
Bennett Cherry

Beth Evens, the director of staffing at Sunshine Hospital, was experiencing an ever-growing list of problems with the hiring policies and procedures she had recently implemented. In an effort to get units more involved in the hiring process and therefore to take more ownership of their hiring decisions, part of the hiring process had been decentralized to the unit level. All position openings continued to be posted and advertised by the staffing group in the human resource department, and application forms were collected, background data verified, and references contacted by the staffing group. However, after this initial processing, applications were turned over to the units with the position to be filled, which were responsible for interviewing and conducting any screening or selection testing necessary to identify the best candidate.

Beth knew this effort to "empower" units in their hiring decisions would take considerable training and transition management. But she firmly believed it would ultimately result in better hiring decisions and more effective staffing management. In an effort to facilitate transition to the new hiring process, she and her staff developed a number of new and innovative training programs on topics such as effective interviewing, structuring hiring decisions, and identifying optimal fit. Although participants in these sessions really seemed to get a lot of valuable information, attendance was voluntary and participation had been sparse. Memos, flowcharts, and "tip" sheets had been sent to all unit managers, but it was unclear whether anyone had paid much attention to these written summaries.

The problems became apparent when applicants started to complain that they never heard back from the people who had done the interviewing. As one applicant stated, "They told me they would call me within a week. It has been over a month and I still haven't heard anything. I have called three times, but no one ever returns my calls." Other applicants complained about the questions they were asked during interviews. Some interviewers appeared to be asking about marital status and children. There had been no lawsuits or complaints filed against the hospital yet, but at this rate Beth knew it would only be a matter of time.

The unit managers were certainly the cause of a number of these problems. In an effort to increase involvement in the training seminars, Beth had talked to a number of the managers. The typical reaction of managers was that with the chronic shortage of staff, the myriad new hospital initiatives, and other demands on their time, attention to staffing was a low priority. One manager suggested that his ideal interview lasted about ten minutes and allowed him to make a quick yes or no decision before the candidate even left the office. Another manager had (quite seriously) suggested that Beth's group offer a training seminar on "how to attract and hire single Canadian nurses," because this group was most likely to accept job offers in the warm southern climate and tend to remain with the hospital for longer periods.

Perhaps the most serious problem was with a manager who had realized the importance of effective staffing decision making only after hiring an employee who caused problems practically from day one. In addition to patient complaints, costly errors, and broken equipment, morale among the other members of the unit had deteriorated to an all-time low. The manager had found that a much more difficult task than terminating the problem employee was rebuilding a productive work climate in the unit after the employee was gone.

Beth had even received complaints from employees who were not directly involved in the hiring process; in fact, the problem was that they were not involved in the hiring process. With the new "unit-empowered" hiring system, many of them had expected to play a greater role. They wanted to be consulted with regard to staffing needs and wanted to be involved in the interviewing. One employee quite accurately observed, "We are the ones who have to train and then work with the new people we hire. This really affects us a lot more directly than it does the unit manager. Shouldn't we be involved in making the hiring decision?"

Beth stared at the wall and asked herself what had gone wrong. Was decentralizing the hiring process and empowering the units unworkable? Her boss, John, vice president of human resources, had told her that it was a great idea when she proposed it more than a year earlier. Maybe she should ask for his input.

After spending fifteen minutes in John's office outlining some of the problems she was experiencing with the new procedure, Beth heard what seemed like overly simplistic advice. John told her that the key to successful human resource management was to know who your customers are *and* what they want.

Beth returned to her office and stood with a marker at her whiteboard. Who were her customers in the staffing function? What did they want from the staffing process?

This case describes a staffing process that generated criticism from applicants, hiring managers, and even coworkers. It also highlights many of the concerns that are salient to these different "customers" of selection. Although perhaps extreme in its entirety, all of the details of this case have been adapted from actual organizational experiences.

Recent research has focused considerable attention on reactions of applicants to selection (for example, Gilliland, 1993, 1995; Smither, Reilly, Millsap, Pearlman, & Stoffey, 1993). This research has demonstrated the importance to applicants of administering job-relevant and consistent selection procedures, treating applicants with dignity and respect, and providing timely and informative feedback on hiring decisions. Although researchers have not given much attention to managers and coworkers as customers of selection, most selection practitioners have probably experienced the challenges of getting organizational members' buy-in on new selection programs. Managers want selection procedures that are quick and simple to administer. Coworkers have a great stake in the outcome of the selection process and want to make sure future colleagues are going to "fit" with the work group.

What happens if we fail to attend to these customers of selection? As the opening case illustrated, applicants may complain about the hiring process. In addition to the time and energy required on our part to deal with these complaints (especially if they progress to legal complaints), disgruntled applicants are less likely to accept job offers or recommend the organization to others and may even turn against the organization's products. On the flip side, a positive hiring experience can lay the foundation for a productive, committed worker. For managers and coworkers, complaints about the selection process can also be problematic. Because managers and coworkers are often the people involved in implementing the selection process, failure to get their buy-in can lead to myriad implementation problems. Problems in the socialization of new hires and work group conflict can also originate from failure to manage the customers of selection.

This chapter addresses the two key questions asked by Beth Evens at the end of the opening case: Who are the customers of selection and what do they want? Although we are drawing from and integrating past research, this chapter is the first effort to organize systematically and discuss the concerns of the different customers of selection. We begin with a discussion of the customers of selection and their interest or "stake" in the selection process. We then examine the importance of attending to each of these customers. The focus of this chapter is on managing the customers of selection. Specifically, we consider the perspective of each customer group in each of the three stages of the selection process (that is, development, assessment, feedback). We conclude the chapter with some summary recommendations for maintaining a successful customer-based selection system.

Who Are the Customers?

A stakeholder conceptualization of organizations suggests that many constituents have interests and needs that are satisfied by an organization. The total quality movement (Dean & Bowen, 1994) has focused attention on the importance of customers as a stakeholder group. The various roles of customers include purchaser, output recipient, user, and beneficiary. When considering total quality in human resource (HR) functions (for example, Bowen & Lawler, 1992), HR staff can be viewed as a service provider. Their main role is to provide service to the customers: line managers who implement HR processes, employees directly affected by HR policies and procedures, and job applicants who experience firsthand the selection and hiring processes. These three groups are also the primary customers of selection. At various points in the selection process, they assume roles of outcome recipient, user, and beneficiary. We will discuss the roles of each of these groups as well as their needs, desires, and goals as stakeholders in the selection process.

HR staff administering the procedures could also be seen as customers of selection, but we prefer to view these individuals as service providers or internal consultants rather than customers.

In light of this internal consultant role, the HR staff must realize that consulting skills play a large part in the success of a customer-focused selection system. Managers and coworkers will look to the selection program managers as experts, and the selection program managers must learn to use the terminology and metrics of the department managers and coworkers both to inform and to persuade. Knowing how to communicate with the customers as well as how to persuade them when necessary are critical consulting skills.

It is also possible to consider external stakeholder groups as potential customers. For example, customers that indirectly receive benefits or feel the consequences of a company's selection procedures could include labor unions representing the interests of employee groups, consumers buying a company's products, and recipients of customer service provided by new employees. Because these groups are only indirectly tied to selection, we will not be considering their roles in this chapter. However, it is possible to extend many of the concepts in this chapter to these external customers.

Line Managers

Line managers often serve an important role in the latter stages of selection as they conduct interviews with job applicants and make the final hiring decisions. Line managers may also provide information to HR on position requirements and staffing needs that aids in the development of selection systems. Based on this input into selection development and the implementation of the latter stages of selection, line managers can be seen as the most direct customers of selection process administration. Since we are identifying line managers as customers or stakeholders of selection, it is important to identify what "stake" this group has in the selection process. What are the needs, desires, and goals of managers when it comes to selection?

Line managers usually have direct responsibility for accomplishing a specific subset of an organization's goals. They also have the authority to direct the work of subordinates. The selection process is important to them to the extent that it enables them to identify high-potential applicants and place these individuals in positions most suited to their skills and abilities. In short, the selection process helps a manager find the right person for the job. Thus, line managers need the selection process to be an accurate and informative indicator of applicant potential.

Because line managers also usually have responsibility and accountability for performance of their unit, they are also customers in that they accrue the benefits of a successful selection process. If the selection process is inefficient and yields poor performers, the line manager suffers. But if an effective selection process is used, the unit's performance will improve and the manager will benefit. In addition, because a line manager's primary role is achieving unit and organizational goals, rather than staffing and selection, many managers want the selection process to be quick and easy to administer.

Coworkers

Coworkers are customers of selection in that they have to interact with and work with the new hires who are evaluated in the selection process. The coworkers experience directly the results of selection. If poor hiring decisions are made, coworkers have to try to deal with the problem new hires. However, if particularly effective hiring decisions are made, the entire image and reputation of the work group can be enhanced. Given the possibility—albeit extreme and unlikely—that a new hire may turn violent and threaten the safety of existing workers, some researchers have considered coworker rights in the selection process (Mael, Connerley, & Morath, 1997). Based on their stake in the outcome of the hiring decision, coworkers should be concerned about the accuracy of the selection process. They may also desire input into the selection process (both in development stages and administration) in order to ensure that their concerns are reasonably represented.

To the extent that employees are organized into work groups or teams, the coworkers' stake increases and they should be given greater input into the selection process. For example, in the case of semiautonomous work teams, coworkers' input and involvement can far outweigh the manager's. At the other end of the continuum, when coworkers have very little shared activity with new hires, they may not want input into the selection process but instead want to be kept informed about hiring decisions. They may simply want answers to the basic questions, such as, Which people have we hired? What are their backgrounds? When do they start?

Applicants

Both line managers and coworkers are internal customers of selection. The primary external customers are the applicants because they are the "recipients" of the selection process and most obviously affected by the hiring decision. Recent research on customers of selection has done a lot in terms of defining the desires, needs, and goals of job applicants (for example, Gilliland, 1993; Smither et al., 1993). To define what an applicant believes to be fair treatment, Gilliland (1993) suggested that applicants are concerned with the *fairness of the selection decision* and the *fairness of the selection process*. Fairness of the decision is based on the belief that the best person received the job. This belief rests on an applicant's perceptions and is clouded by the fact that there are many potential definitions of "best," so it is not unusual to see applicants disagree on the fairness of a selection decision. As far as the fairness of the selection process is concerned, an applicant is looking for fair treatment along three dimensions: an unbiased, job-related selection process that gives the applicant the opportunity to demonstrate his or her capabilities; honest and appropriate interpersonal treatment; and timely and informative feedback throughout the selection process and on the hiring decision.

Perception of fairness is not the only determinant of an applicant's reactions. The outcome of the hiring decision (that is, hired versus rejected) alone has a strong influence on reactions. The relative importance of outcome versus fairness depends on a number of factors, including the individual's expectations of receiving the job and the severity of unfair treatment. The outcome carries more weight when an individual has high expectations of receiving the job (Gilliland, 1994), whereas fairness carries more weight when applicants feel particularly violated by the selection process (Gilliland & Steiner, in press). Most important from the customer service perspective is that fairness matters most when the decision is negative. Considerable research has demonstrated that fair treatment in the selection process or when communicating the rejection decision can lessen the blow of an unfavorable hiring decision (Gilliland, 1994, 1998).

Summary

The three groups of customers and their needs, desires, and goals for selection are summarized in Table 4.1. It is important to realize that these three customer groups are interrelated. For example, supervisors and coworkers who are directly involved in the selection process will play a substantial role in determining applicants' reactions to the process through the questions they ask and the way they communicate with applicants. In addition, applicants who are hired will shape and influence the dynamics of the work unit, thereby directly affecting coworkers and line managers.

The fact that the different customers of selection are interrelated highlights the importance of attending to all three groups. However, it is also possible to identify characteristics of the labor market, the organization, and the position that can influence the relative importance of each customer group. For example, when

**Table 4.1. Customers of Selection
and Their Needs, Desires, and Goals.**

Customer	Needs, Desires, and Goals for Selection
Line managers	• Accurate and informative indicators of applicant potential
	• Quick and easy-to-use selection process
	• Flexibility and accommodation of selection procedures
	• Perceived validity of selection process
Coworkers	• Accurate and informative indicators of applicant potential
	• Input into the selection decision-making process
	• Perceived validity of selection process
Applicants	• Appropriate hiring decision
	• Unbiased, job-related selection process that gives them a chance to demonstrate their potential
	• Honest and sensitive interpersonal treatment
	• Timely and informative feedback

unemployment is relatively low and many jobs are available—as is currently the case in the United States—the importance of attending to applicants as customers increases. With such a market, organizations cannot afford to "turn off" applicants at any stage of the selection process. When it comes to organizational influence on customer groups, the greater the decentralization of decision making the more important it is to attend to line managers and coworkers as customers because they are the people who make the selection process work effectively. In addition, the more workers are empowered or organized into work teams, the greater the need to attend to coworkers as customers of selection. Finally, the position that is being filled by the selection process will also influence the importance of different customer groups. With higher-level managerial and executive positions, involvement from coworkers (that is, other executives) becomes more important. The relevant customers of selection for executive positions may also be expanded to include subordinates (that is, direct reports) and external shareholders.

The important lesson from the stakeholder approach is that we consider the selection process to be a decision process in which many groups have an interest. After identifying who the stakeholders are for a given selection situation, we must identify the relevant interests—that is, the needs, desires, and goals—of each stakeholder group. The final step is to ensure that their interests are represented in the selection process. But before we discuss how to manage their interests, we must address the question of why it is important to attend to these customers' interests.

Why Attend to the Customers?

The most direct answer to the question "Why attend to the customers of selection?" comes from an examination of how these customers can influence the outcomes of the selection process, all the way through to work performance and commitment. In the opening case, Beth Evens was faced with complaints of applicants, the apathy of managers toward the selection process, and perceptions among coworkers that they had been excluded. Even more problematic for the organization was that the selection process had led to patient complaints, costly errors, broken equipment, and deteriorated morale. Across both internal and external customers, Beth Evens had many problems with customer satisfaction.

The idea of taking a customer service orientation has been gaining acceptance in the field of human resource management. Bowen and colleagues (for example, Bowen & Greiner, 1986; Bowen & Lawler, 1992) have argued that in order for HR to be an effective contributor to modern organizations, it must adopt a customer service orientation. If the internal customers (employees and managers) are satisfied with HR, then a large body of the organization supports and recognizes the value of the HR function. However, if they become dissatisfied, then the perceived value of HR decreases and the HR function becomes a prime candidate for cost-cutting reductions and downsizing.

The general value of a customer orientation in HR applies specifically to selection. Unfortunately, research has not directly examined the link between satisfaction among the customers of selection and the perceived (or actual) value of HR. There is, however, considerable research that demonstrates the influence that customers of selection can have on the outcomes of the selection process. There is also some research on the relationship between applicants' reactions to selection and their attitudes on the job, as well as some evidence that reactions of internal customers can "spill over" to services provided to external customers (Gilliland & Troth, 1998; Macan, Avedon, Paese, & Smith, 1994). In this section we consider outcomes associated with selection effectiveness, posthire attitudes and behavior, and spillover effects. The various outcomes influenced by the customers of selection are summarized in Table 4.2.

Selection Effectiveness

In industrial and organizational psychology, selection effectiveness is often defined as the ability of the selection process to predict performance on the job. However, another important indicator of effectiveness is whether the best applicants accept job offers. As previous research has demonstrated, when your top choices turn you down, the overall effectiveness of the selection process is diminished (Murphy, 1986). Similarly, if the applicants who would have been your top choices do not apply or withdraw from the selection process, then the overall effectiveness of hiring is diminished. Finally, with an increasing number of legal challenges from applicants, selection effectiveness can also be defined as the absence of Equal Employment Opportunity Commission (EEOC)

Table 4.2. Positive Consequences
Associated with Customers of Selection.

Selection effectiveness

- Effective prediction as a result of the selection process being correctly administered
- Increased applicant attraction to the organization, decreased withdrawal from the selection process, and increased likelihood of top candidates accepting job offers
- Avoidance of legal challenges associated with discrimination, invasion of privacy, and defamation

Posthire attitudes and behavior

- Increased satsifaction, commitment, and performance of newly hired applicants
- More effective socialization of new hires by coworkers
- Faciliated development of quality relationships between line managers and new hires
- Enhanced team effectiveness

Spillover effects

- Enhanced service delivery to the organization's customers
- Positive company image projected
- Unsuccessful job applicants maintained as customers of the organizaton

---

claims and lawsuits. We consider how the management of selection customers can influence selection effectiveness in terms of effective prediction, applicant attraction, and avoiding legal challenges.

Effective Prediction

Selection specialists devote much time and attention to developing tests and interview questions that demonstrate validity in the prediction of job performance (see Chapter Eleven of this volume for more information). However, this validity can be compromised if the tests or interview questions are not administered correctly. Administration of selection procedures may be the responsibility of line managers or, in some cases, coworkers. With structured tests, administrators can make errors in timing or delivery of instructions that limit the validity of the tests. With structured interviews, administrators have ultimate control over the degree to which they stick to the interview guide in asking questions and scoring responses. Similarly, the validity of the selection procedure can be compromised if applicants are turned off by the selection process. Schmit and Ryan (1992) demonstrate that the validity of cognitive ability tests is lower among individuals with lower test-taking motivation. The bottom line is that if selection customers do not buy into the selection process, the effectiveness of decisions made with that process can be undermined.

Applicant Attraction

A second way to enhance the effectiveness of the selection process is by attracting and retaining the best candidates. If applicants are dissatisfied with the selection process, they may withdraw from it or turn down the job offer. In a study of applicant withdrawal from consideration for police officer positions, Schmit and Ryan (1997) reported that 11.7 percent of applicants who withdrew prior to the selection exam cited perceived unfairness in the hiring process as the reason. Other studies have demonstrated that job applicants who react unfavorably to the selection procedures or to interviewers report being less likely to accept job offers (Macan et al., 1994; Schmitt & Coyle, 1976). Furthermore, the impact of applicants' negative reactions extends beyond the immediate recruiting effort, because applicants are less likely to recommend the organization to others or to reapply for future jobs themselves if they feel they were unfairly treated in the selection process (Gilliland, 1994; Smither et al., 1993). Thus, because both the selection procedures and the personnel administering those procedures can turn applicants off, the internal customers of selection can directly affect reactions and decisions of the external customers.

In traditional selection processes, the focus is on validity, quantitative standards, and effective decision making. But from the customer perspective the organization tries to retain the best applicants throughout the selection process. With today's tight labor market, the customer approach may do more to increase the utility of the selection system than the traditional approach. Further research is needed to investigate this hypothesis.

Avoiding Legal Challenges

In recent years, there have been multimillion dollar discrimination settlements against organizations such as Shoney's Inc., a national restaurant chain, and Lucky Stores Inc., a large grocery retailer. Although the huge dollar amounts of these settlements represent extreme cases, it is clear that organizations today face increased legal challenges from job applicants (for more information, see Chapter Eight). These challenges include discrimination charges, invasion-of-privacy claims, and defamation claims against former employers. Job applicants will try to get justice in the courts when they feel they have not received justice in the hiring process. Recent research suggests that one of the predictors of decisions to file discrimination claims with the EEOC is perceived injustice in the hiring process (Goldman, 1999). Line managers and coworkers involved in the selection process can create this perception of injustice with the questions they ask and the statements they make.

The traditional consideration of legal issues in selection emphasizes the defensibility of different selection procedures. But when selection is approached from a customer perspective, the emphasis is on preventing legal claims from arising. Given the legal costs and the costs to an organization's reputation of defending employment lawsuits, the customer-oriented preventative approach has some clear advantages.

Posthire Attitudes and Behavior

At times, individuals will accept jobs even when they feel they were treated unfairly during the selection process. This is particularly likely if the job is especially desirable or if an applicant has only one job offer. In such situations, negative experiences in the selection process appear to have residual effects. The hiring process represents the first contact a future employee has with an organization. Initial impressions of it and the way it treats its employees are formed at this time, and these impressions can sometimes be long-lasting. Studies by Singer (1992) and Gilliland and Troth (1998) report negative attitudes in areas such as satisfaction and organizational commitment by individuals who feel they were treated unfairly in the selection process. Gilliland (1994) also presented some evidence to suggest that these effects can carry over into job performance.

Not all of the damage from poor attention to selection customers is done to job applicants. Although research has not examined the consequences of line manager and coworker dissatisfaction with the selection process, negative consequences likely exist. For example, coworkers who feel disenfranchised from the selection process may make less of an effort to socialize new employees. In contrast, if coworkers are actively involved in the selection process they may develop a greater stake in the initial socialization of new hires. Research has shown that the quality of the relationship that exists between supervisors and subordinates can begin with the selection interview (Dockery & Steiner, 1990). Thus, line managers' beliefs regarding the selection process may affect their relations with new hires.

Spillover Effects

A final set of consequences associated with customers of selection are related to the external customers of the organization's products and services. Bowen, Gilliland, and Folger (1999) argue that employees who are treated fairly by the organization are more likely to treat external customers fairly, and this, in turn, is associated with customer satisfaction and retention. That is, fair human resource management can lead to fair service delivery (for more on this, see Schneider & Bowen, 1993). The basis for this link is that employees are more likely to go above and beyond the call of duty in interactions with customers when they feel their interests are being addressed by the organization. This link should exist for both coworkers involved in the hiring process and new hires. Attending to coworkers' needs in the hiring process is one way of creating an atmosphere of fair HR management. Furthermore, if customer service is emphasized in interactions with applicants, they are more likely to adopt this service emphasis when they are hired. Companies such as Disney and Southwest Airlines make special efforts to develop a customer service atmosphere in the hiring process that can carry through with new hires on the job.

A more direct link between selection and customer satisfaction with the organization's products and services stems from the fact that job applicants are also potential customers of the organization. As one HR manager from the auto industry stated,

"Regardless of whether or not we hire these people, we want to make sure they continue to buy our cars." It is indeed possible that applicants' perceptions of the selection process may influence their consumer purchase behavior. Macan and colleagues (Macan et. al, 1994) found a relationship (albeit weak) between applicants' perceptions of selection procedure fairness and purchase intentions. This relationship would probably be strongest among those who feel the selection process was a particularly strong violation of their standards or perceived rights.

Clearly, there are many potential benefits of attending to customers of selection. There are also many possible negative consequences if these customers feel dissatisfied with the selection process. The next issue to consider is how to manage customers of selection.

Managing Customers of Selection

Researchers in the area of customer service management emphasize the importance of meeting or exceeding customer expectations (Berry, 1995), expectations both of *what* is delivered to them and *how* it is delivered. This concept can also be applied to customers of selection. For example, when we treat line managers as customers it is important to consider both the selection system being administered and the way in which that system is developed and implemented. In managing customers of selection, it is important to note that their buy-in will affect their perceptions of value of the selection process and their dedication to parts of the process, such as job analysis and interviewing. Credibility and face validity are important considerations in developing and administering any selection system (Landy, 1993).

To provide this perspective, we define the selection process as a series of three interrelated stages: development, assessment, and feedback. *Development* involves the designing and implementing (for example, offering training) of new or updated selection systems. Development is often the work of HR professionals or selection specialists. However, including the customers of selection in the development process may be critical to the success of the selection system. In the *assessment* stage, applicants are screened using the procedures developed in the earlier stage. In this stage, job applicants experience screening procedures, selection tests, and interviews. Line managers are often involved in the assessment process and coworkers may or may not be involved. The *feedback* stage involves providing feedback to applicants on the outcomes of the selection process. However, a critical and often overlooked part of the feedback stage is collecting feedback from different customer groups on the selection process, which can then be used to refine the selection system. Because feedback provides input for the development stage, the three stages of the selection process can be seen as cyclical. Figure 4.1 summarizes the stages of the selection process.

We have defined the customers of selection to be line managers, coworkers, and job applicants. We have also defined the selection process to include the three stages of development, assessment, and feedback. In this section we consider how to manage the needs of the customers during each of these selection stages. Table 4.3 summarizes these recommendations.

Development

A key aspect of a customer-based selection system is inclusion of the three customer groups in its development. This involvement can be achieved through communication and soliciting input. Communication can help establish the importance of developing a new selection system and keep customers informed during the development process. Soliciting input allows the customers' collective "voices" to be heard, so that each group shares its needs and identifies ways to meet them in a cohesive and effective system. The

Figure 4.1. Stages of a Customer-Based Selection System.

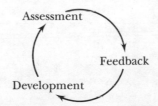

**Table 4.3. Recommendations
for Managing Customers of Selection.**

Stage in Selection	Line Managers and Coworkers	Applicants
Development	• Communicate how and why new selection system is being developed. • Involve customers in development and administration of the selection system. • Allow selection customization in concert with organizational units.	• Include applicant concerns in development of system. • Provide applicants with an understanding of what selection process entails and how it was developed.
Assessment	• Train line managers in the use of the selection system and in effective interviewing and decision making. • Simplify the assessment process to ease administration. • Involve customers in screening and assessment processes.	• Make sure selection procedures are job-related and unbiased. • Give applicants a chance to demonstrate potential. • Make sure selection process is consistently administered. • Treat applicants with honesty and respect. • Allow for two-way communication
Feedback	• Solicit feedback on effectiveness of and satisfaction with selection system.	• Deliver timely and informative feedback to applicants on hiring decision. • Solicit feedback on selection process.

following practices can be used to involve the customer groups (listed in order of progression):

- *Make the initial communication:* Provide communication from the top on the development process.
- *Gather information:* Collect input through open-ended or structured surveys of members of the different customer groups.
- *Expand and synthesize:* Conduct focus groups to elaborate on the issues mentioned in the information-gathering stage and to gain insight into the customer groups' general and specific concerns about the existing selection system.
- *Address customer-oriented issues:* Create a task force specifically to address important issues identified and develop general selection practices to meet customer concerns.
- *Customize selection:* Allow different units to refine (in concert with other organizational units) their own selection systems to meet their individual unit needs.
- *Train users:* Provide training for the line managers and coworkers who will be directly involved in administering the selection system.
- *Inform applicants:* Provide applicants an understanding of what the selection process entails and how it was developed.

Make the Initial Communication

One strong determinant of employees' perceptions of fairness and customers' perceptions of service quality is the information that is provided to justify and explain actions or outcomes (Bowen et al., 1999). In the selection development process, internal customer groups (line managers and coworkers), should be informed about how and why a new selection system is being developed. The higher this communication comes from in an organization's hierarchy, the greater impact it is likely to have on customer groups. Meetings, memos, e-mails, and company newsletters can all be used to highlight the selection system development process. This communication can also pave the way for obtaining input from customers.

Gather Information

A customer-oriented selection system is effective because the concerns of the three most important stakeholder groups are addressed in a comprehensive format. Many researchers have demonstrated that perceptions of procedural fairness increase when individuals are allowed to voice their opinions about the process used to determine outcomes (for example, Thibaut & Walker, 1975). Performance evaluation systems are perceived more positively by employees when they believe they have had opportunities to express their own viewpoints (Dipboye & de Pontbraind, 1981). Sometimes in selection system development, we allow line managers to express their needs and the selection system is altered in response to this input. However, with a true customer-oriented selection system, all customer groups need to be allowed input into the system's development. One flight attendant recently remarked to us: "The way they select flight attendants in this company is just horrible! They only ask them basic interview questions that the applicant can see right through, and answers come flowing out that delight the ears of the interviewer. But then when they get into the airplane and really start interacting with people, is when you have trouble." In this particular organization, the selection system did not include the coworkers' concerns about the system's effectiveness in selecting high customer-oriented employees.

One way of eliciting input from the different customer groups is to create an open-ended survey that provides sufficient structure to allow for ease of answering but does not exclude open-ended comments about particular issues. The survey can ask general questions about satisfaction with and effectiveness of the current selection system, as well as invite group members to offer suggestions for developing a more effective system. The objective at this stage is to uncover the issues and needs of the customer groups and get a *general picture* of the customer's perception of the existing selection system.

Expand and Synthesize

After generating an initial understanding of the perceptions of the current selection system, HR should conduct focus groups in an effort to gain a deeper understanding of the issues brought up in the information-gathering stage. The focus groups allow for more informal roundtable discussions that encourage candid communication about the usability and effectiveness of the current system. Employees may feel more comfortable about expressing their concerns and needs in a group environment than individually.

Two kinds of focus groups can be formed: *single customer* or *mixed customer*. It may be useful to create a focus group composed solely of coworkers in a department. By so doing, the specific concerns of the department may be elicited. However, it may be time consuming to form single customer focus groups with all departments in the organization. A better approach may be to mix different customers in the focus groups. In this way, all the customers' interests will be represented and they can discuss the perceptions that are similar to all and those that are distinct to each group.

It is important to note that focus groups may not be necessary if the information gathered in the first stage reveals that all customer groups are satisfied with the existing system or if the information gathered is complete enough to progress to the next stage—that is, addressing the specific issues. Again, the purpose of using focus groups is to get a more complete picture of the customer-specific concerns about the selection system.

Although some of the information obtained at this stage may be consistent with a usual job analysis, there are some differences. In particular, the means by which this information is attained is unique and the information received is unique. Job analysis is usually a sterile process, whereby a manager informs the HR staff of the requisite needs and characteristics of the available job. After receiving this somewhat impersonal information, the HR staff constructs a selection process that, it is hoped, will yield the best applicant based on the requirements of the job. But what is missing from a usual job analysis is the less subtle information related to the work group or, more generally, the organization. Typically, job analysis limits its scope to "the job" whereas a customer focus extends the analysis to include "the role" that will be assumed by a new employee (for more on the job-role distinction and integration, see Ilgen & Hollenbeck, 1991). Job analysis narrowly defines the necessary requirements of the job but neglects the more ambiguous role requirements. In a customer-focused system, the role requirements are brought into the selection process through the input of the manager and coworkers. Similarly, with a customer focus the selection system may include an organizational analysis (Bowen, Ledford & Nathan, 1991) so that applicants who fit the organization may be identified. So although the customer focus and traditional job analysis do overlap to some extent, the customer focus will yield important subtleties missed by job analysis and will emphasize the manager and coworker groups' voices in the process.

Address Customer-Oriented Issues

The goal of the first two stages is to get a complete and comprehensive understanding of the issues, needs, concerns, and perceptions of the three stakeholder groups. With this information, a task force can be created that will specifically address these issues and develop a general organizational selection system that satisfies them. Along with selection specialists, the task force should have representatives from the three customer groups, with internal customers representing different departments in the organization. There may be some difficulty with including past applicants in the task force. Past applicants who were successful and are currently employees of the company will have a slightly different perspective than people who were not selected for a position. But what motivation does a past applicant who was not selected into the company have for assisting in developing a new selection system? It may be that applicants will not be a well-represented customer group on the system development task force.

Customize Selection

The product of the task force's effort is a general organizational selection system that addresses the main customer concerns. With this base system in hand, line managers and departmental units can begin to specialize their selection systems based on their individual departmental needs. For instance, in addition to the organizational selection system, an accounting department may need to create a more specialized accounting skills test to select the best applicants for an accounts payable position. In another instance, marketing may have representatives involved in initial recruiting and screening and thereby customize the initial process for their needs. The inclusion of customers in the screening process is discussed in the section on assessment that follows. In this way, the individual departments can customize the selection system to meet their needs but also maintain the overall organizational customer-oriented perspective.

Train Users

All line managers and coworkers who will be directly involved in administering the selection system (for example, conducting interviews) should receive training. Recall from the opening case that one of the challenges Beth Evens faced was getting managers to attend the interview training. This challenge can be addressed in at least two ways. First, if customers are involved in the development process they will have more ownership in the selection system and be more likely to participate in training, thus enhancing the effectiveness of this system. Second, it may be possible to make completion of training a mandatory requirement for those involved in making hiring decisions. Although there are potential drawbacks to making any training mandatory, linking input in the selection process with training may help present it as a benefit rather than a cost or imposition on work time.

Inform Applicants

Applicants should be informed about what the selection process entails and how it was developed. This information can help an applicant feel more confident and also justify the selection process. Contrast the widely divergent reactions of these two applicants based on the information they were provided regarding selection processes:

"The process was clearly unfair. I mean I had no problem with the test, but they didn't provide me with any initial information before the test—no discussion of the types of scores they got or what they were looking for."

"Prior to the interview they provided me with a lot of good information on the company and the selection process. Then in the interview, it was just like you are supposed to do when giving a talk. They told me what they would ask me, then they asked the questions."

Research supports the recommendation to provide information. Lounsbury, Bobrow, and Jensen (1989) found that attitudes toward testing were more favorable when people were told how the test related to future job performance. Similarly, Gilliland (1994) found that applicants were more likely to recommend that others apply for a position when they were given a written explanation summarizing why the selection procedure was an effective means of identifying competent individuals.

Information may be conveyed through an information sheet handed to applicants when they submit an application form or as part of a letter that confirms receipt of an application. Alternatively, the initial stages of the selection process may include an oral, video, or computer-based presentation that describes the selection process. Arvey and Sackett (1993) suggest that the reduction in uncertainty that this information provides, particularly with unfamiliar selection procedures, should reduce applicants' beliefs that they performed poorly because they had not known what to expect.

Assessment

Including customers in the development process does a lot for establishing a customer-based selection system. However, the involvement must continue into the assessment stage. In addition, applicants have the most at stake in the assessment stage—they will either get a job offer or be turned down for the job—and therefore have a number of additional concerns. Because line managers and coworkers have very different roles in the assessment stage than do applicants, we will consider managing the assessment stage from the line manager and coworker perspective first and then turn to managing assessment from the applicant perspective.

Line Managers and Coworkers

As in the development stage, involvement is a central issue with line managers and coworkers in the assessment stage. Customarily, this involvement takes the form of having line managers and coworkers conduct the final interviews after the candidate has passed the initial screening and selection. However, it is possible to get involvement in other aspects of the assessment process. The downside of involvement is that many line managers and sometimes coworkers want an assessment process that is quick and easy to administer. Effective selection facilitates the performance of a work unit, but the primary responsibility of that unit is work performance and not selection. As with any support function, time taken away from regular duties should be minimized. When managing customers of selection, it is important to recognize and balance these trade-offs that exist between the customer's competing demands of both involvement and efficiency. We list and then discuss four recommended practices for managing line managers and coworkers as customers in the assessment stage of selection.

- *Include them in the screening process:* Have coworkers assist in the resume or application screening process.
- *Share results of testing:* When possible and permissible, share results of selection testing with line managers.
- *Involve them in conducting interviews:* Involve both line managers and coworkers in conducting interviews with job applicants.
- *Simplify the assessment process:* Simplify the assessment process wherever possible to ease administration.

Include Them in the Screening Process. Screening is often conducted by HR staff. Depending on the organization, this process can include reviewing resumes and job application forms, conducting background checks and verifications, and contacting references. Although a centralized screening process is efficient and possibly helpful from a legal point of view, it can leave the hiring units out of the initial selection processes. Line managers and coworkers may wonder what the complete applicant pool looks like. Without decentralizing the screening process, it still is possible to get customer involvement by having coworkers assist with reviewing resumes and job applications. It is not necessary to involve all coworkers. Instead, including one or two members of the hiring unit will ensure that the unit's views are represented.

Another way to get involvement in the screening process is to seek input from the hiring unit on the criteria used for initial screening. Formal methods for gaining this involvement were discussed in the previous section on selection system development. A final means of involving the hiring unit in screening (albeit in an ad hoc fashion) is to summarize the results of the screening process with members of the hiring unit. For example, information could be shared on the total number of applicants, the number that did not meet basic education and work requirements, the number that were eliminated based on reference checks, and so on. This information-sharing will give line managers and coworkers a greater understanding and appreciation of the screening process.

Share Results of Testing. Another step in selection that could involve line managers is the structured assessment or testing procedures. Like screening, this process is probably coordinated and administered more efficiently through a central HR function. However, results of this testing could be shared with line managers. It is important first to educate these managers on the interpretation of test scores, including what the numbers represent, what sort of error the test scores contain, and how that error limits discrimination between test scores. It is also important to recognize the potential for self-fulfilling prophecy when telling test results to managers. Eden (1990) has demonstrated that when managers are given subordinates' scores on standardized tests, they form expectations about these subordinates' future performance. Further, these expectations can actually increase the performance of high-scoring subordinates and decrease the performance of low-scoring subordinates. Recent research suggests that these expectation-based effects can be limited if information related to test score interpretation is provided (Oz & Eden, 1994).

In addition to sharing test scores with managers, in some situations it may be possible to share scores with coworkers. Doing so is potentially more problematic, however, because of concerns about invasion of privacy. Stigmatization based on high or low test scores of hired individuals would also be a problem if these scores are widely shared with coworkers.

Involve Them in Conducting Interviews. Interviewing is one selection process that can include both line managers and coworkers. In fact, the higher this involvement goes in the organization's hierarchy, the stronger the message it sends about the importance of hiring. Microsoft CEO Bill Gates still gets involved in the hiring process and sometimes even calls people right out of college to encourage them to apply. The director of recruiting at Microsoft summarizes the benefits of this involvement in the following way: "It doesn't seem like something a CEO should be spending his time on, but if Bill and the vice presidents weren't involved, employees would probably think they didn't care, and if they don't, why should we?" (Davies, 1996, p. 123).

Southwest Airlines takes customer involvement one step further. Besides including pilots and flight attendants in group interviews of job applicants, Southwest invites some of its frequent-flyer customers to participate in the interviewing process. A potential advantage of involving internal customer groups in the interview process is more accurate and valid assessments of person–work group fit. However, we know of no research that supports this assertion.

One possible drawback to greater involvement in the interviewing process is that it increases the opportunity for bias and prejudice to enter into hiring decisions. People tend to evaluate others who are similar to themselves more favorably than those who are dissimilar (Dipboye, 1992). If coworkers are selecting members for a work group, the result may be homogeneity and lack of creativity or new perspectives. Two ways to attempt to limit these biases are through careful training of all interviewers and by structuring interview questions and response evaluations.

Simplify the Assessment Process. There may be a limit to all this involvement in the selection process. Line managers and coworkers may feel they are too busy to get actively involved in screening and interviewing. Rather than offering one or two ways to simplify the assessment process, we suggest that a more useful perspective is to evaluate all components of selection from an efficiency standpoint. Although a six-page structured interview may provide a thorough and valid assessment, it will only be effective if the interviewers stick to this structure. In a recent class on selection interviewing, a manager of engineers in a high-technology organization said, "Sure HR provides us with structured interview guides, but we can't be expected to ask all the questions they list. I treat it more like a menu and choose the ones I think will be most useful with a particular applicant."

The lesson is that, when developing any selection system, make sure that the customers will actually take the time to use it. In some cases this may mean compromising a little validity for greater usability.

Applicants

Of the many aspects of customer-based selection systems, the one that has received the most research attention is applicant reaction to selection procedures. Rynes (1993) has examined assessment from a recruiting perspective to see how reactions to selection procedures

can affect the success of recruiting efforts. Gilliland (1993; Gilliland
& Steiner, in press) and others (for example, Smither et al., 1993)
have considered applicant reactions from a fairness perspective
and examined what makes a selection process seem fair or unfair
to applicants. Generally, applicant reactions to assessment can be
divided into issues involving the selection procedures and issues
involving the administration of those procedures. With regard to
selection procedures, applicants are looking for an accurate, unbiased selection process that gives them a chance to demonstrate
their potential. As for the administration of procedures, applicants
are looking for honest, ethical treatment and the opportunity for
two-way communication. The following recommended practices
capture most of the concerns expressed.

- *Job-related assessment:* Selection tests and interview questions
  should appear to be related to the job being filled.
- *Unbiased assessment:* Interview questions and selection procedures should be free from unrelated biases and prejudices.
- *Chance to demonstrate potential:* The selection process should
  give applicants adequate opportunity to demonstrate their
  knowledge, skills, and abilities.
- *Consistent administration:* All job applicants should be treated
  equally and without prejudice or unfair advantage in the selection process.
- *Honest and ethical treatment:* Applicants should be treated truthfully and with respect by interviewers and other selection
  administrators.
- *Interpersonal communication:* The selection process should allow
  for two-way communication between applicants and those involved in the hiring process.

Job-Related Assessment. Applicants clearly prefer selection procedures that they perceive to be related to the job being filled. In a
study of opinions of sixteen commonly used selection procedures,
Kravitz, Stinson, and Chavez (1996) found that work sample tests,
which are transparently job-related, were preferred to all selection
procedures except interviews. In contrast, personality and integrity
tests have been criticized because test content does not appear to

be job-related (Gilliland, 1995). In a direct investigation of the importance of job-related assessment, Steiner and Gilliland (1996) found that perceived face validity was the strongest predictor of favorable selection procedure ratings. Ensuring job-related assessment applies to all selection procedures, including structured tests and interview questions.

The developers of the selection system could face a dilemma when deciding how best to structure the system. That is, should they utilize selection instruments that are shown to be most valid? Or should they use instruments that are perceived as being more fair? (See the "justice dilemma" in Folger & Cropanzano, 1998.) Folger and Cropanzano suggest that it is often possible to solve this problem by substituting fair tests for unfair tests or by modifying existing instruments to improve perceptions of fairness. Although justice dilemmas exist for some selection procedures, for many other procedures no dilemma exists; valid tests are seen as more fair than less valid tests.

Unbiased Assessment. In addition to assessment being job-related, selection procedures should be free from unrelated biases and prejudices. Applicants are particularly sensitive to discriminatory or invasive questions (Rynes, 1993). In fact, Bies and Moag (1986) found that improper questions and prejudicial statements were commonly mentioned causes of unfair recruiting experiences among MBA job candidates. As many of these questions and statements are also legally problematic, managing customer service is not the only reason to keep the selection process free from biases.

Generally, the ways to ensure unbiased assessment include structuring interview questions and training interviewers on appropriate and inappropriate interview questions. Unfortunately, training and awareness may not always be enough to ensure that certain questions are not asked. In one study of college recruiters and job candidates nearly 100 percent of recruiters indicated that questions about spouses were inappropriate, yet 10 percent of candidates who interviewed with these recruiters reported that they were asked questions about spouses (Dew & Steiner, 1997).

Chance to Demonstrate Potential. The selection process should give applicants adequate opportunity to demonstrate their knowledge, skills, and abilities. Applicants prefer selection techniques that they believe give them the opportunity to do so. This also applies to interview questions. Although structuring interview questions is a great way to increase validity and reduce potential bias, it may also cause applicants to feel that they have not been given the opportunity to display their own unique characteristics. Consider this reaction from an applicant who had gone through an unstructured interview: "The interview was a discussion rather than a question-and-answer session. It was very casual. I was able to give them a real idea of who I was and why I was qualified."

Indeed, research has shown that applicants respond more favorably to unstructured interviews than to structured or situational interviews and feel that unstructured interviews allow them greater opportunity to present their abilities (Latham & Finnegan, 1993; Schuler, 1993). One interview approach that could meet the demands of validity and legality as well as the concerns of applicants is discussed by Schuler (1993). He proposes a multimodal interview in which part of it is structured and used for assessment and the other part is unstructured and used to satisfy the applicant's need for input. Keep in mind that the unstructured section of the interview is not wasted or discarded, but instead seen as a valuable opportunity for mutual communication of expectations between the organization and the applicant.

Consistent Administration. Some organizations develop formal or informal hiring policies that give preference to family members and relatives of existing employees. Although it may be argued that these candidates have greater familiarity with the organization and often are more quickly socialized into the organizational culture, giving this preference creates the appearance of inconsistent treatment. It is not uncommon to hear applicants complain that "it is not what you know but who you know that gets you a job." When managing the selection process from an applicant's perspective, all job applicants should be treated equally and without prejudice or unfair advantage. This issue may be particularly problematic for organizations that have adopted affirmative action programs to address underrepresentation. Such preferential treatment will likely violate the beliefs of many applicants about consistent administration and decision making.

Honest and Ethical Treatment. In a study of job applicants who felt they had been unfairly treated by recruiters, the most common complaint was feeling they had been lied to, misled, or deceived (Bies & Moag, 1986). Similarly, research on employment interviews has demonstrated that applicants' perceptions of interviewer sincerity and believability are strongly predictive of affective reactions toward the interview, impressions of the organization, and intention to accept a job offer (for example, Schmitt & Coyle, 1976). The bottom line is that all applicants should be treated truthfully and with respect by interviewers and other selection administrators.

The notion of honest and ethical treatment can be taken one step further. Instead of simply not doing wrong, organizations may benefit from doing right—that is, treating applicants with professionalism and respect in all interactions. For example, Disney ensures positive treatment from the time an applicant walks into the recruiting center, which is a pleasantly decorated "casting center" filled with images of classic Disney characters. In contrast with the subbasement recruiting office usually found in the hospitality industry, Disney sends a message to applicants that they are important and valued as customers.

Interpersonal Communication. A final recommendation for managing applicants as customers during selection is to recall that the selection process is an important time for information-sharing and communication. Identifying the right candidate for the position is only one goal of the selection process. Rynes (1993) asked the question "Who's selecting whom?" in a typical selection situation. With the today's tight labor market, the idea of selling the applicant on the job is more important then ever. Therefore, it is important that the selection process allow for considerable two-way communication. Gilliland (1995) found that a common praise of well-conducted interviews was that they allowed for ample discussion and two-way communication. One MBA student described his best interviewing experience in the following way: "The interviewer and I talked openly about the job and industry. This relieved all the pressure from the interview and made it a very relaxed atmosphere. At the end of the interview, the interviewer had not asked but a few standard questions and felt obligated to ask more. He finished the interview with half a dozen standard questions."

Loss of interpersonal communication may become a problem as selection procedures become increasingly computerized. Martin and Nagao (1989) found that simulated applicants expressed more anger and resentment toward computerized and paper-and-pencil interviewing than toward traditional interviewing involving the same questions. Interpersonal communication was missing from the computer and paper-and-pencil interviewing.

The importance of interpersonal communication is also highlighted in the feedback stage of the selection process.

Feedback

Two types of feedback should be part of this final stage in the selection process. First and most obvious is the feedback to applicants regarding the hiring decision. This is the final opportunity for the organization to do right by its applicant customers. The second type of feedback is that from all customer groups on their reactions to the selection system. We discuss managing each of these feedback processes separately.

Feedback to Applicants

Providing applicants with feedback on the hiring decision is a critical step in the selection process, especially from the applicant's perspective. Before getting this feedback, applicants have beliefs about their performance and expectations about the likelihood of a job offer. Applicants also usually have expectations about when they will get feedback on the hiring decision. The key to managing applicants' reactions during the feedback process is effectively managing these expectations. Our two recommended practices at this stage are the following:

- *Deliver informative feedback:* Provide applicants an explanation or justification with the hiring decision.
- *Deliver timely feedback:* Provide applicants feedback in the promised time frame.

Deliver Informative Feedback. Obviously, applicants are going to be most satisfied with a hiring decision if they are offered a job. However, even when providing negative feedback, information that explains or justifies the hiring decision can improve reactions to it. Bies and Moag (1986) found that the absence of justification was associated with perceptions of unfair recruiting practices. In studies of simulated rejection letters, researchers demonstrated that explanations for rejection decisions improve perceptions of fairness about the hiring decision (for example, Bies & Shapiro, 1988). In an experiment involving actual job applicants, Gilliland (1998) demonstrated that applicants responded more favorably to a rejection decision when they were provided a rejection letter that detailed the hiring decision compared with a standard but polite rejection letter. In fact, those receiving the detailed letter were two and a half times more likely to apply for a job with the organization in the future than those receiving the standard letter.

Deliver Timely Feedback. Timely feedback is important for both successful and unsuccessful applicants. Rynes, Bretz, and Gerhart (1991) asked job applicants what made a once-attractive company unattractive and a significant number of responses were related to delays in the recruiting process. This was particularly true for the more highly qualified applicants. Among unsuccessful applicants, Gilliland (1995) found that failure to receive timely feedback was one of the leading contributors to perceptions of unfairness in the selection process. As the following quote from a job applicant indicates, timeliness has more to do with fulfilling a promise than with actual length of time: "They waited four weeks to tell me no! But they said they would make a decision as soon as I left. Finally, I had to push them for an answer. I wouldn't work for them for anything in the world."

Feedback from Customers

Continuous and candid feedback is an essential component of a customer-based selection system. As with any high-quality process, genuine and informative feedback is needed to keep the system operating at top level. The feedback mechanism provides a cycle of continuous checks and balances for the system's usability and effectiveness. Over time, the feedback could be used continually to refine the system and maintain its effectiveness. In considering how and what feedback to solicit, the following practices can assist in maintaining a customer orientation:

- *Solicit feedback from applicants:* Collect systematic feedback from applicants following (and perhaps during) the selection process.
- *Solicit feedback from internal customer groups:* Seek input from line managers and coworkers regarding the usability and effectiveness of the selection system.

Solicit Feedback from Applicants. At AT&T, the employment group regularly surveys applicants to assess their reactions to the entire selection process. An "applicant satisfaction card" is one way organizations can solicit this feedback. Such a card is similar to customer satisfaction cards commonly found in stores, restaurants, and hotels that ask customers to rate the service (for example, service representatives, food, room) on a number of dimensions. The objective is to attain a simple snapshot of the customer's perceptions of the selection process in a user-friendly format.

Essentially a postcard, the card should be sent to applicants (both successful and unsuccessful) after a selection decision has been made or perhaps during the selection process. It asks them to rate their reactions to the selection system. This can easily be accomplished through rating questions (Likert-type scales) such as these:

I am satisfied with the selection process.

The selection process allowed me to demonstrate my unique qualifications.

I was treated with a high degree of respect and sincerity in the interview(s).

I received adequate feedback on the hiring decision.

The questions asked may be determined by assessing the goals and strategy of the selection system with regard to the applicant group. Different departments may want to tailor the card to meet their own feedback needs as well. Caution should be exercised when asking rejected applicants about fairness or bias, because this may prompt unwanted legal challenges.

In addition to providing valuable feedback, simply asking applicants for their reactions is likely to generate positive feelings. In a hiring situation in which we solicited applicant feedback, one of the applicants wrote the following comment at the bottom of the feedback survey: "Thank you for taking the time to ask for feedback. I applaud your effort to improve your process."

Solicit Feedback from Internal Customer Groups. Feedback should also be collected from line managers and coworkers regarding their reactions to the selection system. This feedback could be collected immediately after hiring occurs, as well as some time after the new hire has been on the job (for example, four months posthire). Customer satisfaction cards similar to the applicant satisfaction cards could be used to collect this feedback. These cards may include questions such as these:

I was able to offer input into the hiring decision.

I believe the selection process was effective at identifying strong candidates.

The selection process seemed overly burdensome. (This is reverse-scored.)

Once again, the questions asked should be based on the goals of the selection system with regard to line managers and coworkers; it may be necessary to develop different questions for these two groups. The value of this card lies in its ability to generate genuine feedback from all customer groups at varying intervals in a user-friendly format.

In addition to using the customer satisfaction card, organizations can collect feedback through roundtable discussions or focus groups involving line managers and coworkers. As with applicants, the value of collecting internal customer feedback comes from both the input it provides into the selection system development process and from the goodwill it generates as a result of asking customers for input. The result is continuous improvement of the system.

Conclusions

In this chapter we have proposed that selection systems be considered from a customer perspective. Although there are many potential customers of selection, we chose to focus on the three primary groups: line managers, coworkers, and applicants. The value of developing a customer-based selection system can be seen in outcomes associated with effective selection and hiring, positive work attitudes and behaviors, and spillover effects onto customers of the organization's products and services.

We discussed managing the customers of selection in the development, assessment, and feedback stages of the selection process. We made similar recommendations for managers and coworkers, noting that coworker involvement should increase as workers become more interdependent, such as when they are in work teams. Here are our main suggestions regarding these two groups as customers of selection:

- Communicate how and why a new selection system is being developed.
- Involve line managers in development and administration of the selection system.
- Train line managers in the use of the selection system and in effective interviewing and decision making.
- Simplify the assessment process to ease administration.
- Solicit feedback on the effectiveness of and satisfaction with the selection system.

As for managing job applicants as customers of selection, we made the following recommendations:

- Include applicant concerns in the development of the selection system.
- Provide applicants with an understanding of what the selection process entails and how it was developed.
- Make sure the selection procedures are job-related and unbiased, and give applicants a chance to demonstrate their potential.
- Make sure the selection process is consistently administered.
- Treat applicants with honesty and respect, and allow for two-way communication.
- Deliver timely and informative feedback to applicants on the hiring decision.
- Solicit feedback from applicants on their reactions to the selection process.

The problems Beth Evens faced in the opening case in this chapter were clearly a result of failing to manage the customers of selection effectively. But an organization should not wait until problems become evident before developing a customer-based selection system. As we stated throughout this chapter, industry leaders like Disney, Microsoft, and Southwest Airlines excel in their hiring processes because they have adopted a customer orientation. Customer-based selection can be an integral component of an organization's competitive human resource advantage.

References

Arvey, R. D., & Sackett, P. R. (1993). Fairness in selection: Current developments and perspectives. In N. Schmitt & W. Borman (Eds.), *Personnel selection in organizations* (pp. 171–202). San Francisco: Jossey-Bass.

Berry, L. (1995). *On great service: A framework for action.* New York: Free Press.

Bies, R. J., & Moag, J. S. (1986). Interactional justice: Communication criteria of fairness. *Research on Negotiation in Organizations, 1,* 43–55.

Bies, R. J., & Shapiro, D. L. (1988). Voice and justification: Their influence on procedural fairness judgments. *Academy of Management Journal, 31,* 676–685.

Bowen, D. E., Gilliland, S. W., & Folger, R. (1999). HRM and service fairness: How being fair with employees spills over to customers. *Organizational Dynamics, 27* (3), 7–23.

Bowen, D. E., & Greiner, L. E. (1986). Moving from production to service in human resources management. *Organizational Dynamics, 15,* 35–53.

Bowen, D. E., & Lawler, E. E., III (1992). Total quality–oriented human resource management. *Organizational Dynamics, 21,* 29–41.

Bowen, D. E., Ledford, G. E., & Nathan, B. R. (1991). Hiring for the organization, not the job. *Academy of Management Executive, 5*(4), 35–51.

Davies, E. M. (1996, February 5). Wired for hiring: Microsoft's slick recruiting machine. *Fortune,* pp. 123–124.

Dean, J. W., Jr., & Bowen, D. E. (1994). Management theory and total quality: Improving research and practice through theory development. *Academy of Management Review, 19,* 392–418.

Dew, A. F., & Steiner, D. D. (1997). *Inappropriate questions in selection interviews: Interviewer knowledge and applicant reactions.* Paper presented at the 12th annual meeting of the Society for Industrial and Organizational Psychology, St. Louis.

Dipboye, R. L. (1992). *Selection interviews: Process perspectives.* Cincinnati: South-Western.

Dipboye, R. L., & de Pontbraind, R. (1981). Correlates of employee reactions to performance appraisals and appraisal systems. *Journal of Applied Psychology, 66,* 248–251.

Dockery, T. M., & Steiner, D. D. (1990). The role of the initial interaction in leader-member exchange. *Group and Organization Studies, 15,* 395–413.

Eden, D. (1990). *Pygmalion in management: Productivity as a self-fulfilling prophecy.* San Francisco: New Lexington Press.

Folger, R., & Cropanzano, R. (1998). *Organizational justice and human resource management.* Thousand Oaks, CA: Sage.

Gilliland, S. W. (1993). The perceived fairness of selection systems: An organizational justice perspective. *Academy of Management Review, 18,* 694–734.

Gilliland, S. W. (1994). Effects of procedural and distributive justice on reactions to a selection system. *Journal of Applied Psychology, 79,* 691–701.

Gilliland, S. W. (1995). Fairness from the applicant's perspective: Reactions to employee selection procedures. *International Journal of Selection and Assessment, 3,* 11–19.

Gilliland, S. W. (1998). *Applicant reactions to rejection letters: A field experiment.* Paper presented at the 13th annual meeting of the Society for Industrial and Organizational Psychology, Dallas.

Gilliland, S. W., & Steiner, D. D. (in press). Causes and consequences of applicant perceptions of unfairness. In R. Cropanzano (Ed.), *Justice in the workplace* (Vol. 2). Hillsdale, NJ: Erlbaum.

Gilliland, S. W., & Troth, M. A. (1998). *Consequences of employee selection system justice.* Manuscript submitted for publication.

Goldman, B. M. (1999). *Employment discrimination–claiming behavior: The effects of organizational justice, social guidance, and perceived discrimination.* Manuscript submitted for publication.

Ilgen, D. R., & Hollenbeck, J. R. (1991). The structure of work: Job design and roles. In M. D. Dunnette & L. M. Hough (Eds.), *Handbook of industrial and organizational psychology* (pp. 165–207). Palo Alto, CA: Consulting Psychologists Press.

Kravitz, D. A., Stinson, V., & Chavez, T. L. (1996). Evaluations of tests used for making selection and promotion decisions. *International Journal of Selection and Assessment, 4,* 24–34.

Landy, F. (1993). Job analysis and job evaluation: The respondent's perspective. In H. Schuler, J. L. Farr, & M. Smith (Eds.), *Personnel selection and assessment: Individual and organizational perspectives* (pp. 75–90). Hillsdale, NJ: Erlbaum.

Latham, G. P., & Finnegan, B. J. (1993). Perceived practicality of unstructured, patterned, and situational interviews. In H. Schuler, J. L. Farr, & M. Smith (Eds.), *Personnel selection and assessment: Individual and organizational perspectives* (pp. 41–55). Hillsdale, NJ: Erlbaum.

Lounsbury, J. W., Bobrow, W., & Jensen, J. B. (1989). Attitudes toward employment testing: Scale development, correlates, and "known-group" validation. *Professional Psychology: Research and Practice, 20,* 340–349.

Macan, T. H., Avedon, M. J., Paese, M., & Smith, D. E. (1994). The effects of applicants' reactions to cognitive ability tests and an assessment center. *Personnel Psychology, 47,* 715–738.

Mael, F. A., Connerley, M. L., & Morath, R. A. (1997). *Caught in the crossfire: Coworkers' stake in hiring decisions.* Paper presented at the 12th annual meeting of the Society for Industrial and Organizational Psychology, St. Louis.

Martin, C. L., & Nagao, D. H. (1989). Some effects of computerized interviewing on job applicant responses. *Journal of Applied Psychology, 74,* 72–80.

Murphy, K. R. (1986). When your top choice turns you down: Effect of rejected offers on the utility of selection tests. *Psychological Bulletin, 99,* 133–138.

Oz, S., & Eden, D. (1994). Restraining the Golem: Boosting performance by changing the interpretation of low scores. *Journal of Applied Psychology, 79,* 744–754.

Rynes, S. L. (1993). Who's selecting whom? Effects of selection practices on applicant attitudes and behaviors. In N. Schmitt & W. Borman (Eds.), *Personnel selection in organizations* (pp. 240–274). San Francisco: Jossey-Bass.

Rynes, S. L., Bretz, R. D., Jr., & Gerhart, B. (1991). The importance of recruitment in job choice: A different way of looking. *Personnel Psychology, 44,* 487–521.

Schmit, M. J., & Ryan, A. M. (1992). Test-taking disposition: A missing link? *Journal of Applied Psychology, 77,* 629–637.

Schmit, M. J., & Ryan, A. M. (1997). Applicant withdrawal: The role of test-taking attitudes and racial differences. *Personnel Psychology, 50,* 855–876.

Schmitt, N., & Coyle, B. W. (1976). Applicant decisions in the employment interview. *Journal of Applied Psychology, 61,* 184–192.

Schneider, B., & Bowen, D. (1993). The service organization: Human resource management is crucial. *Organizational Dynamics, 22,* 39–52.

Schuler, H. (1993). Is there a dilemma between validity and acceptance in the employment interview? In B. Nevo & R. S. Jager (Eds.), *Educational and psychological testing: The test taker's outlook* (pp. 239–250). Toronto: Hogrefe & Huber.

Singer, M. S. (1992). Procedural justice in managerial selection: Identification of fairness determinants and associations of fairness perceptions. *Social Justice Research, 5,* 49–70.

Smither, J. W., Reilly, R. R., Millsap, R. E., Pearlman, K., & Stoffey, R. W. (1993). Applicant reactions to selection procedures. *Personnel Psychology, 46,* 49–76.

Steiner, D. D., & Gilliland, S. W. (1996). Fairness reactions to personnel selection techniques in France and the United States. *Journal of Applied Psychology, 81,* 134–141.

Thibaut, J., & Walker, L. (1975). *Procedural justice: A psychological analysis.* Hillsdale, NJ: Erlbaum.

CHAPTER 5

Selection Programs in a Union Environment: A Commentary

David A. Bownas

As I gathered information for this chapter, I found that several fairly general principles of human behavior seemed to be at work behind the scenes. This should have come as no great surprise, but it's easy for those of us who work in selection to forget that all the principles of psychology we studied as undergraduates apply to us and to those around us.

Precepts of Human Behavior

As an introduction, then, I'll discuss a few of these precepts of behavior.

We're All Just Folks

The kinds of motives that drive union spokespeople in organizations are no different from those that motivate corporate management. Sometimes the different vantage points from which the two groups operate cause them to reach different conclusions about specific outcomes, but the underlying motives are the same. We all try to maximize personal outcomes (such as power, prestige, and influence) and to maximize the outcomes of constituents and other loyal followers.

One purpose of this chapter was to discuss the (usually inappropriate) pressures brought to bear on selection research professionals by labor organizations to influence selection processes. What I found was that these are the same (usually inappropriate) pressures that management so often brings to bear on selection research professionals when their relatives, neighbors, friends, or protégés are being considered for jobs. In fact, when unions find themselves seriously committed to making accurate selection decisions, they usually embrace the same principles of valid selection that professional personnel psychologists do. In short, if this chapter were to be viewed from a "we versus they" perspective, "we" are selection professionals (not management) and "they" are others with personal axes to grind and agendas to pursue (not labor organizations).

Adversariness Abounds

Notwithstanding the slipperiness of the concepts of *we* and *they* in the matter of good employee selection practices, the history of labor-management relations in many organizations is so fraught with conflict that it's difficult to discuss issues of cooperation and disagreement with any degree of neutrality. I found it very hard to write a structured interview form to discuss labor and management perspectives on employee selection practices without falling into adversarial language traps. I needed three or four drafts before I arrived at a dialogue organizer that I wasn't embarrassed to send to a labor representative. During the ensuing discussions with labor leaders, it was a constant struggle for both of us to keep us-versus-them overtones from creeping in. Convincing labor leaders of the utility of fair, objective selection processes (for them as well as for us) will require a good deal of effort. We frequently have to overcome the friction resistance of a history of adversarial relations between labor and management, as well as their more immediate vested interests.

Ultimately, in many ways it's about power. The ability to influence selection, promotion, and retention decisions is a potent commodity. Astute corporate players want a share of this power, and successful union representatives and managers have both mastered the skills of power and influence.

A Tale of Three Perspectives

Figure 5.1 summarizes the similarities and differences among the perspectives of union leaders, corporate managers, and personnel psychologists.

Union Leaders

Union leaders seek to protect the interests of their members, who generally already work in the organization. As a result, unions usually aren't concerned about entry-level hiring, unless there's a substantial pool of out-of-work members to whom they would like to

Figure 5.1. Who Wants What from Employee Selection Procedures.

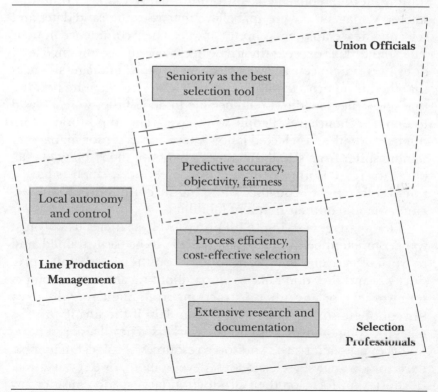

give hiring preference. Unions do, occasionally, lobby for patronage hiring of friends and relatives (theirs or their constituents'). Institutionally, this is handled by employee referral recruitment processes, but labor representatives may become more directly and actively involved in important cases by lobbying and arm-twisting. Again, none of this is very different from the behavior of management folks. Unions usually do feel very strongly about selection processes when the candidate pool includes their members; this includes screening for promotion, for transfer, and for retention during layoffs.

Managers

Corporate managers try to achieve their perceived objectives for their organizational units. Thus, they want to ensure adequate staffing, at their convenience, with minimal red tape or other obstacles. Managers, as a group, believe that assessing candidates and selecting new employees is pretty simple. Their confidence in their assessment skills exceeds their true accuracy, and confidence level doesn't predict accuracy very well. As a result, managers expect that the hiring process will be fast, efficient, and accurate because that's how they feel they would be able to do it if they were allowed to do it for themselves. People who have attained positions of influence (whether as elected labor leaders or as senior managers) seldom suffer from self-doubt, especially about their ability to evaluate (to "read") other people. Thus selection specialists have a tough sell trying to convince these highly confident, variably accurate people of their frequent fallibility.

Line managers trying to fill entry-level vacancies usually just want competent people to appear quickly, to be easily trained, and to work effectively. They want to focus on their work unit's productivity and they don't like to worry about vacant jobs, incompetent workers, or any other distractions from managing the daily flow of operations. Managers will complain if the hiring process takes too long or gives them useless workers. They'll also resent requests to use their scarce workforce resources as subject matter experts for job analysis, selection test development, or test validation. In short, they focus on their production targets and consider any distractions from HR as irritants.

Some managers don't get involved in the test development process and seem to view selection professionals as supply vendors. As long as the quality, quantity, and timeliness of delivery of newly hired workers meet their expectations, they aren't concerned with the details of how they get there. Other managers are intently concerned that the process be done right to ensure they get the quality of workers they want. Others participate in the development process more from curiosity than from pragmatism. In both of the latter cases, managers can be invaluable sources of information and subject matter experts, but they need to be managed and educated through the process. Like union officials, managers occasionally want to grant patronage to friends or relatives.

Selection Professionals

Personnel psychologists usually approach selection more systematically and analytically than either managers or union leaders, because they don't think "reading people" is simple. They try to make selection decisions that enhance total utility for the organization, not individual candidate utility and not individual manager utility. As a result, they often find themselves in conflict with both union leaders and line managers. Furthermore, personnel psychologists aren't immune from the various human pressures themselves when their own friends, relatives, or protégés are being considered.

Challenges in Selection

Selection specialists try to balance predictive accuracy against cost. Often, especially when external candidates with no extensive experience are being considered for jobs, selection procedures will tend toward the distant-sign end of Wernimont and Campbell's (1968) sign-sample continuum. This is the case when all that can be assessed are the aptitudes necessary for learning and performing jobs.

In general, both unions and managers look more favorably on work sample measures and other closer approximations to the sample end of the sign-sample continuum, but unions are likely to be less sensitive than managers to the cost aspects of such selection. On occasion, our union leaders have suggested selecting workers for *all* positions by means of job tryout. From their perspective, this affords equal opportunity for all their members, with final retention based on documented performance. This approach is usually too costly for human resource management in terms of training, development, and performance management resources devoted to employees who don't succeed. Furthermore, taking corrective developmental action with poor performers requires considerable time and emotional effort, and overworked managers can often justify (at least to themselves) focusing on other more tractable and less aversive problems. If a manager avoids dealing with a personnel problem for the duration of a probationary period, the employee's problem behavior becomes harder to improve, and at the extreme, the termination process becomes a much more arduous event.

Selection Procedures

Union reactions to company selection procedures are strongly affected by union-management relations in general. As is often the case, good communication usually facilitates the process. Employees and their representatives are often anxious about job security, so if incumbents will not be affected by a new selection procedure, it's usually easier to get their cooperation by telling them that, and by explaining how the procedure *will* be used and how their input will contribute to the quality of the final product. In some cases, labor-management relations are so poor that no amount of communication about a specific selection procedure can overcome the ambient animosity. In such cases, selection professionals can only cut their losses, develop a professionally acceptable selection procedure using whatever resources they can tap into, and apply their skills to improving overall employee relations.

One case from my company presents a dramatic example of the ways union-management relationships can affect selection programs. In this case, the union's prior experience with a department head who used patronage and threats of demotion to control his workforce created an environment of hostile suspicion. Ultimately, the union negotiated collective bargaining agreement provisions that detailed many aspects of the promotion testing process. The union contract not only specified that objective tests be used to determine promotions but prescribed the number of test items, mandated that one of five alternate forms be chosen by lot at the beginning of each test session (so supervisors couldn't give the answers to their preferred candidates), and specified the weighting to be given the written, oral, and experience (seniority) components of the promotion process. Our efforts to streamline the process were unsuccessful, so we continue to develop five alternate forms of a job knowledge test each time a promotional test is to be given. We use one form and discard 80 percent of the items we developed, even though control over the promotion process has been centralized in a professional HR department for more than fifteen years.

In other, more tractable cases we have met with employees and union leaders to explain the test development process; involved employees in the job analysis, skill-knowledge identification process, and item-writing stages; and generated considerable support for the testing process as a result.

In one other case, we had considerable success allaying the fears of one union local representative while a neighboring representative for the same union covering the same workers in a different location advised his members not to cooperate. Similarly, one company reported that one representative of its supervisors' union strongly supported supervisor participation in identifying candidates for promotion to foreman. He held that no one is more familiar with workers' supervisory potential than their current supervisors. His colleagues, however, felt strongly that, because selection was management's prerogative, the union shouldn't take *any* role in the process, partly to avoid creating bad feeling between two or more potential co-members and partly to avoid sharing any blame for selection errors.

One related concept that's typical of our testing arrangements with some unions is "grandfathering" of testing results. Some (though not all) contracts specify that once employees pass a test and qualify for a job, they don't have to take the test again. This usually doesn't represent a serious burden for the company. If the test is assessing basic abilities that remain stable over time, there's not much point in requiring retesting. Similarly, if the test assesses more specific job skills and knowledge that the worker maintains at a high level of proficiency, retesting is superfluous.

Unions feel most strongly about selection programs that affect their current members. As a result, because unions usually don't object to entry-level selection, they advise their members to co-operate in job analyses and let them participate in concurrent validation studies as long as adequate assurances are given that employees won't be harmed by any adverse information that comes up during criterion measurement. The primary exception to this rule is if the external candidates are union members who have been laid off and don't have seniority rights to the jobs they're applying for. In these situations, unions will advocate vigorously to waive normal selection programs and treat their furloughed members as prequalified job candidates.

Once an employee becomes a dues-paying member of a union, the union generally prefers seniority as the sole criterion for subsequent job moves. Seniority has two attractive features for its proponents: it's completely objective and it comes to all members who have the patience to wait for it. Union representatives can argue for one member and against another on the basis of seniority without disparaging or offending either of them, and unions will go to extreme lengths to avoid being put in the position of articulating disparities between the value of two of their members.

When companies do use selection procedures to choose between union members for union jobs, labor organizations usually prefer the most objective and job-related selection procedures possible. Actual job tryouts, apprenticeships, and selection by successful completion of training programs are the preferred procedures from a union perspective, and work sample tests (hands-on demonstrations of actual job skills) are the least objectionable of testing procedures.

One of our unions endorsed prequalification testing for different construction trade specialties (carpenter, mason, ironworker) after it was satisfied that the tests were challenging but fair exercises of actual job duties and that standardized, objective protocols would be used to evaluate test performance. Most of our union representatives understood the distinction between a standardized test exercise and a standardized evaluation of the test product. They approved the testing program for transferring between specialties only after they saw that the evaluation standards were both objective and realistic. (For example, a four-foot high wall is to be laid level and plumb within one-eighth of an inch; a light fixture is to be wired to be controlled by two three-way switches, with all connections according to national electric code and no ground faults or short circuits.)

Even with selection programs that fall closer to the sign end of the selection procedure continuum, unions are more likely to be comfortable with tests that are standardized, objective, and face-valid. A test that looks like part of the job evokes less anxiety than an equally valid but less cosmetically appealing measure of the same construct. A test that requires no subjective evaluation by the administrator or scorer will be perceived as less susceptible to bias and favoritism. Again, union officials don't want to be put in the position of arbitrating claims between two members, so to the extent that test-scoring rules are standard and objective, unions will be more willing to accept the tests and acquiesce to the results.

When unions do accept testing as a process for screening their members, they tend to prefer either strict top-down rank scoring or a fixed passing score with seniority determining selection order among those who pass. Both these approaches provide a consistent, objective process for making decisions between union members.

Unions also object to tests that are perceived as too difficult. "Excessive difficulty" is operationally defined as a friend, relative, constituent member, or other protégé of a union official failing a test, especially a constituent member who has been performing similar jobs before testing. In one firm, when the payroll timekeeping process was partially automated, a new screening procedure was instituted consisting of a keyboard data-entry exercise and some fairly simple arithmetic and rule-following tests. When nearly half of the former timekeepers failed the test battery, the union objected that the test was too hard and lobbied to have the former timekeepers grandfathered from the testing requirement. As a compromise, some coaching was provided to those who had failed, particularly for the keyboarding skills, and most of the former timekeepers were eventually able to pass the test battery. Several people who had attained only marginal passing scores had difficulty performing the new job, though, and were subsequently disqualified.

Again, concerns about excessive test difficulty aren't limited to union officials. Line managers and corporate executives often find it hard to accept that their referred candidates fail selection tests.

Some companies and unions have established collaborative selection test development projects, but most firms discourage sharing their selection prerogative with unions and most unions wish to avoid putting themselves in the position of choosing between their members. One scenario that has provided a vehicle for labor-management collaboration is selection systems for jointly (union and management) sponsored apprenticeship and other training programs for union members. Union members can contribute enough to such selection systems—in knowledge of candidate skills and work habits—that some companies have overcome their reluctance to share selection decision-making power. Similarly, unions, in some cases, have been concerned enough about the selection of apprentices and trainees for skilled craft and supervisory positions that they have been willing to participate in the screening process and to share responsibility for the quality of recruits.

Professional Credibility

Although in many cases external influences such as contract negotiations and grievance/arbitration outcomes affect the development of selection systems in a union environment, selection research professionals can do some things to smooth relations where testing is concerned. Most of these things revolve around credibility.

There are eight principles for building and maintaining credibility for applied selection research.

Hold to Your Professional Principles

A consistent commitment to accurate prediction of job performance will, eventually, impress itself on union representatives. Once they understand and believe that you are working to predict actual job performance fairly and accurately, they will be more willing to accept both the process and the outcomes.

Recruit Staff Who Understand the Jobs and Have the Trust of the Rank and File

Recruit people for your selection test development staff who have a detailed understanding of the jobs involved and enjoy the trust and confidence of workers and union leaders. Our firm tries to keep a mix of people in its selection research group, including some with a formal I/O psychology and psychometric background and some who have worked as union employees in a variety of trade crafts.

Avoid Association with Certain Corporate Functions

Avoid being associated with or acceding to corporate functions that unions will perceive as having axes to grind. This will vary from setting to setting, and it may not be a problem at all in some organizations.

In some companies unions perceive certain departments, units, or functions as their "enemy" and may perceive other functions as their "friends." The work of selection test development and validation will go much more smoothly, and be viewed with more respect, if the test development function is perceived by both unions and management as belonging to neither of these camps but rather as being above "all that." Again, in some companies it is critical to arrange this, in others it's impossible, and in yet others it doesn't matter at all. This does not mean exiling the personnel research function from the rest of the company, nor interdicting communications from "enemy" departments, "friendly" functions, or the unions themselves. Rather, selection testing is best viewed as a professional, scientific enterprise and should not be perceived by unions as just another mechanism the company will try to use to affect union workers adversely.

Spend Time Listening to Union Members

Spend a lot of time listening to what union members have to say about job tasks, ability and skill requirements, working conditions, and work methods. The more information you have about jobs, the more accurately you can predict performance in them. The more workers feel you're taking them seriously, the more confidence they'll have in the selection process. The more union members perceive that you're using their input in developing tests, the more they'll take emotional ownership of the final product.

Guarantee Confidentiality

Guarantee confidentiality, and do whatever is necessary to ensure that nobody experiences negative repercussions from cooperating with your research. Employees become paranoid very easily when managers begin measuring skills, abilities, and performance levels. Confidentiality means that you won't divulge an individual's scores on any measures. At the very least explain to participants in a validation study why you need to identify them on their test forms and performance measures. If they don't trust you enough to put their names on experimental test materials, it's possible to arrange for a double-blind design, where employees and raters both turn in tests and ratings with coded identification fields and the union local (or some other nonthreatening entity) keeps concordance lists. The union can inform the research unit of which test identification code corresponds to each rating identification code (for example, test answer form number 559 should be linked to supervisory ratings AAD and ABF) without the research unit knowing the name of the employee, and without the union knowing either the test responses or the performance ratings. These procedures are cumbersome, may introduce sources of error, and should be avoided if possible, but if true anonymity is necessary in validation research, this approach makes it possible.

In one concurrent validation study, a consulting firm used invisible ink to precode answer sheets when the employees refused to participate if they had to put their names on the test materials. The employees smuggled an answer sheet out of the testing session, inspected it in the company lab under ultraviolet light, and found the invisible coding. The validation study was aborted, and it was only with the greatest difficulty that a strike was averted. The moral of the story is always and only to tell the truth. If that prevents an empirical validation study, just walk away.

Prefer Measures That Are Close to Actual Work Behavior

Prefer measures that are as close as possible to samples of actual work behavior. Emphasize face validity as much as possible (as well as, not in lieu of, construct validity). From a psychometric standpoint "construct-pure" measures may be preferable, but from a union relations standpoint the choice may be between a face-valid measure that has (merely) acceptable psychometric properties and a factor-analytically pure construct measure that can't be validated because the union instructs its members not to take the test honestly.

Try to Gain Support from Local Union Officials

Enlist the support (or obtain the acquiescence) of local union officials. At the very least, keep local union representatives informed of the research you are doing and the involvement you will ask of their members. Local labor leaders are often opinion leaders for the workforce, and persuading them that your research won't hurt, and should help, their members can gain cooperation from large numbers of their members with relatively little effort on your part. Labor representatives and other opinion leaders are the leverage points for communicating with the workforce at large.

Explain the Test Development Process

Explain the test development and validation process to everyone who will be involved. Be careful to avoid jargon and to use terminology they'll understand, without talking down to anybody. In some settings you'll want to make sure people know of your academic credentials; in other settings, you may want to take extraordinary measures to keep people from finding out that you have a graduate degree. In *most* settings you will want to work to minimize, not accentuate, any status differences between your research staff and the union workers who will be providing your validation research data.

Conclusions

The bad news and the good news is that dealing with unions in developing, validating, and implementing selection processes isn't any different from dealing with all the other groups of interested participants. Union officials are probably no more difficult to persuade, to educate, and to accommodate, on average, than are vice presidents. By doing as professionally competent a job as you can of conducting rigorous, objective validation research, you'll eventually convince your company's labor leaders that you're developing the most fair, objective, and accurate measures possible of candidates' performance contributions. They may not like you for that, but at least they'll respect you.

Reference
Wernimont, P. F., & Campbell, J. P. (1968). Signs, samples, and criteria. *Journal of Applied Psychology, 52,* 372–376.

CHAPTER 6

Selection in Team Contexts

Robert G. Jones
Michael J. Stevens
Donald L. Fischer

Selecting teams requires consideration of problems that are not commonly considered in individual selection practice. Teams are often used to provide flexibility in rapidly changing environments and to relieve organizations from expending some resources on individual manager selection, development, and compensation. By extension, teams themselves need to be able to adapt and shape themselves according to changing demands. Abilities likely to be important for team members in these circumstances include thinking strategically, understanding and accounting for one another's differences, communicating ideas and other information effectively, and negotiating collective courses of action efficiently. Thus, among other things, selection for teams involves taking into account the same sorts of skills that people need in order to get along with others who are culturally and psychologically different from themselves. However, describing "middle level" constructs that adequately cover these general skills for the purpose of selection is complicated by the dynamism of team behavior and by the multiple roles taken by team members over time. As will be seen in this chapter, the implication of this is that approaches to team selection are somewhat different from traditional individual selection.

Teams are dynamic social structures (McGrath, Berdahl, & Arrow, 1995; Donnellon, 1996; Cannon-Bowers & Salas, 1997). Central to this dynamism are the changing roles taken on by team members over time. In fact, there is evidence that, in the course of accomplishing organizational goals, team members engage in negotiations over role definition (Donnellon, 1996; Feldman, 1984; Gabarro, 1987; Jones & Lindley, 1998; Mohrman & Mohrman, 1997; Northcraft, Polzer, Neale, & Kramer, 1995; Walsh, Henderson, & Deighton, 1988), with predictable performance enhancement for teams that manage to clarify their roles (Salas, Mullen, Rozell, & Driskell, 1997; Walsh et al., 1988). Such role definition may include negotiation of who will perform which tasks, how the tasks will be performed, which tasks will be performed, and even which organizational goals will be pursued.

While the extent of team self-management makes some of these role-defining decisions more or less relevant, it seems quite likely that newly constituted teams require different member behaviors than do teams in transition or well-established teams. These different behaviors imply the need for different member skills. For example, a newly constituted task force may engage in long and conflict-laden discussions about which organizational goals define criteria for effective completion of its assigned task. Later, the task force may be more concerned with whether individuals have successfully completed their individual component tasks. The point here is not that these tasks are both performed or that they focus on team and individual levels of analysis respectively. It is that they are done at different points in the team's life cycle. This means that different skill sets are required depending on whether the team has yet defined its role and its members' individual roles.

This aspect of team dynamism has direct implications for selection practices. In this chapter, we argue that approaches to selection will vary depending on whether selecting for new teams, for groups in the process of making a transition to self-management, or for intact high-performing teams. Thus, in terms of approaches to selection, teams are moving targets. Under some circumstances, traditional staffing approaches do make sense; but other circumstances may alter the nature of the selection process. In addition to the usual consideration of *levels* of individual task-related skills, staffing specialists need to consider the breadth of task-related skills within and across members, individual negotiation skills, job preferences, psychological heterogeneity among members, and constituent group representation. Furthermore, the actual process of selection may fall to the self-managed work team. This sort of boundary control

(Cummings, 1978; Trist, 1981) or "empowerment" of teams to make their own decisions (Kirkman & Rosen, 1997) requires a partnership with staffing specialists in order to make the process fair, accurate, and legally defensible.

In this chapter we will first spend time defining what we mean by a team. In addition to the usual conceptual problems with defining the team construct, operational definition is important from a job analysis and needs assessment perspective. Next, selection issues will be identified for new teams (new teams–new members), transitional teams (old members–new team work), and intact teams (old teams–new members). Next, practical problems of selection system validation and evaluation will be considered. We conclude the chapter with a call for continued collaboration between academics and practitioners in order to develop broadly applicable predictor constructs for team selection.

Definitions of Teams

Defining the team construct has importance not only to scientists interested in broadly applicable models but also to practitioners engaged in team selection. This is because construct definition establishes the boundaries for practitioner activities and identifies issues important to the eventual success of selection efforts. For example, selection for maintenance crews may have very different requirements than selection for task forces; basing task-force selection practices on crew-related constructs may reduce the likelihood of the resulting selection program succeeding. Of course, for both science and practice, definition of team work is a group-level corollary for individual job analysis: it is an essential early step in staffing. In this section, we will discuss the parameters of the term *team* for all three purposes (broad construct definition, defining practical boundaries, and team work analysis). It should be noted that traditional job analysis will be expanded here to include team work analysis, which can be used to identify predictor constructs for selection system development and evaluation.

Teams Versus Crews, Work Groups

There are many definitions of teams. We will discuss several (McGrath et al., 1995; Saavedra, Earley, & Van Dyne, 1993; Stevens &

Campion, 1994) in this section. These definitions were chosen because the analytic systems from which they are derived provide practitioners with analytic tools for establishing the likely importance of predictor constructs. For now, and for lack of a better term, we will use the term *team work analysis* to describe the use of these analytic systems in place of traditional, individually oriented *job analysis*. This is because team work analysis encompasses more than task and duty identification. Instead, team work analysis looks for "critical levers" (Tesluk, Mathieu, Zaccaro, & Marks, 1997; Hallam & Campbell, 1992), which are the underlying factors and arrangements essential to team performance. The definition of team work and its underlying critical levers in situ is therefore the object of team work analysis.

Primacy of Members, Tasks, or Tools

McGrath et al. (1995) define teams in terms of the primacy of *members, tasks,* or *tools* to the group's work. Their notion is that *tasks* to be completed are essential to task forces, whereas membership and tools for completing tasks are less "defining" because these groups disband when the task is completed. Crews are groups whose work is largely determined by the technology *(tools)* that they use to complete their work. Crew members are interchangeable, and tasks are largely defined by the tools used to accomplish them. Unlike crews and task forces, membership in teams is more or less permanent, and the completion of their work relies largely on the *members'* characteristics, rather than tools (Arrow, 1998). In essence, team members develop interactions and expectations of one another that can be thought of as a human technology to complete tasks. Thus, teams are work groups whose membership is essential to the effective completion of some ongoing work (tasks using tools).

Task, Goal, or Feedback Interdependence

Saavedra et al. (1993) used a system for describing interdependencies of work groups based on task interdependence, goal interdependence, and feedback interdependence. Their definition of teams is based largely on the extent to which a work group is task-interdependent. In terms of task interdependence, teams are defined as groups that have "simultaneous and multidirectional work flows," such that "members jointly diagnose, problem solve, and collaborate to complete a task" (Saavedra et al., 1993, p. 63). This excludes groups with other types of task interdependencies (for example, sequential work flow) from the definition of team. On the face of it, this sort of exclusionary definition appears too limiting. However, because these authors beg the question of what is the *work* of a team, broader definition is possible.

Other Team Characteristics

In addition to McGrath et al.'s (1995) mapping of team work into tasks and the tools used to accomplish these tasks, other authors (Altman, 1966; Stevens & Campion, 1994; Gehrlein & Dipboye, 1992; Tesluk et al., 1997) have evolved means for classifying team work. As an illustration at the most general level, Stevens and Campion (1994; in press) distinguish between taskwork and team work, from which they derive more specific predictor constructs (see Klimoski, 1993). This is illustrative in the sense that the work of teams involves more than simply completing some set of individually performed tasks. Instead, there are additional coordination (Bowers, Braunn, & Morgan, 1997) and interpersonal facilitation aspects of team work (Van Scotter & Motowidlo, 1996). Using this to inform Saavedra et al.'s (1993) definition, to the extent that work group members depend on one another for information, ideas, social support, or any number of other sorts of team work, they can be referred to as teams even if their task work is less interdependent.

Teams are therefore identifiable by the interdependency and relative permanence of their membership. Team interdependence includes team work (coordination and support) components as well as task-related interdependency. Since the essence of management is the interdependence of two parties for the completion of a piece of work, teams are also by definition self-managing. Unlike crews, membership in teams is not easily interchangeable— which of course has enormous implications for selection decisions, as we will see. Teams also fulfill ongoing functions (as opposed to "one-shot" task forces), though this distinction is less important with respect to staffing decisions.

There are perhaps more commonalities between teams and task forces when teams are defined in this way. A particular concern for task forces that has largely been ignored in understanding team staffing is the need for appropriate representation (Cascio, 1995; Klimoski & Jones, 1995). Specifically, task forces may be constituted with members from critical constituencies such as departments, functional specialties, or labor groups. Whether representational issues are important to teams remains an important question. But there are several reasons to believe that they may make a difference. A few of these include the need for functional liaisons (for example, people with affiliations in marketing and engineering), the need for symbolic (as well as substantive) expertise for purposes of credibility (see Whitmore, 1985; Henry, 1995), the need to equalize potential power differentials in empowered teams (Donnellon, 1996), and the tendency of external allegiances to influence group decisions (Klimoski & Ash, 1974). We will assume that under certain circumstances representation is likely to be important, in addition to taskwork and team work components of team effectiveness.

In the next section, we will consider taskwork–team work–representation requirements to elaborate on selection decision making for teams at different points in their establishment. Individual characteristics that support taskwork and team work will be considered in addition to key representation. These requirements are summarized in Table 6.1.

Selection in Start-Up Teams

Staffing new teams with new members is probably not a very common event, at least for groups that are defined using the definitions of McGrath et al. (1995) and Saavedra et al. (1993). However, staffing teams with a more or less simultaneously assembled group with little or no knowledge of one another is probably common enough that some guidance would be helpful. Furthermore, many of the issues we identify for new teams may also hold for task forces, which are, of course, fairly common work groups. In particular, these are groups with important member-specific knowledge, skills, and abilities (KSAs) as well as general interpersonal

Table 6.1. Key Staffing Considerations at Different Points in Team Life Cycles.

Team Life Cycle	Criterion		
	Task Work	Team Work	Representation
Start-up	• Skill breadth • Skill preferences • Knowledge of teamwork	Individual: • Skills in training and role articulation • Ability to compromise • Comfort with proxies • Emotional competence Heterogeneity/homogeneity: • Problem framing • Strategic outlook • Social pessimism (−) • Authoritarianism • Social dominance • Participative orientation	• Functional area • Group affiliation • Credentials
Transitional	• Skill breadth, learning preferences • Social sensitivity • Cognitive motivation • Speed of processing • Episodic memory • Multiple predictors	Same as start-up, plus: • Conscientiousness level • Knowledge of staffing fundamentals • Innovative/adaptive style homogeneity	Same as start-up, plus: • Organizational or professional connections
Intact	• Knowledge of staffing procedures	Same as transitional, plus: • Knowledge of staffing process effectiveness	Same as transitional

KSA requirements. In addition, representation issues may be important in newly constituted teams.

Task Work Competencies

Skill depth and breadth are likely to affect team effectiveness. Consistent with the considerable literature on team self-management (for example, Hackman, 1987; Campion, Medsker, & Higgs, 1993; Janz, Colquitt, & Noe, 1997), team empowerment usually involves some form of job enrichment, that is, developing or establishing broad skills among individuals in the work group. So in addition to making sure that at least one member of the team has essential task competencies (depth of skills), it is likely that selection for new teams will involve finding people with many relevant task-related KSAs. Also, selection systems might incorporate the ability in team members to instruct each other and develop procedural skills together. In this way, the usual costs of training can be reduced by providing team members the internal skills required to train one another (see Manz & Sims, 1993). At least as important, this approach establishes a considerable self-management component (intertraining) from the very start of the team's life.

There are also some good reasons to expect that initial individual preferences for various types of relevant taskwork will have an impact on team effectiveness. Beyond individual motivational effects of preferences, new teams with broad within-member KSAs will be required to negotiate the tasks that individuals would like to perform or not perform (Graen, 1976). For example, in a research team where all members are able to perform all tasks, some members will enjoy developing research protocols, others will prefer collecting evidence, and others may enjoy data-analytic aspects of the team's work. These preferences are likely to find their way into the role negotiation process in several ways. Perhaps most obvious is the tendency of people to negotiate their roles according to personal preferences. This may not always be desirable, as in the case of a less able person being placed in a role that he or she prefers over a more able person with a lesser preference for that type of work. Awareness of such preferences and deliberately weighing them against abilities would therefore be a useful selection strategy.

A less obvious reason for taking preferences into account may occur when a particular taskwork KSA set is held by only one or two incumbents initially. This minority may be called on to present a case for a particular role to be enacted, based on their knowledge of this role's likely impact on team effectiveness. Minority influence is likely to be greatest where minorities are consistent and extreme (Wood, Lundgren, Ouellette, Busceme, & Blackstone, 1994), and such consistency and extremity often require considerable commitment to a view. This is of course predicated on seeing that role as desirable (a preference) or otherwise important to team functioning. Thus, individual preferences may be important for role negotiation and ultimate team effectiveness.

Team Work Competencies

Several studies have identified personality (Barry & Stewart, 1997; Wagner, Neuman, & Christiansen, 1996; Thoms, Moore, & Scott, 1996; Jordan, Ashkanasy, & Hartel, 1998; Driskell, 1992) and preference (Campion et al., 1993; Eby & Dobbins, 1995; Loher, Vancouver, & Czajka, 1994) as predictors of team member effectiveness and team effectiveness. In particular, four of the big five personality characteristics, including neuroticism, extraversion, agreeableness, and conscientiousness, have been shown to relate to individual performance (Wagner et al., 1996) and self-efficacy beliefs in intact work groups (Thoms et al., 1996) and to experimental group performance (Barry & Stewart, 1997). Egocentricity (Driskell, 1992) and social intelligence (Jordan et al., 1998) have also shown some promise as a predictors of team performance. Stated preferences for team work have been shown to relate to team and individual effectiveness (Eby & Dobbins, 1995; Campion et al., 1993).

Negotiation and Interpersonal Competencies

Although the general notion that certain broad personality characteristics and preferences should influence team performance has merit, we suggest that a more specific level of construct definition provides a more behaviorally relevant basis for prediction. This concept of "lower level" constructs is borrowed from Klimoski (1993), who suggests that broad, general constructs like personality (very broad level of abstraction) encompass more specific personality constructs (for example, the big five) and, ultimately, behavioral constructs. Put differently, little of the current evidence explains why personality characteristics and preferences may influence behaviors and team processes (Waung & Austin, 1997). Several possibilities deserve consideration. Consistent with the view of Hollenbeck, LePine, and Ilgen (1996), the role enactment process is an essential mediator of the personality–team performance relationship.

Following from this, some lower-level individual predictor constructs that might explain team process and performance include:

- Members' ability and willingness to articulate arguments for a role or for the enactment of their preferred role in real time
- Their willingness to compromise or develop role trade-offs ("I'll do this less preferred role for *X* months, then it will be your turn") in the interest of shared strategic outcomes
- Their willingness to trust in other team members' abilities to complete key roles
- Their emotional competence to maintain perspective on their own and others' emotional responses during conflict-laden role negotiations

Some of these are, of course, consistent with the existing literature on broader personality and preference predictors. For example, the extent to which people are willing to compromise and trust others relates to the personality predictor *agreeableness* (Costa & McCrae, 1988, 1992; Hollenbeck et al., 1996). In addition, Smith-Jentsch, Salas, and Baker (1996) have shown some support for the first proposition. Similarly, two studies (McKenna & McHenry, 1992; Waung & Austin, 1997) have provided some support for the second and third, and Jordan et al. (1998) for the fourth predictor construct in team settings.

Because teams are self-managing, some of the same individual characteristics that predict management success may also predict team success. For example, given that negotiation processes are likely to be important to team success, conflict resolution skills that have been shown to predict managerial performance may also be important (Olsen-Buchanan et al., 1998). Commonality with management skills also points to possible similarities in selection methods (that is, simulation-based assessment in addition to paper-and-pencil inventories) for teams.

Team Work KSAs

In addition to skills and preferences, knowledge about the operation of teams may be important to start-up teams. Stevens and Campion (1994; in press) have shown that team work KSAs, which consist primarily of an understanding of effective team processes, predict performance in teams. Some of the process knowledge dimensions included in the instrument they have devised include goal setting, work-sharing arrangements, conflict-resolution strategies, decision-making tools, and sensitivity to group communication. Individual understanding of team work functioning is therefore a potentially important selection issue, particularly for start-up teams.

Heterogeneity

In addition to individual-level behavioral predictors in team settings, predictor constructs that deal with the heterogeneity or mix of individual characteristics may be extremely important to team functioning (Wagner et al., 1996; McKenna & McHenry, 1992). Although the research on demographic heterogeneity (greater or less representation by demographic groups in teams) has shown relationships between heterogeneity (so defined) and team processes (see Galarza & Dipboye, 1996), we agree with Jackson and Ruderman (1995) that demographic diversity is only one type of group heterogeneity.

Following from our preference for establishing team predictor constructs closer to the behavioral domain, we suggest looking beyond broad demographics and social identity to more specific psychological constructs. For example, for some tasks, having greater diversity among team members in terms of problem framing (Galarza & Dipboye, 1996; Jackson, 1992) and social dominance (Shaw & Harkey, 1976; Heslin, 1964) may lead to greater team effectiveness. In contrast, team member homogeneity when it is a question of problem-solving approaches, strategic outlooks, tendency to trust others, and effective ways of dealing with emotions may predict team effectiveness. Taking each of these in turn, we suggest that

- Homogeneity in norms for problem framing and decision making bypass the need for team members to agree on problem definitions, thus facilitating timely problem solving.
- Agreed-on end states and strategies for achieving these reduce the need for discussion of such strategies at each decision point, which again reduces the time to problem resolution.
- Assuming that everyone is aiming for the same ends and shares common strategies, it is also necessary for team members to be able to act independently without either fear of negative feedback or fear that other group members are not fulfilling their important functions. In other words, an individual needs to trust other group members to complete their own tasks and not interfere with his or hers.
- Effective responses to emotional events are implied in various approaches to conflict resolution. For example, ineffective coping with emotional responses might include immediate retaliation in response to perceived slights, which would tend to be divisive in team problem solving.

Although evidence for these hypotheses is scarce and mostly indirect, data from a recent study reported by Stevens and Yarish (in press) provide clearer support for the use of some of these lower-level constructs in team selection. Factor analysis of a personality–biodata inventory used in a team environment yielded five factors that were predictive of production team performance using mean team level and intermember heterogeneity as predictors. These included social dominance, authoritarianism, social pessimism, individual achievement, and participative orientation. Table 6.2 describes the results of this inventory, which is currently being cross-validated.

Representation

Klimoski and Jones (1995) suggest that selection to teams be based on more than abilities, preferences, and personality. *Political selection* (Cascio, 1995), or selection on the basis of representation, may be an important consideration in team staffing. Including team members from important functional areas with known group affiliations

Table 6.2. Correlations Between
Team Personality and Team Effectiveness.

	Performance		Process	
	Effectiveness	Safety	Process	Role Definition
Social dominance (n=38)				
Level	.22	−.01	−.06	.28
Variability	−.45**	−.11	−.12	−.31
Authoritarianism (n=38)				
Level	−.43**	−.41**	−.35*	−.51**
Variability	−.28	−.35*	−.34*	−.43**
Social pessimism (n=41)				
Level	−.30	−.19	−.31*	−.26
Variability	−.37*	−.02	−.09	−.38*
Individual achievement (n=36)				
Level	−.18	−.11	.06	−.32
Variability	−.14	−.15	−.32	−.47**
Participative orientation (n=35)				
Level	−.04	−.17	.18	.07
Variability	−.44**	.12	−.07	.02

Note: n represents number of teams.

*$p < .05$

**$p < .01$

or particular credentials may establish credibility of the team approach in the broader organizational context. What this suggests for people responsible for team staffing is that they consider seeking input from multiple constituencies and specialties to help determine team membership. Although this may actually make the role definition process more difficult—because team members will have diverse viewpoints and constituent accountabilities—in the long run it may increase the organization's acceptance of team formation and team decisions. Still, the inherent difficulties in role definition with this approach may make selection based on personality and preference even more critical. Also, care should be taken to avoid "tokenism" in representational selection.

Selection in Transitional Teams

There are generally two types of transitional teams. The first type occurs when a new work team is created using current but unaffiliated employees. This situation presents many of the same concerns that occur in the formation of new teams with new employees, a subject that was discussed in the previous section. This section will look instead at the second type of transitional team, discussing selection concerns that arise during attempts to change existing groups into self-managing or semiautonomous teams. It will be seen that some of the generalizations for new teams hold for this situation as well, but they will be tempered by differences in the teams' interaction requirements and in the staffing process itself.

Task Work Competencies

For one thing, training will usually be in progress under transitional circumstances. This means that ability to develop necessary KSAs quickly is likely to be very important: new team members will need to be "quick studies" (Fromkin, Klimoski, & Flanagan, 1972). Related to this, selection during transition needs to account for existing-member skills gaps: instead of looking mainly for broad KSAs, fairly specific skills may be targeted. This requires a sort of within-team analysis based on previous role definition. In the process of deciding about new hire roles, existing team members may take the opportunity to "shift" their less-preferred roles to the new hires, which presents considerable challenges to staffing specialists who have been assigned to assist these teams.

In both set-role and shifting-role scenarios, extreme situational specificity is implied in the selection process. This creates a formidable challenge to existing principles and guidelines for selection, because the position, not the job, is the unit of analysis, and selection is therefore not standardized or evaluated across all positions for a particular group of jobs. Positions are defined each time the staffing process is put into motion: after a single job opening occurs, position analysis is done. We do not have any quick solutions to this problem, but extension of sociometric selection (Van Zelst, 1952a, 1952b; Colarelli & Boos, 1992; Jin, 1993) to include teams making their own position descriptions (in addition to hiring decisions) may require some changes to existing guidelines and principles. We will have much more to say about this type of selection in the next section (which discusses selection for intact teams).

Also, there may be a case for consistent use of selection for broad KSAs, even when very specific KSAs are needed. First, this means that all team members are treated alike in the selection process, which reduces the problems of position-based selection. Second, the new team member once hired will have the opportunity to take part in negotiation over "who does what," rather than having existing team members make that decision among themselves. Finally, although broad KSAs will not necessarily deal with specific needs, the new person may not need to be trained to the same extent as someone with fewer, more narrow KSAs.

Regardless, the ability to understand the team's "mental model" of performance quickly (Kraiger & Wenzel, 1997) should be considered an essential ability. When members act as proxies for one another or need to anticipate the behaviors of others, shared mental models of the team's work are likely to enhance team effectiveness (see, for example, Dickinson & McIntyre, 1997). Although the ability to comprehend team mental models is likely to be important, it probably consists of a combination of other abilities and personality characteristics. For example, this ability may extend beyond general taskwork competency (discussed earlier) or social sensitivity (discussed in the next section) in the sense that both are probably required, but neither is in itself likely to be sufficient to predict comprehension of the transitional team's formative mental model of their work. Likewise, cognitive motivation (Cacioppo, Petty, Feinstein, & Jarvis, 1996) may play a role in a new member's ability to comprehend quickly the complexities of the team's evolving mental model, but it is probably not especially useful as a single predictor. Team work KSAs may cover some of the declarative knowledge important to developing shared mental models but may not account for preference and procedural skills. Of course, mental abilities such as speed of processing and episodic memory may contribute to the quick understanding other members' views of the team's work. In general, as with other prediction problems, multiple predictors may be needed to account for the ability to quickly understand team mental models.

Team Work Competencies

Although similar personality and preference issues may influence effectiveness in both new and transitional teams, an additional set of these variables becomes important in transitional teams. These arise from the problem of newcomers gaining acceptance into the transitional team (Graen, 1976; Katz, 1982; Fromkin et al., 1972). It is quite likely that transitional teams will be experiencing some doubts about themselves individually and as a group. This may lead them to experience external stimuli (such as newcomers) as threatening (see Gladstein & Reilly, 1985).

For new members to gain acceptance into the team, they may need not only to establish credibility but also to make themselves appear to be nonthreatening. This might include such things as asking questions (versus making statements) and deferring to others initially. It might also mean being a quick study for recognizing the group's social norms, because violations of norms could be construed as threatening or detrimental to the group's emerging efficacy.

Although there is very little evidence with respect to predictor constructs in this area, three studies (Jordan et al., 1998; Waung & Austin, 1997; Nadig, Jex, & Beehr, 1994) provide some suggestive evidence. Jordan et al. (1998) have developed a measure of emotional intelligence, a multidimensional construct that consists of awareness of one's own and others' emotions, as well as ability to manage others' emotions. These authors suggest that emotional intelligence may serve as a potential predictor of team performance. Waung and Austin (1997) found that team level of conscientiousness influenced norm development, goal choice, and commitment and that these predictably affected performance. Nadig et al. (1994) found that the fit between innovative and adaptive cognitive style had some influence on turnover and strain in simulated teams. These studies posited lower-level constructs as predictors of team effectiveness or (in the case of Waung & Austin, 1997) translated broader constructs into lower-level behavioral constructs. Again, these more behavioral constructs are likely to provide for better prediction than broader (for example, big five) constructs.

Representation

As in new teams, representation may be a key concern in selection for transitional teams. For example, a position on the team may need to be filled as a result of turnover of one or more members with key organizational or professional connections. In this case, in addition to concerns over social sensitivity, KSA breadth, and ability to learn quickly about the team's shared mental model, the new member may need to be selected from the same functional specialty as the previous member. Similarly, teams in transition may discover over time that a key functional specialty is missing from their current KSA mix. When selecting a new member from this specialty, the team may want to be cognizant of the representational "baggage" or agendas that may come with members from this functional specialty. For example, the team may choose someone who is "tapped into" a larger professional or functional network. Or they may choose someone who is deliberately divorced from the professional identity that goes with a functional area.

Implicit in this is that selection decisions for the team are done by the team. This so-called sociometric approach (Van Zelst, 1952a; Colarelli & Boos, 1992) carries with it some potential for representational problems in selection. Consider, for example, a group of team members on a team who all graduated from the same school. This group may exert a strong influence over the team's selection decisions based on school affiliation of potential team members. Such an affiliation may be indicative of a particular approach to problems or to work in general. Consequently, shared mental models may actually be enhanced by a selection based on representation. Or common backgrounds may lead to unfair, ineffective, and costly selection decisions.

Representational sociometric selection may also affect the preferences of team members for working with one another, which in turn may influence team affect. If team members are able to select their "most preferred coworker," then there may be (at least temporarily) an increased sense of potency (Guzzo, Yost, Campbell, &

Shea, 1993) in the team. Similarly, selections made purely on the basis of representation (versus KSAs, personality) may be met with considerable skepticism by members who are looking for a capable and agreeable new teammate.

Regardless of the possible problems or advantages of sociometric selection, this approach is likely to send a message of empowerment to the transitional team. The relative success or failure of the selection process may have an important effect on the team's later behaviors. That is, the feedback from their decision (good choice or bad choice) may help the team to get a better idea of their abilities as a team to make such decisions. It may also alter their later decision routines. In addition to team-level feedback of this sort, recognition of the expertise of individual team members (Henry, 1995; Libby, Trotman, & Zimmer, 1987) may be an important consequence of feedback from the selection process.

For the staff assigned to support the team's sociometric decision, a more or less systematic process can be implemented. Specifically, support staff may want to develop with the team some selection criteria (taskwork, team work, and representational dimensions), assist in recruitment of new members, sit in on the development of a skilled candidate short list, and monitor the final selection process and its conclusion. The staffing professional's role may involve pointing out problems and trade-offs in the team's decision making during meetings. Or more formal training of teams in the staffing process may be required.

Selection in Intact Teams

Ultimately, if a team is largely self-managing, then by definition it will be largely self-staffing. This is why training teams to develop their own staffing plans and procedures during the learning process (the transition stage) may be essential in order to make sure the self-staffing process is fair, legal, and effective. Much of this comes from clear definition by the team of the shared mental model of its work. Because the process of role clarification itself may be important for team effectiveness (Salas et al., 1997), it may be useful to take this step even without any immediate staffing need; a strategic consideration of how to replace each current member might follow from this. In any case, it should be noted that this is more than simple sociometric selection: teams must do their own analysis of needs, writing position descriptions (including KSA, personality, and representational requirements), and recruiting potential candidates before actual selection procedures.

This extension of sociometric selection to include teams making their own decisions through the staffing process may require changes to current guidelines and principles. For example, first, the broader definition of job analysis to include team work analysis requires careful consideration, based on some of the initial research in this domain. Second, and following from this, as team members alter the nature of the team to reflect real or perceived staffing needs, *position-level analysis* may be required. Establishing guidelines for this very small *N* situation presents important challenges to traditional job analysis. Third, explicitly establishing representational requirements, in addition to KSAOs, may be important adjuncts to team work analysis.

It is also important to realize that, despite relative differences in importance of predictors depending on team life cycle, many of the taskwork, team work, and representational requirements of intact high-performing teams are likely to be generalizable. In particular, intact teams may need to concern themselves more with the personality predictors important for transitional teams than with the personality predictors for new teams. Similarly, representational issues in transitional teams are likely to be important for intact teams as well.

Implications for Validation and Evaluation

Evaluating selection systems for teams follows the same logic as evaluating individual selection devices in many cases. But team selection validation also involves challenges associated with program evaluation, levels of analysis, and generalization different from common selection system evaluation for individuals. In this concluding section of the chapter we will first reiterate some of the common evaluation issues (content sampling, criterion referencing, and so on), and then turn to special program evaluation problems—particularly those dealing with team self-staffing. Of course, some of the evaluation issues will be relevant to all stages in the team life cycle, and others more to start-up, transitional, or self-managing teams.

Beyond the Usual Trinity

Landy (1986) referred to the content, criterion-related, and construct validation approaches outlined in the *Principles for the Validation and Use of Personnel Selection Devices* (Society for Industrial and Organizational Psychology, 1987) as the *validation trinity*. His view, which we share, is that segmenting validation into only three types of evidence is an oversimplification. Validation can include many types of evidence (Ghiselli, Campbell, & Zedeck, 1981) and is actually a unitary notion. Nevertheless, it is important to establish that the content of a predictor measure relates to the job (content validation), that it is predictive of important organizational outcomes (criterion-related validation), and that it is associated in a theoretically expected fashion with other indicators (construct validation). These certainly should be standards against which we compare predictor *measures* in team selection.

The question becomes quite a bit more complicated, however, by the fact that individual-level predictor measures are being used to infer and predict team- and even organization-level outcomes. In addition, team characteristics may not be easily translated into individual characteristics. For example, representation of various external groups may be vested in an individual: How well will this individual represent the interests of this external group? What are individual corollaries of team and external organizational representation? We offer several preliminary suggestions for dealing with these and other level-of-analysis problems.

But first, it should be noted that several useful guidelines have been offered when measuring team-level phenomena. These are largely aimed at establishing a case for team (versus individual-level) constructs. They include having a theoretical rationale for establishing a team-level construct, using the team as the implied or explicit subject of measurement, and (for mean level composites) empirically demonstrating high within-group agreement (see Tesluk et al., 1997; James, Demaree, & Wolfe, 1993; Roberts, Hulin, & Rousseau, 1978).

Team Work Analysis

As we discussed in the first section, team work analysis is the corollary for task analysis and worker requirement development. Establishing the nature of the team's work, its interdependencies, and the requirements of the team and its members is an essential first step in establishing predictor constructs. In addition to using traditional job analysis to determine individual task work and KSAs, suggestions have been offered for identifying team-level task work, team work, and their individual and compositional requirements (McGrath, et al. 1995; Tesluk et al., 1997; Saavedra et al., 1993; Gehrlein & Dipboye, 1992; Altman, 1966).

Task Work

First, in addition to understanding individual tasks, understanding interdependent team tasks may be an important step toward developing worker requirements. Very little has been done to elaborate on test methods for discovering the nature of these interdependencies in recent years. However, Altman (1966) provides a review and critique of several group task analysis systems (Roby & Lanzetta, 1958; Hare, 1962; Thibaut & Kelley, 1959; Shaw, 1962). Of the approaches he critiques, Altman argues that only two (Roby & Lanzetta, 1958, and Shaw, 1962) are adequately comprehensive. Roby and Lanzetta describe the inputs and outputs of both groups and tasks in their descriptive, distributive, and functional aspects. Shaw's system (on which Saavedra et al., 1993, base theirs) relies on ten dimensions to describe group tasks. Altman suggests that these are still inadequate because they confuse levels of analysis; he then offers his own approach.

Altman's system uses an actor-referent-object approach, which resembles a facet analysis (Elizur & Guttman, 1976) of a basic task statement. This approach relies on the bottom-up analysis of individual behaviors, followed by analysis of the referents and purposes of tasks. Altman argues that, from these, requirements can be more easily inferred. Using Altman's words, "Tasks can be described in terms of *actors* (person 1, person 2, group, environment) who can initiate interactions, their possible *referents,* or loci of interaction, the available *forms of interaction,* for example, ask, inform, infer, evaluate, and the focus or *objects* (person, group, environment) of interaction. In addition, object properties can be described in terms of their *state-action* (static-dynamic) characteristics, their *temporal locus* (past, present, future)" [emphasis in original] (p. 213). In addition to these facets of group tasks, Altman describes participant relationship dimensions, including "hierarchical relationship, task dependency linkages, temporal linkages and directional relationships among participants" (pp. 214–215).

Although fairly complex, Altman's approach appears to have some promise, at least for providing a heuristic for team task work analysis. Tasks are broken down into dimensions that can then be scaled and evaluated by subject matter experts (SMEs). These dimension ratings, in turn, can be used to infer team and worker requirements. In essence, the approach identifies the individual or group level of tasks (the actor), the level of cognitive complexity involved (interaction form), the recipient (referent) of the group's action, and whether the task is aimed at some present, past, or future state or process (object characteristics).

Another team task work issue that should be considered is mental workload (Bowers et al., 1997). In addition to the usual mental workload associated with completing individual tasks, teams may be required to expend significant resources and time coordinating their activities. This means that the relative mental resources available for individual tasks will be diminished. Although successful self-managing teams have presumably devised ways to deal with this, start-up teams and transitional teams may experience considerable trouble developing efficient ways to balance team and task work (see Jones & Lindley, 1998).

Team Work

With respect to team work, several approaches may have some promise as job-analytic tools. Tesluk et al. (1997) suggest that greater interdependence implies greater need for interpersonal competencies. We have also posited a number of potentially important worker requirements for team work. Identifying the behavioral components that make these more or less important remains a significant issue, and it will ultimately rely on empirical approaches derived from systems like Altman's. Meanwhile, worker-oriented job-analytic methods, such as Abod, Gilbert, and Fleishman (1996) have developed, should prove useful. Using dimensions described here and elsewhere, and relying on SME ratings of the importance of these dimensions, will provide a temporary solution to the larger problem of linking team work behaviors to individual worker requirements.

Beyond this, perhaps the greatest challenge to team work analysis is the derivation of composition requirements. Whether the team should be homogeneous or heterogeneous, for example, is a problem that has received some attention. Galarza and Dipboye's (1996) meta-analytic evidence suggests that production tasks are better served by homogeneity than are creative problem-solving tasks. However, personality and preference diversity may be more important (and more appropriate) as selection constructs than demographic diversity. Therefore, we need to know much more about task moderators of diversity-effectiveness relationships using psychological diversities as predictors.

Ultimately, an analytic method that integrates team structures and functions with demands of team work and psychological composition will aid in this decision making. Currently, several promising field studies provide some initial guidance for developing such a system (Campion et al., 1993; Campion, Papper, & Medsker, 1996; Hyatt & Ruddy, 1997; David, Pearce, & Randolph, 1989; Janz et al., 1997). However, the direct or interactive effects of psychological composition have been largely left out of these studies. Without a clear idea of how psychological composition relates to the task and team work characteristics that influence effectiveness, it will remain difficult to make recommendations for practitioners.

Representation

Given the probable need to account for representational needs, an explicit analysis of these needs before and during the staffing process is probably well-advised. There is very little research to guide representational analysis. Some early work by Davis (1953) provides a starting point for evaluating the networks that exist in organizations.

Similarly, O'Reilly and Roberts (1977) operationalize intergroup links in a field study. In general terms, these analyses should seek to discover key constituencies, functional liaison requirements, needs for symbolic expertise, and potential problems associated with power differentials and external allegiances. In the absence of more systematic methods, it may be advisable to canvas other areas inside and outside the organization with possible stakes in the team selection process.

Criterion-Related Validation

In addition to careful consideration of the content and methods for team staffing, criterion-related validation will still be a feasible evaluation methodology for many selection devices. Our main suggestion with regard to this is to separate criterion-related evaluation of team- and individual-level predictors.

For task-work predictors, the individual level of analysis will be appropriate for most cases. For example, considering individual depth and breadth of performance capacity as well as individual preferences in relation to individual performance criteria is quite appropriate. However, combined analysis of the team's overall KSA breadth in relation to team performance may also be important. This may simply mean treating individual abilities as compensatory with respect to each other and forming a composite, or it may mean doing more complex analyses that take noncompensatory and interactive combinations of members' abilities into account. In addition, the inclusion of preferences for new team selection suggests development of a more complex placement strategy, such as the "cut and fit" approach (Cascio, 1997) that incorporates both KSAs and preferences as predictors.

Similarly, for interpersonal skills and team work KSAs, individual-level prediction is clearly appropriate. However, some predictors derived from team work constructs will require evaluation at the team level. In particular, heterogeneity of teams on personality predictors is by definition a team-level construct. In addition to heterogeneity, levels of these and some member KSA constructs may also have meaning in aggregate (at the team level).

Evaluation of Self-Staffing Teams

Evaluation designs that have more in common with training and other kinds of program evaluation may be required to determine the effectiveness of teams in managing their own staffing decisions. For example, time-series analysis of team effectiveness across selection decisions and process analysis of decision-making routines may be more logical than traditional criterion-related evaluation designs. This is because self-selecting teams are likely to be making very specific decisions, incorporating a number of variables for a given selection decision. Instead of concerning themselves with standard selection devices, they may base their team selection decisions on particular needs of the moment in addition to some of the more general team work requirements we have discussed.

Team Life Cycle Considerations

This issue becomes especially complicated as the team changes through its life cycle. Using traditional criterion-related validation may be very sensible for new teams at both the individual and the team levels. As mentioned earlier, some team work predictors (for example, conflict resolution skills) may be usefully evaluated using criterion-related designs because they are appropriate across situations. Similarly, validation of team-level heterogeneity predictors using criterion-related designs should be useful.

However, if roles are in flux—as in transitional teams, for example—selection procedures may be difficult to validate. As mentioned earlier, self-selecting teams may have even greater reason to alter the bases of decisions about KSAs depending on immediate, position-level analyses (as opposed to job analyses) that may identify very specific needs. For example, the loss of an old team member may leave an effective current team member without an important ally. Selection for the new position may therefore involve peculiar compatibility issues. Establishing criterion-related validity using traditional aggregated data designs may be complicated under these conditions. However, selection methods that use human judges (assessment centers, interviews) may provide flexibility here, by incorporating position needs into the judgment process.

Representation Issues

Perhaps the most difficult task in validation of selection decisions is to justify and evaluate representational requirements. Great caution should be taken to avoid "black box" thinking about representational issues. Substantive reasons (for example, liaison capabilities, functional expertise, or credibility) should probably take precedence over purely symbolic representation.

Construct Validation

Eventually, practitioners will be best served by a comprehensive and parsimonious understanding of team work analysis and predictor constructs. Achievement of such an end would allow for broad generalizability of team predictor constructs and synthetic validation of predictor measures. This is why, in this chapter, we have taken a construct validation approach by developing predictor constructs using existing theories and research on team effectiveness. But our efforts will only succeed if continued efforts are made by academic-practitioner teams to evaluate and clarify predictor constructs and to evaluate the self-staffing process more generally.

It is safe to say that currently we do not know much about team staffing when it comes to most of the constructs discussed in this chapter. With respect to operational problems, such as analyzing team tasks, Altman (1966, p. 209) suggested that "gross conceptualizing must eventually reach down into application and tryout; inductive approaches must reach up to conceptual formulations. So far, there has not been much movement in either direction, probably because of recency of work on the problem. It will be interesting to review this problem again in a few years." Ironically, this was written over thirty years ago, and we still do not know much about team work analysis. We hope that the next thirty years will be more productive.

References
Abod, E. T., Gilbert, J. A., & Fleishman, E. A. (1996). *A job analysis method to assess the interpersonal requirements of work*. Paper presented at the meeting of the Society for Industrial and Organizational Psychology, San Diego.
Altman, I. (1966). Aspects of the criterion problem in small group research II. The analysis of group tasks. *Acta Psychologica, 25,* 199–221.
Arrow, H. (1998). *Teams, crews, and task forces: A structural typology of work groups*. Paper presented at the meeting of the Society for Industrial and Organizational Psychology, Dallas.
Barry, B., & Stewart, G. L. (1997). Composition, process, and performance in self-managed groups: The role of personality. *Journal of Applied Psychology, 82,* 62–78.
Bowers, C. A., Braun, C. C., & Morgan, B. B., Jr. (1997). Team workload: Its meaning and measurement. In M. T. Brannick, E. Salas, & C. Prince (Eds.), *Team performance assessment and measurement*. Hillsdale, NJ: Erlbaum.

Cacioppo, J. T., Petty, R. E., Feinstein, J. A., & Jarvis, W.B.G. (1996). Dispositional differences in cognitive motivation: The life and times of individuals varying in need for cognition. *Psychological Bulletin, 119,* 197–253.

Campion, M. A., Medsker, G. J., & Higgs, A. C. (1993). Relations between work group characteristics and effectiveness: Implications for designing effective work groups. *Personnel Psychology, 46,* 823–850.

Campion, M. A., Papper, E. M., & Medsker, G. J. (1996). Relations between work group characteristics and effectiveness: A replication and extension. *Personnel Psychology, 49,* 429–452.

Cannon-Bowers, J. A., & Salas, E. (1997). A framework for developing team performance measures in training. In M. T. Brannick, E. Salas, & C. Prince (Eds.), *Team performance assessment and measurement.* Hillsdale, NJ: Erlbaum.

Cascio, W. F. (1995). Whither industrial and organizational psychology in a changing world of work? *American Psychologist, 50*(11), 928–939.

Cascio, W. F. (1997). *Applied psychology in personnel management* (5th ed.). Upper Saddle River, NJ: Prentice-Hall.

Colarelli, S. M., & Boos, A. L. (1992). Sociometric and ability-based assignment to work groups: Some implications for personnel selection. *Journal of Organizational Behavior, 13,* 187–196.

Costa, P. T., & McCrae, R. R. (1988). From catalogue to classification: Murray's needs and the five factor model. *Journal of Personality and Social Psychology, 55,* 258–265.

Costa, P. T., & McCrae, R. R. (1992). *NEO revised personality inventory professional manual.* Palo Alto, CA: PAR.

Cummings, T. (1978). Self-regulating work groups: A socio-technical synthesis. *Academy of Management Review, 3,* 625–634.

David, F. R., Pearce, J. A., & Randolph, W. A. (1989). Linking technology and structure to enhance group performance. *Journal of Applied Psychology, 74,* 233–241.

Davis, K. S. (1953). A method for studying communication patterns in organizations. *Personnel Psychology, 6,* 301–312.

Dickinson, T. L., & McIntyre, R. M. (1997). A conceptual framework for team measurement. In M. T. Brannick, E. Salas, & C. Prince (Eds.), *Team performance assessment and measurement.* Hillsdale, NJ: Erlbaum.

Donnellon, A. (1996). *Team talk.* Boston: Harvard Business School Press.

Driskell, J. E. (1992). Collective behavior and team performance. *Human Factors, 34,* 277–288.

Eby, L. T., & Dobbins, G. H. (1995). *Preference for working in teams: An individual and group analysis.* Paper presented at the meeting of the Society for Industrial and Organizational Psychology, Orlando.

Feldman, D. C. (1984). The development and enforcement of group norms. *Academy of Management Review, 9,* 47–53.

Fromkin, H. L., Klimoski, R. J., & Flanagan, M. F. (1972). Race and competence as determinants of acceptance of newcomers in success and failure of work groups. *Organizational Behavior and Human Performance, 7,* 25–42.

Gabarro, J. J. (1987). The development of working relationships. In J. W. Lorsch (Ed.), *Handbook of organizational behavior.* Upper Saddle River, NJ: Prentice-Hall.

Galarza, L., & Dipboye, R. L. (1996). *The effect of group heterogeneity on group performance: A meta-analysis.* Paper presented at the meeting of the Society for Industrial and Organizational Psychology, San Diego.

Gehrlein, T. M., & Dipboye, R. L. (1992). *Dimensions of group tasks in the workplace.* Paper presented at the meeting of the Society for Industrial and Organizational Psychology, Montreal.

Ghiselli, E. E., Campbell, J. P., & Zedeck, S. (1981). *Measurement theory for the behavioral sciences.* New York: Freeman.

Gladstein, D. L., & Reilly, N. P. (1985). Group decision making under threat: The tycoon game. *Academy of Management Journal, 28,* 613–627.

Graen, G. B. (1976). Role making processes within complex organizations. In M. D. Dunnette (Ed.), *Handbook of industrial and organizational psychology.* Skokie, IL: Rand McNally.

Guzzo, R. A., Yost, P. R., Campbell, R. J., & Shea, G. P. (1993). Potency in groups: Articulating a construct. *British Journal of Social Psychology, 32,* 87–106.

Hackman, J. R. (1987). The design of work teams. In J. W. Lorsch (Ed.), *Handbook of organizational behavior,* pp. 315–342. Upper Saddle River, NJ: Prentice-Hall.

Hallam, G. L., & Campbell, D. (1992, April). *Selecting people for teams? Start with a theory of team effectiveness.* Paper presented at the meeting of the Society for Industrial and Organizational Psychology, Montreal.

Hare, A. P. (1962). *Handbook of small group research.* New York: Free Press.

Henry, R. A. (1995). Improving group judgment accuracy: Information sharing and determining the best member. *Organizational Behavior and Human Decision Processes, 62,* 190–197.

Heslin, R. (1964). Predicting group task effectiveness from member characteristics. *Psychological Bulletin, 62,* 248–256.

Hollenbeck, J. R., LePine, J. A., & Ilgen, D. R. (1996). Adapting to roles in decision-making teams. In K. R. Murphy (Ed.), *Individual differences and behavior in organizations.* San Francisco: Jossey-Bass.

Hyatt, D. E., & Ruddy, T. M. (1997). An examination of the relationship between work group characteristics and performance: Once more into the breech. *Personnel Psychology, 50,* 553–585.

Jackson, S. E. (1992). *Diversity in the workplace.* New York: Guilford Press.

Jackson, S. E., & Ruderman, M. N. (1995). Introduction: Perspectives for understanding diverse work teams. In S. E. Jackson & M. N. Ruderman (Eds.), *Diversity in work teams.* Washington, DC: American Psychological Association.

James, L. R., Demaree, R. G., & Wolfe, G. (1993). R_{wg}: An assessment of within-group interrater agreement. *Journal of Applied Psychology, 78,* 306–310.

Janz, B. D., Colquitt, J. A., & Noe, R. A. (1997). Knowledge worker team effectiveness: The role of autonomy, interdependence, team development, and contextual support variables. *Personnel Psychology, 50,* 877–904.

Jin, P. (1993). Work motivation and productivity in voluntarily formed work teams: A field study in China. *Organizational Behavior and Human Decision Processes, 54,* 133–155.

Jones, R. G., & Lindley, W. R. (1998). Issues in the transition to teams. *Journal of Business and Psychology, 13,* 31–40.

Jordan, P. J., Ashkanasy, N. M., & Hartel, C.E.J. (1998, April). *Work group emotional intelligence profile (WEIP): A measurement of emotional intelligence in work teams.* Paper presented at the meeting of the Society for Industrial and Organizational Psychology, Dallas.

Katz, R. (1982). The effects of group longevity on project communication and performance. *Administrative Science Quarterly, 27,* 81–104.

Kirkman, B. L., & Rosen, B. (1997). A model of work team empowerment. In W. A. Pasmore & R. W. Woodman (Eds.), *Research in organizational change and development* (Vol. 10, pp. 131–167).

Klimoski, R. J. (1993). Predictor constructs and their measurement. In N. Schmitt, W. C. Borman, & Associates (Eds.), *Personnel selection in organizations* (Chapter 4). San Francisco: Jossey-Bass.

Klimoski, R. J., & Ash, R. (1974). Accountability and negotiation behavior. *Organizational Behavior and Human Performance, 11,* 409–425.

Klimoski, R. J., & Jones, R. G. (1995). Staffing for effective group decision making: Key issues in matching people and teams. In R. A. Guzzo & E. Salas (Eds.), *Team effectiveness and decision making in organizations* (Chapter 5). San Francisco: Jossey-Bass.

Kraiger, K., & Wenzel, L. H. (1997). Conceptual development and empirical evaluation of measures of shared mental models as indicators of team effectiveness. In M. T. Brannick, E. Salas, & C. Prince (Eds.), *Team performance assessment and measurement.* Hillsdale, NJ: Erlbaum.

Landy, F. J. (1986). Stamp collecting versus science: Validation as hypothesis testing. *American Psychologist, 41*(11), 1183–1192.

Libby, R., Trotman, K. T., & Zimmer, I. (1987). Member variation, recognition of expertise, and group performance. *Journal of Applied Psychology, 72*(1), 81–87.

Loher, B. T., Vancouver, J. B., & Czajka, J. (1994). *Preferences and reactions to teams.* Paper presented at the meeting of the Society for Industrial and Organizational Psychology, Nashville.

Manz, C. C., & Sims, H. P., Jr. (1993). *Business without bosses: How self-managing teams are building high performing companies.* New York: Wiley.

McCrae, R. R., & Costa, P. T. (1989). The structure of interpersonal states: Wiggins' circumplex and the five factor model. *Journal of Personality and Social Psychology, 56,* 586–595.

McGrath, J. E., Berdahl, J. L., & Arrow, H. (1995). Traits, expectations, culture, and clout: The dynamics of diversity in work groups. In S. E. Jackson & M. N. Ruderman (Eds.), *Diversity in work teams: Research paradigms for a changing workplace.* Washington, DC: American Psychological Association.

McKenna, D. D., & McHenry, J. J. (1992). *The chemistry of personality compounds: Effects on team productivity.* Paper presented at the meeting of the Society for Industrial and Organizational Psychology, Montreal.

Mohrman, S. A., & Mohrman, A. M. (1997). Fundamental organizational change as learning: Creating team-based organizations. In W. A. Pasmore & R. W. Woodman (Eds.), *Research in organizational change and development* (Vol. 10, pp. 197–228).

Nadig, V., Jex, S. M., & Beehr, T. A. (1994, April). *Cognitive style and cognitive climate: Effects of fit/non-fit.* Paper presented at the meeting of the Society for Industrial and Organizational Psychology, Nashville.

Northcraft, G. B., Polzer, J. T., Neale, M. A., & Kramer, R. M. (1995). Diversity, social identity, and performance: Emergent social dynamics in cross-functional teams. In S. E. Jackson & M. N. Ruderman (Eds.), *Diversity in work teams.* Washington, DC: American Psychological Association.

Olsen-Buchanan, J. B., Drasgow, F., Moberg, P. J., Mean, A. D., Keenan, P. A., & Donovan, M. A. (1998). Interactive video assessment of conflict resolution skills. *Personnel Psychology, 51,* 1–24.

O'Reilly, C., & Roberts, K. (1977). Task group structure, communication, and effectiveness in three organizations. *Journal of Applied Psychology, 62,* 674–681.

Roberts, K. H., Hulin, C. L., & Rousseau, D. M. (1978). *Developing an interdisciplinary science of organizations.* San Francisco: Jossey-Bass.

Roby, T. B., & Lanzetta, J. T. (1958). Considerations in the analysis of group tasks. *Psychological Bulletin, 55,* 88–101.

Saavedra, R., Earley, P. C., & Van Dyne, L. (1993). Complex interdependence in task-performing groups. *Journal of Applied Psychology, 78,* 61–72.

Salas, E., Mullen, B., Rozell, D., & Driskell, J. E. (1997). *The effects of team building on performance: An integration.* Paper presented at the meeting of the Society for Industrial and Organizational Psychology, St. Louis.

Shaw, M. E. (1962). Scaling group tasks: A method for dimensional analysis. *JSAS Catalogue of Selected Documents in Psychology, 3* (Ms. 294).

Shaw, M. E., & Harkey, B. (1976). Some effects of congruency of member characteristics and group structure upon group behavior. *Journal of Personality and Social Psychology, 34,* 412–418.

Smith-Jentsch, K. A., Salas, E., & Baker, D. P. (1996). Training team performance-related assertiveness. *Personnel Psychology, 49,* 909–936.

Society for Industrial and Organizational Psychology. (1987). *Principles for the validation and use of personnel selection procedures.* College Park, MD: Author.

Stevens, M. J., & Campion, M. A. (1994). The knowledge, skill, and ability requirements for team work: Implications for human resource management. *Journal of Management, 20,* 503–530.

Stevens, M. J., & Campion, M. A. (in press). Staffing work teams: Development and validation of a selection test for team work settings. *Journal of Management.*

Stevens, M. J., & Yarish, M. E. (in press). Training and development for team effectiveness. In *Supporting work team effectiveness.* San Francisco: Jossey-Bass.

Tesluk, P., Mathieu, J. E., Zaccaro, S. J., & Marks, M. (1997). Task and aggregation issues in the analysis and assessment of team performance. In M. T. Brannick, E. Salas, & C. Prince (Eds.), *Team performance assessment and measurement.* Hillsdale, NJ: Erlbaum.

Thibaut, J., & Kelley, H. H. (1959). *The social psychology of groups.* New York: Wiley.

Thoms, P., Moore, K. S., & Scott, K. S. (1996). The relationship between self-efficacy for participating in self-managed work groups and the big five personality dimensions. *Journal of Organizational Behavior, 17,* 349–362.

Trist, E. (1981). *The evolution of socio-technical systems: A conceptual framework and an action research program.* Toronto: Ontario Quality of Working Life Centre.

Van Scotter, J. R., & Motowidlo, S. J. (1996). Interpersonal facilitation and job dedication as separate facets of contextual performance. *Journal of Applied Psychology, 81,* 525–531.

Van Zelst, R. H. (1952a). Sociometrically selected work teams increase productivity. *Personnel Psychology, 5,* 175–185.

Van Zelst, R. H. (1952b). Validation of a sociometric regrouping procedure. *Journal of Abnormal and Social Psychology, 47,* 299–301.

Wagner, S. H., Neuman, G., & Christiansen, N. (1996, April). *The composition of personalities in work teams and team job performance.* Paper presented at the meeting of the Society for Industrial and Organizational Psychology, San Diego.

Walsh, J. P., Henderson, C. M., & Deighton, J. (1988). Negotiated belief structures and decision performance: An empirical investigation. *Organizational Behavior and Human Decision Processes, 42,* 194–216.

Waung, M., & Austin, J. T. (1997). *The effects of conscientiousness on group goal selection, commitment, and quality norm development.* Paper presented at the meeting of the Society for Industrial and Organizational Psychology, St. Louis.

Whitmore, M. D. (1985). The impact of ability and behavioral style on perceptions of credibility and actual influence under conditions of varying solution specificity. Doctoral dissertation, The Ohio State University.

Wood, W., Lundgren, S., Ouellette, J. A., Busceme, S., & Blackstone, T. (1994). Minority influence: A meta-analytic review of social influence processes. *Psychological Bulletin, 115*(3), 323–345.

CHAPTER 7

Cultural Context in Adapting Selection Practices Across Borders

Gill Nyfield
Helen Baron

In writing this chapter we draw on our experience as consultants working for SHL Group plc, an organization that operates in thirty-seven countries around the world, including the Far East, Europe, South Africa, and North America. We work with large international organizations as well as local concerns. From the beginning we have always worked with local psychologists and managers in order to adapt our procedures and instruments to match the local cultural needs of our clients.

This chapter attempts to highlight some key issues that must be tackled in adapting selection procedures across borders. It is not comprehensive—it would need a whole book to describe the way assessment is seen in each country. It is very much a practitioner's view and concentrates on three issues important to those who work in the international arena:

- Trends in selection practices around the world
- Issues to consider in adapting selection procedures for different countries
- Selection of managers to work internationally

Trends in Selection Practices Around the World

It might be expected that selection practices differ from country to country. In a recent survey of large organizations in fourteen different countries that we completed with Anne-Marie Ryan at Michigan State University, one of the surprises was the degree of similarity among practices around the world.

The survey was sent to three hundred large employers in each of fourteen countries, and we received back between 27 and 112 from respondents in each country. The survey was quite detailed. Respondents described their typical recruitment and selection practices for both managers and their largest group of nonmanagers. The figures in this chapter relate mostly to the managerial data. Generally, trends were similar for the nonmanagerial groups, but we have noted a few of the differences in the text. Although these samples are small in some places, the results are very similar to those found in other comparative studies with larger samples in fewer countries (for example, Shackleton & Newell, 1997).

Although the responses showed a consensus about many issues, for each question there were countries that bucked the trend, and each country differed from the consensus in some aspect of standard practice. Of course, by focusing on large employers, who are more likely to be influenced by international trends, we may have received a more consistent picture of world trends and practices within a country than actually exists.

It is also important to remember that any generalizations about practices in a country are just that. They will be untrue of many individual organizations. To say that cognitive ability tests are used widely in the United States or that many selectors in the United States are wary of using cognitive ability tests because of fear of legal challenge are both reasonable generalizations—but each statement alone suggests a more uniform picture of practice than really exists. It is important to resist the natural tendency to generalize more broadly in areas with which we are less familiar and assume more consistency in practice elsewhere than we know exists in our own region.

Caveats aside, the results mirror our experience in working around the world as well as the findings of other such surveys: it is possible to use similar selection procedures around the world. In management selection, we have used an assessment center designed around competencies in many different countries. Both the competencies and exercises transfer to the new culture. What often needs adapting are the behavioral indicators that signal the presence or absence of a competency (see the following section on adapting selection procedures).

Figures 7.1, 7.2, and 7.3 show some of the survey results. (For fuller results see Ryan, McFarland, Baron, & Page, 1999.) The first figure shows that job descriptions are used almost universally, with the exception of Poland. Sifting measures such as educational qualifications and application forms are also widely used. The low use of the application form in Sweden is because of greater use of the curriculum vitae (CV). This finding also raises one of the problems with translation. In most countries our question about application forms was understood to include CVs, but in Sweden the language, although on the face of it similar, excluded the CV. The results for use of biodata are much more variable and may reflect a different interpretation of the term in some countries.

Figure 7.2 shows the use of different selection techniques. Interviews and references are the most common, with tests and exercises used to a lesser extent. Differences are noticeable in the way these techniques are used. Although in most countries one-on-one interviews are most common, in Australia and the Netherlands a panel approach is preferred. A few countries (Belgium, the Netherlands, Poland, and Portugal) report using cognitive tests more often than personality measures, but for other countries the opposite is true. This may be surprising to readers in the United States—where cognitive measures are used most widely—although we have experienced an increasing trend toward the use of personality measures in the United States in the last few years.

Job trials are used relatively infrequently with managers in most countries, but they are more frequently used with lower-level jobs everywhere. References are more popular, but in some countries an employer's reference is preferred and in others a personal reference is preferred. Family connections are generally little used for references.

One of the most well-documented differences in the use of selection methods is the popularity of graphology in France. Around

Figure 7.1. Use of Sifting Measures Across Countries.

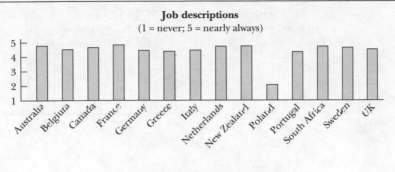

Job descriptions
(1 = never; 5 = nearly always)

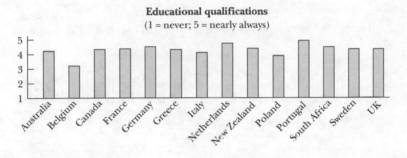

Educational qualifications
(1 = never; 5 = nearly always)

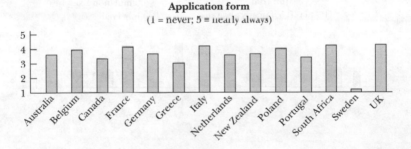

Application form
(1 = never; 5 = nearly always)

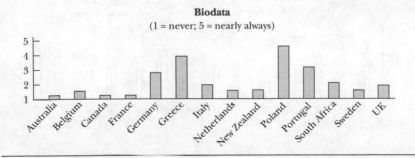

Biodata
(1 = never; 5 = nearly always)

Figure 7.2. Use of Assessment Techniques Across Countries.

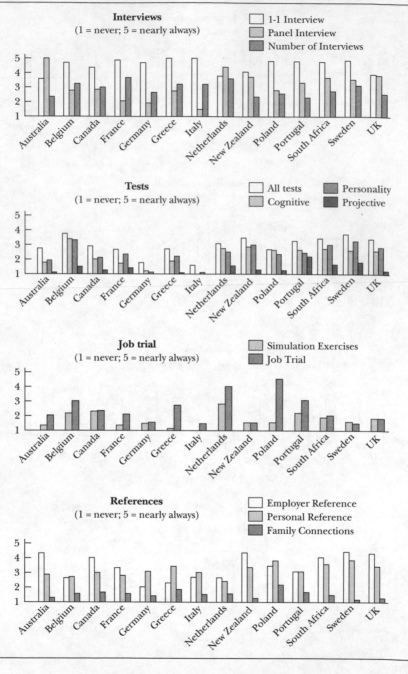

half the companies we surveyed in France included it in managerial selections, with use on a much smaller scale in Belgium (where the French-speaking Walloons often follow French cultural habits) and in South Africa. Shackleton and Newell (1997) found similar results. This is an interesting phenomenon given the failure of studies to show any validity for the technique (for example Ben-Shakhar, 1989). However, it is very much in line with the French approach to making selection decisions. An analytic approach to the individual is evident in the relatively frequent use of projective tests in selection in France, a preference for individual over panel interviews, and the use of more interviews. Our results suggest an average of 3.5 (Figure 7.2), and Di Milia, Smith, and Brown (1993) found 92 percent of their sample of French companies used more than one interview.

The reactions of candidates and local managers are also important. Not surprisingly, a study of the acceptability of different selection procedures among French and U.S. college students showed that French subjects found graphology considerably more acceptable as a selection method than did the American students (Steiner & Gilliland, 1996). Many managers from other countries are astounded that graphology is still used.

Arminas (1998) explains the relatively low use of ability testing in Russia as a function of wariness of less well-known techniques. This indicates that it can be important to show respect for local traditions to retain a positive image of the employing organization among applicants, particularly when selecting in a very competitive market. It is important to listen to and understand the approach used locally and adapt innovations rather than impose a set approach. Imposition may be counterproductive if local managers distrust the approach, and lack of adaptation can make procedures ineffective. We discuss some of these issues in more detail in the next section.

Figure 7.3 looks at some of the process issues in assessment procedures. Again, there are some consistencies across countries. In most countries a candidate for a managerial post can expect to be assessed for around six hours, with the Swedish sample spending longest with candidates (over eight hours on average) and the Polish sample typically taking just over four hours. Around 50 percent of companies in all countries report assigning numerical

Figure 7.3. Process Issues in Assessment Procedures.

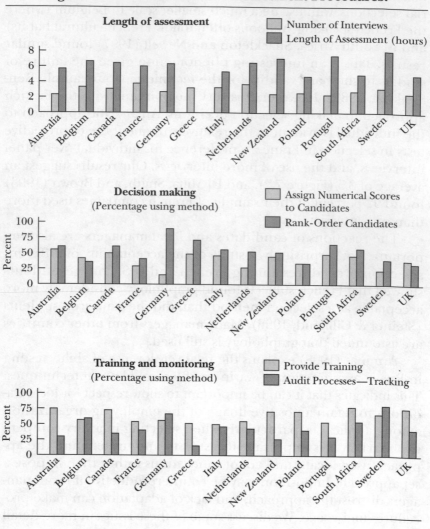

scores to candidates or rank-ordering them. This quantitative approach was most popular in Germany, with France, Poland, Sweden, and the United Kingdom tending to take a more qualitative approach to decision making.

We were surprised at how frequently companies reported providing training and auditing procedures. Training was most used in the predominantly English-speaking countries, with Germany and Sweden being most likely to perform audits of processes.

More generally, differences in practices across the world may result from diverse historical trends as well as differences in country cultures. Cultural differences between nations in business practices have been examined by a number of people, including Hofstede (1991) and Trompenaars and Hampden-Turner (1993). Each suggests dimensions along which cultures can be measured.

Hypotheses of how countries might approach selection decisions can be derived from several of the Trompenaars and Hampden-Turner dimensions. We will discuss some of the findings of our survey, as well as our own experience, in the context of several of these dimensions.

Universalism Versus Particularism

Universalist cultures tend to follow what they see as universal codes of practice and rules. They value literal adherence to contracts and favor rational arguments. *Particularist* cultures put more emphasis on relationships and are willing to bend the rules to accommodate particular circumstances and individual needs. They feel it is important to allow their actions to be influenced by their relationship to others.

Those in a universalist culture would be more likely to take a procedural approach to selection decisions, using objective methods and trying to verify information. In contrast, an organization in a particularist society might focus on getting to know the individual. Selectors might take into account an individual's circumstances—whether he needed a job—as well as the needs of the organization. Wang (1997) describes selection decisions in China as usually relying heavily on economic and personal information with little emphasis on job tasks.

Trompenaars and Hampden-Turner classify Australia, Portugal, Canada, and the Netherlands as strong universalists, whereas countries such as Belgium, France, Greece, and Italy are much more particularist. Our results show the particularist countries tend to use more interviews in selection, and like France, do not favor the panel interview at all (see again Figure 7.2). Only around 20 percent of respondents from these countries indicated that they used a structured interview in contrast to over 50 percent in Australia and Canada. (All countries use more structured interviews with nonmanagerial staff.) For a particularist the interview is a conversation between two individuals, and attempts to structure and "objectivize" the process are likely to be resisted.

In more universalist societies, such as Australia, Germany, Sweden, and the Netherlands, the panel interview is used much more frequently. Organizations in these countries are likely to take more notice of objective evidence such as educational qualifications (see Figure 7.1) and to try to rank-order candidates when making decisions. They are also more likely to engage in a formal audit of their selection process (see Figure 7.3).

When it comes to verifying information, Germany and Greece are significantly more likely to ask for written documentation of credentials than other countries, whereas Belgium and Poland seem much more trusting in this regard. In the Indian subcontinent, candidates come to the interview armed with their certificates and degrees and would feel slighted if these were not examined. An American interviewer might be surprised by a candidate waving credentials, whereas a Pakistani interviewer would be wary of claims to qualifications that a candidate could not support with documentation.

Neutrality Versus Emotion

This dimension is about taking a detached neutral approach as opposed to paying more attention to one's emotional responses. In neutral countries, organizations are likely to prefer a neutral approach to gathering selection data—they might put more emphasis on the candidate's intellectual skills—whereas in an emotional culture, the selector's emotional response to the candidate would have more influence than what the candidate can actually do. The

Japanese and Chinese are renowned for their reserved approach, and in our survey, Poland and New Zealand are strongly neutral in approach. Southern Europeans, Germans, and those in many South American countries are more emotional. Again, the latter are the countries that rely heavily on the one-to-one interview.

Furthermore, our experience is that in these countries the interview is used somewhat differently than in more neutral countries. A Spanish or Indian interviewer may be more influenced by the affective content of the exchange than a northern European. A restrained English presentation or an impenetrable Japanese calmness might be interpreted as dullness or lack of interest; concentration on the facts of an experience might be seen as failing to understand the emotional content.

Of course, just the opposite would occur with a northern European interviewer and a more emotional interviewee. This candidate might seem overexcitable and undependable. The interviewer might be frustrated by the difficulty of gaining a clear account of the candidate's experience in a particular area. It is interesting that training of selectors is more common in the more neutral countries (see again Figure 7.3). Is it the need to be able to see past the presentation to the evidence that requires training, or the importance of controlling one's own emotions in interacting with the candidate in a less natural way?

We noticed a similar difference in the way personality profiles were interpreted around the world. We have found that many Japanese companies look for candidates who have moderate profiles with no extreme scores, whereas European users are often looking for people who are unusually high or low on certain scales—very extroverted or highly conscientious, for example.

Achievement Versus Ascription

Achievement-oriented cultures focus on what individuals have achieved and how effectively they perform. People are judged by what they have done. New managers have to prove themselves to their staff. *Ascriptive* cultures show more respect for position and title. Respect for superiors is important, and often the wisdom of age is highly valued. In selection, achievement-oriented countries are likely to focus more on an individual's experience, college grades, subjects studied, and so on. In an ascriptive society, selectors are likely to be more impressed by an individual's background—whether he or she has studied at a prestigious university or worked for a market-leading company. They might put more weight behind people who can provide impressive references.

The United States, the land of opportunity, is seen as very achievement oriented, whereas the countries of the Middle East and Far East are seen as more ascriptive. In our sample, those in achievement-oriented countries such as Australia, Canada, New Zealand, Sweden, and the United Kingdom were more likely to seek employer references on candidates (see again Figure 7.2) than ascriptive countries such as the Netherlands, Poland, Greece, Italy, and Germany. Canadians in our survey reported almost universally contacting previous employers by phone. In achievement-oriented countries psychometric instruments were also used more often. Cognitive ability tests and personality questionnaires were most commonly used in those countries, and work samples were fairly common with nonmanagerial groups. Sparrow and Hiltrop (1994) suggest that the negative attitudes of the Catholic church toward psychological testing have led to low levels of use in predominantly Catholic countries. Interestingly, when it came to managers, Italy followed the low test use typical of an ascriptive and Catholic country, but this trend was reversed for nonmanagerial staff, where ability test use was quite common. This may be the result of local conditions, where the public sector's importance as an employer and the political need for appointments to be seen to be fair has promoted the use of objective assessment. In Portugal we also found widespread use of tests in both managerial and nonmanagerial grades.

Many of the areas significant to ascriptive cultures were not addressed in our survey. For example, we did not ask people what it was about educational qualifications or previous experience that was important. However, some questions did provide information. Achievement-oriented countries were more likely to use a rank-ordering procedure to make final selection decisions (Figure 7.3). Polish respondents showed a much stronger tendency to use family connections in selection decisions (Figure 7.2) and the scoring of background information with a biodata approach was relatively common in some of the more ascriptive countries (Figure 7.1). We know from our own practice that the importance of attending the correct school and university is high in Japan and elsewhere in the Far East.

Although these are not the only cultural dimensions along which countries differ, they seemed most relevant to selection. Other dimensions may be more pertinent to different aspects of HR management. Individual versus communitarian values influence the way people are managed and rewarded in organizations.

Diffuse cultures tend to merge business and personal matters, and they favor an overview approach to people and issues. Specific cultures are more likely to require people to work toward specific objectives, and they take little interest in employees' private affairs. This dimension also has an impact on the acceptability of feedback on performance. In specific societies—such as the United States—criticism is not taken so personally, and the techniques of 360-degree feedback have wide acceptance. In more diffuse cultures—like China—such an approach is more difficult to use because work performance is not separated from general estimation of self-worth. Any negative feedback on performance is likely to be perceived as a personal criticism.

It is possible to make too much of these differences between countries. The consistencies between the different countries in recruitment and selection are as evident in the charts as are the differences. The use of the interview, job descriptions, educational qualifications, and application forms are near-universal. In all countries, tests, simulations, and job trials are used to some extent, although less frequently. Still, what these instruments are designed to assess and what are seen as their strengths and weaknesses may well differ from country to country.

Adapting the Selection Procedure

Thus, although we have concluded that there are a lot of common practices across the world, selection procedures and instruments do, of course, need to be adapted for the local country. For example, what you include on an application form in the United States may not be the same as in the United Kingdom or France.

Candidates

Before talking about adapting specific selection techniques, it is worth briefly considering the candidates themselves and attracting candidates.

Candidates for the same type of position can differ considerably across countries—in work experience, educational background, and age. Differences may be related to the way the position is perceived, the level of remuneration of the position, and the social status it holds. This has implications for the level of assessment appropriate for each country and has particular impact on global assessment procedures, such as an assessment center where candidates from different countries with very different experiences and expectations of the recruitment process participate together. Some may have more experience with a particular assessment method than others. A common practice now is to offer preparation and practice materials—so that individuals have a better idea of what to expect and how they are to be assessed—and if possible, some actual practice questions for methods such as tests and in-basket exercises.

Candidates for similar jobs differ across countries for a variety of reasons. In some countries, educational or vocational qualifications control the applicant pool very strictly. For example, in the Middle East employers demand, and candidates respect the need for, very specific qualifications. Economic as well as social conditions sometimes result in each stratum of jobs being open only to those of a certain wealth and status. This contrasts strongly with the open systems of countries like the United States, where it is seen as enterprising for a candidate to compete for a job that might seem out of her range. Differences in candidates may also be the result of local economic employment conditions. For example, in Northern Ireland it is very common to find university graduates applying for basic clerical roles. There are just not enough higher-level jobs for the number of students graduating, so they end up competing for positions with much less qualified sixteen- to eighteen-year-olds. Clearly, these differences in the candidate pool will have implications for appropriate sifting techniques. For instance, reasoning tests may be less effective with overqualified groups because job performance differences are less likely to be caused by differences in cognitive ability. When testing, there may be little variance in scores or even ceiling effects on tests.

Methods of attracting candidates also differ. Whereas in most countries recruitment companies will provide employers with a list of suitable candidates for a role, the way in which they, or indeed the employers themselves, attract these candidates in the first place may differ, particularly at senior levels. For example, in the United States search firms are used by most large companies for middle managers and up. The lack of national newspapers makes it difficult to conduct nationwide appeals. However, in countries such as the United Kingdom and in much of Europe national newspapers do exist and have become an extremely well-established way of attracting not only middle-level managers and professionals but also, increasingly, more senior-level staff. Indeed, it is often only the very senior appointments that rely on search agencies alone.

The Internet has had a great impact on attraction of candidates in the last year or two, particularly in the United States. This has provided not just a nationwide "readership" but a worldwide one as well, and the growth of the MonsterBoard and similar recruitment Web sites in the United States demonstrates its success. Use of the Internet and associated technology in other parts of the world has still some way to go to catch up with the United States, but it no doubt will, causing us to reexamine our attraction and selection procedures and tools dramatically in future years.

Local Culture

In adapting selection techniques to the local culture, the use of educational qualifications as a sift illustrates some of the issues that need to be taken into account.

Educational Qualifications

Educational achievements translate poorly across cultures. Most countries have a reasonably demanding high school finishing exam that will often be used locally as a sift for assessment. The French baccalauréat and English "A" levels are examples. However, this type of qualification is much less available in the United States, with many states having only locally administered standards that differ greatly. Is it appropriate to compare a U.S. high school finishing certificate with the baccalauréat, which requires a generally higher standard across subjects, or with "A" levels, which require a high standard (equivalent to at least the first year of college in the United States) but across a much narrower range of subjects? There is an intrinsic difficulty here: without a real knowledge of the educational qualifications of different countries, how they compare, what proportion of populations achieve different standards, and what the expected standard for entrance to different job levels would be, the selector is not going to be able to make sensible recommendations that can work across cultures.

Cognitive Tests

When working with psychometric tests, cultural adaptation is almost as large a task as the initial development process. Many users naively assume that a good translator is all that is required. We have developed considerable knowledge in adapting tests across the many cultures we operate in. In fact, the process of translation and adaptation provides a set of items that must be considered in the same way as the results of the initial item-writing process. Translation should therefore be conducted involving bilingual local psychologists and subject matter experts rather than just professional translators. The items need to be reviewed and put to trial, both for the usual psychometric properties and for suitability to the culture.

Experience has shown that what seems like universally acceptable content matter can prove to be inappropriate in surprising ways. For example, a series of numerical reasoning items around a table of life expectancies could not be used in Italy, where the content of the table was felt to be far too close to the taboo subject of death. A verbal reasoning passage about simple health and safety requirements did not work in some Asian countries because of incredulity that employers would make provision for the workers before ensuring the safety of expensive equipment. It may be thought that nonverbal tests are less open to these problems, but even here issues occasionally arise. Orthodox Jewish candidates in Israel object to shapes based around a cross, and pictures of pigs are unacceptable to Muslims.

On a more general basis, it is wise if possible to avoid questions relating to specific places, use of time (twelve-hour versus twenty-four-hour clock), measurements (metric verses imperial), and currency (different currencies, orders of magnitude of amounts, and also the effects of any dramatic changes in the economic situation such as devaluation). Omitting these areas can make the questions seem a little sterile, and so often a balance is needed with very careful use of data.

The International Committee on Test Standards is producing standards on translating instruments. From a practical point of view these are very exacting (Hambleton, in press). There is a substantial problem of showing equivalence of measurement after translation. The question of norms also needs to be addressed. Are we sure that different language versions of the test are of the same difficulty? Is it enough for the candidates to be at the seventieth percentile in their own country group or should there be a common standard? If an education system emphasizes a particular part of the syllabus, this can lead to generally better test scores in that area. Should this higher level of performance be neutralized through local norms (candidates from other countries could perform as well if they had had the same opportunities) or be noticed in common norms (candidates with more background can perform at a higher level)? It is not always possible to provide perfect answers to these sorts of questions, but knowledge of where differences are likely to arise can at least allow selectors to make informed choices.

Personality Measures

If such questions arise with ability tests, how much more so with personality instruments? Surprisingly, in addition to considerable evidence that the main underlying constructs of personality—such as the big five—hold across cultures (Paunonen, Jackson, Trzebinski, & Forsterling, 1992; Barrett, Petrides, Eysenck, & Eysenck, 1998), it is our experience that more detailed basic constructs also commonly exist.

SHL has developed the Occupational Personality Questionnaire (OPQ), a thirty-scale work-oriented behavioral questionnaire that is used by many thousands of companies in more than forty countries across the world. It is available in twenty-seven languages:

American English	German	Norwegian
Arabic	Greek	Polish
Canadian French	Hungarian	Portuguese
Cantonese	Italian	Romanian
Czech	Indonesian	Russian
Danish	Japanese	Spanish
Dutch	Korean	Swedish
Finnish	Mandarin	U.K. English
French	Mexican Spanish	Vietnamese

In addition, the U.K. English version is used in Australia, Hong Kong, India, Ireland, New Zealand, Singapore, and South Africa.

We have found that it is possible to have questionnaires that work similarly across cultures and indeed validate equally well across cultures. In an international study comparing British, American, and Turkish managers, similar scales correlated with a series of performance dimensions (Nyfield, Gibbons, Baron, & Robertson, 1995). For instance, managers rated as more innovative in approach were significantly more extroverted and less conscientious in all three countries.

However, sometimes the way personality constructs express themselves in different cultures is very different. Going to a party may be interpreted as an extroverted activity in the United States. In Malaysia it can reflect attachment to traditional ways, because parties are more likely to be family events than drunken "raves." The use of idioms can make questionnaires seem more user-friendly, but idioms tend not to adapt to translation. "I like to beat my colleagues" relates to competitiveness in the United Kingdom and the United States, but it has a considerable more physical meaning in the Far East!

Items like "tend to have old-fashioned values" have a different meaning in cultures where traditional values are still highly supported. For instance, in much of the Far East and among some groups of New Zealanders, agreeing would not necessarily mean you favor existing or established approaches in work.

Response Style
One of the greatest differences we have found between cultures is response style. Traditionally, personality questionnaires have used

some form of multiple-choice rating scales for a normative response–type format. For example, look at the following statements:

I am assertive in groups.

I like to help others.

I can sell ideas to others.

I manage to relax easily.

A normative approach might ask candidates to rate each statement on a five-point scale, from "strongly agree" to "strongly disagree." However, for selection purposes people in some cultures will tend to answer as they think the employer would like them to be, rather than as they see themselves. This behavior is often the result of a strong cultural value on pleasing others as much as an attempt to fake good answers. This is particularly so in the Far East and in southern Europe, where responses tend to favor one end of the scale strongly, making the questionnaire less useful. Interestingly, the United States is one of the places where we find that normative questionnaires work best.

To overcome this response pattern we have used *ipsative*-style questionnaires for most parts of the world. Here candidates read the same four statements but are asked to choose the ones that are most and least true of themselves. Essentially, people rank their behaviors. This approach can be problematic with small numbers of scales, but over a large number (thirty in our case) it provides very similar profiles and validation evidence to the normative style (Baron, 1996; Bartram, 1996; Saville, Nyfield, Sik, & Hackston, 1991). It has enabled companies to use personality data in their selection decisions when it just was not possible before.

Simulation Exercises

For assessment methods such as group activities and in-baskets, although the exercises and tasks typically work well across countries (with local adaptation) the assessors need to be aware of the different behaviors that candidates will exhibit to demonstrate competencies such as leadership and assertiveness. An illustration of this can be seen in the behavior of some Indian managers in a group exercise at a development center. They talked constantly,

one over another, in a manner that to our British view was both
rude and counterproductive to any serious discussion. But local assessors explained that this was the way discussion went on normally.
A person who waited for a turn to speak would never manage to
make a contribution. People were expected to speak and listen simultaneously, and the persuasive individual managed in the end to
dominate the discussion. The Indian managers needed to have an
assertive presence and interpersonal skills, but the indicators we
would have usually looked for were inappropriate in this context.

Another example of different behavioral indicators can be seen
in cultures where it is not acceptable to disagree openly. Candidates will nominally assent to everything that others are saying but
will also present a reasoned argument for what they believe, even
if it is the opposite point of view. It is therefore important for assessors to be aware of these differences. Ideally, assessors should
be drawn from the countries represented by the candidates. Conclusions of those less familiar with the culture should be discussed
openly to ensure they are appropriate.

Interviews

The interview is widely used everywhere. However, its purpose and
objectives can differ greatly across countries. Many of the different
trends have been discussed in the first section of this chapter. For
the interviewer from another country it requires the greatest degree of cultural sensitivity to interview elsewhere. The candidate's
behavior must be evaluated correctly, but the interviewer's behavior must be appropriate as well. The way the candidate is met and
greeted, how questions are asked, the body language used, what is
said and what is left unspoken—all are subject to strong cultural
conventions. Local managers can be useful informants about the
correct nuances of behavior.

In certain parts of the world it is not thought acceptable to comment on how well one has done on a task. When asked how well
something has gone or, indeed, to identify their strengths, candidates in the Middle East will often reply that their boss would be the
most appropriate person to answer the question! Other examples
of culture-specific practices are bowing, use of first name or family
name, and touching or shaking hands.

The interview is used not just as a selection tool but features in many management processes such as goal setting, performance management, and review. The same sorts of issues will arise in these contexts. An American employee is likely to engage in active negotiation over goals or performance review ratings. The same processes in the Philippines or Japan are likely to show the employee taking a more passive role and accepting the manager's suggestions. This behavior is a result of deference to higher status as well as the expectation that a manager will set appropriate goals and assess the employee fairly. It does not mean that the employee is lacking in self-confidence or unable to take a more active approach when required.

Legal Issues

Laws concerning recruitment and selection differ around the world. In many countries the system is totally unregulated. In others there are requirements to register vacancies with government offices, notify appointments, and the like. Statutes may relate to how information is stored or give certain groups (for example, the long-term unemployed) precedence. Often the most bureaucratic requirements are the least respected, but it is important to clarify any local regulations.

Equal opportunities statutes, where they exist, usually have the greatest impact on selection procedures. This is particularly so in the United States, where strong legislation combined with a tradition of individuals claiming their rights has led many employers to be very defensive in their procedures. Outsiders recruiting in the United States for the first time would do well to get legal advice.

European Union countries have had legislation outlawing gender bias in selection and employment for some time, although not all countries enforce it with equal vigor. The United Kingdom and Australia both have wider-reaching legislation that has been relatively actively enforced for some years, and this is an increasing trend elsewhere. For instance, both Ireland and Hong Kong have recently passed laws in this area.

Although there are common themes, not all legislation covers the same areas. Gender, race, age, disability, religious affiliation, and trade union membership may or may not be covered. Also, traditional discrimination practices can lead to different emphases. The United States has always preferred the energy of youth, so age-discrimination legislation protects those over forty. In Australia young people have had difficulty finding employment, so in that country age legislation protects the young. Irish legislation specifically protects those from traveling communities.

Selecting Managers to Work Internationally

Today's more global economy means that, increasingly, companies have operations in more than one country. Multinationals are now coping not only with their organizational culture but also with a variety of country cultures. This has the greatest impact at senior levels. When identifying and developing senior managers of the future, companies now seek people who are more international in outlook and can effectively work across the different cultures. Flexibility in succession planning creates a drive to allow the movement of managers from one country to another. All these factors are increasing the number of managers required to work internationally, yet many organizations are coping with a high failure rate with staff on foreign assignments.

Understanding what makes a successful international manager can help companies make better selections for these roles. A study carried out by Dr. Sue Henley at SHL to identify the relevant competencies involved over a hundred international managers. Data were collected using repertory grid techniques and identified eleven major competency groupings that appear critical to success in the international arena. They are listed in the following paragraphs in order of importance.

Flexibility

As would be expected, flexibility refers to the ability to be flexible and to tolerate situations where there is a lot of ambiguity. Those who are very rigid and structured in their approach and dislike changing their plans at short notice tend to be less able to adapt to the needs of another culture.

Open-Mindedness

More successful managers are open-minded and willing to adopt new ideas and different ways of doing things. They are more inquisitive and also seen as less orthodox.

Adaptability

As expected, more successful managers are seen as more adaptable. They are often generalists rather than specialists and take a broad view instead of interpreting information from just one perspective. They are able and willing to take on a wide variety of tasks and are likely to have had broad, cross-functional career paths. They can also successfully manage people across a range of functions.

Interpersonal Sensitivity

Those who are more successful are seen as more sensitive to others. They tend to be thoughtful and considerate, to be influenced by the needs of others, and to care for the welfare of employees and the wider community. They listen well and are willing to compromise, having understood the issues from other people's points of view.

Cultural Sensitivity

Good international managers are not only culturally aware but exhibit strong sensitivity in their behavior, which always takes into account the local factors.

Sociability

Successful managers are sociable individuals. They relate easily to many types of people and are socially skilled and diplomatic. They are seen as good communicators, delivering information clearly, frequently, and proactively. They also readily engage people in conversation and are able to put them at ease. They tend to have a large network of friends and contacts and like working with others—for example, in teams—whether socially or at work.

Strategic and Visionary Thinking

More effective managers are seen as taking a strategic and broader view. They have and are able to communicate a clear vision of the business.

Leadership Skills

Effective managers are described as strong and willing leaders. They easily take on the role and are prepared to provide direction, being decisive and wanting to be in control of events. However, their style is participative and consultative rather than authoritarian, involving others in a relaxed and nonstatus-conscious fashion.

Energy

Successful managers are seen as having considerable energy, and they are ambitious. They have high personal standards and are willing to work hard to achieve their objectives. They have drive and determination and tend to succeed in difficult situations.

Intellectual Capability

Successful managers are seen as above average in intellect. They are interested in information; they actively seek it and approach problem solving in an analytical manner.

Resilience

Effective managers are resilient individuals. They are not easily put off and readily bounce back from setbacks. They are optimistic in outlook and have a "can-do" mentality.

Other, less strong factors found were the following:

Political Awareness and Sensitivity

Effective managers are more sensitive to the internal politics of an organization. They are aware of the issues and tend to use them to their advantage.

Commercial Orientation and Experience

Having a strong commercial awareness and being knowledgeable about operating businesses in different countries, preferably through actual experience, is an advantage.

Family Support

Lastly, a noncompetency factor was identified as being key to a successful placement. Although having family support does not, of course, guarantee success, a lack of family support was a commonly cited reason for failure. This is now a well-acknowledged issue, and organizations tend to provide support facilities for both the manager and the family to minimize the risk.

These characteristics resemble those found by other researchers. For example, the Institute of Personnel and Development (1997), having reviewed a number of case studies, concluded that strategic awareness, adaptability, and sensitivity to different cultures were the most important. Ronen (1989) produced a similar list. There is much in common between these lists of competencies for an international manager and competencies generally associated with being a good manager; however, the priorities are different. Key areas for international managers are often of only moderate importance for other managers. However, it is interesting that some of these characteristics are becoming more important for the effectiveness of managers who continue to work in their own countries. Perhaps because many organizations are constantly changing, managers are working in unfamiliar environments, and this accounts for the increased importance of being able to learn, being flexible, and being open-minded.

However, one big difference for managers working domestically or abroad relates to family support. As indicated earlier, lack of family support is often cited as a reason for failure of international managers, but this rarely appears in lists of factors affecting nationally based managers. Other differences might include a greater emphasis on leadership among local managers than among those based internationally.

The implications of this kind of research are that there are additional issues to consider when selecting people for international assignments. The positive side is that very few of the competencies depend on actual foreign experience. It should be possible to develop and then select individuals who have a high probability of success as managers abroad.

Conclusion

Selection across borders can be very different from selection in a single country, although overall the similarities among countries are stronger than the differences. Sensitivity to the way competencies express themselves in different cultural domains is important, as is a good local knowledge of relevant educational and employment practices.

Trends suggest that the international business world is becoming more uniform. The increasingly global nature of markets means that few firms can afford to ignore what happens outside their borders. Many are now operating, as well as buying and selling products, in more than one country. The multinational corporation has an increasing role in the economies of most nations.

Over the years we have noticed a continual process of harmonization of approaches to selection across the world. Organizations show an ever-increasing interest in how things are done elsewhere—at least those organizations that talk to international consultants like ourselves. Particularly noticeable at the moment is the interest in Western approaches in the countries of Eastern Europe following the breakup of the Soviet Union.

Improvements in communications technology, such as e-mail, the Internet, and videoconferencing, enable offices of an organization across the world to be in constant touch. The head office can exert more effective control on local operations, and staff from different parts of the world can share ideas more easily.

A result of all this internationalization is that business practices from one country, including recruitment and selection, are becoming more familiar in other countries. Large firms often try to transport their ways of doing things to operations in other countries, and managers in less developed countries may try to emulate what they see these high-profile organizations do.

The drive to become more economically effective is also influencing the ways in which organizations assess their staff. Keeping ahead of the competition through technological solutions is more difficult with the wider availability and faster spread of innovations, so the attention is now turning to improving the quality of the people employed in order to provide the business with a competitive edge. This is creating a worldwide shift toward more objective assessment methods; even the most particularist and ascriptive cultures are paying more attention to specific competencies required for effective performance.

People are also becoming more mobile. The European Union has made it much easier for nationals of individual member countries to work in other member countries. Despite a tightening of entry restrictions in many nations, the number of people seeking to work abroad is increasing, with a marked drift toward the more developed economies.

All these factors mean that organizations are more likely to find that they need to assess people from different backgrounds and cultures. They are also fostering the development of more common selection practices. However, for all that the world is growing smaller and practices more similar, cultural differences between nations will remain. The implication for adapting selection procedures is that substantial changes are less likely to be needed when working in another country, but subtler adaptations will still be important and might more easily be overlooked.

References

Arminas, D. (1998, July 16). Staffing problems tax Russian minds. *Personnel Today,* pp. 11–12.

Baron, H. (1996). Strengths and limitations of ipsative measurement. *Journal of Occupational and Organizational Psychology, 69,* 49–56.

Barrett, P. T., Petrides, K. V., Eysenck, S.B.G., & Eysenck, H. J. (1998). The Eysenck personality questionnaire: An examination of the factorial similarity of P, E, N, and L across 34 countries. *Personality and Individual Differences, 25,* 805–819.

Bartram, D. (1996). The relationships between ipsatised and normative measures of personality. *Journal of Occupational and Organizational Psychology, 69,* 25–39.

Ben-Shakhar, G. (1989). Nonconventional methods in personnel selection. In P. Herriot (Ed.), *Assessment and selection in organizations* (pp. 469–485). New York: Wiley.

Di Milia, L., Smith, P. A., & Brown, D. F. (1993). Management selection in Australia: A comparison with British and French findings. *International Journal of Selection and Assessment, 2*(2), 80–90.

Hambleton, R. K. (in press). Guidelines for adapting educational and psychological tests. *Bulletin of the International Test Commission.*

Hofstede, G. (1991). *Cultures and organizations: Software of the mind.* New York: McGraw-Hill.

Institute of Personnel and Development. (1997). *The IPD guide on international management development.* London: Author.

Nyfield, G., Gibbons, P. J., Baron, H., & Robertson, I. (1995). *The cross-cultural validity of management assessment methods.* Paper presented at the tenth annual Society for Industrial and Organizational Psychology conference, Orlando.

Paunonen, S. V., Jackson, D. N., Trzebinski, J., & Forsterling, F. (1992). Personality structure across cultures: A multimethod evaluation. *Journal of Personality and Social Psychology, 62,* 447–456.

Ronen, S. (1989). Training the international assignee. In I. E. Goldstone (Ed.), *Training and development in organizations.* San Francisco: Jossey-Bass.

Ryan, A. M., McFarland, L., Baron, H., & Page, R. (1999). An international look at selection practices: Nation and culture as explanations for variability in practice. *Personnel Psychology, 52,* 359–391.

Saville, P., Nyfield, G., Sik, G., & Hackston, J. (1991). *Enhancing the person-job match through personality assessment.* Paper presented at the annual conference of the American Psychological Association, San Francisco.

Shackleton, V., & Newell, S. (1997). International assessment and selection. In N. Anderson & P. Herriot (Eds.), *International handbook of assessment and selection* (pp. 81–95). New York: Wiley.

Sparrow, P., & Hiltrop, J. M. (1994). *European human resource management in transition.* Upper Saddle River, NJ: Prentice Hall.

Steiner, D. D., & Gilliland, S. W. (1996). Fairness reactions to personnel selection techniques in France and the United States. *Journal of Applied Psychology, 81*(2), 134–141.

Trompenaars, F., & Hampden-Turner, C. (1993). *Riding the waves of culture.* London: Nicholas Brealey.

Wang, Z. (1997). Integrated personnel selection, appraisal, and decisions: A Chinese approach. In N. Anderson & P. Herriot (Eds.), *International handbook of assessment and selection* (pp. 63–79). New York: Wiley.

Regulatory Context

Employment Risk Management

James C. Sharf
David P. Jones

It is in the employer's interest to obtain as much information about an applicant as is both legally and practically possible. Until relatively recently, most of this information has been gathered in face-to-face interviews. Increasingly, however, employers have ready access to a wealth of applicant information in commercial electronic databases. Whether the queries come face-to-face or through an electronic database, gathering information about applicants or incumbent employees is not without risk.

To give practical risk-management guidance to employment decision makers, we begin this chapter by identifying shifts in the risk of employment litigation. We use two recent surveys of employment decision-making procedures as the basis for assigning risk. We then prioritize risk-management strategies, beginning with not asking preemployment medical questions and avoiding questions either prohibited by law or likely to invite litigation.

Limiting applicant pool record keeping to "qualified applicants" is a critical facet of employment risk management. Thus, we

Note: We wish to thank David Copus of the Washington office of Jones, Day, Reavis & Pogue for the litigation trend analyses, and Judith McElya of the Houston office of Aon Financial Services Group of Aon Risk Services for her case law and settlement summaries.

summarize federal employment-decision record-keeping obligations. In this context, we discuss contemporary enforcement agency advocacy requiring federal contractors to ask the race and sex of every potential applicant. Finally, in summarizing employment decision risks, we enumerate the dollar incentives driving employment litigation and the terms of major class action settlements and judgments.

Dollar Incentives and Employers' Increased Risk

This section discusses a number of trends in employment litigation. Since Title VII was passed as part of the federal Civil Rights Act of 1964, trends in employment litigation have significantly shifted (Highberger, 1996):

- Of surprise to most employers, private sector employment litigation over the past two decades has been more likely to be brought under common law torts than under federal or state equal employment opportunity (EEO) statutes. (It should be noted that in the public sector, claims are more likely to be brought on constitutional than common law grounds.)
- Plaintiffs' attorneys will allege disparate treatment so they can argue before a jury, where they are twice as likely to win as when arguing before a judge.
- Common law settlements and judgments pay more in punitive and compensatory damages than capped awards available under federal statutes.
- Incumbents and former employees are almost seven times more likely to sue than applicants for employment.
- Employers are four hundred times more likely to be sued by private plaintiffs' attorneys than by the U.S. Equal Employment Opportunity Commission (EEOC).

Developments in Employment Law in Recent Decades

Before Congress passed the Civil Rights Act of 1991 (CRA '91), Title VII and the Americans with Disabilities Act (ADA) employment discrimination claims were only heard before a judge, never a jury. Monetary awards under these federal statutes were equitable, "make-whole" relief limited to reinstatement and reimbursement for back pay.

Up until 1989, a post–Civil War statute known as Section 1981 of 42 U.S. Code (U.S.C.) had been broadly used by plaintiffs' attorneys to obtain uncapped pain and suffering awards and punitive damages when racial disparate treatment was found in employment decisions. *Disparate treatment* is defined legally as intentionally treating similarly situated individuals differently on the basis of a prohibited classification such as race, sex, and so on. In 1989, however, the Supreme Court's decision in *Patterson v. McLean Credit Union* held that Section 1981 was limited to the making of contracts. Thereafter, only hiring decisions could be challenged under Section 1981 (Gregory, 1988; Nager & Bilich, 1994).

Over the past two decades there has been a growing precedent of uncapped compensatory and punitive tort damages awarded by juries to plaintiffs who successfully challenged employment decisions under common law. *Common law* is a system of precedents based solely on judges' decisions, which are independently made without the constraint of legislatively enacted statutes. For example, because no statutes are involved when arguing a tort claim involving pain and suffering, the presiding judge decides what the law is and makes his or her call according to the way he or she sees the fact situation. Although common law precedents are cited in the decision (if they exist), when they don't, the common law judge decides what the law is to be.

Generally, common law claims involve either the making of a contract or noncontract claims, known as *torts*. Tort claims do not deal with contracts such as the decision to hire or fire someone. Rather, employment torts deal with civil wrongs against a person, such as pain and suffering resulting from an employment decision or "discharge in violation of public policy." Tort claims are most frequently argued by plaintiffs challenging employers' layoff decisions.

What is confounding about trying to generalize from the precedent of common law decisions is that each state and the District of Columbia has its own set of judge-interpreted precedents. So a common law precedent in California may not provide much guidance for a different fact situation argued under common law in California, much less any guidance at all in Rhode Island (Cathcart & Snyderman, 1992; Copus, 1996).

It is the unpredictability of outcomes when dealing with common law decisions that gives risk managers heartburn. According to David Copus, a former EEOC litigator (1996, p. 56), "Tort theories pose enormous risks for all employers because of the increasing creativity of plaintiffs' lawyers, the increasing willingness of common law judges to find ways to permit plaintiffs to recover tort damages, and the essentially unlimited nature of tort damages. The risks from tort liability far exceed the risks posed by federal statutory civil rights violations in almost every case."

Civil Rights Act of 1991

Section 102 of the CRA '91 changed the monetary incentives for plaintiffs' attorneys by now allowing for monetary compensatory and punitive damages in both Title VII and ADA cases involving *intentional* discrimination (disparate treatment). Title VII and ADA plaintiffs get a jury trial when damages are sought for employment decisions in which intentional discrimination is alleged.

Under the CRA '91, compensatory damages include "future pecuniary losses, emotional pain, suffering, inconvenience, mental anguish, loss of enjoyment of life, and other nonpecuniary losses" (CRA § 102[b][3]). These damages are in addition to equitable make-whole relief, such as reinstatement and back pay, which had previously been available. Punitive damages are now awarded where the plaintiff can demonstrate that the employer acted with "malice" or with "reckless indifference" (Cathcart & Snyderman, 1992).

Discrimination Claims Brought Under Common Law

As Figure 8.1 shows, between 1989 and 1995, 57 percent of *all* employment discrimination claims were brought under common law (Copus, 1996).

More than half of all employment discrimination claims in recent years were not based on federal EEO statutes. In addition to claims of discrimination, common law claims also included intentional infliction of pain and suffering, and to a lesser extent, invasion of privacy. Even with the availability of monetary damages

**Figure 8.1. Share of Employment Claims
Based on Federal Statutes and Common Law, 1989–1995.**

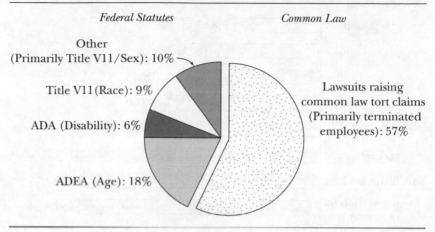

Federal Statutes

Common Law

Other
(Primarily Title V11/Sex): 10%

Title V11(Race): 9%

ADA (Disability): 6%

ADEA (Age): 18%

Lawsuits raising
common law tort claims
(Primarily terminated
employees): 57%

under Title VII, tort damage claims are still brought under common law in a civil trial before a jury because there is no cap on monetary awards (Feliu, 1994). In contrast, the CRA '91 caps individual claims at between $50,000 and $300,000, depending on the size of the employer.

Figure 8.1 shows that 43 percent of the cases were brought under federal EEO statutes; 18 percent involved claims of age discrimination, 9 percent race, 6 percent disability, and 10 percent "other" (primarily sex discrimination). (In the public sector, constitutional claims at both the state and federal levels are the equivalent of common law claims in the private sector.)

Figure 8.2 shows that common law awards were well above the $408,719 average award when combining both statutory and common law claims (Copus, 1996). Given the absence of monetary caps under common law, it would hardly be in the plaintiff's interest (to say nothing about the contingent-fee lawyer's interest) to fail to bring charges primarily on common law grounds alone or on both common law *and* statutory grounds. Figure 8.1 shows the plaintiffs' attorney's preference for alleging employment discrimination claims under common law and Figure 8.2 convincingly shows the dollar reason why this is so.

**Figure 8.2. Average Jury Verdicts for
Winning Plaintiffs, by Type, 1988–1995.**

Disability	$183,598
Race	$242,278
Sex	$264,278
Age	$300,060
Average: Common law and statute	$408,719
Sexual harassment	$417,041
Tort (common law)	$498,075
Breach of contract (common law)	$502,291

$0 $200,000 $400,000 $600,000

Source: Copus, 1996, p. 83. Used by permission.

Discrimination Claims Brought Under Federal Statutes

Table 8.1 reveals employment discrimination trends during the 1990s based on federal statutes. Note that the percent of charges adds up to more than 100 percent because individuals usually file claims on more than one basis (for example, race and sex).

Based on these numbers, the least likely charges (accounting for about 2 percent each) are religious discrimination under Title VII and comparable worth arguments brought under the Equal Pay Act of 1963 (29 U.S.C.). National origin claims have decreased somewhat over the past decade, remaining relatively constant at about 8 percent. Disability claims became actionable in 1992 and now account for slightly more than 20 percent of all charges, a level that has been relatively constant for the past five years. Retaliation claims have increased year by year to the point where today they make up about 20 percent of all claims. Sex discrimination accounts for 30 percent of claims, a figure that has remained constant over the decade.

What is notable about the information in Table 8.1 is the declining percentage of race claims. Although race discrimination

Table 8.1. Charge Statistics from the U.S. Equal Employment Opportunity Commission, 1990–1997.

	FY 1990	FY 1991	FY 1992	FY 1993	FY 1994	FY 1995	FY 1996	FY 1997
Total charges*	62,135	63,898	72,302	87,942	91,189	87,529	77,990	80,680
Race	29,121	27,981	29,548	31,695	31,656	29,986	26,287	29,199
	46.7%	43.8%	40.9%	36.0%	34.8%	34.3%	33.8%	36.2%
Sex	17,815	17,672	21,796	23,919	25,860	26,181	23,813	24,728
	28.5%	27.7%	30.1%	27.2%	28.4%	29.9%	30.6%	30.7%
National origin	7,236	6,692	7,434	7,454	7,414	7,035	6,687	6,712
	11.6%	10.5%	10.3%	8.5%	8.1%	8.0%	8.6%	8.3%
Religion	1,147	1,192	1,388	1,449	1,546	1,581	1,564	1,709
	1.8%	1.9%	1.9%	1.6%	1.7%	1.8%	2.0%	2.1%
Retaliation	7,579	7,906	10,932	12,644	14,415	15,342	14,412	18,113
	12.1%	12.4%	14.4%	14.4%	15.8%	17.5%	18.5%	22.5%
Age	14,719	17,550	19,573	19,809	19,618	17,416	15,719	15,785
	23.6%	27.5%	27.1%	22.5%	21.5%	19.9%	20.2%	19.6%
Disability**	na	na	**1,048	15,274	18,859	19,798	18,046	18,108
			1.4%	17.4%	20.7%	22.6%	23.1%	22.4%
Equal Pay Act	1,345	1,187	1,294	1,328	1,381	1,275	969	1,134
	2.2%	1.9%	1.8%	1.5%	1.5%	1.5%	1.2%	1.4%

*Total charges reflect the number of individual charge filings. Because individuals often file charges under multiple bases, the number of total charges for any given fiscal year will be less than the total for the eight bases listed.

**EEOC began enforcing the Americans with Disabilities Act on July 26, 1992.

Source: U.S. Equal Employment Opportunity Commission, 1997.

accounted for 36 percent of the charges in fiscal year 1997, this figure has steadily declined since the beginning of the decade.

The EEOC's Batting Average

Notwithstanding several highly publicized class-action cases, for most employers the EEOC is not the threat that it once was when it comes to the risk of litigation. An examination of all charges filed with the EEOC in 1994 reveals that "no cause" and "administratively closed" each accounted for about 30 percent of all charges (the latter usually consisting of the charging party's failure to respond to EEOC correspondence). A quarter of all charges were added to the backlog. This means that 88 percent of all charges either went into the backlog, were administratively closed, or were dismissed for lack of merit. Eleven percent were "otherwise disposed of," which includes finding a violation. What is most revealing are the following two statistics: in less than 1 percent of the cases was settlement reached after the commission issued a "cause" finding, and the commission filed suit in less than one-half of 1 percent of the cases (Copus, 1996).

If we compare the trends in Figure 8.1 and Table 8.1, we can see that because fewer than half of all discrimination claims were brought under federal statute and less than half of 1 percent of those involved the EEOC bringing suit, this means that the commission was a party in less than a quarter of 1 percent of EEO litigation. In other words, four hundred claims are filed by private plaintiffs' attorneys for each case brought by the EEOC. According to an employment attorney who has worked for both plaintiffs and respondents, "Created by Congress with the best of intentions, thirty years later, the EEOC has become little more than a paper-shuffling agency" (Copus, 1996).

Assigning Risk to Employment Decisions

In 1996–97, a corporate sample from the Fortune 100 was asked to document their use of objective selection procedures (Tippins & Wunder, 1997). Forty-three corporations responded, documenting seventy-seven selection systems. The sampled industries included aerospace, automotive, banking, chemicals, computing services, consumer products, electric utilities, electronics, energy, fast food, financial services, government, industry association, insurance, manufacturing, publishing, retailing, software, telecommunications, and transportation. The largest numbers of participants were from the energy, insurance, and telecommunications industries.

Objective measures (primarily employment tests) were used in 40 percent of their selection systems. The results of the Tippins and Wunder survey of the Fortune 100 correspond quite nicely with the results of a 1996 membership survey conducted by the American Management Association, which are shown in Tables 8.2 and 8.3.

Table 8.2 shows that employment tests were used by 44 percent of AMA survey participants. Table 8.3 shows the distribution of employment test use by business category.

Not surprisingly, tests were used half as often as the universal employment interview. As shown in Figure 8.3, interviews continue to be the universal workhorse of employment decision making,

**Table 8.2. Frequency of
Psychological Testing Among AMA Members, 1996.**

	(Number of Members)			
Type	Applicants	Employees	Applicants/ Employees	Percentage
Cognitive ability test	236	137	253	27.9
Interest inventory	70	70	101	11.1
Managerial assessment	145	120	183	20.2
Personality instrument	152	94	175	19.3
Physical ability test	105	53	118	13.0
Any psychological testing	320	277	440	44.2
No psychological testing	—	—	506	55.8
Total	—	—	946	100.0

Table 8.3. Psychological Testing Among AMA Members, by Business Category, 1996.

Test Type	Manufacture	Finance	Wholesale/ Retail	Business/ Professional Service	Public Administration	Nonprofit Organizations	Other
Cognitive ability test	31.7	29.8	29.4	25.4	46.7	20.8	21.7
Interest inventory	10.7	14.9	9.8	14.9	—	12.5	9.6
Managerial assessment	21.7	19.1	25.5	20.9	33.3	15.0	17.5
Personality measurement	20.5	17.0	27.5	22.4	33.3	10.0	18.7
Physical ability test	16.3	6.4	11.8	9.0	20.0	6.7	12.7
Any psychological testing	41.7	40.4	39.2	37.3	66.7	30.0	33.7
Total percentage	100.0	100.0	100.0	100.0	100.0	100.0	100.0
(Number)	(429)	(47)	(51)	(67)	(15)	(120)	(166)

Source: American Management Association, 1997, Table PSY, Table AIS4. Reprinted from 1997 AMA SURVEY OF WORKPLACE MONITORING AND TESTING. Copyright © 1997 American Management Association International. Reprinted by permission of American Management Association International, New York, NY. All rights reserved. http:www.amanet.org

used in 99 percent of the sampled selection systems. Within that sample, 40 percent of employers conducted campus interviews.

According to the Tippins and Wunder (1997) survey results shown in Figure 8.3, the second and third most frequently used assessments were inquiries about resumes, experience, and education, which were conducted in 71 percent of the programs, and employment tests, which were utilized in 40 percent. These sources of information were complemented by background checks, which were conducted in 36 percent of the programs. References were checked 28 percent of the time. Three of these sources of information, including interviews, resumes, and references, are an increasing source of risk because of legal developments.

Risks Assigned by Statutes

Table 8.4 shows the EEOC's fiscal year 1997 charges summarized by statute and basis codes. The right-hand column (percentage charges

Figure 8.3. Objective Measures Used by Fortune 100 Employers.

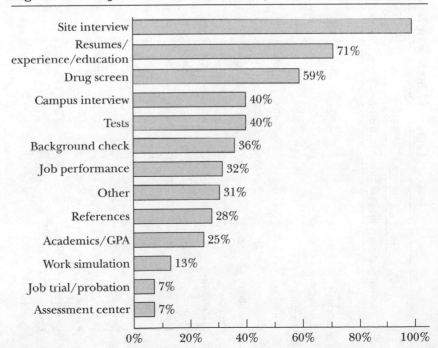

Table 8.4. Statute or Basis Summary by Issues, 1997.

	Issues	Title VII Race	Religion	Origin	Retaliation	Sex	Other	Total VII	Total EPA	Total ADEA	Total ADA	Other STAT	Total Issues	Total CHGS	% VII CHGS	% CHGS	
A1	Advertising	18	0	3	3	18	2	26	0	7	4	0	37	31	.0	.0	A1
B1	Benefits	391	19	101	266	398	21	841	43	492	412	0	1788	1476	.4	1.8	B1
B1	Ben. Ret/Pen	46	9	19	35	44	4	118	9	282	72	0	481	384	.2	.5	B1
B3	Benefits-Ins	34	1	14	34	58	3	102	2	84	184	0	372	308	.2	.4	B3
D1	Demotion	1228	40	260	729	1008	39	2314	62	803	586	0	3765	3058	3.9	3.8	D1
D2	Discharge	13714	878	3314	7438	10369	409	26566	276	7743	9743	0	44328	38159	45.2	47.2	D2
D3	Discipline	3129	161	637	2093	1658	78	5242	47	923	1074	0	7286	6209	8.9	7.7	D3
E1	Exclusion	71	6	39	73	59	6	162	6	24	19	0	211	178	.3	.2	E1
H1	Harassment	5759	529	1778	4720	4592	225	11458	155	1992	2507	0	16112	13497	19.5	16.7	H1
H2	Hiring	2312	153	574	592	1300	119	3798	20	2074	1433	0	7325	6244	6.5	7.7	H2
I1	Intimidation	913	71	269	1051	992	53	2054	33	341	367	0	2795	2345	3.5	2.9	I1
J1	Job Class	153	4	30	70	104	3	242	17	47	55	0	361	295	.4	.4	J1
L1	Layoff	881	41	373	387	711	34	1809	28	1137	655	0	3629	2976	3.1	3.7	L1
M1	Maternity	51	4	13	46	528	2	534	5	1	23	0	563	534	.9	.7	M1
O1	Other	1039	65	251	657	698	93	1950	40	445	588	2	3025	2549	3.3	3.2	O1
P1	Paternity	4	0	1	0	6	0	9	1	2	0	0	12	10	.0	.0	P1
P3	Promotion	4763	131	866	1759	2536	224	7164	162	1603	720	0	9649	8194	12.2	10.1	P3
P4	Med. Ind/Exam	8	4	1	7	11	3	24	0	11	108	0	143	111	.0	.1	P4
Q1	Qualification	83	3	16	54	53	4	135	9	37	31	0	212	162	.2	.2	Q1

R1 Recall	169	4	39	68	105	3	308	4	155	197	0	664	541	.5	.7
R2 Ref Unfavor	50	6	21	160	45	2	213	3	38	84	0	338	292	.4	.4
R3 Referral	86	7	16	39	28	3	138	0	23	34	0	195	177	.2	.2
R4 Reinstatement	147	11	32	102	132	7	321	1	135	575	0	1032	816	.5	1.0
R5 Retire Unvol	22	10	11	20	15	5	63	0	234	90	0	387	298	.1	.4
R6 Reas Accom	584	195	150	467	571	33	1427	17	657	5828	0	7929	6034	2.4	7.5
S1 Segreg Fac.	24	3	5	20	14	1	39	0	1	1	0	41	39	.1	.0
S2 Segreg Loc.	6	0	0	3	0	0	6	0	0	0	0	6	6	.0	.0
S3 Seniority	94	1	19	33	60	6	158	6	73	49	0	286	231	.3	.3
S4 Sex Harass	720	85	217	4397	9114	45	9314	135	282	343	1	10075	9332	15.8	11.5
S5 Suspension	1364	67	250	765	652	42	2213	15	288	567	0	2973	2587	3.8	3.2
T1 Tenure	32	10	22	34	51	2	85	5	23	12	0	125	98	.1	.1
T2 Terms of Emp	7115	367	1577	4511	5129	283	12893	291	2465	2660	0	18309	15363	21.9	19.0
T3 Testing	131	3	20	22	60	11	175	0	33	30	0	238	206	.3	.3
T4 Training	689	19	115	262	340	34	1031	12	234	131	0	1408	1191	1.8	1.5
U1 Union Rep	200	10	22	87	102	9	313	2	85	145	0	545	441	.5	.5
W1 Wages	2996	100	622	1387	2491	111	5496	1000	1033	685	0	8214	6403	9.3	7.9
Total Issues	48999	3017	11697	32391	44052	1919	98741	2406	23807	29902	3	198193			
Total Charges	29330	1712	6723	16368	24790	1014	58839	1136	15814	18133	0	0	80896		
% Total Charges	36.3	2.1	8.3	20.2	30.6	1.3	72.7	1.4	19.5	22.4	.0				

[CHGS]) summarizes across Title VII, the Equal Pay Act, the Age Discrimination in Employment Act, and the Americans with Disabilities Act claims. Hiring accounted for only 7.7 percent of all claims, whereas discharge accounted for 47.2 percent. This means that as far as assigning risk, an employer is almost seven times more likely to be sued by an incumbent or former employee than by an applicant (Bulger & Gessner, 1992; Burns, 1996; Davidson, 1995; Mesritz, 1995; Werner & Bolino, 1997).

Although used in 40 percent of the sampled Fortune 100 employment decision-making systems and by 44 percent of AMA member employers, objective testing procedures didn't even show up on the commission's radar, accounting for less than one-half of 1 percent of all charges. This lowered risk profile for employment testing was confirmed in a separate but related survey of reported court decisions involving employment tests over the past decade. The trend has been steadily downward from a high of about two dozen cases per year at the beginning of the decade to only five cases nationwide in 1996 in which testing was at issue (Pyburn, 1996).

Risks Assigned to Interviews

As Figure 8.3 shows, interviews are the most common component of employment decision making. Although Table 8.4 shows that challenges to hiring decisions represent only 7 percent of the charges, it is nevertheless likely that casual interviews will be displaced in favor of more structured patterned interviews (Burnett, Fan, Motowidlo, & Degroot, 1998; Williamson, Campion, Malos, Roehling, & Campion, 1997). What are the reasons for this?

Nonstandardized, casual interviews are challenged under the disparate treatment theory of discrimination, in which it is alleged that the employer intentionally treated people differently with regard to a prohibited classification (race, sex, and so on). Under the CRA '91, as previously discussed, disparate treatment Title VII claims alleging intentional discrimination are heard before a jury. Punitive and compensatory damages are available. The same is true for common law claims, but without monetary caps. For these reasons, plaintiffs' attorneys will pursue disparate treatment class actions built on nonstandardized assessments such as the casual interview (see the paragraph on Home Depot in Exhibit 8.6).

All the plaintiff who claims intentional discrimination (disparate treatment) needs to show is that similarly situated individuals were treated differently with regard to a prohibited factor such as race or sex. In the absence of a standardized interview protocol with recorded observations, the employer has the burden of showing that protected class members applying for the same job were treated the same. A plaintiff's attorney will capitalize on such a fact situation because the employer can't prove with any certainty that persons were treated the same, that is, that the same questions were asked from one casual interview to the next.

In contrast to casual interviews, standardized interviews, like objective tests, are analyzed under the disparate impact (adverse impact) theory of discrimination. Treating similarly situated individuals differently (intent) is *not* at issue. Rather the issue is one of statistical disparities resulting from standardized use of an objective selection procedure. More important, disparate impact challenges involving objective selection procedures are tried before a judge, not a jury. Compensatory and punitive damages are not available when disparate impact is proven. Rather, only equitable, make-whole damages of back pay and reinstatement are available under disparate impact claims.

In our experience, employment attorneys prefer to argue disparate impact cases before a judge rather than disparate treatment cases before a jury if for no other reason than the judge is less likely to be swayed by emotional testimony presented by plaintiffs. Plaintiffs' attorneys obviously view juries as more sympathetic than judges. As Richard Seymour of the Lawyers' Committee for Civil Rights Under Law succinctly puts it: "Judges don't work on factory floors. They often don't have a clue about the way the real world works" (Price, 1997). In 1994, the latest year for which figures are available, plaintiffs won 43.3 percent of all employment discrimination cases heard by juries but just 22.1 percent of those heard by judges (Myerson, 1997).

Categories of Prohibited Preemployment Questions

Return with us for a moment to the less litigious days of yore, when the personnel department (now known as human resources) did not have to navigate risk-management shoals with guidance from employment attorneys. In those days, the typical application form asked for an explanation about any problems the person had with the law. Interviewers inquired routinely not only about the person's health but likely also about the health of family members. References used to be checked with the expectation of gaining an insight into the applicant's finances, character, and other personal information. That was then; this is now.

As a society we have become at once both increasingly dependent on computers and apprehensive about who has access to the wealth of personal information contained in them. One need look no further for evidence of our increased reliance on electronic, paperless transactions than the popularity of direct payroll deposits, which have all but eliminated the paper paycheck. We are increasingly defined in today's economy by digitized personal information.

The federal government now gets from employers the name of every new hire. "Smartcards" for paying tolls leave the driver's electronic trail. Internet browsing behavior is retrievable, credit card purchase data are resold by telemarketers, cellular calls are scanned, and video cameras record behavior in public places (Safire, 1998).

Digitized Personal Information

For employers, commercially available electronic databases provide inexpensive access not just to the resume that the applicant controls but also to extensive unedited information about a person's education, finances, military service, employment, arrests, convictions, and worker's compensation history.

Credit records, for example, usually contain personal information provided when opening a bank account or applying for a credit card. They also include information such as employment history and previous credit problems. Credit records are also frequently a source of even more personal information based on interviews with references, neighbors, and landlords and may include unedited anecdotal reports on habits and lifestyle choices (Parliman & Dolan, 1990). The one thing common to all these potential sources of information is that they are invasive of personal privacy (Burns, 1994;

Fast, 1993; Jenero & Males-Riordan, 1992; Mael, Connerley, & Morath, 1996; Sharf, 1994; Shepard, Duston, & Russell, 1989; see also Duffy, 1982).

Like the federal government, most states have enacted fair employment practice statutes that prohibit discrimination by private employers based on race, color, religion, sex, national origin, or disability. State antidiscrimination laws, by and large, are construed to track Title VII of the Civil Rights Act of 1964, the Civil Rights Act of 1991, and the Americans with Disabilities Act. Hence, should an employer's use of selection procedures violate Title VII or the ADA, the employer very likely also will have violated the relevant state antidiscrimination law (Mook, 1996; see also Black, 1994). But in many ways, states impose even greater constraints on employers than do federal statutes. Many also deal with invasions of privacy (Jones, Ash, & Soto, 1990; Sharf, 1994).

There are presently ten states with constitutional or statutory privacy protections extended to both private and public employers. Probably the best known among them is California, because of the national press coverage of a recent invasion-of-privacy case. Even in states where there is neither a constitutional nor a statutory basis defining privacy rights, courts have nonetheless found common law grounds for protecting individuals against invasion of privacy (*Bennett v. Nelson*, 1959; *Rhodes v. Graham*, 1931; *Hamberger v. Eastman*, 1965; *K-Mart v. Trotti*, 1984; *Pavesich v. New England Life Insurance*, 1994; see also *Feldleit v. Long Island Railroad*, 1989).

Probably the best known invasion-of-privacy challenge to psychological testing is the Soroka case, which was brought under state constitutional challenge in California (*Soroka v. Dayton Hudson*, 1991). The Soroka court of appeals found that Dayton Hudson's use of the Minnesota Multiphasic Personality Inventory (MMPI) and the California Psychological Inventory to test store security applicants violated both their state constitutional right to privacy and state discrimination laws.

The Soroka court held that questions about a person's sexual and religious beliefs were not job-related. Under the applicable state laws, Dayton Hudson's burden in defending such questions was to show a "compelling interest," which it failed to do (see also *McKenna v. Fargo*, 1979).

Federal Agency Restrictions in Sweeping Databases

At the federal level over a quarter of a century ago, Congress passed the Privacy Act of 1974, which directed federal agencies to "collect information to the greatest extent practicable directly from the subject individual when the information may result in adverse determinations about an individual's rights, benefits, and privileges under federal programs." By the early 1970s, Congress was sufficiently concerned about invasions of privacy to limit federal agencies' sweeping of electronic databases for information about job applicants.

State and Local Restrictions on Preemployment Inquiries

State and local jurisdictions are free to prohibit personnel practices that are not prohibited by federal law. They may not, however, authorize employment practices that would violate federal laws. As a result, many state fair-employment practice agencies have promulgated guidelines for preemployment inquiries that prohibit specific questions that would not violate federal laws.

**Exhibit 8.1. Personal History Questions
Prohibited at State and Local Levels.**

Age, application falsification, arrests, birthplace/citizenship, bonding, childcare, children, convictions/court records, credit rating, dependents, economic status/bankruptcy, education, experience, family, garnishment records, health, hospitalization/doctor's care, language skills, lowest salary accepted, marital status, military service, maiden name, national origin/ancestry, notice in case of emergency, organizations, performance ability, physical condition/handicap, physical description/photograph, political affiliation, pregnancy, race/color, references, relatives, religion, rent/own car/home, residence, residence/duration of, sex, sexual preference, special qualifications, spouse's work, widowed/divorced/separated, work schedules.

Source: Ash, 1994. Modified and reproduced by special permission of the publisher, Consulting Psychologists Press, Palo Alto, CA 94303 from *Biodata Handbook*. Edited by Garnett S. Stokes, Michael D. Mumford, and William A. Owens. Copyright 1994 by Consulting Psychologists Press, Inc. All rights reserved. Further reproduction is prohibited without the Publisher's written consent.

Although acceptable under federal law, as shown in Exhibit 8.1 numerous specific questions that an applicant would have been asked to answer in years past are now prohibited by statute, regulation, and guidelines at the various state and local levels of government.

An employer with operations in more than one jurisdiction is increasingly challenged to stay abreast of such laws. With citizens' ever-increasing privacy concerns, it is likely that such prohibitions will multiply, making employment systems managers' jobs even more complicated.

Exhibit 8.2 shows questions prohibited even where there is validity evidence that applicants' answers are job-related—that is, are helpful in predicting which person will perform better on the job. Prohibited questions, even though valid, generally fall into categories involving personal information (such as marital status), health, finances, and socioeconomic status (Sharf, 1994).

**Exhibit 8.2. Personal History Questions
Valid for Sales Jobs but Prohibited at State and Local Levels.**

"Own or rent home" prohibited in CA, CO, ID, KS, MN, NV, NJ, SD, RI, UT, WA, WV, and WI.

"Age or date of birth" prohibited in AK, AZ, CA, HI, ID, IA, KS, NY, OH, RI, SD, UT, DC, WV, ME, MI, MN, NV, NH, and NJ.

"Marital status" prohibited in AZ, CA, CO, MA, NV, NH, NJ, UT, WA, and WV.

"General health or illness" prohibited in CA, CO, MI, NV, OH, UT, and WA.

"Reside with parents or relatives" prohibited in CA, CO, HI, IN, ME, MA, MI, NV, NH, NJ, UT, and WA.

"Current or past assets or credit" prohibited in AZ, CA, CO, ID, IL, KS, MN, NV, NJ, RI, UT, WV, and WI.

Restrictions on Use of Arrest and Conviction Records

Twenty-seven states have enacted laws governing employers' use of arrest records (Hahn, 1991). For example, it is a civil rights violation under Illinois law for an employer to inquire on a written application whether a job applicant has ever been arrested. California not only prohibits obtaining arrest information from applicants themselves but also provides that employers may not "seek from any source, whatsoever, or utilize as a factor in determining any condition of employment . . . any record of arrest or detention which did not result in conviction" (Hahn, 1991, p. 50).

Restrictions on Checking Credit History

The federal Fair Credit Reporting Act (FCRA) covers employers' use of credit histories for making employment decisions. An adverse employment decision based on a credit history requires that the affected individual be notified and given the name and address of the reporting agency. The employer may not obtain a credit report under "false pretenses." If the employer seeks an *investigative consumer report,* which is defined by statute as a report containing "information on a consumer's character, general reputation, personal characteristics, or mode of living . . . obtained through personal interviews with neighbors, friends, or (other) associates of the consumer," the employer must give written notice to the applicant or employee within three days. An adverse employment decision is not necessary to trigger the notification requirement, only the fact that the investigative consumer report has been sought. If the person requests, the employer must inform the consumer within five days about the nature and scope of the investigation. The credit reporting agency cannot report adverse information including arrests, convictions, tax liens, suits, and judgments more than seven years old, except when the person's starting annual salary exceeds $20,000. Furthermore, the consumer is entitled to get the name of the recipient of any consumer report made within the preceding two years (Hahn, 1991).

The FCRA creates a private right of action with liability, including actual damages and attorney fees for negligent violations and punitive damages for willful violations. In 1990, for example, the ninth circuit found a California employer had violated both state and federal laws when it withdrew an offer of employment upon obtaining a bad credit report *(Comeaux v. Brown & Williamson)*. Under state law, the employer had failed to condition its employment offer upon obtaining a clear credit rating. The employer had offered the applicant a position contingent upon his taking a physical exam, resigning his current position, and moving his place of residence closer to the employer's operations. Before the applicant could begin work, however, the employer refused to honor its commitment to employ him, basing the decision on a bad credit report received in the interim. The employer was also held to have violated the FCRA in obtaining the applicant's credit report under false pretenses.

The EEOC's Position on Credit History

The EEOC holds, and a number of courts have agreed, that it is unlawful to deny employment based on a poor credit rating (EEOC Decision Nos. 72–0427, Aug. 31, 1971; 76–65, Nov. 21, 1975; 74–02, July 10, 1973; and 72–1176, Feb. 28, 1972). (See also *Johnson v. Pike Corp. of America*, 1971.)

Disparate Impact of Arrest and Credit Information

Wholly aside from FCRA restrictions governing the requesting of and subsequent use of credit histories by employers, the same information is susceptible to disparate impact challenge under Title VII.

In *United States v. City of Chicago* (1974), the U.S. Department of Justice successfully challenged the Chicago police department's background investigations assessing applicants' "bad character, dissolute habits, and immoral conduct." This determination was based on information regarding an applicant's arrests, convictions, traffic citations, family member arrests for serious crimes, education, employment, military service, driving history, and financial condition. The court of appeals affirmed the district court's opinion that the use of this information affected minority applicants and that the department's criteria were too subjective: "The vagueness of the governing criteria and the defendant's failure to offer any articulable standards to guide the application of these criteria make it impossible to determine whether the background investigation actually served to select applicants according to real differences in job-related qualifications" (Hahn, 1991, p. 55).

In *Gregory v. Litton Systems* (1973), the court struck down the employer's policy of disqualifying frequently arrested persons from employment. In *Reynolds v. Sheet Metal Workers Local 102* (1981), the employer's claim that it had not used information about arrests in making employment decisions was rejected. The court reasoned that because the information was sought on the application form and in interviews, it must have been considered.

The EEOC's Position on Arrest Records

The EEOC's position is that even if the employer does not consider information on arrests in making employment decisions, "the mere request for such information both tends to discourage applications by those with arrest records and tends to induce false or incomplete answers for which the applicant may be penalized" (EEOC Decision No. 74–02, July 10, 1973).

Restrictions on Use of Convictions

Seeking to be more specific than the Chicago police department in rejecting convicted applicants, the Missouri Pacific railroad offered the following justifications: fear of cargo theft, handling of company funds, bonding requirements, possible impeachment of an employee witness, possible liability for hiring persons with known violent tendencies, employment disruption caused by recidivism, and alleged lack of moral character.

In *Green v. Missouri Pacific Railway Co.* (1975), the court concluded that the defendant's conviction policy swept too broadly in that it would be impossible to know if a conviction had any bearing on a particular job requirement without knowing the specific crime that had been committed. The court concluded that although the reasons the employer advanced "can serve as relevant considerations in making individual hiring decisions, they in no way justify an absolute policy which sweeps so broadly" (see also *Butts v. Nichols*, 1974).

However, courts have been willing to uphold use of conviction information when it is not a ground for automatic disqualification (*Hill v. U.S. Postal Service*, 1981; *Richardson v. Hotel Corp. of America*, 1972).

EEOC's Position on Conviction Records

The EEOC's position is that blanket disqualifications for criminal convictions are unlawful. It does allow employers "to evaluate, on an individual basis, the record of a person who has been convicted of a crime against the requirements of a specific job" (EEOC Decision No. 78–44, Oct. 2, 1978). The EEOC calls for consideration of the number of offenses and circumstances of each offense, the length of time intervening between the conviction for the offense, the individual's employment history, and the individual's efforts at rehabilitation.

Based on these court decisions and regulatory guidance, an across-the-board policy of automatically disqualifying all applicants convicted of any crime for all positions would be least likely to pass judicial muster.

Restrictions on Considering Workers' Compensation History

Many states prohibit retaliation against an employee who files a workers' compensation claim. A number of states prohibit adverse employment decisions based on *any* previous workers' compensation claim.

Prohibited Preemployment Medical and Psychiatric Questions

Regulations issued by the EEOC interpreting the Americans with Disabilities Act clearly limit an employer's inquiring at the preoffer stage about an applicant's medical and psychiatric history. Prohibited categories of questions covered by ADA regulations are summarized in Exhibit 8.3.

The ADA's ban on preemployment medical inquiries likely means that an employer may not routinely ask applicants if they will need an accommodation to perform essential functions of the job. Employers may ask if applicants can meet attendance standards and about their attendance record. Employers may not, however, ask about the use of sick leave because that question may disclose a person's disability.

At the postoffer stage, such medical questions may be asked and medical exams conducted, provided the same procedure is required of all applicants for the same job and provided this information is kept in separate, confidential files.

Exhibit 8.3. Preemployment Offer Questions
Prohibited Under Americans with Disabilities Act.

I. Excerpts from *ADA Enforcement Guidance*, Equal Employment Opportunity Commission, 1995.

Preoffer Stage. An employer may not ask *disability-related questions* or require a medical examination preoffer even if it intends to look at the answers or results only at the postoffer stage. Once a conditional job offer is made, the employer may ask disability-related questions and require medical examinations as long as this is done for all entering employees in that job category. If the question or examination screens out an individual because of a disability, the employer must demonstrate that the reason for the rejection is "job-related and consistent with business necessity" (p. 2).

If the individual is screened out for *safety reasons,* the employer must demonstrate that the individual poses a "direct threat" . . . a significant risk of substantial harm to him/herself or others, and that the risk cannot be reduced below the direct threat level through reasonable accommodation (p. 3).

At the preoffer stage, an employer cannot ask questions that are likely to elicit information about a disability (p. 4).

An employer may ask about an applicant's prior attendance record . . . (and) questions designed to detect whether an applicant abused his/her leave. . . . An employer may *not* ask *how many days an applicant was sick* because these questions relate directly to the severity of an individual's impairments (p. 8).

An employer may not ask applicants about *job-related injuries* or *workers' compensation history* . . . (but) may ask about current illegal use of drugs (p. 10).

An employer: may ask about prior illegal drug use, (However) past addiction to illegal drugs or controlled substances is a covered disability . . . but past casual use is not a covered disability; may ask "Have you ever used illegal drugs?"; may *not* ask *"how often did you use illegal drugs in the past?"* . . . (because) questions that ask how much the applicant used drugs in the past are likely to elicit information about whether the applicant was a past drug addict (p. 11).

An employer may ask whether s/he drinks alcohol or whether s/he has been arrested for DUI because these questions do not reveal whether someone has alcoholism (pp. 11–12).

An employer may not ask questions asking *how much alcohol an applicant drinks* . . . (because such questions) are likely to elicit information about whether the applicant has alcoholism (p. 12).

Exhibit 8.3. Preemployment Offer Questions
Prohibited Under Americans with Disabilities Act, Cont'd.

An employer may not ask a third party . . . any questions that it could not directly ask the applicant (p. 13).

An employer may *not* seek information at the pre-offer stage about *physical or mental impairments or health* (p. 14). (Asking) whether an applicant has *paranoid tendencies, or is depressed* . . . is a medical examination . . . (prohibited at the pre-employment offer stage) (p. 15).

An employer may give psychological examinations unless the particular examination is medical . . . if they provide evidence that would lead to identifying a mental disorder or impairment *(listed in DSM III)* (p. 16).

Postoffer Stage. After giving a job offer to an applicant, an employer may ask disability-related questions and perform medical examinations . . . and ask about an individual's workers' comp history, prior sick leave usage, illnesses/diseases/impairments, and general physical and mental health. (A)n employer (may) ask post-offer disability-related questions *provided:* all entering employees in the same job category (are asked) . . . and if an individual is screened out because of disability, the employer must show that the exclusionary criterion is "job-related and consistent with business necessity" (p. 18) (emphasis added).

II. Excerpts from *Enforcement Guidance on the Americans with Disabilities Act and Psychiatric Disabilities,* **Equal Employment Opportunity Commission, 1997.**

Under the ADA, the term *disability* means: "(a) A physical or mental impairment that substantially limits one or more of the major life activities of (an) individual; (b) a record of such an impairment; (c) being regarded as having such an impairment." "Mental impairment" includes "any mental or psychological disorder such as . . . emotional or mental illness" . . . including major depression, . . . anxiety disorders (which include panic disorder) . . . and personality disorders . . . found in DSM-IV (p. 2).

Stress is not automatically a mental impairment . . . (although) it may be related to a mental impairment (p. 4). *Interacting with others,* as a major life activity, is not substantially limited just because an individual is irritable or has some trouble getting along with a supervisor or coworker. *Sleeping* is not substantially limited just because an individual has some trouble getting to sleep or occasionally sleeps fitfully (p. 5).

An impairment is "substantially limiting" if it lasts for more than several months and significantly restricts the performance of one or more major life activities during that time (p. 8) (emphasis added).

Exhibit 8.4 summarizes record-keeping requirements for the Age Discrimination in Employment Act (ADEA), ADA, and Title VII. Record-keeping requirements for federal contractors are discussed in the following section.

We conclude that two trends seem likely to collide, very likely at the employer's expense. The availability of information on applicants will in the short term become even less expensive to access. In the long term, however, use for employment purposes of much of this readily available information—including credit histories, health records, arrest and conviction records—will become prohibitively expensive because of likely litigation.

In addition, privacy concerns will likely result in ever more restrictive legislation. Because state and local governments have been most responsive to privacy concerns, it is likely that employers with geographically dispersed operations will have an increasingly demanding and expensive job keeping ahead of these strictures.

Record Keeping and Scorekeeping

This section begins by reviewing the Department of Labor's Office of Federal Contract Compliance Programs' (OFCCP) enforcement of Executive Order (EO) 11246. OFCCP has proposed obligating federal contractors to identify the race and sex of everyone who either expressed interest in the employer via the Internet or whose resume is part of an electronic database queried by an employer.

OFCCP's expansive record-keeping burden on federal contractors will inevitably be decided by the courts. Having control over who is and who is not a "qualified applicant" is likely the difference in orders of magnitude (hundreds versus thousands) when a class action of aggrieved potential applicants is certified by the court. The difference in distinguishing between an "interested person" and a "qualified applicant" for record-keeping purposes is a dollar figure usually with at least six zeros. The problem of defining who is a bona fide applicant is at least as old as federal EEO enforcement, with no definition sufficiently generic to describe most employers' record-keeping practices.

Finally, this section concludes with "scorekeeping" since the CRA '91 became effective. Discussed are the dollar settlements that are giving plaintiffs' attorneys an incentive. Also listed are settlements,

Exhibit 8.4. Statutory Record-Keeping Requirements.

Age Discrimination in Employment Act

The ADEA requires retention of payroll records containing the name, address, date of birth, occupation, rate of pay, and weekly compensation for each employee for a period of three years. Job postings, advertisements, applications, resumes, test papers, job orders, promotions, demotions, and results of physical examinations must be kept for one year. 29 CFR § 1627.3.

The Americans with Disabilities Act

The ADA requires retention of records dealing with all individuals with a disability. The records which must be kept for one year *after the decision is made* involve: applications, requests for reasonable accommodation, hiring, promotion, demotion, transfer, training, layoff, termination, and compensation decisions. Records containing medical information about a disabled employee's condition must be maintained in separate, confidential files to be disclosed only to supervisors in order to inform them about necessary accommodations, to medical professionals in order to allow treatment, or to government officials in order to ensure compliance with the law. ADA PP 102, 42 USC § 12112 (d) (3) (B).

Title VII of the Civil Rights Act of 1964

Employers must retain records concerning selection including a chronological list containing each applicant's name, address, date of application, sex, race or national origin, test papers, and interview records for a period of two years from the date of application, or for the period of apprenticeship, whichever is longer. An employer must maintain written records regarding any discrimination charge including: correspondence with individuals and enforcement agencies; employment records involving charging parties and all other employees holding *similar* positions; application records and test papers involving charging parties and all applicants for the *same* position. 43 FR 38290 *et seq.*, August 25, 1978.

dollar figures, and summaries of employment discrimination decisions and settlements exceeding $15 million.

Regulatory Basis for Identifying Applicant's Race and Sex

The record-keeping burden here is OFCCP's proposal obligating employers to identify the race and sex of *anyone* who may have indicated an interest in employment. Such interest may be expressed over the Internet by clicking on a Web site. OFCCP has also proposed that employers may be liable for identifying the race and sex of everyone in an electronic database when they look at a resume from outsourced recruiting vendors such as America's Job Bank, Resumix, Restrac, or PeopleSoft (Pollock, 1998).

Obviously, if an employer does not know a person's race or sex the likelihood of making employment decisions on the basis of job-related skills and abilities is enhanced. For those entities such as OFCCP, whose existence depends on counting by race and sex, a color-blind or gender-blind policy has never been an option. Hence the reason to contrast OFCCP's advocacy with regulatory requirements and the precedent of case law.

EEOC's Position on Identifying an Applicant's Race or Sex

The "Uniform Guidelines on Employee Selection Procedures" (1978) were adopted by the following federal agencies, each of which adopted them into its own regulations: the Equal Employment Opportunity Commission, the Civil Service Commission (now Office of Personnel Management), the Department of Labor, and the Department of Justice. In Section 16(Q), the "Uniform Guidelines" obligate an employer to determine whether any selection procedure has an adverse impact on classes covered by Title VII of the Civil Rights Act of 1964: "A 'selection procedure' is defined as: any measure, combination of measures, or procedure used as a basis for any employment decision. Selection procedures include the full range of assessment techniques from traditional paper and pencil tests, performance tests, training programs, or probationary periods and physical, educational, and work experience requirements through informal or casual interviews and un-scored application forms" (1978).

Employers are obligated to determine if the selection rate for any group is less than 80 percent of the best selection rate (the "Four-Fifths Rule") in Section 4(D). Necessarily, the employer has to determine the race and sex of both the people selected and the applicant pools from which the people were selected.

Subsequently, the federal agencies published a supplementary "Questions and Answers" (Federal Register, 1979) to clarify further certain unresolved issues, including Question and Answer 15, which provided guidance on who was to be considered an applicant (p. 11998):

Question: What is meant by the terms applicant and candidate as they are used in the "Uniform Guidelines"?

Answer: The precise definition of the term applicant depends upon the user's recruitment and selection procedures. The concept of an applicant is that of a person who has indicated an interest in being considered for hiring, promotion, or other employment opportunities. This interest might be expressed by completing an application form, or might be expressed orally, depending upon the employer's practice. The term candidate has been included to cover those situations where the initial step by the user involves consideration of current employees for promotion, or training, or other employment opportunities, without inviting applications.

OFCCP's Proposal to Require Keeping Race and Sex Records

Of late, OFCCP has taken an aggressive enforcement posture requiring federal contractors to document the race and sex of everyone expressing an interest in employment without regard to whether that person meets minimum qualifications for the position in question. In other words, if a person clicks on an employer's Web site it is a sufficient expression of interest in employment to obligate the employer to identify that person's race and sex and to maintain this information.

OFCCP's rationale for keeping race and sex adverse-impact data is the cornerstone of the enforcement of EO 11246. To understand how expansive the record-keeping burden is, start with the fact that minimum qualification requirements are subject to adverse impact analysis under the "Uniform Guidelines": "Each user should maintain and have available for inspection records of other information which will disclose the impact which its tests and other selection procedures have upon employment opportunities of persons by identifiable race, sex, or ethnic group" (Uniform Guidelines, Sec. 4A) and "Users of selection procedures . . . should maintain and have available for each job records or other information showing whether the total selection process for that job has an adverse impact" (Uniform Guidelines, Sec. 15A)[2].

OFCCP's proposal requiring employers to identify the race and sex of every interested person is not supported by a careful reading of "Uniform Guidelines" Question and Answer 88 (Federal Register, 1979, p. 12008):

Question: How should a user collect data on race, sex, or ethnic classifications for purposes of determining the impact of selection procedures?

Answer: The "Guidelines" have not specified any particular procedure, and the enforcement agencies will accept different procedures that capture the necessary information . . . self-identification may be appropriate.

The legal distinction here is one between "permissive" and "required." The "Uniform Guidelines" say an employer *may* collect race and sex information through self-identification but do not require employers to do so. Hence, OFCCP is imposing a regulatory record-keeping burden where none exists, and as such, will likely be forced into public hearings under the Administrative Procedure Act.

Court's Acceptance of Qualified Applicant Limitations

First of all, courts have not limited adverse impact analysis to the employer's actual applicants. The precedent of at least two Supreme Court adverse impact decisions support looking beyond applicant flow statistics to workforce and labor market comparisons. Recall that Griggs permitted the plaintiffs to show the adverse impact of the high school diploma requirement based on U.S. census data for that region of North Carolina, not on the utility's applicant flow statistics (*Griggs v. Duke Power,* 1971).

Similarly, in *Dothard v. Rawlinson* (1977), the plaintiff successfully argued, based on nationwide height and weight distributions, that women would have been adversely affected had they applied as female prison guards. The Supreme Court agreed with the plaintiff's argument that applicant flow statistics were misleading (no women had applied) because the minimum physical requirements had a "chilling effect." The self-recognized inability to meet the minimum requirements, the Court concluded, had discouraged women from applying (see also *Bradley v. Pizzaco,* 1991; *Jones v. Pepsi-Cola Metro Bottling,* 1994; and *Quigley v. Braniff Airways,* 1979).

The Supreme Court has further held in Hazelwood, Teamsters, and Wards Cove that workforce and labor market comparisons are to be made "between the employer's workforce and the *qualified* populations in the relevant labor market" without defining further what "qualified" meant (emphasis added) (*Hazelwood School District v. United States,* 1977; *International Brotherhood of Teamsters v. United States,* 1977; *Wards Cove Packing Co. v. Antonio,* 1989). (See also *Cerrato v. San Francisco Community College,* 1994; *EEOC v. Olson's Dairy Queens,* 1993; *Hester v. Southern Railway,* 1974; *Krodel v. Young,* 1984; *Pouncy v. Prudential Ins. Co.,* 1982; and *Taylor v. USAir,* 1991.)

A pragmatic risk-management strategy containing class-action exposure would entail defining demonstrably job-related minimum standards to limit the population of interested parties to the more manageable number of qualified applicants. The success of a minimum employment standards policy will turn on carefully documenting why exceptions were made. This is because during the discovery phase of litigation, a good plaintiff's attorney will attempt to argue that "exceptions swallow the rule" and that the employer's stated objective was merely pretext for discrimination. When the "exceptions" turn out consistently to be white and male, the employer's burden becomes heavier indeed.

Scorekeeping

A good rule of thumb in American business is that if you want to get management's attention, attach a dollar figure to your presentation.

This section of the chapter does just that. It should get management's attention!

According to the Administrative Office for U.S. Courts, since the Civil Rights Act of 1991 went into effect job-discrimination lawsuits have been growing at over 20 percent a year (Grimsley, 1997). Of significance is the growth in class actions. According to the Administrative Office, in 1995 and 1996 plaintiffs' attorneys filed a total of 133 employment discrimination class actions in federal courts. When a court grants class action status to a suit, it's a pivotal moment in the case. Instead of defending a handful of individual claims, the company has hundreds or even thousands of claims at stake in one suit. According to Jeffrey Norris, president of the Equal Employment Advisory Council, a group that represents mainly Fortune 300 firms on employment issues, "Once the case is certified as a class action, the employer has lost virtually any leverage they had to negotiate a reasonable settlement" (Price, 1997). Figure 8.4 shows the dollar amounts of recent class-action settlements.

An Incentive for Plaintiffs' Attorneys

According to Walt Connolly, a leading class-action employment defense attorney: "When companies like Texaco, Home Depot, and Publix pay outrageous amounts of money—far beyond the value of a case—other plaintiffs' law firms figure it's worthwhile. I have plaintiffs' lawyers in class actions asking for settlement dollars that exceed what they could get if we tried the case and lost" (Price, 1997, p. A1).

Settling early out of court doesn't necessarily end a firm's woes. According to David Fram of the National Employment Law Institute in Washington, D.C.: "Once you settle a lawsuit, there is a fair likelihood that it is going to get out, even if you have a confidentiality agreement. Firms that settle easily invite more lawsuits" (Price, 1997, p. A1).

One "success story" illustrating the dollar incentives driving class action litigation is a Bay Area law firm that has surpassed $600 million in class action awards since passage of the CRA '91 (Segal, 1997). The firm's typical fees range between one-fifth and one-third of class action settlements, and its winning strategy has been to treat

Figure 8.4. EEO Settlement Dollar Amounts (in Millions).

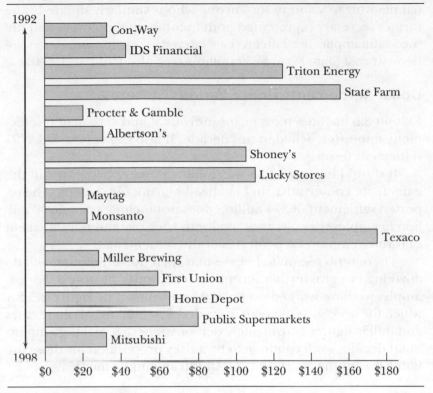

civil rights litigation as a business, where other public interest law firms treat it as a mission. It invests in labor market analyses, for example, before deciding to sue, usually a national employer.

One of the firm's recent multimillion dollar settlements involving an insurance company started when one of the senior partners noticed that all the insurance agents in a company's television ad were men. Following up on his hunch, he had paralegals go through yellow page listings to find a female agent. They found none. To steer clear of ABA ethics rules prohibiting the solicitation of clients, the attorney got newspaper coverage in which he alleged that sex discrimination was rampant at some large insurers. When a former secretary of the targeted firm saw the article and read between the lines, she contacted the law firm. That was this plaintiff attorney's silver bullet, because class action rules allow an individual plaintiff to stand in for anyone who is similarly situated. The former secretary represented both incumbent employees and unsuccessful applicants. Fifteen years later, this sex discrimination settlement cost State Farm $239 million (see also Holden, 1993).

Dollar Settlements Under Various Statutes

Exhibit 8.5 includes most major individual and class action settlement amounts reached in this decade. It also shows post–CRA '91 settlement terms.

It should be noted that the dollar estimates presented in the exhibit are conservative. In Lockheed-Martin, for example, the reported settlement of $14 million does not include some $200 million in employer's costs associated with back pay and reinstatement of former employees, per terms of the settlement.

There is no reason to believe that such dollar amounts will do anything but give further incentive to plaintiffs' attorneys. For example, we have worked on several cases shown in Figure 8.5 for which the average settlement exceeded $50 million! All these cases and dollar figures convincingly demonstrate that making employment decisions will continue to be a risky proposition for those unfamiliar with the constraints of American employment law.

Discussion

The Civil Rights Act of 1991 appeared to change the risk-management strategy of American employers with the introduction of jury trials for intentional acts of discrimination and the expansion of damages available under Title VII and the ADA. In fact, employers were already beset with common law tort claims, the dollar settlement amount of which clearly exceeds settlements under federal statutes.

Employers can escape jury trials under Title VII by avoiding the appearance of disparate treatment—that is, treating similarly situated persons differently with regard to a prohibited classification. One effective risk-management strategy is to replace the casual interview with structured interviews.

The EEOC's already limited role has been further diminished by the CRA '91. Before the CRA '91, federal law enforcement

Exhibit 8.5. EEO Settlement Dollar Amounts by Statutes.

Company	Year	Settlement/Verdict (Dollars)
Age Discrimination:		
Westinghouse	1997	14,000,000
First Union	1997	58,500,000
K-mart	1997	7,500,000
Lockheed-Martin	1996	14,000,000
Airborne Express	1996	3,300,000
Maytag	1995	16,500,000
Con-Way	1992	27,000,000
IDS Financial	1992	35,000,000
Defamation:		
Procter & Gamble	1993	15,500,000
Disability Discrimination:		
Complete Auto	1997	5,500,000
Coca-Cola	1995	7,100,000
Privacy Rights Violation:		
Target Stores	1993	2,000,000
Race Discrimination:		
Texaco	1996	176,100,000
Adams Mark Hotel	1995	4,910,000
U.S. Labor Department	1994	4,900,000
Arkansas State	1993	2,300,000
Du Pont	1993	14,000,000
Illinois Central	1993	10,000,000
Shoney's	1993	105,000,000
Retaliatory Discharge:		
Miller Brewing	1997	26,600,000
Triton Energy	1992	124,000,000
Sex Discrimination:		
Home Depot	1997	65,000,000
Publix Supermarkets	1997	81,500,000
Hooters	1997	3,750,000

Exhibit 8.5. EEO Settlement Dollar Amounts by Statutes, Cont'd.

Company	Year	Settlement/Verdict (Dollars)
Lucky Stores	1994	107,250,000
J. R Simplot	1992	10,300,000
State Farm	1992	157,000,000
Sexual Harassment:		
Astra USA	1998	9,900,000
Baker & McKenzie	1994	6,900,000
California Acrylic	1993	1,000,000
Mitsubishi Motors	1998	34,000,000
Wage Violations:		
Southern New Eng.	1995	7,800,000
Sex and Race Discrimination:		
Albertson's	1993	29,500,000
Age, Race, and Disability Discrimination:		
Monsanto	1996	18,250,000

emphasized conciliation, with EEOC personnel bringing the parties to the table to reach settlements. The CRA '91 now encourages private plaintiffs' attorneys to pursue class actions with monetary damages that had been previously available only through civil trials seeking tort damages under common law. With the exception of a handful of showcase settlements, EEOC has largely taken a backseat to the monetary dynamics encouraging private plaintiffs' attorneys to seek out class-action opportunities.

Plaintiffs can increasingly be expected to make tort common law claims their first choice, if not their exclusive choice, when alleging that employment decision-making systems are discriminatory. Common law claims were, and continue to be, the argument of choice even after passage of the CRA '91 because of the absence of monetary caps on compensatory and punitive damages. This will likely remain so until such time as Congress takes up meaningful, comprehensive tort reform by broadly capping damage awards.

Instrumental to managing risk is controlling what records are kept. Risk will be better managed by an employer's controlling the definition of who is a qualified applicant, because the enforcement agencies are proposing record keeping for *all* who might have expressed an employment interest in one way or another. Courts will ultimately have to decide whether a person assumes the legal status of applicant merely by expressing interest in an employer. Risk will also be managed by closely attending to record retention requirements, because such information is essential to determining the size of an affected class when challenges inevitably arise.

Finally, in an effort to get management's attention, we report summaries of dollar amounts and terms of major individual and class action settlements since passage of the Civil Rights Act of 1991 (see Exhibit 8.6). The more difficult problems for risk managers will be both keeping ahead of statutory restrictions on prohibited questions and keeping current with common law precedents in each and every state in which employment decisions are made. One of the authors recently advised a client whose "attitudes toward legalization of drugs" questions were found to adversely affect liberals under the California Labor Code (*Thompson v. Borg-Warner*).

Conclusion

Employment decision making is more highly regulated than most employment managers could dream in even their worst nightmares. Recently in a remarkably candid comment, Judge Sporkin of the U.S. District Court for the District of Columbia complained that federal trial judges "are becoming personnel czars of virtually every one of this nation's public and private institutions."

The ever-confounding web of employment regulations permeates all levels of government. Where there are regulations, there is enforcement. Where there is enforcement, litigation is inevitable, whether brought by an enforcement agency or by private attorneys. As previously discussed, employment litigation is four hundred times more likely to be initiated by private plaintiffs' attorneys than by an enforcement agency. (It should be noted, however, that when an enforcement agency goes to court, it is less likely to be dismissed or have adverse summary judgments.) Plaintiffs' attorneys are encouraged to bring class action claims both under federal and state

Exhibit 8.6. Post–CRA '91 Class Action Settlement Terms.

Mitsubishi
In September 1997, 27 women settled a private suit for $9.5 million.
In June 1998, EEOC settled a class action in which Mitsubishi agreed
to pay an additional $34 million to a class of several hundred women
employed at their Normal, IL, auto plant. The claims involved a sexual
hostile work environment. *(September 1997)*

Astra USA
Astra USA Inc. settled charges of sexual harassment with the EEOC
agreeing to pay $9.9 million to be split among former and current
employees with valid claims as identified by the EEOC. The suit alleged
ASTRA executives harassed female employees and subjected female
sales representatives to "demands to attend private dinners and parties,
unwanted touching, propositioning, grabbing, kissing, and comments
of a sexual nature." Other charges included allegations that female
sales reps were encouraged to wear bikinis at "Beach Olympics" at some
sales meetings. Employees who acquiesced to these demands received
favorable treatment and those who complained or refused to cover up
were retaliated against. Astra agreed to pay $9.9 million to the claim-
ants and agreed to court-supervised monitoring of its employment
practices. *(February 6, 1998)*

Hunter Tylo v. Spelling Production
A Los Angeles jury awarded Tylo $4.89 million in her pregnancy dis-
crimination suit. The jury found that Spelling wrongfully terminated
Tylo due to her pregnancy. The jury found that Tylo was still qualified
for the "vixen" role she was hired for prior to becoming pregnant despite Spelling's allegations to the contrary. *(December 22, 1997)*

Home Depot
This retailer agreed on September 22, 1997, to pay $65 million to settle
sex discrimination claims by a potential class of 200,000 current and
former employees. Home Depot will also pay an additional $44.5 mil-
lion in plaintiffs' attorney fees. *(September 22, 1997)*

Westinghouse Electric/Northrop Grumman
Westinghouse Electric Corp. and Northrup Grumman Corp. settled
two age discrimination suits with the EEOC for $14 million. One suit
involved claims by 259 employees of Westinghouse's defense and electronics business who were laid off in February 1991. Northrup is assuming partial financial responsibility because it purchased Westinghouse's

Exhibit 8.6. Post–CRA '91 Class Action Settlement Terms, Cont'd.

defense and electronic business in March 1996. The settlement also resolved 548 age discrimination claims under EEOC investigation involving Westinghouse employees laid off between 1992 and 1996. *(October 31, 1997)*

First Union Corporation
The nation's sixth largest bank agreed October 7, 1997, to pay $58.5 million in damages to 239 former employees to settle an age discrimination suit. The plaintiffs worked for two banks acquired by First Union and claimed First Union unfairly fired them and replaced them with younger, lower-paid workers. *(October 7, 1997)*

Hooters
Hooters, a restaurant chain, agreed on October 1, 1997, to pay $3.75 million to settle a class action claim brought by 7 male job applicants. While not agreeing to hire male waiters, Hooters did agree to make more bartender and host positions available to males. *(October 1, 1997)*

K-mart
The retailer agreed to pay 80 former store managers demoted from 1990 to 1992, $7.5 million in a settlement announced September 23, 1997. Plaintiffs alleged they were demoted due to their age. As part of the settlement, K-mart will give the EEOC access to hiring and training information. *(September 23, 1997)*

Miller Brewing
A Wisconsin state court jury awarded $26.6 million to a Miller Brewing executive, Jerold MacKenzie, fired following a co-worker's sexual harassment allegation against him. The jury supported MacKenzie's claim that Miller interfered with his employment by this firing and by an earlier action taken against him. *(July 15, 1997)*

Publix Supermarkets
This grocery store chain agreed in January 1997 to pay 150,000 current and former employees $81.5 million to settle their gender bias suit. The class alleged that women were systematically denied desirable job assignments, training, and management opportunities. *(January 1997)*

Complete Auto Transit
On January 8, 1997, the EEOC won its biggest verdict to date when a federal jury awarded a man suffering from epilepsy about $5.5 million for being discriminated against on his job. The jury found that Complete

Exhibit 8.6. Post–CRA '91 Class Action Settlement Terms, Cont'd.

Auto Transit violated the disabilities law by not transferring an employee into another job after he suffered an epileptic seizure. The verdict included $4.3 million in punitive damages and $960,000 in back pay. To date, it is the largest award the commission has ever obtained for an individual plaintiff. (*January 8, 1997*)

Lockheed Martin

A federal judge gave preliminary settlement approval on November 21, 1996, in a massive age discrimination suit brought by the EEOC. The total settlement is valued at $200 million over five years including $13 million in cash payments to about 2,039 laid-off workers and jobs for 450 of them, plus training, job search help, and promises from company management not to discriminate or retaliate. *(November 21, 1996)*

Monsanto

In June 1996, Monsanto paid $18.25 million to settle this two-year-old suit filed in St. Louis by 43 former salespeople for Ortho lawn and gardening products. The plaintiffs alleged they were discriminated against because of either their age, race, or disability. (*June, 1996*)

Airborne Express

In April 1996, John Kelley, 49, a former executive fired by Airborne, was awarded $3.33 million by a Boston federal judge. Kelley was fired as a regional manager for the Northeast region in 1993, only three months after receiving a superior performance evaluation. The judge found Airborne improperly considered Kelley's age in the decision. *(April 1996)*

Adams Mark Hotel

On December 5, 1995, HBE Corporation, parent of the Adams Mark Hotel chain sustained a $4.91 million jury verdict in a claim brought by the EEOC. The St. Louis, Missouri, jury found that the hotel passed over a black employment manager for promotion because of his race. A white personnel manager who recommended the black manager for promotion was also fired when he refused to fire the black manager. *(December 5, 1995)*

Maytag

Maytag Corporation settled a class-action age discrimination lawsuit in 1995 involving approximately 800 individuals. The suit alleged Maytag promised not to close the Ranson plant yet later did. In a press release,

Exhibit 8.6. Post–CRA '91 Class Action Settlement Terms, Cont'd.

Maytag officials said, "We reluctantly agreed to settle this case even though we believe our actions in closing the plant were lawful, prudent, and reasonable. Yet, as the facts and circumstances evolved, the potential risks associated with a jury trial in Jefferson County, West Virginia, exceeded our earlier evaluation" (*National Law Journal*, Aug. 28, 1995). *(August 1995)*

Coca-Cola
A Dallas jury on July 3, 1995 awarded a former Coca-Cola executive $7.1 million ($6.0 million punitives were later capped by the judge at $300,000) after finding that the company violated the Americans with Disabilities Act when it terminated the executive while he was in alcohol rehabilitation treatment. *(July 3, 1995)*

U.S. Labor Department
The Labor Department agreed to pay an estimated $4.9 million in 1994 to settle a suit that accused the agency of race discrimination against its own black employees. The agreement covers an estimated 350 to 400 employees. *(September 1994)*

Albertson's
On November 22, 1993, Albertson's Inc. a California-based food and drug chain, reached a tentative $29.5 million settlement of sex and race discrimination charges. It was alleged that Albertson's had assigned female and Hispanic employees to low-paying jobs by denying them promotions and access to training programs and by offering women and Hispanics part-time rather than full-time employment. Of the $29.5 million, $23.5 million was allocated to damage claims and $4.5 million represented attorneys' fees. *(November 22, 1993)*

Arkansas State Hospital
On September 27, 1993, a federal judge approved a $2 million settlement of a lawsuit filed by black employees and former employees who claimed that they were discriminated against because of their race. Plaintiffs' attorneys fees amounted to almost $300,000. *(September 27, 1993)*

Du Pont
On August 13, 1993, Du Pont settled a race discrimination suit challenging the seniority system of a Du Pont manufacturing plant in Louisville, Kentucky, for $14 million. A federal court had earlier ruled that the company violated Title VII of the Civil Rights Act of 1964 by

Exhibit 8.6. Post–CRA '91 Class Action Settlement Terms, Cont'd.

relegating black workers to certain job classifications and by putting
up barriers to their promotion to other jobs. The settlement includes
$13.4 million in back pay and $1.7 million in attorneys' fees and costs.
(August 13, 1993)

Target Stores
On July 9, 1993, Target Stores agreed to pay more than $2 million to
settle a class action lawsuit brought by job applicants who were required
to answer intimate personal questions in a preemployment psychological examination. The applicants charged that the test violated their
constitutional privacy rights as well as state labor laws. *(July 9, 1993)*

Baker & McKenzie
In August 1994, a San Francisco jury found the Baker & McKenzie law
firm along with a senior partner liable for $6.9 million in damages re-
lated to the sexual harassment of a former secretary. The trial judge
upheld the finding but reduced the punitive damage award. The case
was later settled confidentially after the appellate court remanded the
case for new trial. *(August 1994)*

Lucky Stores
A San Francisco federal judge approved a $107.25 million damage settle-
ment in 1994 in a class action sex discrimination suit filed against Lucky
Stores. The August 1992 case alleged that Lucky discriminated against
20,000 women in assignments, scheduling, and promotions at its northern California division stores. In the case, Judge Patel said she would not
call the award "modest" but it was well within the range of reasonableness given the length and complexity of the case. *(January 1994)*

Illinois Central Gulf Railroad
On June 8, 1993, Illinois Central Corporation agreed to pay $10 million
to settle a class action lawsuit alleging that the railroad discriminated
against blacks in its hiring practices during a track rehabilitation project. The settlement, approved by the federal court in Illinois, included
claims for back pay, damages for emotional distress, interest, attorneys'
fees, and costs. *(June 8, 1993)*

California Acrylic Industries
On May 17, 1993, a Los Angeles jury awarded $1 million to a male
worker who accused a female supervisor of persistent sexual harass-

Exhibit 8.6. Post–CRA '91 Class Action Settlement Terms, Cont'd.

ment. The complaint alleged that the male employee was sexually harassed "on an almost daily basis" for over five years by his female supervisor, who was the chief financial officer and director of personnel for Cal-Spas, a Pomona, California–based company. The jury awarded $375,000 for emotional distress, $550,000 in punitive damages, and $90,000 in economic losses. *(May 17, 1993)*

Shoney's
On January 25, 1993, a federal judge approved a $105 million settlement of a class action employment race discrimination suit against Shoney's Inc., a Nashville-based company that operates one of the nation's largest restaurant chains. Legal fees, expenses, and court costs pushed the total to $132 million. *(January 25, 1993)*

J. R. Simplot
On April 23, 1993, the J. R. Simplot Company, an agricultural processing firm headquartered in Boise, Idaho, reached a tentative $10.3 million class action settlement of sex discrimination claims. The lawsuit, originally brought by 15 former Simplot employees, alleges sex discrimination in pay and promotional practices by Simplot. The class of 1,000 present and former salaried Simplot employees will receive $4.8 million. Another $500,000 will be provided to the 15 named class representatives. Additionally, Simplot will allocate $1 million in each of the next five years for equity adjustments on salaries and bonuses as well as employees training fees. *(April 23, 1993)*

Con-Way International
In August 1992, John Moody, 65, was awarded $27 million in a Fort Worth, Texas, age discrimination case. Moody, a regional manager, was transferred to Fort Worth from Michigan in 1985, then demoted while two younger men were promoted ahead of him. Con-Way is a subsidiary of Consolidated Freightways, Inc. *(August 1992)*

IDS Financial Services
IDS Financial Services, Inc. agreed to pay $35 million to 32 former executives to settle an age discrimination lawsuit. The class action lawsuit claimed that in the 1980s, executives over age 40 were replaced by younger, less experienced people as part of a plan to reduce the average age of middle managers. IDS admitted no wrongdoing in the settlement made in 1992. *(August 1992)*

Exhibit 8.6. Post–CRA '91 Class Action Settlement Terms, Cont'd.

State Farm Insurance
On April 28, 1992, State Farm Insurance Company settled a sex discrimination class action for $157 million. The settlement comes after a federal judge ruled against the Bloomington, Illnois–based company in a suit alleging sex discrimination in its hiring practices. Before settling on the $157 million figure, an average of $193,000 for each of the remaining plaintiffs, the company had paid out an estimated $33 million to resolve previously settled cases. *(April 28, 1992)*

Claims data note: There are currently no reliable sources to track employment-related jury verdicts or settlements (which are usually confidential). However, according to the Ohio-based organization Jury Verdict Research, average compensatory damages in employment liability cases nationwide in 1995 was about $532,000 for wrongful termination not based on discrimination; $502,000 for work-related gender discrimination; $198,000 for racial discrimination; $159,000 for handicap discrimination; and $120,000 for sexual harassment.

These figures do not include legal expenses or punitive damages.

The average verdicts (including punitive and legal costs) in California employment-law cases rose from about $778,000 in 1992 to $1.9 million in 1994.

statutes and under common law. Most discrimination cases this decade have been brought under common law, where dollar settlements consistently exceed those brought under federal and state statutes.

The use of demonstrably job-related employment tests is a winning strategy for minimizing the risk of employment litigation. Forty-plus percent of employment decisions in the private sector are based on the results of employment tests. Litigation challenging employment test use, however, occurs in less than one-half of 1 percent of all discrimination claims. So the tides have turned from the post-Griggs days, when employers abandoned the casual use of employment tests. Legally defensible employment testing is now one of the safest harbors offering shelter from the howling gales of class-action EEO litigation.

On the basis of trends discussed in this chapter and "hostile work environment" court decisions, we are reluctantly forced to agree with *The Economist* ("Men, Women," 1998): "The Supreme Court completed its 1997–98 term by greatly extending the scope of antidiscrimination laws in a way that will not only increase the burdens on employers but could well turn the American workplace into the most highly regulated in the world."

Regulation begets litigation, and litigation is spelled *r-i-s-k*. Good news if you are an employment attorney; bad news if you are not.

References

Administrative Procedure Act, 5 U.S.C. § 554.

Age Discrimination in Employment Act (ADEA), 29 U.S.C.

American Management Association. (1997). *Survey on workplace testing and monitoring.*

Americans with Disabilities Act (ADA), 42 U.S.C. (1990).

Ash, P. (1994). The legality of preemployment inquiries: A guide to state and other jurisdictional rules and regulations. In G. Stokes, M. Mumford, & W. Owens (Eds.), *Biodata handbook: Theory, research, and use of biographical information in selection and performance prediction.* Palo Alto, CA: CPP Books. (Original work published 1988)

Bennett v. Nelson, 151 A.2d 476 (Pa. 1959).

Black, K. (1994). Personality screening in employment. *American Business Law Journal, 3,* 69–83.

Bradley v. Pizzaco, 939 F.2d 613 (8th Cir. 1991).

Bulger, B., & Gessner, C. (1992). Sign of the times: Implementing reductions in force. *Employee Relations Law Journal, 17*(3), 431–448.

Burnett, J., Fan, C., Motowidlo, S., & Degroot, T. (1998). Interview notes and validity. *Personnel Psychology, 51,* 375–396.

Burns, J. (1994). Employee privacy. *Employee Relations Law Journal, 20*(1), 161–171.

Burns, J. (1996). Use and abuse of performance appraisals. *Employee Relations Law Journal, 22*(2), 165–170.

Butts v. Nichols, 381 F. Supp. 573 (S.D. Iowa 1974).

Cathcart, D., & Snyderman, M. (1992). The Civil Rights Act of 1991. *The Labor Lawyer, 8,* 850.

Cerrato v. San Francisco Community College, 26 F.2d 976 (9th Cir. 1994).

Civil Rights Act of 1964 (Title VII), 42 U.S.C. § 2000 (1964).

Civil Rights Act of 1991 (CRA '91), Pub. L. No. 102–118, 105 Stat. 1071 (1991).

Comeaux v. Brown & Williamson Tobacco, 915 F.2d 1264 (1990).

Copus, D. (1996). *Employment law 101 deskbook.* Larkspur, CA: National Employment Law Institute.

Davidson, J. (1995). The temptation of performance appraisal abuse in employment litigation. *Virginia Law Review, 81,* 1605–1629.

Dothard v. Rawlinson, 433 U.S. 321 (1977).

Duffy, D. (1982). Privacy v. disclosure: Balancing employee and employer rights. *Employee Relations Law Journal, 7,* 594–609.

Eichenseer v. Reserve Life Insurance, 894 F.2d 1414 (5th Cir. 1994).

Equal Employment Opportunity Commission v. Olson's Dairy Queens, 989 F.2d 168 (5th Cir. 1993).

Equal Opportunity Commission (EEOC). (1995, Oct. 10). *ADA enforcement guidance: Preemployment disability-related questions and medical examinations.* Washington, DC: Author.

Equal Opportunity Commission (EEOC). (1997, Mar. 25). *Enforcement guidance on the Americans with Disabilities Act and psychiatric disabilities.* Washington, DC: Author.

Fast, S. (1993). Breach of employee confidentiality: Moving toward a common-law tort remedy. *University of Pennsylvania Law Review, 142,* 431.

Federal Register. (1979, Mar. 2). *44* (43).

Feldleit v. Long Island Railroad, 732 F. Supp. 892 (E.D. N.Y. 1989).

Feliu, A. (1994). Workplace violence and the duty to care: The scope of an employer's obligation to protect against the violent employee. *Employee Relations Law Journal, 20*(3), 381–405.

Green v. Missouri Pacific Railway, 523 F.2d 1290 (8th Cir. 1975).

Gregory v. Litton Systems, 316 F. Supp. 401 (C.D. Cal. 1970); 472 F.2d 631 (9th Cir. 1973).

Gregory, D. (1988). Reducing the risk of negligence in hiring. *Employee Relations Law Journal, 14,* 31–40.

Griggs v. Duke Power Company, 401 U.S. 424, 430 (1971).

Grimsley, K. (1997, May 12). Worker bias cases are rising steadily. *Washington Post,* pp. A1, A10.

Hahn, J. (1991). Preemployment information services: Employers beware? *Employee Relations Law Journal, 17*(1), 45–69.

Hamberger v. Eastman, 106 N.H. 107, 206 A.2d 239 (N.H. 1965).

Hazelwood School District v. United States, 433 U.S. 310 (1977).

Hester v. Southern Railway, 497 F.2d 1379 (5th Cir. 1974).

Highberger, W. (1996). Current evidentiary issues in employment litigation. *Employee Relations Law Journal, 22*(1), 31–56.

Hill v. U.S. Postal Service, 522 F. Supp. 1283 (S.D. N.Y. 1981).

Holden, B. (1993, June 10). A law firm shows civil rights can be a lucrative business. *Wall Street Journal,* p. A1.

International Brotherhood of Teamsters v. United States, 431 U.S. 324 (1977).

Jenero, K., & Males-Riordan, L. (1992). Electronic monitoring of employees and the elusive "right to privacy." *Employee Relations Law Journal, 18*(1), 74–75.

Johnson v. Pike Corporation of America, 332 F. Supp. 490 (C.D. Cal. 1971).

Jones, J., Ash, P., & Soto, C. (1990). Employment privacy rights and pre-employment honesty tests. *Employee Relations Law Journal, 15*(4), 561–575.

Jones v. Pepsi-Cola Metro Bottling, 871 F. Supp. 310 (E.D. Mich. 1994).

K-Mart v. Trotti, 677 S.W.2d 632 (Texas Civ. App. 1984).

Krodel v. Young, 748 F.2d 710 (D.C. Dir. 1984).

Mael, F., Connerley, M., & Morath, R. (1996). None of your business: Parameters of biodata invasiveness. *Personnel Psychology, 49,* 613–650.

McKenna v. Fargo, 451 F. Supp. 1355 (D.N.J. 1978), aff'd 601 F.2d 575 (3rd Cir. 1979).

Men, women, work, and law: An even more dangerous mixture than before, thanks to the Supreme Court. (1998, July 4). *The Economist,* pp. 21–22.

Mesritz, G. (1995). Update on recent trends in the law: The Age Discrimination in Employment Act. *Employee Relations Law Journal, 21*(1), 107–119.

Mitchell, T. (1994). Are weighted application data valid and legal? In G. Stokes, M. Mumford, & W. Owens (Eds.), *Biodata handbook: Theory, research, and use of biographical information in selection and performance prediction.* Palo Alto, CA: CPP Books.

Mook, J. (1996). Personality testing in today's workplace: Avoiding the legal pitfalls. *Employee Relations Law Journal, 22*(3), 65–88.

Myerson, A. (1997, Jan. 12). As federal bias cases drop, workers take up the fight. *The New York Times,* pp. A1, A14.

Nager, G., & Bilich, E. (1994). The Civil Rights Act of 1991 going forward. *Employee Relations Law Journal, 20*(2), 237–251.

Parliman, R., & Dolan, T. (1990, Summer). Preemployment information services: How useful are they? *Employment Relations Today, 17,* 127.

Patterson v. McLean Credit Union, 491 U.S. 164 (1989).

Pavesich v. New England Life Insurance, 122 Ga. 190, 50 S.W. 65 (1994).

Pollock, E. (1998, July 30). Inhuman resources: For job seekers these days, computer scanners are a vexing first hurdle. *Wall Street Journal,* p. A1.

Pouncy v. Prudential Insurance Company, 668 F.2d 803 (5th Cir. 1982).

Price, D. (1997, Oct. 13). Job-bias lawsuits skyrocket: Lawyers step up to take advantage of 1991 law. *Investor's Business Daily,* p. A1.

Privacy Act of 1974, 45 U.S.C. 552(e)(2).

Pyburn, K. (1996, Apr.). Trend in cases involving employment tests. Paper presented at the Personnel Testing Council of Northern California, Sacramento.

Questions and answers. (1979). *Federal Register, 44,* 11996.

Quigley v. Braniff Airways, 85 F.R.D. 80 (N.D. Tex. 1979).

Reynolds v. Sheet Metal Workers Local 102, 498 F. Supp. 952 (D.D.C. 1980); 702 F.2d 221 (D.C. Cir. 1981).

Rhodes v. Graham, 238 Ky. 225, 37 S.W.2d 46 (Ky. 1931).

Richardson v. Hotel Corporation of America, 332 F. Supp. 519 (E.D. La. 1971); 468 F.2d 951 (5th Cir. 1972).

Safire, W. Nobody's business. (1998, Jan. 8). *The New York Times,* p. A29.

Segal, D. (1997, Jan. 27). Lawyers stake a claim on bias lawsuits. *Washington Post,* p. A1.

Sharf, J. (1994). The impact of legal and equal employment opportunity issues on personal history inquiries. In G. Stokes, M. Mumford, & W. Owens (Eds.), *Biodata handbook: Theory, research, and use of biographical information in selection and performance prediction.* Palo Alto, CA: CPP Books.

Shepard, I., Duston, R., & Russell, K. (1989). *Workplace privacy: Employee testing, surveillance, wrongful discharge, and other areas of vulnerability* (2nd ed.). Washington, DC: Bureau of National Affairs.

Soroka v. Dayton Hudson Corporation, 235 Cal. App. 3d 654 (1991).

Taylor v. USAir, 56 FEP Cases 366 (W.D. Pa. 1991).

Thompson v. Borg-Warner, Case No. C-94–4015 (MHR; U.S.D.C. Northern District of California).

Tippins, N., & Wunder, S. (1997, Apr.). *Entry-level management and professional selection: Best and most common practices (Are they the same?).* Workshop presented at the meeting of the Society for Industrial and Organizational Psychology, St. Louis.

Uniform guidelines on employee selection procedures. Section 3D. (1978). *Federal Register, 43,* 38209.

United States v. City of Chicago, 385 F. Supp. 540 (N.D. Ill. 1974).

Wards Cove Packing v. Antonio, 490 U.S. 642 (1989).

Werner, J., & Bolino, M. (1997). Explaining U.S. courts of appeals decisions involving performance appraisal: Accuracy, fairness, and validation. *Personnel Psychology, 50,* 1–24.

Williamson, L., Campion, J., Malos, S., Roehling, M., & Campion, M. (1997). Employment interview on trial: Linking interview structure with litigation outcomes. *Journal of Applied Psychology, 82*(6), 900–912.

CHAPTER 9

Accommodations for Persons with Disabilities

Wanda J. Campbell
Maureen E. Reilly

The most far-reaching statute relating to the protection of individuals with disabilities in the workplace is the Americans with Disabilities Act (ADA), which was enacted on July 26, 1990. Although this chapter focuses on the ADA, employers should be aware that other statutes also provide protection in the workplace for individuals with disabilities. Section 504 of the Rehabilitation Act of 1973 (29 U.S.C. § 794[d]) protects federal employees from disability-related discrimination, and many states also prohibit disability discrimination in their human rights laws. The substantive standards for determining liability under the Rehabilitation Act are the same as those applicable under the ADA. State laws, however, may differ from the ADA in significant ways.

The passage of the ADA was received with mixed reactions by many psychologists involved in the development and implementation of employment tests. Psychologists endeavor to develop assessment systems that give all candidates the same opportunity to demonstrate their knowledge, skills, and abilities as they relate to the job. However, the ADA mandates that a segment of the population be provided accommodations in the testing process to eliminate bias attributable to a demonstrated disability. While there is strong support for the spirit of the law, the practicalities of implementing it have been a real challenge.

The ADA applies to the selection process and any resulting employment relationship. This chapter will address the issues that the ADA presents in the selection process—in particular in employment testing. Issues relating to modifying the work environment and the job to accommodate disabled employees will be addressed only insofar as they pertain to the selection process. The primary focus of this chapter will be twofold: to present the legal requirements of the ADA as they relate to employment testing, and to describe some of the ways in which practitioners from across the country have adapted their selection procedures to comply with it. This chapter will also discuss the benefits and disadvantages of approaches adopted by different organizations when dealing with disability-related issues in the selection process.

The information concerning how organizations approach ADA testing issues is based on interviews conducted by senior author Wanda Campbell with a wide range of private organizations, as well as with state and local governmental agencies.

Factors That Influence Decisions Concerning Accommodations

The ADA prohibits discrimination against individuals with disabilities by covered employers, public services, public accommodations, and telecommunications. The employment provisions of the act (Title I), which went into effect on July 26, 1992, prohibit discrimination against individuals on the basis of their disabilities, both on the job and in the employment selection process (42 U.S.C. § 12112[a]). This prohibition, as it pertains to selection decisions, is broadly construed to include all types of selection criteria, such as safety and lifting restrictions, hearing and vision requirements, and employment tests (29 C.F.R. App. § 1630.10). Moreover, the statute is broader than most other federal antidiscrimination statutes, because the ADA not only prohibits discrimination by employers but also imposes affirmative obligations relating to the manner in which employers treat both their employees and applicants for employment. Specifically, an employer may have an affirmative duty to provide reasonable accommodations to a disabled employee so that he or she can perform the essential functions of the job (42 U.S.C. § 12112[b][5][A]; 29 C.F.R. § 1630.9). This duty to reasonably accommodate an employee also extends to the selection process (29 C.F.R. App. §§ 1630.10–11). The details of these requirements will be discussed in the following sections.

Coverage Issues Under the ADA

Most private employers, as well as employment agencies, labor organizations, and state and local governments, are covered by Title I (42 U.S.C. § 12111[5]). The employment provisions apply to all employers with fifteen or more full-time employees. Covered employers are prohibited from discriminating against individuals with disabilities. The ADA also prohibits discrimination against individuals who may not themselves be disabled but have a known association or relationship with a disabled individual (42 U.S.C. § 12112[b][4]). However, not all individuals with disabilities are covered by the ADA. Instead, the ADA limits its protection to *qualified individuals with disabilities* (42 U.S.C. § 12112). In order to understand this proscription, it is necessary to understand how the statute defines both *disability* and *qualified*.

Defining Disability

Not all disabilities are covered by the ADA. A disability is covered only if it is a physical or mental impairment that substantially limits one or more major life activities. Individuals are also disabled under the ADA if they have a record of a physical or mental impairment that substantially limits one or more major life activities or if they are regarded as having such an impairment (42 U.S.C. § 12102[2]). Major life activities include functions such as caring for oneself, performing manual tasks, walking, seeing, hearing, speaking, breathing, learning, working, and reading (29 C.F.R. § 1630.2[I]). With respect to psychiatric disorders, major life activities may also include thinking, concentrating, interacting with others, speaking, and sleeping (EEOC, 1997).

In addition to restricting covered disabilities to those that substantially limit a major life activity, the ADA specifically excludes certain conditions from its coverage to eliminate or avoid any debate about whether they are covered disabilities. Such excluded conditions include current illegal drug use; homosexuality and bisexuality; sexual behavior and gender identity disorders; compulsive gambling, kleptomania, and pyromania; predisposition to illness; temporary, nonchronic impairments; personality traits; environmental, cultural, or economic disadvantages; advanced age; and pregnancy (42 U.S.C. § 12211).

Determining When an Individual with a Disability Is Qualified

An individual with a disability is not covered by Title I of the ADA unless he or she is *qualified* for the job (42 U.S.C. § 12112[a]). In order to be a qualified individual with a disability, the candidate must satisfy the prerequisites of the job (skills, education, and other job-related experience) and be able, with or without reasonable accommodation, to perform the essential functions of the job (42 U.S.C. § 12111[8]; 29 C.F.R. § 1630.2[m]). Because employment tests are designed to measure the knowledge, skills, and abilities (KSAs) necessary to perform the job, successful performance on employee selection tests is relevant to whether a candidate is qualified. Candidates who are unable to pass the selection test may not be viewed as qualified. However, if an employment test adversely affects the opportunities for selection for an individual with a disability, then the employer must demonstrate that the skill being measured by the test is job-related (29 C.F.R. App. § 1630.10). The employer may also be required to provide the disabled candidate with reasonable accommodations in the test-taking process (29 C.F.R. App. § 1630.11). Alternatively, the employer may demonstrate that it would not be possible to provide a reasonable accommodation for the disability at issue.

Identifying Essential Functions

As noted, an individual is considered a "qualified individual" with a disability only if he or she can, with or without a reasonable accommodation, perform the essential functions of the job. Under the ADA, job duties are divided into two basic categories: *essential* job functions and *nonessential* (or marginal) job functions. The term essential functions refers to fundamental job duties (29 C.F.R. § 1630.2[n]). To identify essential job functions, the focus should be on the purpose of the function and the result to be accomplished rather than on the manner in which the function is presently or traditionally performed. Although consideration may be given to the manner in which a job is currently performed, that method is not determinative and should not be considered an essential function unless there is no other way to perform the job without undue hardship.

In its regulations interpreting the ADA, the Equal Employment Opportunity Commission (EEOC) has cited three factors as indicators of the essential nature of a function (29 C.F.R. § 1630.2[n][2] and Appendix):

- Whether the purpose of the position is to perform that function
- The number of other employees available to perform the function
- The relative skill and ability required to perform the function

Information relating to the essential functions of the job is routinely gathered through job analysis procedures. To the extent that the job analysis is also the basis for the development of a valid test, it can provide strong evidence that the test in fact measures the essential functions of the job. However, employers should be aware that the EEOC has advised that the ADA does not require the use of job analysis, nor does the EEOC consider all job analysis techniques to be appropriate for assessing the essential functions of the job. For example, according to the EEOC, a job analysis method that categorizes tasks according to their relation to people, data, and objects, although well-suited for setting wage rates, may not sufficiently identify the essential functions of a particular job (see Title I *Technical Assistance Manual* § 2.3[b]). In addition, according to the EEOC, the KSA method used to develop selection procedures does not account for the fact that individuals with disabilities may be able to perform an essential function by using different skills or abilities. Job analysis techniques that do capture the essential functions of the job focus instead on the purpose of the job and the importance of the functions that achieve that purpose. Measures of importance, frequency, and time spent are useful in this regard.

Employers are not required to conduct a job analysis in order to identify the essential functions of the job. Other forms of evidence that help identify essential functions include:

- Whether the position exists for the purpose of performing the function
- Time spent performing the function
- Work experience of employees who currently perform similar jobs
- Nature of work, employer's organizational structure
- Whether it is a highly specialized function
- Consequence of not requiring the function
- Terms of a collective bargaining agreement
- Employer's judgment
- Written job descriptions (29 C.F.R. § 1630.2[n][3])

Prohibited Discrimination in Selection

The EEOC regulations interpreting the ADA explicitly address employment tests: "It is unlawful for a covered entity to use qualification standards, employment tests, or other selection criteria that screen out or tend to screen out an individual with a disability or a class of individuals with disabilities, on the basis of disability, unless the standard, test, or other selection criteria . . . is shown to be job-related for the position in question and is consistent with business necessity" (29 C.F.R. § 1630.10; see also 29 C.F.R. pt. 1630 App. § 1630.10 ["job criteria that even unintentionally screen out . . . individuals with disabilities . . . may not be used"]).

Selection criteria addressed by this standard include, for example, education and work experience requirements, physical and mental requirements, safety requirements, paper-and-pencil tests, physical or psychological tests, interview questions, and performance rating systems (29 C.F.R. pt. 1630; App. § 1630.10).

In order for a selection factor to be job related and consistent with business necessity, it must be a legitimate measure or qualification for the specific job to which it is being applied, and for ADA purposes, relate to the job's essential functions (Title I *Technical Assistance Manual* § 4.3). For example, an employer may ask candidates for a clerical position if they have a driver's license because from time to time they may be expected to deliver packages to the post office or run an errand. Although this question is job related, it appears to pertain to an incidental function rather than an essential function of the job, and for that reason, under the ADA might not be justified by business necessity.

An employer is required to show that a test is job related and consistent with business necessity only if it screens out candidates with disabilities *because of* those disabilities (29 C.F.R. App. § 1630.10; Title I *Technical Assistance Manual* § 5.6). Thus, if a candidate with dyslexia fails a pole-climbing performance test for a telephone repair job, it is not likely to be because of his or her reading disability.

Preemployment Inquiries and Medical Examinations

On May 19, 1994, the EEOC issued enforcement guidance on preemployment inquiries under the ADA. The purpose of the guidance was to provide more specific information regarding the ADA's restrictions on an employer's use of disability-related inquiries and medical examinations. On October 15, 1995, the EEOC issued further enforcement guidance on preemployment disability-related questions and medical examinations, which were published in the November 9 BNA Daily Labor Report (EEOC, 1995).

The ADA's restrictions on disability-related questions and medical examinations are intended to prevent the use of information about an applicant's physical or mental condition to exclude the applicant on that basis alone before his or her ability to perform the job at issue is evaluated. Thus, the ADA's restrictions vary depending on whether the applicant is at the preoffer or postoffer stage of the application process. An employer may not ask a disability-related question or conduct a medical examination until after the applicant is given a conditional job offer (42 U.S.C. § 12112[d]). According to the EEOC's recent guidance, the test for whether a question is disability-related is whether it is likely to elicit information about a disability (EEOC, 1995). This issue is discussed in greater detail in Chapter Eight of this volume, which discusses invasion of privacy.

The EEOC guidance defines a *medical examination* as a "procedure or test that seeks information about an individual's physical or mental impairments or health" (EEOC, 1995, p. 1106). Factors that indicate that an examination is medical whether it is administered by a health professional or the results are interpreted by a health professional, is designed to reveal physical or mental impairments, and is invasive, for example, by requiring the drawing of blood, urine, or breath.

Some employers have expressed the concern that physical agility and fitness tests may be considered preemployment medical examinations and, therefore, be forbidden by the ADA. The critical issue in these situations is whether the test involves physiological or biological measures. An employer may require an applicant to take an agility test, in which the applicant demonstrates the ability to perform actual or simulated job tasks, or a physical fitness test, in which the applicant's performance of physical tasks, such as running or lifting, is measured. Neither the agility nor the physical fitness test will be considered a medical examination unless the employer measures the applicant's physiological or biological responses to performance. For example, if a messenger service tests an applicant's ability to run one mile and at the end of the run takes the applicant's blood pressure and heart rate, the test will be considered a medical examination (EEOC, 1995).

An employer also can require applicants to provide medical certification from a physician that they can safely perform a physical ability test. This is lawful at the preemployment stage provided that the certificate only elicits a statement from the physician that the test can (or cannot) be safely performed. The certificate must not elicit disability-related information. The employer also can require applicants to agree to assume liability in the event that they are injured while performing a physical ability test (EEOC, 1995).

Some psychological tests also qualify as preemployment medical examinations and, therefore, are prohibited by the statute unless a preliminary offer of employment has been made (EEOC, 1995). If an employer administers a psychological test purportedly to determine the applicant's habits (not mental illness), but the test results are interpreted by a psychologist and the test is the type designed and used by psychologists to reveal mental or emotional illnesses, it may constitute a medical examination. Thus, in the case of *Barnes v. Cochran* (1997) the United States District Court for the Southern District of Florida held that the administration of preemployment psychological examinations, including the Minnesota Multiphasic Personality Inventory (MMPI) and the California Personality Inventory, violated the ADA. If, however, the employer administers a test for the purpose of measuring honesty, tastes, or habits—such as a personality test—it probably will not constitute a medical examination.

Polygraph examinations under the ADA are not themselves medical examinations, although provisions of other federal or state laws may limit their use. However, the administration of a polygraph test must not include disability-related questions (EEOC, 1995). After making a conditional offer of employment to an applicant, an employer may ask disability-related questions and perform medical examinations and may condition the job offer on the results of those questions or medical examinations. The employer may ask about an applicant's workers' compensation history (for certain limited purposes), prior use of sick leave, and any illnesses, diseases, impairments, or general health. But if the employer chooses to ask these questions or administer a medical examination, the employer must take the same action on the results with all employees in the same job category. If the employer asks these questions and decides not to hire the applicant, then the reason for rejecting the applicant must be job-related and consistent with business necessity (EEOC, 1995). Finally, all information obtained through such questioning must be kept confidential.

Reasonable Accommodation for Employment Tests

The ADA specifically includes provisions for the modification of selection procedures, jobs, the work environment, and the manner or circumstances in which jobs are customarily performed to enable qualified individuals with disabilities to enjoy equal employment opportunity. EEOC regulations specify three categories of accommodation: to ensure equal opportunity in the application process, to facilitate performance of essential functions of the position, and to make available equal benefits and privileges of employment (29 C.F.R. § 1630.2[o][1]). As a preliminary matter, the physical space of the work environment must be accessible to individuals with disabilities. This includes the employment office, test administration room, rest rooms, and water fountains, as well as the actual workplace, training rooms, and break rooms. Next, organizations have an affirmative duty to make the job itself accessible by providing reasonable accommodations to enable disabled individuals to apply for, and subsequently perform the essential functions of, the job. An employer need not provide such accommodations, however, if doing so would pose undue hardship on the employer or if the employee or candidate presents a direct threat to his own health or safety or the heath or safety of those around him (47 U.S.C. § 12113[b]).

Initiation of the Accommodation Process

An employer's duty to provide a reasonable accommodation applies only to *known* disabilities. Although the employer is responsible for notifying job applicants and employees of its obligation to provide accommodation by posting notices containing the provisions of the act in conspicuous places on the premises, it is generally the responsibility of the applicant or employee with a disability to inform the employer that he or she needs an accommodation. This applies to the need for accommodations in the testing process as well as on the job. (For example, see *Fussell v. Georgia Ports Authority,* 1997, where the court held that the employer had no duty to accommodate an applicant on a firearm proficiency test because it lacked knowledge of the candidate's disability and need for accommodation.)

Moreover, it is the candidate's obligation to request an accommodation within a reasonable period of time before the administration of the test. An employer generally is not required to provide a testing accommodation unless it is aware of the candidate's needs in advance. As already noted, employers should take steps to ensure that candidates are aware of the opportunity for accommodations prior to the administration of the test. Although employers are prohibited from asking candidates whether they have a disability under the ADA, they can notify applicants that they must request an accommodation within a reasonable period of time prior to the test date and that they must provide appropriate documentation of their need for accommodation (EEOC, 1995).

In the case of *Morisky v. Broward County* (1996), the Eleventh Circuit discussed the candidate's obligation to make her disability and need for accommodation known. Morisky applied for a janitorial position with Broward County, Florida. The job announcement stated that a written test was required and that candidates needing accommodation for disabilities should notify the staff. Although Morisky stated in her application that she could not read and had taken special education courses, she did not inform the county that she had a disability or required an accommodation for the test. Instead, she arrived for the test with a vocational counselor who requested permission to administer the test to her orally. When the request was denied, Morisky filed suit, alleging that the county failed to reasonably accommodate her disability. The court rejected Morisky's claim, holding that because the county never knew about her disability it could not have discriminated against her on that basis. Morisky's statements in her application (that she could not read and had taken special education classes) were "vague [and] conclusory statements revealing an unspecified incapacity," and accordingly, were "not sufficient to put an employer on notice of its obligations under the ADA" (*Morisky v. Broward County,* 1996, p. 448).

One problem that applicants with disabilities face is that they may lack sufficient information about the selection process to know that they may need a testing accommodation, and if so, how to request one. Many organizations address this concern by providing candidates with a brochure containing an outline of the testing process and examples of the types of questions that could be expected on the various test components. It is useful for these brochures also to indicate the number of questions posed and the length of time that will be provided for the test. These pamphlets give candidates an opportunity in advance of the test to review the requirements and consult with experts on their disability concerning the type of accommodation that would be best for them.

It is a unique challenge to describe computerized tests to candidates. One organization has prepared demonstration software that can be presented to candidates with disabilities to give them an idea of what the test will be like. The demonstration software also can be loaned to firms that provide technologically advanced accommodations, such as screen readers, without jeopardizing test security.

After the initial application process, the next opportunity for candidates with disabilities to identify themselves usually occurs when the selection test is scheduled. A common way to inform candidates of the opportunity for accommodations is by including a statement in the instructional materials such as, "If you require an accommodation under the Americans with Disabilities Act, please complete and return the attached form." By referencing the ADA, or disabilities generally, the organization reduces the likelihood that candidates will misunderstand what is meant by an accommodation. (At least one confused candidate misinterpreted an invitation to request disability accommodations to be a mechanism to obtain hotel accommodations.) A specific reference to the ADA may also reduce requests for accommodation from nondisabled candidates for whom English is not the primary language.

Some organizations choose to schedule candidates for testing by telephone. This is another opportunity to communicate the availability of accommodations for disabilities. It is useful to have a prepared script to ensure that information is properly conveyed and to avoid inadvertent unlawful inquiries about a candidate's disabilities. The ADA explicitly prohibits employers from asking a candidate whether he or she has a disability (42 U.S.C. § 12112[d][2][A]). Some human resources employees may not understand the distinction between, "Do you require an accommodation under the ADA?" and "Are you disabled?" The former is lawful; the latter is prohibited. Furthermore, if a candidate later challenges what was asked during the scheduling, the company representative who recited the information from memory has a more difficult task than the one who read a script.

Untimely Self-Identification

Despite an organization's best efforts, it is not unusual for candidates with disabilities to wait to identify their need for accommodation until after the testing process has begun, and in some cases, until after completing the test or receiving the results. Based on senior author Wanda Campbell's experience, and that of other practitioners across the country, this phenomenon appears to occur most often with learning-disabled candidates. One explanation is that a candidate with a hidden disability may believe that her chances of being selected will be enhanced if her disability remains unknown. Another is that the candidate simply underestimated the difficulty of the task.

Many organizations faced with this situation require the candidate to wait the required time period between test administrations—often six months or longer—and then retake the test with an agreed-upon accommodation. Some organizations permit applicants to retest before the expiration of the waiting period, based on the rationale that the initial test results were unreliable because the disabled candidate took the test without an appropriate accommodation. Accelerating the retest is a more attractive option if the organization has alternate forms of the test. Test administrators should be advised that when candidates identify themselves after the start of the test but before its completion, they should retrieve the test material immediately so that the candidate is not exposed to any other test components. This will facilitate a more accurate reassessment, particularly if the candidate will be retested before the expiration of the waiting period.

Evidence Requirements

All organizations contacted require that candidates provide evidence of their need for the accommodation when their disability is not apparent. Organizations are far less likely to request documentation if the disability is obvious, such as missing limbs. Requesting documentation of an obvious disability was thought to make the organization appear ridiculous if not punitive so long as the accommodation requested was reasonable. Organizations also require documentation when a candidate requests an accommodation that does not appear appropriate for the disability at issue (for example, a hearing-impaired candidate requesting unlimited time to take an arithmetic test).

Some organizations have expressed confusion about whether the documentation should address the presence of the disability or be restricted to a specification of the recommended accommodation. Some employers believe that they should refrain from asking a candidate to identify his or her disability, even after a request for accommodation has been made. The EEOC's 1995 guidance on preemployment inquiries put this issue to rest. In that guidance, the EEOC specifically instructs that "if the need for accommodation is not obvious, an employer may ask an applicant for reasonable documentation about his/her disability if the applicant requests reasonable accommodation for the hiring process" (p. 1104). This is a permissible inquiry because not all claimed disabilities are covered by the ADA, as noted earlier in this chapter. Unless the candidate identifies and provides documentation relating to his or her disability, the employer has no way of knowing whether it has a duty to accommodate. (See also *Argen v. New York State Board,* 1994, where the court held that the board properly concluded that the candidate for the bar examination was not disabled under the ADA and therefore properly denied his request for double time when taking the test.) As a practical matter, documentation often specifies both the disability and the recommended accommodation. For example, candidates with long-term disabilities may possess and provide historical records of special accommodations as provided in individualized education plans (IEPs) from their elementary or secondary schools. Although relevant, these data are not outcome-determinative.

Documentation should be provided on official letterhead by an appropriate qualified professional. Qualifications differ depending on the disability. Questions of appropriateness may at times be judgment calls. Many organizations will not accept a recommendation for an accommodation for a learning disability from a physician unless the physician has credentials or training relating to learning disabilities. A few organizations are hesitant to reject documentation from a physician because of the fear that a jury might react negatively to their decision if challenged in court.

Some documentation has a longer accepted "shelf life" than other documentation. Documentation of physical conditions such as blindness may be relatively impervious to change. However, candidates with learning disabilities may find the disabling effects mitigated over time as they gain proficiency in compensating strategies; in contrast, degenerative conditions such as multiple sclerosis may become more disabling with time. Therefore, out-of-date documentation could result in either over- or underaccommodation. Most employers are sensitive to the costs associated with obtaining documentation and will accept existing documentation whenever possible.

Most organizations require candidates to produce documentation of need for accommodation before they make the accommodation available. Only after the document is approved by the company will the test be scheduled. A few employers do not require documentation until after the candidate has been successful on an employment test. The rationale for the latter approach is that if the candidate is not successful on the test even with the accommodation, then she will not be selected, and thus, the need for documentation of the requested accommodation is immaterial. This is analogous to some organizations' requiring candidates to provide proof of a degree upon selection for a position.

Duty to Accommodate in the Selection Process

Once a candidate has requested an accommodation and provided the required documentation, the employer must determine whether an accommodation is appropriate, and if so, what type of accommodation. An employer's duty here is to provide reasonable accommodations in the administration of selection tests for individuals with disabilities that impair sensory, manual, or speaking skills and interfere with their ability to take the test (42 U.S.C. § 12112[b][7]). The extent of this obligation is limited by the purpose of the test and whether the employer can accommodate the disability on the job (42 U.S.C. § 12113[a]; 29 C.F.R., App. § 1630.11). Thus, an employer is not required to provide accommodations in the administration of the test if the skill impaired is the particular skill that the test is intended to measure and is related to performance of the essential functions of the job. A test that relates to the essential functions of the job is job-related (29 C.F.R. App. § 1630.10). (See *Ethridge v. State of Alabama,* 1994, where the court held that a handgun test for police officer selection is job-related and necessary to "ensure the safety of police officers and the community"; also *Valle v. City of Chicago,* 1997, where the court held that the police department prerequisite that candidates must run 1.5 miles in a specified time cannot be enforced against a disabled candidate unless it is related to the essential functions of the job.) In such a case, however, the results of the test cannot be used to exclude the disabled applicant from the job unless no reasonable accommodation *on the job* would enable the applicant to perform those functions. (For example, in *Etheridge v. State of Alabama,* 1994, the court held that the employer is not required to accommodate a police officer applicant for a handgun test because shooting with two hands is an essential function of job for which a reasonable accommodation is not available.)

To understand the process of evaluating accommodation requests for tests, consider a written examination of procedures for performing certain tasks as an auto mechanic. A candidate has dyslexia and has requested as an accommodation that the examination be administered orally. The essential function of the job that is being measured by the test is knowledge of auto mechanics, not the ability to read and comprehend written material. Accordingly, the employer may accommodate this candidate's learning disability in the test-taking process. In contrast, for certain public safety jobs it is important that the job incumbent be able to read and comprehend written and oral instructions quickly in potentially life-threatening situations. For those jobs, an employer may be justified in denying a testing accommodation for a candidate with dyslexia. (See *Burke v. Virginia*, 1997, where the court held that no testing accommodation was required for a police officer applicant with dyslexia.)

Reasonable accommodations must be determined on a case-by-case basis. As with job accommodations, an employer is not required to provide the applicant with his or her first choice. Rather, the accommodation need only be one that is reasonable based on that individual's sensory, manual, or speaking disability (29 C.F.R. § 1630.11). If an individual refuses a reasonable accommodation necessary to perform essential job functions and as a result cannot perform those functions, then the individual may be terminated or refused an offer of employment (29 C.F.R. App. § 1630.9[d]). Likewise, if a candidate refuses a reasonable accommodation on an employment test or other selection procedure, then the employer can subject the candidate to the same requirement as nondisabled candidates (29 C.F.R. App. § 1630.11).

Accommodations in Testing for Groups of Jobs

Organizations that do broad-based testing for groups of jobs face special challenges with the ADA. All the knowledge, skills, and abilities measured by these broad tests may not be necessary for some of the jobs in the grouping to which the test applies. In other words, they may not meet the job-related requirement of the ADA. In contrast, when an employer provides an accommodation that results in excluding some constructs from measurement, then it is left without knowing whether that candidate is qualified to perform certain positions. Thus, the organization not only loses information about its candidates but must track each disabled candidate's test accommodations, which may be an onerous administrative burden, especially for a large employer.

Organizations that choose to waive a selection test for disabled candidates effectively move the qualification question to the next step—determining the ability of the candidates to perform the essential functions of the job with or without accommodation. A benefit of this approach is that the psychologist does not have to deal with the problem of identifying appropriate job accommodations. A disadvantage is that those who are now confronted with the problem may be less well-equipped to deal with it. Line managers who have not had experience with disabled candidates are often unaware of the many types of available accommodations and therefore underestimate what applicants with disabilities can do—which is exactly what the ADA is designed to counteract.

Limitations on the Duty to Accommodate

There are several limitations on the duty to accommodate.

Undue Hardship

An employer is not required to make an accommodation for a disability if doing so would create an undue hardship (42 U.S.C. § 12112[b][5][A]). *Undue hardship* refers to an accommodation that would be unduly costly, extensive, or substantial, or would fundamentally alter the nature of the business (42 U.S.C. § 12111[10]). Even if a particular accommodation would impose undue hardship, however, the employer must consider whether there are alternative accommodations that would not impose such hardship (29 C.F.R. App. § 1630.156[d]). Many accommodations for testing—such as extending the time to take the test or enlarging the test—involve little monetary expense. Others can be more onerous, such as making modifications to computer-administered tests to work with screen readers. The undue hardship exception has been interpreted narrowly, and employers should not refuse accommodation on the basis of undue hardship hastily.

Direct Threat to Health and Safety

Individuals with disabilities may be excluded from a job on the basis of their disability without the need for reasonable accommodation where there is significant risk of substantial harm to the health and safety of the candidate or of others (29 C.F.R. § 1630.2[r]). Generally, an employer may not exclude candidates from a job based on a category of disability that is usually associated with certain safety concerns. Instead, the employer must determine on a case-by-case basis if a disabled individual poses a direct threat. Under the ADA, a direct threat exists only under the following circumstances:

- There is specific, identifiable, nonspeculative, and current risk.
- The risk cannot be based on stereotypes, patronizing attitudes, or irrational fears.
- There is high probability that harm will occur.
- Potential harm must be severe.
- Determination must be based on most current medical knowledge, best objective evidence.
- Reasonable accommodation will not reduce or eliminate risk.

It may be appropriate to exclude an individual from a test because, due to the nature of that individual's disability, participation in the test presents a significant risk of substantial harm to the health and safety of that individual or others. For example, in *Ethridge v. State of Alabama* (1994), a candidate was excluded from the police academy because he was unable to fire a handgun using two hands. In that case, the court held that an accommodation was not required, because two-handed firing is an essential function of the job for which no reasonable accommodation is available. Moreover, the court found that a separate justification for removing the plaintiff from the training academy was that his inability to handle his weapon using two hands presented a substantial risk of harm both to himself and to the other candidates at the academy.

Litigating ADA Claims

As is the case with other employment discrimination statutes such as Title VII, several different legal theories are available to a plaintiff who has filed suit under the ADA. In addition, an ADA plaintiff may initiate these actions as an individual or, under certain circumstances, on behalf of a group of similarly situated people. The types of claims available under the ADA, as well as the types of relief that are available for those claims, are discussed in the following sections.

Legal Theories and Burdens of Proof

Disabled candidates may challenge a selection process on three different theories: they were treated differently because of their disability, a neutral practice had an adverse impact on them, or the employer failed to reasonably accommodate their disability in the selection process.

Discriminatory Treatment

The ADA prohibits adverse employment decisions when those decisions are based on a qualified individual's actual or perceived disability (42 U.S.C. §§ 12112[a], 12112[b][3], and [4]). In disparate treatment claims, most courts apply a modified version of the "burden shifting" framework set forth by the Supreme Court in *McDonnell Douglas Corp. v. Green,* 1973, which courts have applied to both Title VII and ADEA disparate treatment actions (*Weigel v. Target Stores,* 1997). Under this framework, the plaintiff must demonstrate that he or she is a disabled person within the meaning of the ADA, is qualified (meets job qualifications and is able to perform essential functions of job with or without reasonable accommodation), and was excluded from the job because of the disability. (See *Milton v. Scrivner,* 1995; *Wilson v. Pennsylvania State Police Department,* 1997; *Bultemeyer v. Fort Wayne Community Schools,* 1996; *Valle v. City of Chicago,* 1997.) Once the plaintiff has met this burden, the defendant must produce evidence that the adverse action was taken for a legitimate, nondiscriminatory reason. The burden on the employer at this stage is one of production, not of persuasion. That is, the employer need not prove that the articulated nondiscriminatory reasons are true but only present evidence that, if believed by the trier of fact, would support a conclusion that the employer did not commit unlawful discrimination. Once the employer has established its reason, the burden of proof remains with the plaintiff, who must persuade the trier of fact that the employer's articulated explanation is really a pretext for discrimination.

Discriminatory Impact

In addition to disparate treatment claims, the ADA also permits claims of disparate impact. A theory of disparate impact applies to situations where a facially neutral practice has a disproportionately negative impact on individuals with disabilities. Recently, one court described that in the context of the ADA disparate impact applics to the following situations: individuals have been classified based on their disabilities in a manner that affects their employment opportunities; standards have been applied to employees or candidates in a way that discriminates against those with disabilities; individuals have been denied benefits based on a disability; and individuals with disabilities have been screened out of jobs based on criteria that are not job-related or based on business necessity (*Horth v. General Dynamics Land Systems,* 1997).

The analysis for disparate impact claims under the ADA is comparable to the analysis for disparate impact claims under Title VII (*Tanca v. Nordberg,* 1997). In order to prevail under a disparate impact theory, the plaintiff must first prove that a neutral practice has a disproportionate negative impact on an individual or class of individuals with disabilities. Unlike Title VII cases, statistical proof of adverse impact is usually infeasible in ADA cases, and such proof is not always required (29 C.F.R. § 1630.10). Unlike race and gender classifications, individual disabilities are not fungible and cannot always be grouped together for purposes of assessing discrimination.

Once the plaintiff establishes his or her burden and thus a prima facie case of disparate impact, the burden shifts to the employer to demonstrate that the challenged practice is job-related and consistent with business necessity. This is done by showing that the selection criteria concern essential functions of the job. If the employer meets this burden, the plaintiff can still prevail by showing that a less discriminatory yet equally effective and valid selection procedure is available. In the context of the ADA, the plaintiff may attempt to meet this burden by showing that a reasonable accommodation is available for his or her disability. (*Cox v. New England Telephone & Telegraph,* 1993, for example, applied similar analysis to a state antidiscrimination statute.)

Most selection tests do not include criteria that on their face exclude candidates from consideration on the basis of a disability. Rather, the tests involve neutral criteria that may have the effect of excluding those candidates because of their disabilities. Accordingly, most selection practices will be challenged on the theory of disparate impact.

Failure to Accommodate

In addition to the disparate impact and disparate treatment theories of discrimination that parallel Title VII jurisprudence, plaintiffs can also challenge selection procedures on the basis that the employer failed to make reasonable accommodations for their disabilities in the selection process itself. In order to prevail under this theory, plaintiffs must demonstrate that they are disabled as defined by the ADA, that the employer was aware of the disability and the need for accommodation yet failed to provide an accommodation, and that they were qualified for the position in question (*Fussell v. Georgia Ports Authority,* 1997). Some courts also require plaintiffs specifically to identify, as part of their burden of production, a reasonable accommodation that would allow them to perform the job duties (*Willis v. Conopco,* 1997). The burden then shifts to the employer to prove that the accommodation is not reasonable or that providing the proffered accommodation would create an undue hardship.

Class Actions

A class action is when one or more named plaintiffs sue on behalf of a larger group of individuals of which they are a part as well as on their own behalf. Even though each individual class member does not actively participate in the lawsuit, they may all be entitled to relief if the named plaintiff prevails. In federal court, a class action is permissible only under the following circumstances:

- The class is so numerous that joinder of all members is impracticable.
- There are questions of law or fact common to the class.
- The claims or defenses of the representative parties are typical of the claims or defenses of the class.
- The representative parties will fairly and adequately protect the interests of the class (Federal Rules of Civil Procedure, 23[a], 1998).

A number of employers have successfully defeated motions for class certification in ADA litigation on the basis that, as a prerequisite to asserting a claim under the ADA, each plaintiff must establish that he or she is disabled. This question is necessarily resolved in an individualized, case-by-case inquiry and cannot be done on a classwide basis. Likewise, determining whether the employer has made reasonable accommodations requires an individualized analysis of the particular characteristics of the disability when it comes to the essential functions of the particular job. The need for these individualized fact-driven determinations make ADA claims generally inappropriate for class disposition. (See *Burkett v. United States Postal Service,* 1997, where the court held that a Rehabilitation Act class consisting of all applicants who were denied employment on medical grounds is inappropriate because it would require a series of minitrials as to whether each class member was perceived to be disabled, and *Davoll v. Webb,* 1995, where the court held that a class consisting of all members of a police department who have or will have disabilities is inappropriate because individual determination is required about whether the class member who suffered a work-related injury is disabled under the act.)

However, at least some courts have concluded that class actions may be appropriate under circumstances where a policy on its face violates the ADA or when a procedure not apparent on the face of the policy violates the ADA. In these cases, the question of whether class members are disabled is not a core issue to the relief sought. Accordingly, courts have certified classes—for example, for claims challenging medical layoff policies and vision standards for job applicants (see *Hendricks-Robinson v. Excel Corporation,* 1997, where the court held that class action is appropriate because the plaintiffs were attacking the policy itself as violating the ADA, and *Wilson v. Pennsylvania State Police Department,* 1997, where the court certified the class because all potential class members were denied employment because of visual impairments, but limited class certification to issues of liability and injunctive relief and rejected certification on issues of damages).

Most employment testing practices are challenged under the ADA on the theory of disparate impact. Although class actions are not uncommon for disparate impact claims under Title VII, they are much less likely for similar claims under the ADA. Because there is such wide variation in disabilities, it is unlikely that a single test will affect enough candidates with the same category of disability to meet the numerosity requirement for class actions. In addition, challenges of testing practices are likely to be accompanied by claims that the employer failed to make a particular accommodation in the administration of the test. This individualized inquiry will probably make the case inappropriate for a class-based disposition.

Potential Liability

Title I of the ADA provides that the remedies available for violations of the Act are the same as those available for violations of Title VII (42 U.S.C. § 12117[a]). Under Title VII, the court has the power to enjoin the unlawful practice and also award appropriate affirmative relief including (but not limited to) reinstatement or hiring of plaintiffs, with or without back pay or any other equitable relief as the court deems appropriate. Back pay includes fringe benefits and is limited to two years prior to the filing of the charge with the EEOC, and it is offset by other wages earned (or earnable with reasonable diligence) during that time period (42 U.S.C. § 2000e-5[g]). Front pay for future losses may be available in place of reinstatement. In addition, in the case of intentional discrimination (that is, disparate treatment claims but not disparate impact claims), compensatory and punitive damages may be available (42 U.S.C. § 1981a[b]). Compensatory damages generally represent nonpecuniary losses, including emotional pain, suffering, inconvenience, mental anguish, and loss of enjoyment of life, whereas punitive damages represent a sum that is intended to punish the employer for its conduct and deter repetition. In order to recover punitive damages, a plaintiff must demonstrate that the employer engaged in the unlawful conduct "with malice or with reckless indifference to the federally protected rights of an aggrieved individual" (42 U.S.C. § 1981a[b]). Damages are not available in an ADA action alleging a failure to accommodate if the employer proves it engaged in good-faith efforts to identify and make available a reasonable accommodation (42 U.S.C. § 1981a[a][3]). Punitive damages are not available if the defendant is a government, government agency, or political subdivision (42 U.S.C. § 1981a[b]).

The total recovery available for compensatory and punitive damages combined is limited to $300,000 for employers with more than 500 employees, $200,000 for employers with 201 to 500 employees,

$100,000 for employers with 101 to 200 employees, and $50,000 for employers with 15 to 100 employees (42 U.S.C. § 1981a[b][3]). This is the maximum *combined* per plaintiff allowable recovery for compensatory and punitive damages.

Although some plaintiffs have attempted to argue that the cap is separate for each type of damage award, this has been flatly rejected by the courts. (See, for example, *Hogan v. Bangor & Aroostook R.R.*, 1995.) Challenges to standardized selection procedures usually are brought under a theory of disparate impact, and thus compensatory and punitive damages are not available. Some claims may constitute disparate treatment if the procedure is facially discriminatory, such as a vision standard. In those cases, however, it is unlikely that a plaintiff will meet the standard required for punitive damages. Finally, in addition to equitable remedies, compensatory damages, and punitive damages, a prevailing plaintiff also can recover reasonable attorneys' fees (42 U.S.C. § 2000e-5[k]).

Entitlement to a Jury Trial

As a result of the passage of the Civil Rights Act of 1991, jury trials are now available under Title VII, as well as the ADA, whenever compensatory and punitive damages are available. If a selection procedure is challenged under a disparate impact theory, as they often are, neither a jury trial nor compensatory or punitive damages is available.

Psychometric Research on Testing Accommodations

Most organizations do not have a sufficient number of candidates with the same disability to enable them to perform meaningful analyses of the impact of accommodations on the psychometric characteristics of the test. In addition, even among candidates with the same nominal disability, there are often substantial differences in the extent of the disability as well as in the appropriate accommodations. Despite these challenges, the Educational Testing Service (ETS) and the United States Office of Personnel Management (OPM) have conducted research that is instructive for private employers. The sections that follow will first describe ETS's research on the comparability of standard testing and testing with accommodation. Next, research by OPM on the administration of tests for various types of disabilities will be presented.

Education Testing Service Research

Willingham (1988) described two challenges faced by ETS when conducting research on the comparability of test scores for disabled and nondisabled candidates. The first was a criterion problem. Grading varies across college programs, and it is possible that the college programs that are developed to meet the special needs of students with disabilities may differ in their grading from traditional programs. The second problem faced was the accurate classification of disabled candidates with respect to the nature and severity of their disability. This was a particular problem with learning disabilities. Four types of disabilities were explored in the ETS research: learning disabilities, visual impairments, hearing impairments, and physical disabilities.

Bennett, Rock, Kaplan, and Jirele (1988) compared candidates with disabilities to nondisabled candidates on performance level, test completion rates, reliability, and differential item functioning. Four types of test formats were used in the administration of the SAT:

- A regular edition of the test was administered with extra time; sometimes adaptive devices such as magnification were also provided. This test format was used by examinees in all four disability categories.
- A large type edition was used by visually impaired and learning-disabled examinees.
- A braille edition was used by visually impaired examinees.
- A cassette and regular edition of the test were used for learning-disabled examinees.

Accommodations available included separate testing locations, extra time, additional space, additional rest periods, a reader, a recorder, a sign language interpreter for communication of test instructions, and other arrangements.

Table 9.1 summarizes the findings for differences between disabled and nondisabled students on score level, completion rate, reliability, and differential item functioning for the SAT. All values in the table are weighted averages taken across two samples of students who took a different form of the SAT.

Performance on the GRE was studied among three groups of students: visually impaired students who took the national adminis-

Table 9.1. SAT Results Showing Psychometric Differences Between Disabled and Nondisabled Students.

Type of Impairment	Score Level Verbal	Math	Completion Rates Verbal	Math	Diff. Item Funct. Verbal	Math
Visual impairment						
Regular type				+1.35		
Large type			+1.21	+1.32		
Braille		−.53	+.25	+1.20		Neg.
Physical impairment						
Regular type			+.21	+1.30		
Learning disabled						
Regular type	−.48	−.50		+1.22		Pos.
Large type	−.64	−.74				
Cassette	−.81	−.93	+1.22			
Cassette and regular type	−.69	−.81				
Hearing impairment						
Regular type	−1.18	−.73	+1.22	+1.35		Pos.

Notes: Score level reflects differences of .2 or greater in standard deviation units from the mean for nondisabled examinees tested during the same time period.

Completion rates reflect ratio of the percentage of members in each disability group completing the test to the same value for nondisabled examinees taking the test.

Diff. item funct. Reflects differences in differential item functioning. "Pos." means that disabled students performed better than nondisabled students; "Neg." means that disabled students performed worse than nondisabled students.

Source: From Bennett et al., in *Testing Handicapped People.* Copyright © 1988 by Allyn & Bacon. Adapted by permission.

tration; visually impaired students who took the extended time, large-type administration; and physically disabled examinees who took the national administration.

Score Level

Visually impaired students' scores on the SAT and GRE were comparable to those of nondisabled students. Students with physical disabilities scored comparably on the SAT when given special administrations, but performed less well than nondisabled students on the GRE national administration. The performance of learning-disabled and hearing-impaired students was lowest for all of the groups examined. As expected, the performance of hearing-impaired students was lowest on the verbal component of the SAT.

Completion Rates

As a group, disabled candidates who took the SAT under non-standard conditions completed more of the test than their nondisabled counterparts. Physically and visually disabled students tested on the GRE as part of the national administration completed a comparable number of verbal questions but fewer quantitative and analytical questions than their nondisabled counterparts.

Reliability

Reliability was estimated by the standard error of measurement because of its insensitivity to range variation. These measures were comparable across all four disabled groups and the group given the standardized administration.

Differential Item Analyses

These analyses assessed whether particular test items were differentially difficult or easy, given overall test performance. For the most part there was little evidence of differential item difficulty. Visually impaired students who took the braille version of the SAT had more difficulty with certain types of items, such as those containing figures and number systems such as the tally system. By contrast, some items were differentially easy for students with hearing impairments and learning disabilities. Because the "easy" items were at the end of the test, it is possible that this effect resulted from the higher completion rates for disabled students.

Other research issues investigated by ETS were factor structure, predictive validity, and timing studies.

Factor Structure

Rock, Bennett, Kaplan, and Jirele (1988) discovered that the factor structures for disabled and nondisabled students were generally comparable. One difference was that the verbal and quantitative factors were less highly related for the disabled students than for the nondisabled. It is possible that the disabled may develop these abilities differentially in compensating for their disability. Alternatively, a speed factor common to both the verbal and mathematical parts in the standard administration may account for the relationship (Willingham, 1988). The overall similarity in the factor structures suggests that the accommodations were successful in eliminating irrelevant sources of difficulty for the candidates with disabilities.

Predictive Validity

Braun, Ragosta, and Kaplan (1986, 1988) found that except for hearing-impaired students, SAT scores from special administrations tended somewhat to overpredict college performance of students with disabilities. Greatest overprediction occurred with high-scoring learning-disabled students. The overprediction was found to be positively related to the amount of time students were given to take the test. More recent research by Ragosta, Braun, and Kaplan (1991) confirmed the previous findings. Willingham (1988) suggests that factors such as problems with managing the disability and poor quality support systems may intervene in the relationship between test and academic performance. Another point that Willingham makes is that, by definition, learning-disabled students are individuals whose academic performance does not equal that expected based on their ability.

Office of Personnel Management Research

The OPM, previously known as the United States Civil Service Commission, is charged with developing selection procedures for the federal government. This organization has had a long-standing interest in the comparability of tests for disabled and nondisabled candidates (Shultz & Boynton, 1958; Stunkel, 1957). Candidates for jobs with the federal government are rank-ordered on the basis of their test scores, and the selecting official is required to choose from among the top three candidates. OPM began a major research program on testing accommodations in the early 1970s in connection with the development of the Professional and Administrative Career Examination (PACE).

Hearing Impairments

The United States Civil Service Commission developed two equivalent forms of the PACE exam for deaf candidates (Nester & Sapinkopf, 1982). Because prelingually deaf candidates usually have difficulty reading and communicating in traditional spoken language, the instructions were simplified and sample questions were included to ensure that they understood what was expected of them. To the extent possible, the verbal content of subtests not designed to measure verbal ability was minimized. Specifically, tabular items replaced inference items that had a heavy verbal component on the deduction subtest. On the number subtest, computational items replaced reasoning items. Deaf candidates performed at a lower level than their hearing counterparts on the verbal-oriented subtests but performed at a higher level on the other three subtests. The pattern of correlations between verbal and nonverbal subtests was substantially lower than that for nondisabled candidates.

Visual Impairments

The United States Civil Service Commission also developed two equivalent forms of the PACE exam for visually impaired applicants (Sapinkopf, 1978). Questions that depend on visual experience (such as figural questions) were deleted and replaced by questions measuring the same construct that had been used experimentally with a sighted population.

Visually impaired and sighted candidates performed differentially on the various test components. Visually impaired candidates performed better than sighted candidates on a test of induction. The visually impaired candidates' test had twice as many letter series questions to make up for the deleted figure analogies items.

By contrast, the visually impaired candidates scored lower than the sighted candidates on the deductive test. The deductive test for the visually impaired deleted the tabular items and replaced them with inference items.

Organizational Approaches to Accommodation Issues

Organizations differ in the policies and procedures they have established to provide testing accommodations. The sections that follow describe considerations when identifying the individuals authorized to grant accommodation requests and options with respect to flagging scores. Thereafter, different types of accommodations are described along with the experiences of organizations that have used them.

Centralizing-Decentralizing Accommodation Request Approval

When an accommodation has the potential to alter the interpretation of scores, virtually all organizations require that the accommodation be approved by an individual with an advanced degree in industrial-organizational psychology or a related field. Some organizations permit test administrators to make "on-the-spot" accommodations. In these cases, generally, the test administrators receive written guidance describing the types of accommodations they are permitted to make and those that require higher approval. Other organizations require that all accommodations receive approval from a psychologist.

Permitting test administrators to make some limited decisions on low-impact accommodations is most attractive in those instances where testing is decentralized and test administrators do not have ready access to a psychologist. There are, however, problems associated with empowering test administrators. For example, one test administrator told a candidate who requested an accommodation immediately before testing began that it was too late and then proceeded to administer the test as usual. In contrast, it is very difficult to control the actions of geographically dispersed test administrators. The prudent course is to provide the test administrators with as much training as possible and describe in careful detail what they may and may not do. The simplest instructions are to contact the psychologist immediately whenever a request for accommodation is made.

Flagging Scores

The *Standards for Educational and Psychological Testing* (AERA, APA, & NCME, 1985) stress that caution must be exercised in interpreting the validity of modified tests in the absence of data. Although it seems prudent, the standard provides no practical guidance to the practitioner. Most if not all of us have concerns about the effect of certain types of accommodations on test validity. The important issue is what we do about it.

One option is to "flag" the scores. Flagging scores can have two meanings: to identify the scores in a secure database in the hopes of some day being able to conduct meaningful research, and to advise the selecting official that the test score was earned through nonstandard administration. The second option clearly appears to run afoul of the law because it effectively notifies the decision maker that the test taker has a disability. Particularly to the extent that the individual has not requested an accommodation on the *job* (versus the test), this may be an unlawful release of disability-related information.

Many organizations maintain a secure record of scores earned in a nonstandard administration and the nature of the administration. Some exclude these scores from psychometric analyses of the test data, although this is not universal. None of the organizations in any way advises selecting officials that a test score was earned with an accommodation. Although some psychologists have concerns about the fairness of this to the selecting official, the potential legal risk of flagging the scores is viewed as too great to do otherwise.

Distinguishing Between Levels of Accommodations

Many of the organizations contacted distinguish between accommodations that are likely to alter the psychometric interpretation of the scores and those that are not likely to have such an effect.

Examples of innocuous accommodations include such things as adjusting table height to accommodate a wheelchair and providing straight-backed chairs for candidates with back problems. Examples of accommodations that may have the effect of potentially altering the interpretation are discussed in the sections that follow and are summarized in Table 9.2.

Making Psychometrically Complex Accommodations

Nester (1984, 1993) categorizes these accommodations as modifications to the testing medium, time limits, and test content. The sections that follow describe these types of accommodations and incorporate experiences of organizations across the country. For a comprehensive guide to administering tests to candidates with disabilities, see Eyde, Nester, Heaton, and Nelson (1994).

Modified Testing Medium

The test medium is the method by which information is communicated to the candidates. Examples of modifications include braille, large print, reader, and audiocassette.

Braille. Translating test material into braille is not unlike translating into a foreign language. Just as there are dialects in languages, there are several braille codes. The most common code is Grade 2, which enables candidates to read material more quickly than the more cumbersome Grade 1. Thus, test materials should be printed in Grade 2 braille.

When translating test material into braille, it is useful to have a specialist in services to the blind review the translation against the standard version to ensure correspondence. Material usually presented in tables can be problematic. Some blind candidates prefer to have this information presented linearly; others prefer that the columns be retained. One organization presents the tabular information in both formats and gives blind candidates the choice of format.

Test security is an issue with tests that have been translated into braille. Translation companies may be preferred over volunteer groups because the firms can exert greater control over the individuals performing the work. In addition, if there is a security breach, there are likely to be more avenues of redress with a

**Table 9.2. Summary of
Psychometrically Complex Accommodations.**

Accommodation	Recommendations and Considerations
Testing medium Braille	• Print test materials in Grade 2 braille. • Have specialists in services to the blind review the test materials before use to reduce unexpected problems. • Take care in the handling and storage of braille test materials so that the embossed dots are not flattened.
Enlarged print	• Take care that enlargement does not alter pagination so that illogical page breaks occur. • Provide larger work surfaces to accommodate larger pages if necessary. • Larger print also means larger circles. Have the candidate mark the circles in some fashion but not completely blacken them. • Enlarged print on a computer screen reduces the amount of material that can be viewed on the screen. Use a large screen, if possible.
Readers	• Use readers who are trained test administrators and not friends or relatives of the candidate. • Be sure that readers are patient and able to read well and speak clearly. • Be sure that readers do not try to identify the correct answer because it may alter their voice inflection. • Allow extended time limits to accommodate communication between the reader and the candidate.
Recorders	• Be sure that recorders repeat the answer before marking it on the test. • Tape the session to reduce doubt about the answer indicated by the candidate to particular questions.

**Table 9.2. Summary of
Psychometrically Complex Accommodations, Cont'd.**

Accommodation	Recommendations and Considerations
Time limits	
Extended time	• This is the most frequently requested accommodation; requires separate testing session. • This has little effect on power tests; can result in severe distortion of scores on speeded tests. • Most requests granted are for double time or less. • You may wish to base denials of requested time on essential job functions rather than psychometric principles.
Test content	
Eliminated components	• Consider whether the test component eliminated is related to an essential job function.
Work sample	• It is difficult to establish criterion for success. You often must distinguish between those who are and are not able to perform the work.
Probationary hire	• You must be able to collect good measures of job performance. • Discharging an employee is more difficult than not hiring a candidate.
Testing waiver	• This is the least desirable accommodation because there is no information on qualifications. • This may weaken the business-necessity defense for using testing to select non-disabled candidates.

for-profit corporation than with a volunteer group. The fewest number of people possible should be used to perform the translation and all test materials, braille and originals, should be stored in a secure location when work is not in progress. Contractual protection should be obtained.

Transporting and storing braille materials require extra care to ensure that the embossed dots are not flattened. The tests should be covered in multiple levels of protective covering to guard against damage from shipping. When storing braille tests, heavy objects, like other tests, should not be placed on top of them.

Enlarged Print. The organizations that translate materials to braille may also be able to enlarge the test. Or the materials can be enlarged on a photocopier to a font size selected by the candidate. Care should be taken if the enlargement alters the pagination. Using more pages is preferable to introducing illogical page breaks in related materials. Substantial page additions may require extensions in the amount of time allotted to take the test.

Enlarged paper-and-pencil tests may require larger than normal work surfaces for the candidates. In addition, when tests are enlarged, so are the circles that candidates blacken. Alternatives such as checking the circle of the selected response option are preferable to having the candidate waste time blackening larger circles. If tests are scanned, the responses should be copied onto a scannable form by a test administrator and double-checked by a second person. The enlarged test should be retained in case there are questions about the candidate's answers.

Enlargement is also possible for tests administered on a computer. This may be accomplished by an attachment to the monitor or by software that enables the user to select the desired font. One difficulty with enlarging material on a monitor is that it reduces the amount of material that can be viewed on a screen, thus potentially making the test more difficult. It is best to use one of the larger monitors in these applications. As of this writing, thirty-inch monitors are available.

Enlarged print may be used by visually impaired candidates as well as by some with learning disabilities.

Readers. Readers should be test administrators and not friends or relatives of the candidate. It is essential that these people be able to read well and speak clearly. It also is important for readers to have a great deal of patience, because these administrations can be tedious.

Before administering each test component, the candidate and test administrator should discuss the test format, the order in which the candidate would like material read, and ways to distinguish among the material. If the candidate finds that the requested order is not optimal, it should be altered as specified by the candidate. It also may be necessary for the test administrator to reread specific portions of the test. (Sighted candidates can change the order in which they read material and reread material as often as desired.) It is essential that all response options read by the reader be given equal emphasis. Eyde et al. (1994) provide extensive instructions for readers.

Readers may be used for candidates with visual impairments or learning disabilities. These tests are often administered with generous or no time limits because of the directional communication between the reader and the candidate.

A recent lawsuit relating to the Law School Admissions Test (LSAT) addressed the issue of readers as an accommodation in the testing process. In April 1997, three blind law students and the National Federation of the Blind filed suit against the Law School Admission Council (LSAC), alleging that the LSAC violated the ADA by, among other things, refusing to allow the students to provide their own readers for the LSAT. The court never ruled on this issue because the case was settled. However, as part of the settlement, the LSAC agreed to allow blind and visually impaired test takers to meet with, approve, and take a practice test with readers selected by the LSAC.

Recorders. Test administrators who function as recorders need to ensure that they correctly understand the response option selected by the candidate. This may be done by repeating the letter and the text of the response option selected. Some organizations tape the session to ensure that the responses selected by the candidate were recorded correctly. Recorders may be required by visually impaired or physically disabled candidates.

Modified Time Limits

Extension of the time limit is probably the most frequently requested accommodation. The appropriateness of this accommodation is determined in large part by the type of test being administered. If the test is a "power test" or a noncognitive instrument, then requests for additional time may have very little impact on the psychometric interpretation of the test scores. In contrast, if the test is a speeded test, such as those used for many clerical jobs, then the extension of time will substantially alter the meaning for the scores. Between these two extremes are many cognitive ability tests, which are predominantly power tests but do introduce some element of speed.

All organizations contacted extend the time limits for job knowledge and cognitive ability tests that are not primarily speed tests when appropriate documentation is provided. Most of the time extensions are for double time or less. Many organizations are very reluctant to extend the time beyond twice the standard time allotted, although one organization has extended the time by as much as four times the standard. In the latter case the candidate was still unsuccessful.

Organizations that wish to place a ceiling on the time extension should consider basing this decision on the essential functions of the job. Denial of recommended requests for extended time for reasons of psychometric purity or administrative convenience are risky from practical and legal perspectives. Although validating statistics are based on relationships among data for large numbers of people, the ADA requires consideration of accommodations in light of the unique situation of each disabled candidate.

Some organizations will grant unlimited time when the test is administered in braille or by a reader. The braille format takes longer to read than printed material. In the case of tests administered by a reader, candidates should not be penalized for time spent discussing how to read the material and identifying the sections of the material to be reread. It is simply not feasible to be turning on and off timing devices for these conversations.

Speeded tests provide the greatest challenge for psychologists and have yielded the most diverse responses. A few organizations indicate that candidates unable to take speeded tests without accommodation are unable to perform the essential functions of the job. Some organizations waive the speeded test components and apply greater weight to the nonspeeded subtests in a compensatory scoring equation. A few organizations develop work samples to replace the speeded components. One organization makes no accommodations and tells candidates to do the best they can. A final organization treats speeded tests as power tests, granting most time extensions.

Time-limit extensions are requested most often for candidates with learning disabilities and visual impairments. Hearing-impaired candidates usually do not request additional time unless the test has substantial verbal requirements.

Modified Test Content

Generally, changes in test content are the last resort in accommodations. OPM is the only organization of which we are aware that has developed alternative versions of tests for blind and hearing-impaired candidates (Nester & Sapinkopf, 1982; Sapinkopf, 1978). Most organizations lack a sufficient number of candidates with these disabilities to justify the expense.

Some organizations that use a compensatory selection system will waive the test components that the candidate cannot take with accommodation and prorate the scores on the other components. Consideration should be given to whether the test component reflects an essential job component, such as the ability of a drafter to work with printed diagrams. A promising but time-consuming alternative is to create a work sample to determine the candidate's ability to perform essential job functions. Criteria for determining success or failure on the work sample can be problematic. In some positions requiring limited abilities, however, the primary distinctions are between being able to do the job and not.

A related solution used by a few organizations is to hire the disabled candidate on a probationary basis. If the candidate cannot perform the job by the end of the probationary period, his employment is terminated. The risk associated with this alternative is that the candidate is usually in a stronger position to wage an employment discrimination battle than if he were an applicant. Documenting poor performance is time consuming and unpleasant. In addition, those who work with the disabled candidate may not uniformly share management's perspective on his or her performance.

Most organizations agree that the least desirable solution is to waive testing completely. Some test performance information, however imperfect, is better than no information. In addition, waiving the test may weaken the business-necessity defense for using testing to select nondisabled candidates. The argument will be, "If you can hire disabled candidates without testing, why do you need to test the other people?"

Accommodations in Perspective

The purpose of a reasonable accommodation is to reduce or eliminate the biasing effects of the disability with respect to test or job performance. In effect, systematic error variance is reduced with the goal of achieving a more accurate assessment. A difficulty encountered with testing accommodations, however, is that their effects are uncertain and will remain so, notwithstanding repeated calls for research on their effects. The drafters of the ADA correctly captured the unique quality of the disabled individual. Individuals differ in the magnitude of their disability, and individuals with comparable levels of a given disability have devised unique ways to accommodate it. The law thus correctly calls for individualized treatment of each candidate. Therefore, coming to terms with the ADA has two implications for psychologists: our traditional approaches for conducting research in this area will fall short of our desires for precision, and we need to become comfortable in dealing with the ambiguity. The remainder of this section will focus on different aspects of the accommodation decision.

A concern of some psychologists is that granting an accommodation will result in overprediction for the disabled candidate. The predictive research conducted by ETS reinforces this concern, particularly as it applies to learning-disabled candidates, the largest group of disabled candidates requesting accommodation. The problem is that we do not know at what point the line between under- and overprediction is crossed. Thus, the choice is not between overprediction and an accurate assessment; rather it is between under- or overprediction. The decision should be governed by legal issues, practical issues, and corporate culture.

Legal Issues

Testing issues involving the ADA, like Title VII, require consideration of both psychometric and legal issues. Often these two issues are mutually reinforcing, as in the case of the psychological principle of standardization and its legal implication of avoiding disparate treatment. Other times legal considerations may argue counter to psychometric principles. From a legal perspective, the risk under the ADA lies with inadequate accommodations and the attendant underprediction. Therefore, from a legal standpoint, those who are litigation-averse may favor overprediction because the ADA does not provide the opportunity for "reverse discrimination" suits.

Another legal issue to be considered is that a dispute involving an accommodation under the ADA is not tried with a psychologist on the bench or with a group of psychologists on the jury. At most, psychologists will appear as expert witnesses, often at least one on either side of the debate. Therefore, the appearance of reasonableness and fairness is critical—and, arguably, more important than the psychometric considerations that neither the judge nor the jury may understand or appreciate. Thus, before psychologists reject requests for accommodation, they should consider how their decisions may appear to those who will be passing judgment in a court of law.

Practical Issues

It is important for practitioners to remember that requests for accommodation occur relatively infrequently. Estimates provided by practitioners surveyed nationwide were that the frequency of requests for accommodation was less than one-half of 1 percent of all candidates tested. Therefore, accommodation decisions that favor the candidate fairly often are not likely to have severe detrimental effects on the organization's well-being.

It also is useful to compare ADA accommodations with other low-frequency deviations from standardization. Despite the best efforts of practitioners, stopwatches sometimes fail and test administrators occasionally make mistakes. When those anomalies occur, we do our best to undo their effects, recognizing that absolute accuracy is not achievable. When faced with these types of situations, senior author Wanda Campbell has always erred in the direction of the candidate.

Corporate Culture

Just as ADA accommodations are not the only example of imprecision in administration procedures, the effect of overprediction is not a new experience for psychologists. Long before the passage of the ADA, psychologists were aware that the use of a single regression line could result in the apparent overprediction of the performance of some minority candidates. Accommodations under the

ADA are simply a new twist on an old problem: how to balance conflicting and competing goals. The balance that is struck should be influenced by the corporate culture and the attendant goals. Some organizations are very socially conscious and will take proactive steps to expand employment opportunities for the disabled. Such organizations are likely to favor any request for accommodation that appears reasonable. Whether the motivation is corporate responsibility or "headline phobia," the result is that societal considerations and not psychometrics are controlling. In other organizations, the philosophy is simply to abide by the law as written and do only what is required. Such organizations may put a premium on psychometric considerations and focus on hiring the candidate with the greatest likelihood of success. The orientation of the organization with respect to these sometimes competing goals is a strategic decision usually made at a level above the industrial psychologist. Therefore, practitioners need to be aware of their organization's values *before* they make decisions on accommodations to be provided and those to be denied. Making accommodation decisions in a vacuum is a high-risk proposition for the psychologist because the psychometric decision may not yield the result favored by the organization.

Conclusion

The research and case law discussed in this chapter demonstrate that employers face a variety of challenges in order to bring their selection practices into compliance with the ADA. First, they must ensure that their practices do not unlawfully discriminate against individuals with disabilities. Next, they must determine the conditions under which they have a duty to provide accommodations. Finally, they must choose solutions that accommodate a candidate's disability yet still permit a valid assessment of that candidate's qualifications for the job.

Beyond the minimum requirements of the law, the scope and variety of approaches to accommodation issues are shaped by each individual organization's mission and philosophy. This chapter has provided guidance on how an employer can maneuver this labyrinth of issues and still achieve its goals for selection. Additional information on accommodating candidates with disabilities is shown in Exhibit 9.1.

Exhibit 9.1.   Information on the Americans with Disabilities Act and the Employment of Candidates with Disabilities.

Job Accommodation Network

The President's Committee on Employment of People with Disabilities
West Virginia University
918 Chestnut Ridge Road, Suite 1, P.O. Box 6080
Morgantown, WV 26506–0680
(800) 526–7234
(800) ADA-WORK (V/TT)
(304) 293–7186 (V/TT)
(800) 526–2262 (from Canada; V/TT)
(800) DIAL-JAN (Computer Bulletin Board)
www.janweb.icdi.wvu.edu

President's Committee on Employment of People with Disabilities
1331 F Street NW
Washington, DC 20004
(202) 376–6200 (V)
(202) 376–6205 (TDD)
www.pcepd.gov

ADA Information Center for the Mid-Atlantic Region
451 Hungerford Drive, Suite 607
Rockville, MD 20850
(301) 217–0124
(800) 949–4232
www.adainfo.org
E-mail: adainfo@transcen.org

TransCen, Inc.
451 Hungerford Drive
Suite 700
Rockville, MD 20850
(301) 424–2002
(301) 251–3762 (Fax)

U.S. Equal Employment Opportunity Commission
Office of Communications and Legislative Affairs
1801 L Street NW
Washington, DC 20507
(800) 669-EEOC (V)

**Exhibit 9.1. Information on the Americans with Disabilities Act
and the Employment of Candidates with Disabilities, Cont'd.**

(800) 800–3302 (TDD)
(202) 663–4900 (V)
(202) 663–4494 (TDD)
www.eeoc.gov

Learning Disabilities

Learning Disabilities Association of America (LD)
4156 Library Road
Pittsburgh, PA 15234
(412) 341–1515
(412) 341–8077

Distance Learning Link (LD, ADD)
University of Georgia
534 Alderhold Hall
Athens, GA 30602
(706) 542–1300

International Dyslexia Association (LD)
Chester Building
8600 LaSalle Road
Suite 382
Baltimore, MD 21286–2044
(410) 296–0232
(410) 321–5069 (Fax)

Hearing Impairments

National Association of the Deaf
814 Thayer Avenue
Silver Spring, MD 20910
(301) 587–1788 (V)
(301) 587–1789 (TTY)
www.nad.org

National Information Center on Deafness–Gallaudet University
800 Florida Avenue NE
Washington, DC 20002–3695
(202) 651–5051 (V)
(202) 651–5052 (TT)

Exhibit 9.1. Information on the Americans with Disabilities Act and the Employment of Candidates with Disabilities, Cont'd.

www.gallaudet.edu/~nied
E-mail: nicd@gallux.gallaudet.edu

Visual Impairments

American Council of the Blind
1155 15th Street NW
Suite 720
Washington, DC 20005
(202) 467–5081
(800) 424–8666

American Foundation for the Blind
11 Penn Plaza, Suite 300
New York, NY 10001
(212) 502–7600
(800) 232–5463
www.afb.org

National Federation of the Blind
1800 Johnson Street
Baltimore, MD 21230
(410) 659–9314

The Lighthouse, Inc.
800 Second Avenue
New York, NY 10017
(212) 808–0077 (V/TT)
Physical Impairments
AIDS Action Council/National Aids Network
1875 Connecticut Avenue NW, Suite 700
Washington, DC 20009
(202) 986–1300
(202) 986–1345 (Fax)

American Amputee Foundation, Inc.
P.O. Box 250218 Hillcrest Station
Little Rock, AR 72225
(501) 666–2523

Exhibit 9.1. Information on the Americans with Disabilities Act and the Employment of Candidates with Disabilities, Cont'd.

Arthritis Foundation
1330 West Peachtree Street
Atlanta, GA 30309
(404) 872–7100
(800) 283–7800
www.arthritis.org

American Cancer Society National Office
1599 Clifton Road NE
Atlanta, GA 30329–4251
(800) ACS-2345

Cancer Information Service
Building 31, Room 10A-07
31 Center Drive, MSC 2580
Bethesda, MD 20892–2580
(800) 4-CANCER

National Cancer Institute
Office of Cancer
Communication Building 31, Room 10A24 9000
Rockville, MD 20892
(800) 4-CANCER

American Heart Association (AHA)
7272 Greenville Avenue
Dallas, TX 75231
(800) 242–8721
(800) 242–1793
(214) 706–1179
(214) 706–1341 (Fax)

National Multiple Sclerosis Society
733 3rd Avenue, 6th Floor
New York, NY 10017
(800) 344–4867
(212) 986–3240
www.arbon.com/nmss/

Exhibit 9.1. Information on the Americans with Disabilities Act and the Employment of Candidates with Disabilities, Cont'd.

Mental Disabilities

American Psychiatric Association
Box SF98, 1400 K Street NW
Washington, DC 20005
(202) 682–6000
(202) 682–6850 (Fax)
www.psych.org
E-mail: apa@psych.org

American Psychological Association
750 First Street NE
Washington, DC 20002–4242
(202) 336–5500
www.apa.org
E-mail: executiveoffice@apa.org, centralprograms@apa.org

Anxiety Disorders Association of America
11900 Parklawn Drive, Suite 100
Rockville, MD 20852–2624
(301) 231–9350
(301) 231–7392
www.adaa.org

National Alliance for the Mentally Ill (NAMI)
200 North Glebe Road, Suite 1015
Arlington, VA 22203–3754
(800) 950-NAMI
www.nami.org
E-mail: membership@nami.org

National Mental Health Association
1021 Prince Street
Alexandria, VA 22314
(703) 684–7722
(703) 684–5968 (Fax)
www.NMHA.org

References

Americans with Disabilities Act, 42 U.S.C. § 12101 (1990) *et seq.*

American Educational Research Association (AERA), American Psychological Association (APA), and National Council on Measurement in Education (NCME). (1985). *Standards for educational and psychological testing.* Washington, DC: American Psychological Association.

Argen v. New York State Board, 860 F. Supp. 84 (W.D. N.Y. 1994).

Barnes v. Cochran, 944 F. Supp. 897 (S.D. Fla. 1996), aff'd mem., 130 F.3d 443 (11th Cir. 1997).

Bennett, R. E., Rock, D. A., Kaplan, B. A., & Jirele, T. (1988). Psychometric characteristics. In W. W. Willingham, M. Ragosta, R. E. Bennett, H. Braun, D. A. Rock, & D. E. Powers (Eds.), *Testing handicapped people.* Boston: Allyn & Bacon.

Braun, H., Ragosta, M., & Kaplan, B. A. (1986). *The predictive validity of the Scholastic Aptitude Test for disabled students* (Research Rep. 86–38). Princeton, NJ: Educational Testing Service.

Braun, H., Ragosta, M., & Kaplan, B. A. (1988). Predictive validity. In W. W. Willingham, M. Ragosta, R. E. Bennett, H. Braun, D. A. Rock, & D. E. Powers (Eds.), *Testing handicapped people.* Needham Heights, MA: Allyn & Bacon.

Bultemeyer v. Fort Wayne Community Schools, 100 F.3d 1281, 1284 (7th Cir. 1996).

Burke v. Virginia, 938 F. Supp. 320 (E.D. Va. 1996), aff'd, 114 F.3d 1175 (4th Cir. 1997).

Burkett v. United States Postal Service, 175 F.R.D. 220, 223–24 (N.D. W.Va. 1997).

Cox v. New England Telephone & Telegraph, 607 N.E.2d 1035 (Mass. 1993).

Davoll v. Webb, 160 F.R.D. 142 (D. Colo. 1995).

Ethridge v. State of Alabama, 860 F. Supp. 808 (M.D. Ala. 1994).

Equal Employment Opportunity Commission (EEOC). (1991). Americans with Disabilities Act Regulations 29 C.F.R. § 1630.

Equal Employment Opportunity Commission (EEOC). (1995, Nov. 9). Guidance on preemployment disability-related inquiries and medical examinations under the ADA. 46 Daily Labor Report (BNA), 70:1103–1107.

Equal Employment Opportunity Commission (EEOC). (1997, Mar. 27). EEOC Guidance on psychiatric disabilities and the Americans with Disabilities Act. 59 Daily Labor Report (BNA) E-1.

Eyde, L. D., Nester, M. A., Heaton, S. M., & Nelson, A. V. (1994). *Guide for administering written employment examinations to persons with disabilities* (PRDC–94–11). Washington, DC: U.S. Office of Personnel Management.

Federal Rules of Civil Procedure 23(a) (1998).

Fussell v. Georgia Ports Authority, 48906 F. Supp. 1561 (S.D. Ga. 1995), aff'd mem., 106 F.3d 417 (11th Cir. 1997).

Hendricks-Robinson v. Excel Corporation, 972 F. Supp. 464 (C.D. Ill. 1997).

Hogan v. Bangor & Aroostook R.R., 61 F.3d 1034 (1st Cir. 1995).

Horth v. General Dynamics Land Systems, 960 F. Supp. 873, 881 n.10. (M.D. Pa. 1997).

Milton v. Scrivner, Inc., 53 F.3d 1118, 1123 (10th Cir. 1995).

Morisky v. Broward County, 80 F.3d 445 (11th Cir. 1996).

Nester, M. A. (1984). Employment testing for handicapped people. *Public Personnel Management, 13,* 417–434.

Nester, M. A. (1993). Psychometric testing and reasonable accommodation for persons with disabilities. *Rehabilitation Psychology, 38*(2), 75–85.

Nester, M. A., & Sapinkopf, R. C. (1982). *A federal employment test modified for deaf applicants* (OPRD 82–7). Washington, DC: U.S. Office of Personnel Management.

Ragosta, M., Braun, H., & Kaplan, B. (1991). *Performance and persistence: A validity study of the SAT for students with disabilities* (College Board Rep. No. 91–3 and ETS Research Rep. No. 91–41). New York: College Entrance Examination Board.

Rehabilitation Act of 1973, as amended, §504, 29 U.S.C. §794(d) (1978).

Rock, D. A., Bennett, R. E., Kaplan, B. A., & Jirele, T. (1988). Construct validity. In W. W. Willingham, M. Ragosta, R. E. Bennett, H. Braun, D. A. Rock, & D. E. Powers (Eds.), *Testing handicapped people.* Needham Heights, MA: Allyn & Bacon.

Sapinkopf, R. C. (1978). *Statistical characteristics of the written test for the Professional and Administrative Career Examination (PACE) for visually handicapped applicants* (TM 78–1). Washington, DC: U.S. Civil Service Commission.

Shultz, M., & Boynton, M. (1958). Typing tests: Visual copy vs. recordings. *Public Personnel Review, 19,* 24–27.

Stunkel, E. R. (1957). The performance of deaf and hearing college students on verbal and non-verbal intelligence tests. *American Annals of the Deaf, 102,* 342–355.

Tanca v. Nordberg, 98 F.3d 680, 683 (1st Cir. 1996) (citing H.R. Rep. No. 40(II), 102d Cong., 1st Sess. 4 [1991]), cert. denied, 117 S. Ct. 1253 (1997).

Valle v. City of Chicago, 982 F. Supp. 560, 562 (N.D. Ill. 1997).

Weigel v. Target Stores, 122 F.3d 461 (7th Cir. 1997).

White, K. O. (1978). *Testing the handicapped for employment purposes: Adaptations for persons with motor handicaps* (PS 78–4). Washington, DC:

Personnel Research and Development Center, U.S. Civil Service Commission.

Willingham, W. W. (1988). Discussion and conclusions. In W. W. Willingham, M. Ragosta, R. E. Bennett, H. Braun, D. A. Rock, & D. E. Powers (Eds.), *Testing handicapped people*. Needham Heights, MA: Allyn & Bacon.

Willis v. Conopco, 108 F.3d 282, 285 (11th Cir. 1997).

Wilson v. Pennsylvania State Police Department, 964 F. Supp. 898 (E.D. Pa. 1997).

PART 3

Professional Context

The Relationship Between I/O Psychology and Public Policy: A Commentary

Sheldon Zedeck
Irwin L. Goldstein

The purpose of this chapter is to discuss the role of research in support of public policy. In particular, we have been charged with exploring the professional and social factors that influence the effectiveness and appropriateness of research intended to advance specific public policies. We will pursue this mission by, first, reviewing the objectives of industrial/organizational (I/O) psychology; second, discussing the relationship between public policy and I/O psychology; and third, identifying areas of public policy in which I/O psychologists have a contribution to make. Our goal is to raise issues and to highlight factors that should be considered as I/O psychologists work in their various specializations.

Because our domain of interest—work—is dominant in the lives of all in one fashion or another, it should be obvious that I/O psychology has implications for public policy. However, there is no

Note: We thank Wayne Cascio and Frank Landy for their comments on initial drafts of this chapter. We also sincerely acknowledge Jerry Kehoe for his input, insight, and contributions from the chapter's inception through completion. The views, opinions, and positions expressed, however, are ours alone.

definite, unequivocal position on the relationship between I/O psychology and public policy. Rather, it is a reality about which we must be aware and informed. We hope that the following discourse sheds light on the topic.

Roles of I/O Psychologists

A commonly accepted description of an I/O psychologist is that he or she is a behavioral scientist who studies human behavior in the workplace (Society for Industrial and Organizational Psychology [SIOP], 1995). In general, I/O psychologists promote human welfare through various applications of psychology to all types of organizations. They derive principles of individual, group, and organizational behavior through research; the field of I/O psychology develops scientific knowledge and applies it to the solutions of problems at work.

This description or definition has been labeled the *scientist-practitioner model.* The underlying premises are that I/O psychologists are scientists who attempt to find answers to questions or identify solutions to problems and do so from a scientific and empirical perspective. In other words, they are trained both as scientists and as practitioners. This description is consistent with that of the role of psychology promulgated by the American Psychological Association in its "Ethical Principles of Psychologists and Code of Conduct" (APA, 1992), which states: "Psychologists work to develop a valid and reliable body of scientific knowledge based on research. . . . Their goal is to broaden knowledge of behavior and, where appropriate, to apply it pragmatically to improve the condition of both the individual and society. . . . They also strive to help the public in developing informed judgments and choices concerning human behavior" (p. 1599).

To accomplish their work, I/O psychologists generally use the following methodology: study the issue, including observation, interview, and other data-gathering techniques; study the literature pertaining to the problem; formulate hypotheses that propose or suggest relationships between variables (such as the relationship between a potential predictor of performance, a test, and an actual measure of job performance); conduct research to test the hypotheses; analyze the results; and present conclusions and recommendations. The heart of this methodology is on the *scientific method*.

When we adopt the preceding descriptions and definitions as I/O psychologists, it influences the role we take in public policy, as we will discuss later. For many, the description implies that I/O psychologists should be neutral on public policy issues. Let us contrast our role as I/O psychologists with our role as private citizens. As private citizens, we have every right to participate in the establishment of public policy. We can present our various views along a variety of dimensions—such as liberal or conservative philosophy—to our elected leaders and attempt to influence the direction of our country.

In contrast, we believe our role as I/O psychologists is to present the evidence and let the consequences (implementation of our recommendations) be whatever they may (as long as the implementation is consistent with the results of our research). Furthermore, it is entirely appropriate for us to be advocates for action as long as we rely on scientific evidence and are honest in our appraisal of that evidence. The evidence presented—which is often an account of what the literature on the topic has reported—should be unbiased. Contradictory evidence, when it exists, should also be reported. The purpose of the presentation should be to help policymakers avoid making faulty assumptions about human behavior (for example, Barrett & Morris, 1993).

It is our position that public policy has driven much research in our field and has strengthened the science and the profession (for example, Jarrett & Fairbank, 1987; DeLeon, 1986; Payton, 1984). We will examine this position in the following section.

Public Policy and I/O Psychologists

Public policy evolves from the identification of a social problem or social conflict and is often made manifest in the adoption of a law, legal strategy, or business strategy. That is, our leaders (government, business, political, religious, and others) identify a problem—such as the appropriate means for maximizing human resources in the workplace—and as a result develop laws or strategies to address it. When the problems are addressed by legislation, such as the Civil Rights Acts of 1964 and 1991, the laws shape the public policy.

Characteristics of Public Policy

In many ways, the laws represent the formulation of public policy. Accordingly, they are explicit about the roles to be played by constituencies concerned with the policy (which, for work-related issues, includes I/O psychologists). Even in the legal framework, there is no simple statement regarding the establishment of policy. For example, consider the three branches of government. Congress, the legislative branch of our federal government, passes laws. The Supreme Court, the judicial branch, interprets those laws. And departments such as the Department of Labor or the Department of Justice—the executive branch—issue "guidelines" that suggest means by which the laws are to be enacted. (This division of policy formulation will be illustrated later in this chapter when we discuss the civil rights acts, how courts have interpreted them, and the selection guidelines that were postulated by federal agencies.) The obvious point of this kind of division is that strategies for implementing policy are neither clear-cut nor universally accepted!

It may appear from this description of the evolution of public policy that the issue that underlies the policy is straightforward and obvious. In fact, however, issues can be presented along a continuum, ranging from those that reflect basic social values to those that address practical problems for targeted populations. It is likely that people will have varying levels of agreement and disagreement about where on the continuum policy issues fall. For example, in the United States there is probably little disagreement about who has the right to vote, which is a basic social value. (Of course, even with such issues, there are some people who do not accept the basic value. But at the least, the majority of the population accepts this as a basic social value.) At the other end of the continuum, there is likely to be more disagreement on topics such as immigration policy (a practical issue).

Do I/O psychologists function differently depending on where on the continuum a particular issue falls? We don't think so. We present the continuum idea to suggest that there are differences among policy issues and that policymakers are likely to view the I/O psychologist's contribution and recommended strategies for implementing a policy differently depending on where on the continuum they themselves place the issue.

Role of I/O Psychology in Public Policy

Laws and policies should reflect convergence of public sentiment about an issue and be clear about the social objective to be accomplished. In contrast, the means by which the problem may be addressed are often ambiguous. Unfortunately, the development of public policy is not necessarily based on systematic analyses of the issues involved.

What is the role of I/O psychology in the workplace "public policy arena?" I/O psychologists and professionals in other disciplines can identify and predict social problems in need of a public policy. For example, we can study and forecast the skill and ability levels of the high school graduate in the year 2000 and suggest that new or alternative training programs be adopted by organizations to meet their human resource needs of the future. It is even possible that our examination of the required skills in the workplace can lead to recommendations for the kind of education needed in the public schools. The most recent relevant example here is the need for large numbers of computer scientists, systems analysts, and programmers to work in the growing information technology industries. In 1994, President Clinton signed the School to Work Opportunity Act (Stamps, 1996), a program designed to assist the states in developing school-to-work systems that would prepare students for high-skill, high-wage jobs. It encourages the development of partnerships between schools, work organizations, and labor unions. The I/O psychologist's role in this problem is to study a workplace issue and suggest a potential solution or solutions. Our role is also to conduct research and provide evidence. We need to provide the evidence for the extent of the problem and for the expectation that proposed solutions will work. We must be diligent in our efforts to ensure that policy deliberations are informed by sound research. As scientists, we may think that our professional activities are uninhibited by the law, but we need to be practical and move the situation along. In contrast, it is the role of policymakers to determine whether the problem is of such magnitude that a public policy is needed. If so, a policy can be adopted by executive order, by passage of a law, or by increased allocation of funds for research and development.

Again, as individuals we have every right to communicate our views and attempt to influence our nation's leaders on these policies. But the focus for I/O psychologists is on *framing the question so that it is testable, finding the answers, and recommending solutions.* In this case, what skill and ability levels in the workplace will be needed in the next millennium? And why is there a deficiency in the skill and ability levels of our high school graduates? As I/O psychologists, we focus on how to address and solve the problem; we present the state of knowledge in the relevant field and how it applies to the particular case.

The preceding discussion offers what appears to be a straightforward role in the policy arena for I/O psychologists—to be scientists and practitioners and present unbiased research evidence and suggestions for implementing programs that address an issue. That role becomes most interesting and is highlighted when there is controversy in the profession and among decision makers over the problem and its potential solution. Controversy in the policy arena often stems from tensions between the involved constituencies. For example, the national debate on affirmative action and the means for implementing it (assuming one agrees that there should be an affirmative action policy) reflects the tension between those advocating free-market principles of maximizing productivity and the freedom of an employer to choose its employees and those who wish to increase the number of ethnic minorities and women in the mainstream economy. This debate pits the organizational goal of productivity maximization against a societal goal of equitable, unbiased treatment. What should the I/O psychologist do in this situation? Is there a point where a sufficient amount of research that we view as reasonable and appropriate would cause us to move to a role of advocacy?

Levels of Involvement

One way to view our role is to consider that an I/O psychologist can get involved at different levels. At Level 1, the lowest level, I/O psychologists conduct research, gather evidence, and find answers to problems. This represents, in some ways, the "ivory tower" role that has been ascribed to many academics. At Level 2, I/O psychologists not only communicate the evidence to obvious interested parties, such as colleagues, but also attempt to communicate the evidence to decision makers, such as government policymakers. At Level 3, our role increases to that of *advocate* for actions to be taken, based on the evidence. There might be other levels, particularly when our conclusions are based on evidence that is not clear or is not completely supported. In such situations, we question whether I/O psychologists should be involved as representatives of our discipline, although as private citizens they all have the right to make that choice.

By presenting these levels we are attempting to draw attention to the notion that we can function as I/O psychologists, as scientists only, or we can become advocates for particular positions. We strongly believe that our domain of interest—understanding work behavior—calls for us to be advocates. But as we will reaffirm later in this chapter, our advocacy needs to be based on the evidence.

I/O Psychologists as Advocates

Thus, as much as we may pretend otherwise, a dilemma such as the affirmative action debate causes us to become advocates. But what is the relationship between advocacy and the scientist-practitioner model? Merton (1973) articulated four norms of science:

- Scientific accomplishments must be judged by impersonal criteria.
- Scientific information should be publicly shared.
- Researchers need to proceed objectively, putting aside personal biases and prejudices.
- The scientific community should hold new findings to strict levels of scrutiny through peer review, replication, and the testing of rival hypotheses.

If we adhere to these principles, we do *not* need to be uncomfortable in advocating solutions. Nor do we need to depart from the "scientific method." We can be advocates and propose alternative strategies, or even compromises, for implementing policies. Our advocacy would be based on our interpretation of data and results. Our advocacy, however, should not be based on *selective* use and emphasis of evidence to promote a position. In other words, it would not be proper for an I/O psychologist as a professional to take an advocacy role in situations where the evidence is not clear.

Advocacy is normatively defensible and acceptable provided that it occurs with an explicitly advocacy-based organization or an explicitly adversarial system of disputing (MacCoun, 1998).

Our science has been productive, and we know much about the world of work. As Glass (1976) and Hunter and Schmidt (1990) have implied in their writings on meta-analysis, we know much more than we have been able to demonstrate. The consequence of our research is that some solutions will appear better than others. If we are to function as scientists, then the consequence is that we function as advocates based on data rather than as advocates based on personal values or opinions. We need to communicate the research results and advocate for what we think is the best or at least the better solution.

An Example of Advocacy

To illustrate the role of I/O psychologists in the public policy arena, we will describe a situation when we, the authors, were part of a team asked to consult in a particular situation. The problem pertained to a desire to increase minority representation in an organization that relied on typical employment tests (for example, cognitive ability tests), which resulted in underrepresentation of minorities (compared with their representation in the community labor pool). One compromise solution was *banding* (see Cascio, Outtz, Zedeck, & Goldstein, 1991, for a description of this strategy).

The data on cognitive ability tests, though shown to be valid and appropriate for use in situations that are consistent with professional and legal guidelines, have also shown close to a one standard deviation difference between white and African American applicants on these tests (Hartigan & Wigdor, 1989; Schmitt, Clause, & Pulakos, 1996). This difference has resulted in a higher rejection rate among African Americans for many jobs that require some kind of cognitive ability; the problem is particularly acute in the public sector, where cognitive ability testing has been the primary means by which applicants are hired and where applicants are usually hired in top-down order, with highest scorer hired first. Through the Civil Rights Act of 1964, the government fostered a policy of equal employment opportunity for gender, racial, and other protected groups. The federal "Uniform Guidelines on Employee Selection Procedures" ("Uniform Guidelines," 1978) spell out what to do when there is adverse impact as a result of the selection test and the means by which organizations are to validate their selection tests.

In essence, the Civil Rights Act of 1964 called for equal opportunity; this is a public policy statement that reflects a commonly held social value. If tests were shown to have adverse impact and not to be valid, certain remedies were imposed by the courts, one of which is a *consent decree*. Consent decrees could call for the development of new, valid tests as well as the establishment of goals and timetables for increasing minority representation.

One of the sections in the "Uniform Guidelines" called for the organization to consider alternatives to the test in question, provided the alternatives were equally valid. As a consequence, I/O psychologists have spent considerable research time and effort exploring alternatives to various testing formats, because the continued use of traditional cognitive ability testing results in some degree to maintenance of the status quo or underrepresentation of minorities. The status quo is contrary to the implicit public policy of the Civil Rights Act, which was to increase minority representation in the employment workforce. What could be the role of I/O psychologists in such a situation?

First, I/O psychologists could spend time developing alternatives to cognitive ability testing that are equally or more valid and have less of an adverse impact. Some success with this approach has been reported by H. Goldstein and his colleagues (Goldstein, Yusko, Braverman, Smith, & Chung, 1998), who examined the value of video-based testing. Second, I/O psychologists could spend time improving the cognitive ability tests that currently exist in the hopes of increasing or maintaining their validity while at the same time reducing their adverse impact. Third, they could try to determine the effectiveness of composite selection procedures that combine cognitive testing with other types of predictor information in the hopes that the combination would increase explanatory power of the performance criterion and reduce the adverse impact of the selection process.

Based on the history of cognitive ability testing, we personally are not optimistic that the effort needed would yield a payoff, and thus we would prefer to concentrate on the first option (video-based testing) or the third option (a combination of different predictor types). A fourth option that does not focus on type of test stimulus is to explore alternative ways of interpreting test scores. It is this last approach that we will use to further the discussion on selection research and public policy.

A group of I/O psychologists (for example, Cascio et al., 1991) examined the situation in a particular setting: selection of entry-level firefighters and promotion of firefighters to higher ranks. There had not been new hires or merit-based promotions for many years. (At the outset of the project, racial minorities made up only about 10 percent of the fire department and there were almost no women firefighters.) The situation had deteriorated to the point where there was such a shortage of firefighters that each firefighting apparatus was responding to calls with one firefighter less than deemed appropriate. The legal resolution of the situation was to implement a consent decree that specified a timetable and goals for hiring minorities.

This is an example of a public policy that incorporates social values as well as a practical issue—the need to meet the requirements of the consent decree. The consent decree was monitored by a U.S. district court. The underlying position for the courts and city officials was to implement a public policy of a more diversified fire department. Cascio et al. (1991) proposed banding as a way to interpret test scores, a way to use valid tests in a different manner than traditionally used (that is, top-down hiring).

Banding is an attempt to use the foundation of our science and its methods and measurement theory (such as determining the reliability and degree of error of measurement in our tests) to provide a broader candidate pool from which an organization can choose employees. It yields a broader pool for selection because selection from the candidate pool may not necessarily be in top-down order. Secondary criteria, such as experience, training, the organization's perceived need to be diverse (for example, to accommodate community policing programs), and other such factors can be used to select from the candidates in the band.

Cascio et al. (1991) recognized that banding would yield predicted performance outcomes that would be less than optimum or that would be expected to be achieved by top-down scoring. Nevertheless, proponents of banding were able to show the magnitude of the potential loss from the compromise strategy (banding as opposed to top-down selection), and the organization was able to decide for itself whether to implement the recommended strategy.

The banding strategy was adopted by the jurisdiction not only for its fire department but also for its police department. This decision for the police department was appealed by the union and eventually reviewed by the Ninth Circuit Court of Appeals (*Officers for Justice v. Civil Service Commission of the City and County of San Francisco*, 1993), which found "that the efforts exerted in this process culminated in a unique and innovative program which succeeds in addressing past harms to minorities while minimizing future harmful effects on non-minority candidates. The successful efforts of all parties and the district court in reaching this resolution are to be lauded" (p. 9055).

Needless to say, a number of I/O psychologists oppose banding on psychometric and logical grounds. It was, however, the organization's decision to use banding in order to come closer to the desired public policy and to meet its obligations as set forth in the consent decree. Banding has created sufficient interest that the Scientific Affairs Committee of SIOP issued a report (SIOP, 1994) evaluating banding methods. The committee noted that the evaluation of banding methods depends on the objectives being pursued by test users and that the various technical issues do not represent an insurmountable obstacle to the use of banding in a specific situation. Rather, the decision to use it depends on the careful evaluation of the "costs and benefits of either ignoring or paying attention to small differences in applicants' test scores" (p. 86). In addition, a special issue of *Human Performance* (Hogan, 1995) was devoted to the topic, and a symposium on banding was held at the 1997 SIOP meetings in Dallas (Campion, 1998). It is interesting to note that most if not all of the participants at the symposium, including some who had been critical of banding, acknowledged that it was a reasonable strategy; there remained disagreement, however, on how to group scores from a measurement procedure into a band.

Issues in the Advocacy Role

The I/O psychologists examined several issues as they attempted to facilitate the public policy mandated by the legal system in the situation described in the previous section. First, were there alternative ways for interpreting scores, other than top-down scoring? Second, what were the pros and cons of the different alternatives? Third, given that banding was judged to be a reasonable alternative, how should the width of the band be established? The proponents of banding explored the literature, considered alternative referral strategies such as "the rule of three," "within-group norming," and banding. They decided on banding because it had a foundation in psychometrics and was not based on personal choice or values or on arbitrary decision rules.

In other words, the I/O psychologists who proposed the implementation of banding did so on the basis of what they saw as scientifically justified grounds. It was a strategy based on their understanding of tests—how tests are constructed, what their intended purpose is, the degree of reliability and validity found for the instrument, and the way in which test scores will be used. The strategy was discussed and adopted based on its merits and potential consequences (such as the negative consequence of claims of reverse discrimination) independent of the results it would yield in the particular situation (that is, it is possible to use banding and still have adverse impact after hiring is completed).

A point to be noted is that the I/O psychologists involved were not asked to make the public policy but rather to determine ways in which a policy could be implemented. The recommendations made by the team of I/O psychologists were based on their interpretation of the science that pertained to the underlying personnel issue; they applied that knowledge to a particular issue that needed to be addressed by the city. Thus, we attempted to resolve a social value issue (equal opportunity) and a practical issue (underrepresentation of minorities) by proposing a method that was value-free. There were no guarantees that the public policy would be achieved by adopting the banding strategy. What was offered was, in our opinion, a scientifically based method to make selections that could result in the achievement of a desired public policy. We did not address the social value issue of equal opportunity but rather provided a means for selecting employees that could accomplish an organization's goals.

In this case, science was neutral on the topic of social values, equal opportunity, and so on. And that is the way we intended it to be! The neutrality of science lies in its methodology. As psychologists and lay citizens, we have personal value systems and opinions on the issues of equal opportunity, but we must be vigilant and ensure that our personal opinions and values do not interfere with *how* we do our work. There is no denying the fact, however, that our personal opinions influence whether we *will* undertake the work. Given the task proposed to us by the city, we could have declined the consulting job if it was not consistent with our personal views. We all have this option; we may choose to work as I/O psychologists for Company X but not for Company Y because we dislike Company Y's policies, image, trade relations, and so on. But once we accept the job or consulting arrangement, the methodology and data should determine our actions.

A related public policy issue for the above-described situation pertains to the possibility of the perception of reverse discrimination when banding is used. The perception, based on traditional use of testing, is that if a lower score is selected before a higher score, then merit is not the basis for the hiring decision. If the lower-scoring individual is a minority and the higher-scoring individual is a majority, then the latter is likely to perceive reverse discrimination. The role here for the I/O psychologist is to educate the policy leaders and those being directly affected by the policy— the employees or candidates. The proponents of banding assert that all those within a band can be considered equivalent in their likely performance on the job. Accordingly, the scores of the two candidates are not considered to be meaningfully different, and as a consequence, either one can be selected. Explaining the strategy—its pros and cons—provides information to the policy leaders as they make the decision whether to implement. Explaining the strategy to those directly affected—the candidates—also provides needed information, though given the emotion surrounding the issue, the information is not always heard.

Professional Factors

What are the professional factors involved in taking this kind of position? Basically, we rely on our literature and our interpretation of methods, data, and results. Clearly, I/O psychologists may assume many different roles when they work on these types of issues. The I/O psychologist could be employed by an organization that is the defendant in litigation, by the plaintiff, or even by the court itself or other groups that have an interest in the issue. When representing any one of these groups, the I/O psychologist must employ the same set of standards, based on his or her understanding of the science and knowledge in our field. The group being represented may not wish to use the information that the I/O psychologist offers or even to employ that individual. But that should not deter the I/O psychologist from providing information based on professional standards and not on personal standards and values.

We view it as inappropriate to criticize I/O psychologists based on who employs them as long as they maintain professional standards. Many of the issues that I/O psychologists study involve a blend of truth conflicts and conflicts of interest (MacCoun, 1998). Truth conflicts involve a blend of attempts to seek the truth or the correct answer. Here, researchers are interested in basic findings that can contribute to the literature and increase understanding of phenomena. They are not interested in the implications of their research. For others, the organization has a mission and is operating in a zero-sum game regarding the distribution of outcomes. Here, the researcher may have a conflict of interest regarding how the distribution should be made. Although it may be difficult for people to separate out their personal views and values from their role as I/O psychologists, we believe it is critical to rely as much as possible on research knowledge and professional standards alone. We need to understand our different potential roles and then separate our personal, value-based advocacy from our role as researchers. Weimer and Vining (1992) identify three different professional models in the field of public policy: *objective technician,* who maintains a distance from clients but lets the data speak for themselves and avoids recommendations; *client's advocate,* who exploits ambiguity in the data to strike a balance between loyalty to the facts and loyalty to a client's interests; and *issue advocate,* who explicitly draws on research opportunistically in order to promote broader values or policy objectives. If we seek to criticize, we should identify the model we are using. There is nothing wrong with different standards for judging data and results; there is also nothing wrong with being an advocate, provided we are aware of and understand our professional standards and position and make them explicit. Fostering hypothesis competition and alternative views can simultaneously serve the search for "truth," but we need to be certain to articulate the boundary between being an adversary or an advocate and being a scientist (MacCoun, 1998).

The decision to be an advocate also relates to how and where we publish our knowledge. We believe that the appropriate forum for the presentation, publication, and discussion of knowledge is in the professional and scientific journals and in conferences sponsored by our professional associations. The public media—such as newspapers and TV and radio shows—should be used to inform the lay public about the work we do and to present findings and a body of knowledge that have undergone peer review in our professional journals. The public media, however, should not be an arena in which we attack other professionals in one-sided presentations in ways that would never be acceptable in our profession and which are merely attacks on an individual's values rather than a fair discussion of the scientific evidence.

Social Factors

What are the social factors to be considered? Basically, I/O psychologists react to a social situation. To return to the banding example, we reacted to a situation in which the policy was to integrate a workforce by valid means. We operated within the constraints of the Civil Rights Act of 1964, the constraints of the consent decree, and the stated desire of the elected public officials to obtain a diverse workforce, where selection into the organization would be based on merit.

Another social factor pertains to change—change in attitudes, values, beliefs, and so on over time. Social, political, and personal beliefs and interests change over time, and consequently, give rise to changes in the evolution of public policy related to selection. For example, when the Civil Rights Act was passed in 1964 it was assumed that affirmative action was a necessary and reasonable policy. According to the "Uniform Guidelines" (1978), affirmative action involves a series of activities that the employer can undertake to ensure that positions are genuinely and equally accessible to qualified persons without regard to sex, racial, or ethnic characteristics. Actions may include establishing goals or specially designed recruitment programs; making systematic efforts to organize work and redesign jobs to facilitate entry and progress within careers; increasing pools of candidates; and making other such attempts to increase the number of protected groups eligible for consideration in the employment or promotion process. The policy's focus was on *voluntary* actions to achieve equal employment opportunity and to provide opportunities to minorities that would allow them to compete with majority members for workplace positions.

Now, thirty-five years later, the mood in the country has changed. The role of affirmative action plans is being questioned by government leaders, business leaders, and the population at large. Should the role be any different now for the I/O psychologist? Not really, except that as researchers we should be monitoring and paying closer attention to attitudes than we may have done previously. The role for I/O psychologists in the affirmative action debate is consistent with our role in situations in which there is a definite public policy: review the literature on affirmative action, study its definition and operationalization, evaluate its impact on behavior and attitudes, and perhaps, evaluate its economic contribution to society. Consequently, we can provide information to policymakers about the impact of affirmative action on behavior and attitudes and identify the changes in the population's attitudes. In part, SIOP has fulfilled this role, as evidenced by its report entitled *Affirmative Action: A Review of Psychological and Behavioral Research* (SIOP, 1997), which studies the literature on the nature of affirmative action, attitudes, individual differences, behavioral effects, economic effects, and limitations of current knowledge. This report is a source that should be considered by policymakers who want to understand affirmative action.

Direct Impact on Public Policy

In the context in which we function—the world of work—we are often asked to address issues that have social, practical, and public policy implications. In such situations, we can have a direct impact on public policy, and our research directly informs public policy. Research on personnel matters *is* policy-relevant research. When we conduct research on a particular topic, accumulate much evidence about the issue, and subsequently examine meta-analyses of the findings, we often report what the consensual view is on an issue. Consensus is the "food for thought" for policymakers. Accordingly, our research findings are what the policymakers are (or should be) interested in seeing and using when deciding on solutions to the problems. However, we agree with MacCoun (1998), who cautioned that we should not be so naive about the gaps between our research findings and the inputs needed for sound policy formulation; policymakers need also to consider the economics and politics of the policy.

Indirect Impact on Public Policy

Most of what we have presented to this point addressed our direct role in public policy, that is, responding to social situations that can benefit from our science and knowledge base. Another influence on public policy is indirect. Organizations in either the public or private sector, even when not responding to laws or requests for input on public policy, still have an effect on public policy. An organization that develops a selection system and uses it to make decisions is formulating and implementing its own public policy. The organization is the agent of change by determining the way it wants work to be accomplished, the type of worker it needs, who gets hired and has employment (and, consequently, who remains unemployed), and other such issues. Depending on its hiring criteria, policy implications derive from the fact that the organization also is defining training needs for the future. That is, the organization that decides to hire candidates with the computer skills necessary to operate the equipment in the plant is also stating that future applicants will need such skills and therefore training ought to be developed to meet those needs. This decision by the organization has the potential to affect how educational systems construct their curricula and how funds might be allocated to develop and deliver training programs. Also, there could be an impact on the benefits provided to future employees in order to attract them to the organization. This kind of impact stems from concern about what motivates candidates to select organizations, including family-job relationships.

In essence, the organization by its actions has an indirect as well as a direct impact on public policy.

Intentional Influence on Public Policy

At a more general level of discussion, should I/O psychologists *intentionally* become active in public policy issues? As stated earlier, our research has direct and indirect effects on public policy issues.

Most of those effects have been reactive. Much of our research on testing, selection, test fairness, validity generalization, and other such topics has occurred because we have responded to real-world issues, many of them stemming from public crises. Similar statements can be made by those in other applied fields, such as human factors engineering, consumer behavior, and so on. We pose for consideration the notion that perhaps I/O psychologists should take a more proactive role in public policy.

Our research domain—the world of work—cannot be separated from public policy. We have heard numerous discussions by SIOP executive committee members over the years lamenting the fact that we are ignored when important social and public issues are debated. The solution is to be more proactive and more vocal about how our research can affect behavior in the world of work. Perhaps those who are writing on topics that have public policy implications should be requested to include in the discussion section of their article a few paragraphs on the implications of their findings. This would be a positive change in the way in which we operate. But we need to keep in mind that we do not have sole claim on the public policy arena. Other disciplines have much to contribute to public policy discussions; in other words, we also need to be more interdisciplinary in our research. Finally, we should not be so naive as to think that all public policy is based on research; politics, economics, and religion are important contributors to the scene.

I/O Psychology and Specific Public Policy Domains

The preceding discussion focused on a particular area in selection research in which I/O psychology can contribute to public policy. The following presents other topics in selection research as well as other arenas in which I/O psychology relates to social issues and may have public policy implications.

Americans with Disabilities Act

The Americans with Disabilities Act of 1990 calls for employers to provide reasonable accommodations in the test process and on the job for persons who need such adjustments because of a sensory, manual, or speaking disability, but who can otherwise perform the essential functions of the job.

This act is interesting because although it represents a public policy there is little to guide us when it comes to definitions of some disabilities or appropriate accommodations for specific disabilities. The I/O psychologist can contribute by defining behavior and determining whether that behavior is a disability as implied by the act. Also, based on our understanding of and ability to study jobs, I/O psychologists should explore the link between various disabilities, their relationship to task performance, and appropriate accommodation, if any, for the problem.

The questions for I/O psychologists become these: What is the effective design of alternative predictors or what accommodation is needed for the disabled to be able to perform on a traditional predictor? In some instances, this is a relatively easy challenge, such as when written material can be read to a person with a visual disability. (Nevertheless, we still need to determine the change in validity, if any, when the mode of test presentation changes.)

However, in most instances, the preparation of reasonable accommodation is done as an afterthought. There is little research on which type of accommodation permits the individual with a disability to perform up to his or her capability. We suspect the lack of attention to these issues stems in part from the fact that most accommodations are developed only when an individual is in need of one, rather than during the class action suits that often occur in employment discrimination cases involving race or gender. However, increasing numbers of individuals with disabilities are becoming aware of opportunities to be productive citizens, and organizations need their talents. More research on selection systems that maximize opportunities for these individuals is needed.

Goals 2000: Educate America Act of 1994

This act established a national skill standards board to stimulate the development of a voluntary national system of skill standards, assessments, and certifications. These standards must be nondiscriminatory and consistent with civil rights law. The assessment systems under this law are required to use multiple methods, including, where appropriate, oral and written evaluations, portfolio assessments, and performance tests.

This law has obvious prescriptions for contributions from I/O psychologists. Much can be done with respect to identification of the requisite skills, their measurement, and means by which training can be provided to achieve the skills. If methods suggested by I/O psychologists for conducting the assessments have disparate impact on protected groups, what do we do? The response, again, is to look for alternatives that would yield equally valid results.

Immigration Issues

The influx of minorities into the workforce is so high that it is predicted that in some states, such as California, ethnic minorities will make up the majority of the workforce. The proportion of our nation's population born in foreign countries continues to climb. A Census Bureau study conducted in 1997 (Vobejda, 1998) indicated that U.S. residents born outside the country made up 9.7 percent of the population, a larger segment than at any time in the last five decades.

What issues does this pose for I/O psychologists? Many job candidates will not have English as their first language and therefore may be at a disadvantage when taking employment tests. In work contexts where the ability to read English is not necessary, a solution is to have alternative modes of testing (for example, minimizing or eliminating reliance on the written word as a test stimulus and instead using video- or audio-based testing) or develop the examination in the language of the candidates. Either of these solutions has a higher cost to the organization than the more traditional multiple-choice paper-and-pencil test. Who pays for the development of these alternatives? The I/O psychologist should develop the alternatives and identify their utility in light of costs and benefits.

Another aspect of the immigration issue involves hiring immigrants when there are shortages of native candidates. At one time, there was a shortage of hospital nurses. The federal government responded to the need by permitting the immigration of thousands of nurses from Great Britain and the Philippines. The original legislation (Chavez, 1998) stipulated that these individuals would be permitted to spend a set number of years in the United

States, but eventually the time period was waived and the nurses were allowed to remain. Similar issues are currently at play with immigrant workers in technology jobs because of industry pressure to fill these jobs.

Critics of this approach argue that technology companies and educational institutions are not doing enough to attract and train American workers with basic computer skills. Clearly, there are serious issues regarding selection and training opportunities both for the present populations and for future workers. This is made even more complicated because the growth of the workforce has slowed. This slowdown has also occurred in a number of other countries, such as Sweden and Germany, where the population growth rate is virtually nil. In Sweden, this has led to a heavy emphasis on training programs. In Germany, it has led to interlocking agreements between schools and industry with national coordinating committees to ensure standardization and consistency.

Certainly, this situation leads to important questions about the proper mix of selection and training systems to create the most productive system. It leads to questions about teaching skills and abilities to our own population rather than employing immigration policy as an alternative solution. And it raises questions about the diversity of the workforce and how organizations can work with an increasingly complex mix of workers with different histories, values, and beliefs and still maintain a satisfied and productive workforce.

Workforce Diversity

As noted above, the U.S. workforce is becoming increasingly diverse because of the number of immigrants entering the United States. However, that is only one aspect of diversity. The aging of the population, the increase in ethnic and racial minorities, and the increase in the numbers of working women all contribute to the diversity of the workforce. Yet we have learned very little about adapting the workplace to a diverse workforce. For example, there is very little information on the performance of older individuals. Cognitive performance is a strong predictor of work behavior, but older individuals show measurable declines in some cognitive functioning indicators, such as reasoning and memory factors. Yet except for tasks that require speed and short-term memory factors, the relationship between age and job performance is positive, at least for some workers under the age of sixty-five. We need to know a lot more about the relationship between predictors that might be used in the selection of older individuals and work performance (for example, Cascio, 1998; Landy, 1992). It may be that the type of predictors that need to be utilized need to be modified in terms of the criterion space that we need to measure.

Similarly, every indicator points to the growing proportion of the workforce that will be made up of ethnic and racial minorities. Many of these individuals have not been given access to the types of educational opportunities they will need in order to compete effectively on the types of traditional predictors that we have used in selecting individuals. Yet there is a growing realization that we need these individuals in the workforce and cannot plan for a productive society without them. Again, the question of which predictors to use to give these individuals opportunities in the workplace needs to be considered. There also need to be further questions about the criterion space that defines success for the organization.

It is becoming quite obvious that having an all-white workforce may make a statement that will not result in organizational success. The question is how that translates into the prediction equation at the individual level.

Education: Focus on K–12

Many are concerned that schoolchildren today are not prepared to enter the world of work, or for that matter, to be successful at the university level. I/O psychologists can obviously present information on the requisite skills and competencies needed to be successful in various jobs; we can also determine how to assess competency achievement. We can study the links between job and skill competency needs and educational programs designed to develop the skills. We can study the hierarchical nature of abilities and skills to determine which ones form the foundation for higher-level abilities and skills. All of this information can be used by policymakers when they allocate funding to different levels of education.

As it is, analysts are suggesting that the criteria for success for competing in the workplace are changing (Secretary's Commission on Achieving Necessary Skills, 1991). Interpersonal criteria such as "works well with others" are being added to our requisite-skill list, as are others such as "participates as member of a team" and "teaches others new skills."

With our understanding of job analysis, I/O psychologists can be at the center of determining the new skills required to compete in the workplace as well as the developmental analyses of when such skills should be fostered and the best way for teaching them. Mentoring partnerships between schools and local businesses will be necessary to develop a productive workforce. This further suggests the need to develop effective work internship and apprentice programs as well as work-based learning opportunities for both teachers and students. As I/O psychologists, we will need to expand our horizons in new ways, such as understanding the developmental psychology of youth.

International Work

With the global economy a dominant issue for multinational organizations, the I/O psychologist can contribute by presenting evidence on values, beliefs, customs, and mores that will facilitate living in different cultures (see Chapter Seven of this volume). We can also study the issues surrounding acceptance of foreign workers into the U.S. work domain. In other words, I/O psychologists can study the interrelationships among workers from all countries, with respect to attitudes, acceptance, stereotypes, teamwork, and other relevant dimensions.

Work-Family Relationships

As the nature of the workforce and the centrality of work in family life both change (Galinsky, Bond, & Friedman, 1993), I/O psychologists need to increase their research into issues beyond the workplace. Obvious areas in which policymakers are interested are scheduling and the programs that affect scheduling, attendance, and work performance. I/O psychologists should provide research on the benefits and liabilities of telecommuting and flexible scheduling programs. Research is also needed on the demand for elder care.

Family factors are playing a greater role in a worker's decision to make a commitment to a job and an organization; consequently, a greater understanding of workers' attitudes and values is called for. More needs to be known about the impact of organizational policies on attitudes and behavior of workers.

Conclusion

One of the implications of our adopting the scientist-practitioner model is that we are active in researching and resolving social issues and questions. In this regard, I/O psychologists should use the scientific method to develop research that is responsive to these issues and questions. We do not believe that this means that the I/O psychologist is relegated only to speaking with other scientists and interested colleagues. It is entirely appropriate for us as I/O psychologists to be advocates for action, as long as we rely on scientific evidence and are honest in our appraisal of that evidence.

Another critical role for the I/O psychologist is to suggest methods to collect new evidence needed to understand particular issues. Indeed, we believe that I/O psychologists have much to offer in the public policy arena on many important issues that relate to work behavior, such as workforce diversity, school-to-work issues, immigration, the aging population, and so on.

Finally, we believe that it is perfectly appropriate for us as citizens to be advocates for positions for which we do not have evidence or when we do not personally accept the systematic evidence that has been collected. In those cases, however, we should make it clear that we are speaking as individual citizens—and not in our role as I/O psychologists.

References
American Psychological Association (APA). (1992). Ethical principles of psychologists and code of conduct. *American Psychologist, 47,* 1597–1611.
Americans with Disabilities Act of 1990, 42 U.S.C. Sec. 933.

Barrett, G. V., & Morris, S. B. (1993). The American Psychological Association's amicus curiae brief in Price Waterhouse v. Hopkins. *Law and Human Behavior, 17,* 201–215.

Campion, M. A. (1998, Apr.) *The controversy over score banding in personnel selection.* Symposium conducted at the meeting of the Society of Industrial and Organizational Psychology, Dallas.

Cascio, W. F. (1998, Aug.) *Is age a proxy for declines in performance among workers over 65?* Paper presented at the meeting of the International Congress of Applied Psychology, San Francisco.

Cascio, W. F., Outtz, J., Zedeck, S., & Goldstein, I. L. (1991). Statistical implications of six methods of test score use in personnel selection. *Human Performance, 4,* 233–264.

Chavez, L. (1998, Aug. 2). Guest workers might ease immigration flow. *USA Today,* p. 11A.

Civil Rights Act of 1964, U.S.C. Stat. 253 (1964).

Civil Rights Act of 1991, Pub. L. No. 102–166, 105. Stat. 1075 (1991).

DeLeon, P. H. (1986). Increasing the society contribution of organized psychology. *American Psychologist, 41,* 466–174.

Equal Employment Opportunity Commission, Civil Service Commission, Department of Labor, and Department of Justice. (1978). Uniform guidelines on employee selection procedures. Section 3D. *Federal Register, 43*(166), 38295–38309.

Galinsky, E., Bond, T., & Friedman, D. E. (1993). *National study of the changing workforce.* New York: Families and Work Institute.

Glass, G. V. (1976). Primary, secondary, and meta-analysis of research. *Educational Researcher, 5,* 3–8.

Goals 2000: Educate America Act of 1994, 20 U.S.C. Sec. 5801.

Goldstein, H. W., Yusko, K. P., Braverman, E. P., Smith, D. B., & Chung, B. (1998). The role of cognitive ability in the subgroup differences and incremental validity of assessment center exercises. *Personnel Psychology, 51,* 357–374.

Hartigan, J. A., & Wigdor, A. K. (1989). *Fairness in employment testing.* Washington, DC: National Academy Press.

Hogan, J. (1995). [Special issue]. *Human Performance, 8*(3).

Hunter, J. E., & Schmidt, F. L. (1990). *Methods of meta-analysis.* Thousand Oaks, CA: Sage.

Jarrett, R. B., & Fairbank, J. A. (1987). Psychologists' views: APA's advocacy of and resource expenditure on social and professional issues. *Professional Psychology: Research and Practice, 18,* 643–646.

Landy, F. J. (1992). *Alternatives to chronological age in determining standards of suitability for public safety jobs.* Report submitted to the U.S. Equal Opportunity Commission, Washington, DC.

MacCoun, R. J. (1998). Biases in the interpretation and use of research results. *Annual Review of Psychology, 49,* 259–287.

Merton, R. K. (1973). *The sociology of science.* Chicago: University of Chicago Press.

Officers for Justice v. Civil Service Commission of the City and County of San Francisco, 979 F.2nd 721 (9th Cir. 1992); cert. denied 61 U.S. L.W. 3367, 113 S. Ct. 1645 (1993).

Payton, C. R. (1984). Who must do the hard things? *American Psychologist, 39,* 391–397.

Schmitt, N., Clause, C. S., & Pulakos, E. D. (1996). Subgroup differences associated with different measures of some common job-relevant constructs. In C. R. Cooper & I. T. Robertson (Eds.), *International review of industrial and organizational psychology* (Vol. 11, pp. 115–140). New York: Wiley.

Secretary's Commission on Achieving Necessary Skills. (1991). *What work requires of schools.* Washington, DC: U.S. Government Printing Office.

Society for Industrial and Organizational Psychology (SIOP). (1994). An evaluation of banding methods in personnel selection. *Industrial and Organizational Psychologist, 32*(1), 80–86.

Society for Industrial and Organizational Psychology (SIOP). (1995). *Graduate training programs in industrial/organizational psychology and related fields.* Bowling Green, OH: Author.

Society for Industrial and Organizational Psychology (SIOP). (1997). *Affirmative action: A review of psychological and behavioral research.* Bowling Green, OH: Author.

Stamps, D. (1996, June). Will school-to-work work? *Training, 6,* 72–81.

Vobejda, B. (1998, Jan. 9). Survey: U.S. population about 10 percent foreign-born. *Washington Post,* pp. A1, A7.

Weimer, D. L., & Vining, A. R. (1992). *Policy analysis: Concepts and practice.* Upper Saddle River, NJ: Prentice-Hall.

CHAPTER 11

Research and Practice in Selection

Jerard F. Kehoe

This chapter describes the relationship between research and practice in selection psychology today, identifies factors that influence the practice decisions that selection program managers make, and suggests research and professional agendas to support selection program management practice. The purpose is to enhance our professional community's understanding of the multiple considerations that influence the management of selection programs. A better understanding can help focus research on issues central to effective selection, can help selection program managers balance the integration of these multiple considerations, and can help the industrial-organizational (I/O) psychology profession to strengthen its support of selection program management by focusing on a dialogue about the relationships between practice, research, and governing standards and principles.

The Relationship Between Research and Practice in Selection Psychology

A central theme of this chapter is that professionally responsible selection practice decisions depend on a broader set of considerations than our standards of scientific research. Selection program management decisions are not the same as research-based scientific conclusions. Paradoxically, this distinction may have been masked somewhat by the historically close link between selection research and the procedures commonly used in practice. Selection practice decisions are routinely based on accumulated experience, expertise, and judgment that aggregate research results, local organizational conditions, sociopolitical considerations, and legal risks. In contrast, the legal and professional standards that govern these decisions emphasize the importance of local ad hoc studies to justify selection practice decisions.

The Scientist-Practitioner Model Applied to Selection

The scientist-practitioner model is generally accepted as the professional model to which we aspire when designing our training programs, maintaining our professional community, and focusing on our research and delivering our solutions. Although there would be little point in seeking to change this, my perspective is that the distinguishing roles are research and practice, not science and practice. If we agree that the purpose of I/O psychology science is to provide solutions to important organizational problems, then it is clear that research and practice have interdependent but distinct roles. These two roles together constitute the science of personnel selection practiced by a professional community of scientist-psychologists who are defined by their common training, methodology, and interests. Research and practice are distinguished more by their purposes and outputs than by their methods. Indeed, the scientific method of observing, theorizing, and testing is a problem-solving "tool kit" that is applied to both research and practice in the domain of selection. This is true in part because the external standards for research publication and for practice defensibility impose essentially the same methodological criteria.

Among the behavioral sciences, the link between research and practice is perhaps closest in industrial-organizational psychology, and in personnel selection in particular. This close link exists because personnel selection in practice uses fundamentally the same selection procedures as those most frequently investigated in our research; the procedures we implement in our selection practice are to a great extent the same as or highly similar to the measurement processes we target in our research. Tests of verbal reasoning and assessments of conscientiousness as designed for employment applications are frequently the same in research and in practice.

Contrast this with the experience of our clinical cousins. Nearly half a century ago, the Boulder conference (Raimy, 1950) established a scientist-practitioner model as the foundation for training in professional clinical practice. Since then, Psy.D. training programs have grown to the extent that in 1993 nearly a quarter of the doctorates awarded in clinical psychology were Psy.D.s (Rice, 1997). The companion debate, recently driven by managed care, has been to address growing concerns in the clinical profession about the development of professional practice guidelines (Nathan, 1998). Because of the debate over such guidelines, the link between the science and practice of clinical psychology has been closely scrutinized (Rice, 1997). At the heart of this dialogue is the question of the extent to which research can or should compel clinical judgment at the moment of service delivery. The debate is not so much about whether research has addressed the most important questions but rather about whether clinical research is even commensurable with clinical practice (Peterson, 1991; Stricker & Trierweiler, 1995; Stricker, 1997).

Although there has been considerable concern about differences between the contexts of I/O practice and I/O research (Levy-Leboyer, 1988; Dunnette, 1990; McIntyre, 1990; Murphy & Saal, 1990), it is fair to say that in our professional community we have not experienced such a fundamental division. The concerns expressed over research and practice in I/O psychology relate to a lack of participation by practitioners in the research process (Dunnette, 1990); pressures in organizational settings for quick, oversimplified solutions to complex problems that presumably reduce the practitioner's opportunity to be careful and research-based (McIntyre, 1990); and differences between academic and organizational performance demands and reward contingencies for I/O psychologists (Hackman, 1985; Guion, 1988).

Selection Research in the 1990s

One of the purposes of this chapter is to elaborate on distinctions between research and practice that should be a source of concern and action for individual psychologists and for our professional community. Information about the content of recent research in our field is an appropriate and valuable starting point for this discussion.

At the beginning of this decade, Dunnette (1990) presented profiles of published I/O researchers as part of his discussion of the relationship between research and practice. A key finding was that the number of nonacademic I/O psychologists was shrinking among published authors, particularly among those whose work appeared in the *Journal of Applied Psychology (JAP)* and *Personnel Psychology (PP)*. One of Dunnette's premises was that a healthy professional relationship between research and practice would require that practitioners increase their participation in the research endeavor. A related issue that deserves at least equal attention and may be more susceptible to the influence of our professional community is the content of published research, regardless of author affiliation. Table 11.1 profiles research content categories in *JAP* and *PP* from 1990 through 1997.

This research profile offers some insights into the current relationship between selection research and practice. Selection research activity continues, and the measurement and testing foundations of selection research remain in the 1990s. Selection practice continues to be directly informed by the continuing volume of research on such procedures as interviews, ability tests, disposition and temperament inventories, and predictor composites. It is primarily in this way that the research and practice of selection psychology has been closely linked.

The articles focusing on selection-related issues most frequently deal with disposition-temperament and group differences, followed by cognitive ability, and then utility, interviews, and personal reactions to recruiting, selection, and related processes. A more modest number of articles deal with experience, biodata, and selection procedure technology.

Most of these categories correspond directly to particular types of selection procedures. Only the utility and experience categories are not about particular selection procedures, although there is considerable overlap between the experience and interview categories. It is this continuing research focus on application-based issues and on specific types of selection procedures used in research largely as they are used in practice that creates a close link between research and practice in selection psychology. Similarly, the significant research volume on contextual issues, such as group differences, utility, and perceptions, is driven by issues associated with the application of selection procedures in organizations.

Table 11.1. Research Content
of *JAP* and *PP* Articles, 1990–1997.

Content of Article	Number of Articles[a]	Percentage of Articles[b]
Related to the workplace	696	75
Individual job behavior/performance	241	26
Selection	200	22
Measurement	200	22
Research related to selection procedures:		
Disposition/temperament	66	7
Cognitive ability	49	5
Interviews	33	4
Biodata	17	2
Experience	16	2
Selection procedure technology	14	2
Research related to selection context:		
Group differences	64	7
Utility	34	4
Perceptions/reactions	27	3
Disabilities	3	0
Selection program design as dependent variable	2	0
Type of study:		
Local study	812	88
Aggregate of separate studies	90	10

[a]926 research articles were published in *JAP* and *PP* from 1990 through 1997.
[b]Percentages less than 0.5 are shown as 0.

Selection research not only is largely about selection tools and their applications but also has advanced the knowledge base considerably. The research on personality has established a growing foundation of validity evidence (Hough, Eaton, Dunnette, Kamp, & McCloy, 1990; Barrick & Mount, 1991; Tett, Jackson, & Rothstein, 1991) and has begun to address one of the most significant application issues: faking or socially desirable responding (Hough et al., 1990; Ones, Viswesvaran, & Reiss, 1996). Similarly, the advances in biodata relate to the generalizability of validity across situations

(Rothstein, Schmidt, Erwin, Owens, & Sparks, 1990). *JAP* and *PP* research on cognitive ability has not focused primarily on measurement or construct issues but rather on applications-oriented issues, such as incremental predictive validity results (McHenry, Hough, Toquam, Hanson, & Ashworth, 1990) and reasons for and methods for minimizing group differences on cognitive measures (Schmitt, Rogers, Chan, Sheppard, & Jennings, 1997; DeShon, Smith, Chan, & Schmitt, 1998). The research on interviews has shown perhaps the most dramatic advance of all based on meta-analytic results that have reversed once commonly held beliefs about the level of interview validity, particularly in unstructured interviews (McDaniel, Whetzel, Schmidt, & Maurer, 1994; Huffcutt & Roth, 1998). These results also create a considerable challenge for our selection-oriented theorizing because they are about a method that most often has a poor or absent specification of the constructs being measured. Although this may at first seem problematic only for our theorizing, it is also problematic ultimately for our practice, because the ability to generalize to practice situations depends on construct-level specification and understanding. This seems to be particularly true for less structured interviews that now appear to have the capability of much higher validity than previously thought. How? What would it take to expect the same result in my organization?

The group differences research has been driven by two major developments. First, the Civil Rights Act of 1991 further constrained the options organizations have for minimizing the adverse impact of valid selection systems. As a result, strategies such as banding (Cascio, Outtz, Zedeck, & Goldstein, 1991; Murphy, 1994; Kehoe & Tenopyr, 1994) have been developed and evaluated in an effort to find alternative solutions. Second, the emergence of persuasive and generalizable validity evidence for disposition-temperament and interviews, which generally yield much smaller group differences than ability tests, has created an active and important line of research focusing on the effects of combined predictors on group selection rates and performance (Sackett & Roth, 1996; Schmitt, Rogers et al., 1997).

Similarly, the utility research has taken a direction largely dictated by practice. In addition to addressing the problems of utility estimation, recent research also has looked at the meaning of utility estimates for organization managers (Latham & Whyte, 1994; Carson, Becker, & Henderson, 1998) and the relevance of traditional utility estimation to complex organizational decision-making processes (Russell, Colella, & Bobko, 1993).

The relatively recent line of practice-oriented research on personal reactions to recruiting and selection processes continues to be popular, focusing on perceptions of justice, fairness, and attributions about organizations based on recruiting and selection practices.

In contrast, essentially no selection research has been published in *JAP* and *PP* on the relationships between disabilities and selection procedures. One explanation might be that the research traditions most closely associated with disabilities are in the education and health sciences. Nevertheless, determining and managing selection practice accommodations for people with disabilities is an increasingly significant part of selection program management. Chapter Nine in this volume discusses what is known about disability accommodation issues in an effort to organize the practice issues and inform practitioners about those issues.

This profile of the research that has appeared in *JAP* and *PP* indicates that selection research continues to be about the tools and procedures of selection as well as certain directly related contextual issues. But with a very small number of exceptions, it is not about the organizational process of selection program management. Why do some successful organizations avoid professionally designed and supported selection programs? What are the organizational barriers to the effective and enduring implementation of systematic selection programs? What are the factors that selection practitioners must routinely balance in their efforts to implement enduring and effective selection practices? Are professional selection practices more or less likely to be embraced at different stages of organizational development and evolution? These questions address the organizational factors that frequently determine the presence or absence of selection practices. They are representative of the context in which many selection practitioners work both in organizations and as consultants to organizations.

Two recent studies reported on surveys about the influence of organizational factors on selection practices. Rynes, Orlitzky, and Bretz (1997) described the tendency of organizations with less dynamic business environments, older workforces, and growth-oriented short-term staffing strategies to rely more heavily on the recruitment and selection of experienced new hires than college recruits. Similarly, in a survey of assessment center practices, Spychalski, Quinones, Gaugler, and Pohley (1997) reported that assessment center practices varied by type of industry and purpose. In addition to these studies that addressed the relationship between organizational characteristics and specific selection practices, earlier studies proposed broader models of the relationship between higher-level organizational attributes and the use of a wide range of human resource practices. Johns (1993) modeled the implementation of professional HR practices as organizational administrative innovation that is not strongly affected by technical merit. Rather, other influences, such as imitation, political influence, and legal and environmental threat, tend to affect organizational decisions to adopt such practices. Jackson, Schuler, and Rivero (1989) summarized organizational characteristics that are predictive of the adoption of various personnel practices. Although neither of these broader treatments focuses specifically on selection practices, both provide models of the influence of organizational attributes on the adoption of comparable HR practices that should provide a reasonable framework for further research on the subject.

Finally, it is particularly noteworthy that the 1990s have seen an increasing rate of articles that aggregate research across multiple studies and derive generalizable conclusions. From 1990 through 1993, 7.5 percent of the *JAP* and *PP* articles either aggregated previous results or developed or evaluated a methodology for doing so. From 1994 through 1997 that increased to 12.5 percent, fueled mostly by the near-tripling of such articles in *PP*. It might seem evident that aggregating results to form generalizable conclusions is important, but it is particularly significant for the practice of selection psychology that generalizable conclusions be documented, presented, and acknowledged by our scientific community.

Dimensions of the Research-Practice Relationship in Selection Psychology

Research and practice roles vary on a number of dimensions. It is helpful to describe these dimensions in order to understand the suggestions made later in this chapter for a practice-oriented research agenda and a practice-oriented professional agenda. In considering these dimensions and the salient attributes of the research and practice roles, let us imagine the different roles held by different people. Table 11.2 shows characteristics of the research and practice roles on five dimensions and evaluates the commensurability of the two roles on each dimension. This proposed set of dimensions is intended to identify characteristics of research and practice that are particularly salient to this discussion. Clearly, many more similarities and differences could be identified for most dimensions. The ones chosen for inclusion in the table are intended to be representative only.

The concept of commensurability is being borrowed from the dialogue about research and practice in the clinical profession. In that dialogue (Stricker, 1997), *commensurability* refers to the extent to which two systems—in this case, research and practice—share common paradigms and languages for knowing and self-correcting. In the case of selection research and practice, commensurability would imply that a singular paradigm for knowing and, by extension, a singular professional community could sustain the professional requirements of both research and practice. One would be relevant to the other.

Governance

The practice of selection psychology usually must balance competing legal, political, social, and scientific imperatives. Professional, regulatory, and organizational governance has been established to provide practice guidance regarding these interests. Similarly, governance has been developed for our research endeavors to publicize the relevant scientific and ethical imperatives and guide researchers' professional decisions. As Table 11.2 shows, the governance of research and practice are highly commensurable. That is, significant sets of standards are held in common and those that on their face are different tend to be reasonably comparable in the nature of the requirements. For example, ethics for research and ethics for practice both emphasize the interests of the recipient and are rooted in the Ethical Principles of Psychologists and Code of Conduct (see APA, 1992). Although at first this may seem to be a trivial observation, it is very likely a critical commonality that has enabled a single professional community to sustain both roles.

Table 11.2. Characteristics of Research and Practice Roles in Selection Psychology.

Dimension	Research		Practice	Commensurability
		Role		
Governance	APA ethical research	↑	Ethical principles for psychologists	High
	Publication standards	↑	Standards for educational/psychological testing	
	Local research committee	↑	SIOP principles for validation and use	
			SIOP ethical practice	
			Fed/Local Laws/Regulations	
			Organization standards	
Use of research and theory	Form conclusions	↑	Define body of knowledge	High
	Raise questions		Inform decisions	
	Generalize across		Determine solutions	
			Generalize to particular	
Critical skills	Peer communication	↑	Graduate Training	High
	Research management		Hierachical communication	
			Relationship management	
Community identity	Work colleagues are research oriented	↑	Organization of psychologists	Moderate
	Psychology is the common interest		Work colleagues are solution oriented	
			Organization is the common interest	
Employer relationship	Nondirective		Directive	Low
	Secondary		Primary	
	Longer cycles		Shorter cycles	
	Controls many rewards		Controls most rewards	

Similarly, researchers and practitioners are both subject to their local organizational standards, although these may vary considerably. For researchers, these standards are frequently formalized in a research committee review of proposed local research projects. For practitioners, similar standards may be less formalized but equally pressing in the organizational culture and values. Finally, even the "Uniform Guidelines on Employee Selection Procedures" (1978), which express legal standards for the practice of employment selection, are based on the same principles of scientific inquiry that would generally govern the publication review process for researchers. In all probability, it is this common language of validation research methodology embraced by the "Uniform Guidelines" that has led our profession not to seek revisions to it during two decades in which there will have been three sets of joint "Standards for Educational and Psychological Testing" and at least two sets of SIOP "Principles for the Validation and Use of Personnel Selection Procedures" (SIOP, 1987).

However, despite these similarities there are fundamental differences that have extraordinary consequences for the governance of research and practice. One key distinction between the governance of research and practice is the control over and potential cost of the consequences. The governance environment of research generally allows that self-correction can provide reasonable resolutions, frequently guided by a common interest. Research methods can be revised to accommodate research committee conclusions; manuscripts and analyses can be redone in response to reviewer concerns. The legal context for selection practice is quite different. In the event of a legal challenge to a selection procedure the ensuing processes are generally adversarial, they represent a fundamental conflict, professional colleagues can be enlisted for the specific purpose of arguing that flaws invalidate the conclusion of validity, and they are decided by a third party who frequently is not an expert. And they can be tremendously costly.

Ironically, this problem for practice—that consequences can be severe and out of one's control—is exacerbated by the focus of the "Uniform Guidelines" on the methodological rigor of validation studies, which creates the compelling expectation that local studies of prescribed rigor should be the usual strategy to demonstrate job relevance. Although the "Uniform Guidelines" do provide for reliance on other validity studies, they do so with a cautionary tone: *"Use of other validity studies. A. Validity studies not conducted by the user.* Users may, under certain circumstances, support the use of selection procedures by validity studies conducted by other users or conducted by test publishers or distributors and described in test manuals" ("Uniform Guidelines," 1978, Section 7).

The circumstances include the prescription that the other studies meet "Uniform Guidelines" requirements (1978, Section 14B, p. 26) for criterion validity studies, such as requiring that sample validities be statistically significant at the .05 level and that incumbents in the other studies "perform substantially the same major work behaviors" as those shown by job analyses in the other jobs and the jobs in question. Of course, neither of these requirements is consistent with the current body of knowledge on the predictive validity of cognitive ability tests. The effect is to put considerable pressure on selection program managers to gamble on local studies as the justification for selection procedures.

SIOP's "Principles" (1987) express research *and* practice principles that somewhat more closely reflect the manner in which practice makes appropriate use of research. They achieve this by occasionally relying on accumulative conclusions to shape the principles. For example, the discussion of differential prediction rely on two accumulative conclusions, one regarding the internal consistency of competing models of predictive bias and the other the then-current evidence of the absence of differential prediction for women and men and for major ethnic groups on cognitive tests. In this way, the Principles more accurately reflect the manner in which practice derives its necessary conclusions from research.

Nevertheless, like the "Uniform Guidelines," SIOP's Principles are expressed primarily as principles for the design and execution of rigorous validation studies. The Principles would better reflect practice's scientific conclusion process by first describing general guidelines for scientifically sound generalizations from all sources of empirical evidence. Such an approach could draw on Cook and Campbell's (1979) treatment of validity to support the primacy of generalizability as the fundamental criterion of research design, including processes for generalization based on accumulation across studies as well as generalization from individual studies. Furthermore, an initial focus on generalization would provide an appropriate opportunity to emphasize the fundamental unity of validation processes, drawing attention to the importance of constructs as the basis for generalizing across methods and situations. Such a presentation, which would begin with a treatment of principles for generalization (integrating the treatment of meta-analysis, validity generalization, and scientific inference) and follow with principles for validation study design, would avoid the present implication that local studies are necessary to justify local selection procedures.

Regulations emphasizing scientifically rigorous guidelines for generalizable conclusions about test validity based on all relevant evidence would create a considerably different demand on practice decisions and would be more consistent with the appropriate scientific process required of practice decisions that is described in the next paragraphs. Such regulations would emphasize local study methodology in the absence of suitable aggregate evidence. This change in emphasis could lessen the risk to practitioners that results from being forced to rely on less conclusive local studies as the primary source of supporting evidence.

Use of Research and Theory

Given the close relationship between the focus of selection research on selection procedures and the use of those same procedures for practice, Table 11.2 shows that research and practice both rely on research and theory to define and organize the body of knowledge that constitutes selection psychology. Beyond that fundamental commonality, specific differences are identified to help focus on an important distinction between the value of research and theory for research and for practice. These differences, however, do not imply a need for different paradigms. Rather, given a common paradigm, they focus on practice's special need for accumulative results, whereas research benefits from both individual study results and accumulative results.

In a research role, psychologists use previous research to form conclusions, raise questions, and generalize across conditions of interest. In a practice role, selection psychologists depend on previous research to determine solutions, inform decisions, and generalize to the particular set of conditions in the organization. The needs of practice are to decide on and implement solutions; the needs of researchers are to create information, raise possibilities, and expand the horizon of questions. Practice is about reaching closure; research is about opening for discovery. Both seek to come to a conclusion; however, research has no need to fix a conclusion but rather always to expand on it. In contrast, practice must fix a conclusion into an application that remains relatively unchanging. Individual studies can serve the purpose of research very effectively. They can narrow the possibilities and create others. They can identify the next question or method to shape the direction of ongoing research. Because the research role is continuous, individual studies fit well, usually without the risk of overemphasis. In contrast, because the practice role is episodic around design, implementation, and maintenance of selection solutions, individual studies to justify those solutions run a great risk of being overstated, and practitioners (and regulators) run a great risk of attaching too much value to individual studies, which are virtually always less conclusive than an aggregation of studies.

Practice's need for closure and decision is not well-served by individual studies. We know that this is true not only as a matter of scientific principle but also, in I/O psychology, as an empirical result of considerable research in the last two decades about the variability of individual studies and the conclusiveness of aggregated results.

Critical Skills

In addition to governance and the use of research and theory, critical skills reflect the paradigm by which knowledge is acquired in research and practice. Qualitative differences in the skills required for research and practice would be an indication of a lack of commensurability in these two roles. The presence of such differences would imply that these two roles are more likely two disciplines. However, the common focus of research and practice on the measurement and predictive validity properties of selection procedures and criteria ensures that a broad set of skills associated with scientific inquiry provides a common foundation for research and practice. This common foundation is taught initially in I/O psychology graduate programs and extended by participation in the professional community.

Frequently, other work management skills are cited as important, particularly for practitioners in nonacademic organizations. For example, Cullen, Klemp, and Rosini (1981) identified eight non-technical competencies for organizational effectiveness psychologists in organizations: strong self-concept, professional self-image, ability to develop common understanding, personal influence, diagnostic skills, tactical planning ability, tactical flexibility, and results orientation. My own experience in both academic and nonacademic organizations is that these nontechnical skills vary only in the particular organizational context. So, for example, as shown in Table 11.2, communication skills in an academic setting might be described as "peer" communication skills, whereas in a business organization they might be described as "hierarchical" communication skills. Each context demands a somewhat different communication focus, but the skill to be learned very likely is derived from highly similar composites of aptitudes and motivations.

Table 11.2 shows another example centering on self-management skills, which in one setting focus on the activity of research and in the other on relationships. Such contextual differences are unlikely to represent qualitatively or substantively different skills. A reasonable hypothesis is that the same context-neutral competency survey administered to researchers and to practitioners would identify very similar work and organizational management skills and would be generally similar to other standard models of management skills, including planning and organizing, communicating, enabling others, and so on.

Community Identity

Table 11.2 shows that the commensurability of research and practice varies on a number of dimensions. Three of those dimensions—governance, use of research and theory, and critical skills—define the scientific singularity of our profession. Other, less central dimensions are identified because they can have implications for strategic decisions that our profession can make to serve all members more effectively. Low commensurability on the less central dimensions does not threaten the fundamental scientific singularity of our profession.

A significant difference can exist between professional identities when the research and practice roles are carried out in different organizational settings. With the important exception of large consulting houses, most research is carried out as an academic activity by those employed in academic organizations, whereas virtually all practice is carried out as a nonacademic activity in organizations. It is likely that the principle community differences are that academic work settings provide large communities that are oriented toward education and research with smaller but still-substantial communities oriented toward psychology. Nonacademic settings are much more likely to be a community of managers who are oriented toward business solutions and the organization. These different community identities are not inherent to the research and practice roles but are correlates with workplace setting. They are not relevant to the professional commensurability of research and practice, but they are important differences that may influence participation in our professional community and the importance people attach to professional activities. As a result, our profession is wise to attend to them.

Employer Relationship

Similar to community identity, employer relationships are correlates of the frequent work setting differences between research and practice. They are noted in Table 11.2 because they can be very different and have significant impact on the participation of nonacademicians in professional activities. To the extent that practice is in nonacademic settings, the practitioner's employer relationship is more likely to be primary (compared with the professional relationship) and directed toward the interests of the organization.

A possible consequence of the significant differences in community and employer relationships is that the communication of research to our profession is largely through the lens of the research role rather than the practice role. If so, it may not be surprising that our professional principles tend to reflect the researcher's emphasis on the study as the "coin of the realm" rather than the practitioner's emphasis on conclusions or statements of accumulated knowledge. It is telling that, in two of the principal volumes designed to communicate our knowledge base, nearly 90 percent of the authors were academicians, although virtually all had practice experience. Twenty-four of the twenty-seven authors in Schmitt and Borman's *Personnel Selection in Organizations* (1993) and fifty-seven of the sixty-four authors in Dunnette and Hough's four-volume work *Handbook of Industrial and Organizational Psychology* (1990) were affiliated primarily with academic institutions. Indeed, only one author in each volume worked in a nonconsulting, private company. An intended contribution of this volume about selection—in which eight of eleven chapters are authored by professionals in nonacademic settings—is that a critical mass of professional practitioners' perspectives about selection research will identify common themes that will help to advance the practice of selection with the necessary supporting research.

A Proposed Practice-Oriented Professional Agenda

Exhibit 11.1 shows a proposed agenda for our professional society that addresses the three most important professional needs of our practice role, needs that follow directly from the analysis of the relationship between research and practice. The first two address the continual need for focused, conclusive, and effectively communicated research that addresses the important and accessible selection issues given the current state of research and methodology. The last is for a governance structure for the practice of selection that gives greater weight to our accumulated body of knowledge as the basis for local selection practice decisions. These needs of research content, communication, and governance are highly interactive; the first and second are interdependent, and both influence the third.

Research

Two proposals are made for our profession's role in directing and organizing research. First, a "problems-oriented" conference and review process should be convened, modeled after the methodology-oriented 1981 conference at the Center for Creative Leadership. That conference resulted in six monographs (Campbell, Daft, & Hulin, 1982; Hakel, Sorcher, Beer, & Moses, 1982; Hunter, Schmidt, & Jackson, 1982; James, Mulaik, & Brett, 1982; McGrath, Martin, & Kulka, 1982; and Van Maanen, Dabbs, & Faulkner, 1982) that crystallized key methodological themes. The monographs on meta-analysis and causal modeling were instrumental in making those techniques more generally understood and available both for application and for further refinement. Although this conference also

Exhibit 11.1. A Proposed
Practice-Oriented Professional Agenda.

Research	Goal: To increase the effectiveness with which published research provides information leading to solutions to organizations' most important selection problems.

Possible activities:

- Convene a conference to focus research on the most important organizational problems including selection.

- Coordinate and support research consortia to address important problems in a focused, timely manner.

Communication	Goal: To communicate important research conclusions to the selection profession in a manner and frequency that strongly supports professionally responsible selection practices.

Possible activities:

- Develop a SIOP publication series to report and endorse important conclusions about important organizational problems including selection.

Governance	Goal: To revise SIOP's own principles and influence other standards and regulations to emphasize the primacy of generalized conclusions from accumulated research as an appropriate basis for selection practice.

Possible activities:

- Update SIOP's principles to reflect the growth in the knowledge base and to express the primacy of generalization from accummulated research as an appropriate basis for selection practices.

- Undertake an influence process to urge the updating of the "Uniform Guidelines" to reflect the advances in knowledge and the primacy of generalization.

addressed methodological issues associated with research in applied settings and applicable research, the focus was on methodological concerns more than on the content of the important problems. A successor conference would be well-positioned now to create energy for identifying our most important organizational problems. This is a particularly good moment for such a conference, especially one that at least in part would focus on the practice of selection.

The research on the validity and content of selection procedures has reached an advanced stage. Measures of disposition and temperament appropriate to the employment setting are now available, demonstrating meaningful levels of validity. The interview process is demonstrating more predictive power than previously believed, although the measurement properties still need considerable attention (for example, Huffcutt, Roth, & McDaniel, 1996). Research is addressing the inevitable complexities and promise of selection systems based on the relationships of multiple predictors to multiple criteria (for example, Murphy & Schiarella, 1997). Promising advanced building blocks are now in place to enable effective inquiries into our most important questions. In addition, with a few notable exceptions, such as Project A, leading-edge research with significant scope and conclusiveness continues to depend on the occasional opportunity, usually with the larger consulting firms. Perhaps because we are a relatively small professional community, our science and practice have been well-served by the collaborative and public nature of these types of efforts. However, our profession could advance practice significantly by providing direction and structure to collaborative research efforts that address our most significant organizational problems.

Communication

It is not the purpose of this suggested agenda item simply to improve the flow or amount or even the clarity of information to our professional membership. Rather, the purpose is to convey professional acknowledgment and, as warranted, endorsement of key research conclusions that have implications for practice. This type of public statement is important for practice. The value is not so much that such summaries would ease the task of integrating substantial amounts of research but rather that they make public that a particular conclusion is reasonable and backed by the credibility of a respected professional organization. Of course, endorsement and conclusion do not necessarily imply consensus, but they do imply reasonableness of conclusion based on careful, integrated aggregation and evaluation of the relevant research. Because practice is routinely challenged to demonstrate the rationale for a selection practice with significant consequences at stake, practice has a special need for independent, influential summary statements of research-based professional judgment.

The purpose of this agenda item extends beyond communication. An appropriate role for our professional organization is to aggregate and interpret our research base with a collective authority. But this is not a new role. SIOP's Principles serve this same function at least in part. The difference between the principles and communications of the sort being proposed here is that the Principles convey *standards* for professionally responsible actions, whereas communications about research conclusions would represent publicly acknowledged information based on collective professional judgment that practitioners could rely on to make responsible practice decisions.

Governance

Standards that govern selection practice, particularly the "Uniform Guidelines" and the SIOP "Principles," focus on scientific standards for conducting relatively dependable and repeatable research studies. This is readily observed by noting that the current versions of both are organized around the three types of validity studies. In this sense, the action that is being governed by the "Uniform Guidelines" and the SIOP "Principles" is the conduct of research studies. (The "Standards" are different [AERA, APA, & NCME, 1985]. Although there are clusters of standards that focus on studies themselves—for example, standards 1.11 through 1.22 in the validity section, most focus on specific applications and issues relating to the use of tests. The actions being governed by the standards are test uses more than studies of tests.) As a result, these governing standards clearly imply the primacy of local studies. Indeed, the "Uniform Guidelines" even specify the outline for the documentation of such studies. The wisdom of this prescription is that it ensures the accumulation of knowledge in the long run; the problem with this prescription is that it forces practitioners into high-risk behavior with respect to individual selection practices.

For individual practitioners, the "Uniform Guidelines" and the SIOP "Principles" do not adequately acknowledge the appropriateness and, indeed, primacy of the alternative to ad hoc local studies. This alternative is scientific inference leading to professionally responsible conclusions based on the accumulation of research on the practice issue at hand. Generalization is an integral part of the scientific process, and it is particularly representative of the practitioner's needs not only because of the frequent difficulty in conducting sound ad hoc studies in organizations but also because of the now well-established variability of individual study results, indicating that even well-designed individual studies alone are not likely to provide an adequate basis for a practice decision. The purpose of this proposed governance agenda item is to revise the SIOP "Principles" and influence a revision of the "Uniform Guidelines" to reflect the appropriateness of generalization from accumulated research as a scientifically sound and primary basis for practice decisions.

A Proposed Practice-Oriented Research Agenda

Perhaps the most important role of a science-based professional community is to provide direction and reinforcement that lead research to important issues. Exhibit 11.2 summarizes a proposed agenda for research questions that are currently important to selection program management.

This agenda is organized into four levels: the individual, the selection procedure, the selection system, and the organization. As discussed earlier, selection research in the 1990s has continued the traditionally strong focus on measurement and selection procedures, with a growing focus on selection systems and little focus on organization-level issues. Certainly, a primary purpose of the proposed agenda is to draw attention to the systems and organization-level issues intrinsic to the practice of selection psychology. Also, it is worth noting that this proposal is mainly about research in the

Exhibit 11.2. A Proposed Practice-Oriented Research Agenda.

Focus of Analysis	Key Research Question

Individual	• Experience
	  – What are the dimensions of experience?
	  – Can experience be a surrogate for ability or personality?
	• Personality
	  – Are biodata and personality inventories about the same things?
	  – Are subfactors necessary for validity?
	• Should individual rights or preferences preclude some valid selection?

Selection procedure	• Interviews
	  – What do or can they measure?
	  – What methodology is necessary for validity?
	• Can personality assessment avoid invasiveness and response bias?

Selection system	• How are multiple predictors related to multiple criteria?
	  – Are there even more types of validity evidence?
	  – Is a new, general form of differential prediction needed?
	• Can job analysis diagnose valid selection constructs?

Organization	• How much can or do selection practices affect organization-level results? – The McDonalds experiment: Do organizations adapt to different selection practices? • Do organization characteristics affect choice or tolerance of selection? • How do selection systems "fit" with other HR systems?

usual sense of scientific investigation, although a few topics are best addressed through professional dialogue to further understanding and definition.

Individual Focus

Three topics are noted here: experience, personality, and rights and preferences. The first two reflect the current need to understand better how experience and personality relate to performance. The third is about an issue of socioprofessional judgment: Are some valid predictors inappropriate for selection application?

Experience

The questions about experience arise from measurement and practice issues. The overall measurement issues are the same as those comprehensively addressed by Tesluk and Jacobs (1998): What is the dimensionality of experience and what is its relationship to future work performance? But there are specific practice questions that can be addressed by more narrowly focused research. For example, could experience assessment be a surrogate for other test-based assessments, such as cognitive ability and disposition and temperament, either because experience can be used to measure those other attributes or because experience overlaps in the prediction of the same criteria as ability or personality? This research topic would seek to extend the earlier modeling work of McDaniel, Schmidt, and Hunter (1988), which represented experience as a source of job knowledge independent of cognitive ability.

In addition, research on experience should address a frequent problem in the management of selection programs: test-based assessments such as cognitive tests and personality inventories are often dissatisfying to job candidates, and particularly candidates already in the organization, who often strongly prefer that their track record of performance and organizational citizenship be considered sufficient for any selection decision. There frequently is strong pressure on selection program managers, particularly for internal selection, to base selection on evidence that has some direct relationship to past performance and behavior in the organization. Research on the dimensionality of experience and associated assessment methodology would enable selection programs to capitalize on experience information where incremental value is not likely to be lost by the avoidance of test-based procedures.

Personality

The personality questions reflect the continued extension of the current streams of research about disposition and temperament and performance. In particular, the accumulating research indicates that the facets of personality that predict performance are at the subfactor level of the "big five" structure (Hough et al., 1990; Hogan & Roberts, 1996; Raymark, Schmit, & Guion, 1997). But the labels for these subfactors are usually instrument-specific. In order to investigate and codify the generalizability of subfactor validity, it will be necessary to arrive at a common understanding of the meaning of the subfactors. In effect, practice has a need to know the "little ten or fifteen" facets that demonstrate generalizable validity. A similar issue in practice decisions is the meaning and validity of clusters of facets organized around performance constructs such as service, sales, workplace integrity, and teamwork. What facets belong in these composites? What job features are diagnostic of these composites being appropriate?

Validity

Is validity sufficient? There has been relatively little public discussion about this issue in the selection profession, perhaps because it is more policy than science and has only recently emerged as a result of discussions on faking, or socially desirable responding, on personality inventories. The question is this: Are there features of selection procedures that would preclude the use of a valid, legal selection procedure? In the extreme, the answer is certainly yes. Physical ability tests that jeopardize the health of applicants are clearly inappropriate. But this question is not about extreme examples. It is about conditions well within the mainstream of professional practice. This issue is placed in the individual research focus because ultimately the judgment rests on the impact of such selection procedures on individuals and the judgment of professionals, organizations, and the affected individuals about that impact. Following are three examples of such situations.

Example A. Is it appropriate to use selection procedures in which candidates can deliberately choose to answer inaccurately in order to gain an advantage over candidates who answer as instructed? This, of course, is the dilemma facing users of self-report personality inventories, on which deliberately inaccurate responding is known to increase scores on scales that have a socially desirable direction. Another version of this same question is whether it is appropriate to disallow a selection procedure score where there is evidence that the candidate deliberately responded inaccurately to gain an advantage. In the personality case, should a "high lie" score cancel the candidate's result?

Example B. Is it appropriate to select candidates based on their volitional but established interests? In other words, should a candidate's preferences or interests be held against her? If it is generally inappropriate to select candidates based on interests, does it follow that it is inappropriate to select candidates based on other personal qualities, such as optimism? Of course, the fact that selection is frequently based on personal qualities such as optimism implies that there is general agreement on the appropriateness of such practices. A related twist is the question of whether candidates should be fully informed about how their test results will be used in the selection process. The core issue here is whether mere predictive value is sufficient to justify the use of a selection procedure. Although we might all disagree with this fairly extreme version of the core issue, are there conditions that we as a profession might agree should limit the appropriateness of any selection procedure? Or is this issue always to be resolved at the local level?

Example C. Is it appropriate to select poorer scorers over better scorers where the scores are generally believed to have a preferred direction? For example, if an organization believes or has evidence that the highest-scoring applicants who subsequently tend to be the highest-performing employees also tend to leave the job at a higher rate than lower-scoring candidates, is it appropriate to select the lower-scoring candidates in order to minimize turnover at the expense of expected performance? To be sure, this is not a question of whether organizations have the right to weigh one metric more heavily than another. Rather, the question is whether individuals have any right to be protected from or at least well-informed about unexpected treatment by selection processes.

Two themes about appropriateness run through these examples. One theme is the extent to which candidates can choose response strategies based on some belief about desired responses. This possibility creates a potential threat to the validity of such selection procedures and also raises the possibility of a job-irrelevant advantage for those with insight into the desired responses. In principle, the solution to this problem is to develop selection procedures that are immune to response strategies that can create a job-irrelevant advantage. The other theme is somewhat more problematic and rooted in values rather than selection technology; that is, is it appropriate to make employment decisions based on personal attributes that do not reflect any degree of capacity to perform but do reflect tendencies to behave in certain ways, even though such behavior is generally volitional? For example, even if high scorers tend to have higher turnover rates, they certainly are capable of staying.

Selection Procedure Focus

Generally, research on selection procedures is very active and diverse, and practice has been well-served by that traditionally strong line of research. Only a few topics will be identified here to draw attention to particularly salient practice issues.

Interviews

The emerging evidence indicating that interviews have higher and more generalizable validity than previously believed represents both a promise and a challenge for the selection profession. It is a promise because interviews are such common and popularly accepted procedures. It is a challenge because there is good reason to believe that less structured interviews have little or no generalizable validity. As a class of selection procedures, they are less objective and less rigorously designed and administered, and they have less well-specified measurement properties. However, the general result is well demonstrated that structure does enhance validity, but less structure does not eliminate validity (Huffcutt et al., 1996; McDaniel et. al, 1994). Indeed, less structured interviews can have substantial true validity, estimated by McDaniel et al. to be .33, which is at the high end of estimated true validities of scored personality assessments. Campion, Palmer, and Campion (1997) presented a comprehensive analysis of the components of interview structure that provides a useful template for practitioners to develop effective interviews.

Given these advances, the most significant question for practice is about the content of interviews that accounts for the generalizable validity. Although some research has addressed this issue (for example, Huffcutt et al., 1996), much less is known about interview content than about interview structure. Indeed, part of the dilemma resulting from the demonstration of substantial interview validity is that it appears to be relatively independent of what is measured and more dependent on how it is measured (that is, structure). Because selection programs often incorporate both interviews and other test-based procedures, the added value of interviews depends on an understanding of their relationship to other types of selection criteria. This type of construct validation of interviews is needed for practitioners to make informed decisions about the use of combinations of selection criteria, including interviews.

Personality Assessment

Two key methodological advances would provide significant relief for selection practitioners considering self-reported personality inventories. Personality assessment methods that avoid perceived invasiveness and do not invite construct-invalid response strategies would diffuse two of the biggest concerns about the use of such instruments. This may be an example of a methodology that suits the research context well but is not optimal for the selection practice context. If so, it is an unusual case in the domain of selection research, where to a great extent selection instruments serve research and practice applications without needing to be adapted in any fundamental way.

Selection System Focus

Perhaps the single most significant research issue for selection practice is specifying the relationship between multiple predictors and multiple criteria. The focus on selection system is directed primarily at the various elements of this many-to-many relationship between selection and performance. This is an important need in selection practice because this multiplicity is precisely the context in which many selection program decisions are made.

Multiple Predictors, Multiple Criteria

Recently, significant research has begun to address two important issues associated with multiple predictors. Murphy and Schiarella (1997) evaluated properties of the correlation between linear combinations of predictors and criteria. Their observation, based on a Monte Carlo study, was that the level of such composite validities (a selection system) varied considerably as a function of the weights associated with predictors and performance dimensions. This research represents a number of selection issues as they are managed in practice. As this research is advanced, several important implementation questions can be addressed. For example, this approach to validity should enable meaningful estimates of maximum validity. It should allow comparative evaluations of competing selection and performance profiles that may be used to define optimal or maximal performance and selection profiles.

In addition, recent research (Sackett & Roth, 1996; Schmitt et. al, 1997) has investigated the impact of predictor composites and associated weights on the adverse impact of selection decisions on protected groups. This critical issue is central to perhaps the most contentious aspect of selection practices. More will be said in the following paragraphs about the implications of multivariate predictor-criterion relationships for group differences and differential prediction methodology for assessing predictive bias.

New Types of Validity Evidence

System-level approaches to selection problems may require a new language about validity. Consider the relationship between a predictor assessing cognitive ability and each of several criteria. Specifically, consider a customer service example. A selection test of verbal comprehension might be correlated with each of several criteria. One common criterion for cognitive ability predictors is training mastery, frequently assessed by an end-of-training achievement test. Another frequent criterion is a supervisor's overall performance rating. A third criterion might be some measure of customer satisfaction provided directly by customers. A fourth possible criterion is some measure of work citizenship, such as number of days tardy. Finally, a fifth criterion might be a linear combination of all important facets of performance and work behavior.

A number of points can be made. First, some criteria have more a priori construct relevance to verbal comprehension than do others. In this customer service case, training mastery is likely to be viewed as more construct-relevant to verbal comprehension than is a direct measure of customer satisfaction. The correlation with training mastery is likely to be viewed as construct-validity evidence, whereas an equal correlation with customer satisfaction would have less value for confirming the construct validity of the measure of verbal comprehension. Furthermore, some criteria, such as days tardy, may be so irrelevant to verbal comprehension that a correlation might not even be viewed as an index of validity. Borrowing from Seligman's (1995) discussion of science and practice in the clinical profession, we might distinguish between validity evidence that reflects the *efficacy* of a selection procedure from other validity evidence that reflects the *effectiveness* of that selection procedure. Efficacy refers to evidence that the selection procedure correlates with or causes facets of performance that are thought to depend on the same construct as the selection procedure assesses. It is evidence about the meaning attributable to the selection procedure. Effectiveness refers to the extent to which the selection procedure is related to a desired overall outcome in the targeted application. It is evidence about the extent of desired effect in the applied setting. A highly efficacious selection procedure may have little effectiveness if the criterion for the efficacy evidence is relatively unimportant in producing the valued overall outcome. In contrast, it is hard to imagine how an effective selection procedure could lack efficacy. A validation study should determine which type of evidence—efficacy or effectiveness—is more appropriate. For example, validity analyses conducted to estimate the economic utility of a selection procedure would call for effectiveness validity.

The distinction between efficacy evidence and effectiveness evidence can also be used to draw attention to the type of validity evidence that serves the selection program manager's need for validity conclusions that may be generalized to her organization.

The difference between the evidence supporting cognitive tests and interviews is an important example. The evidence for the validity of cognitive tests reflects high efficaciousness because the underlying constructs are well-specified and their link to performance is well-specified. This construct-based rationale for demonstrated validity provides selection program managers the sound scientific basis for generalizing evidence from other organizations and situations to their organizations. For example, the rationale by which verbal comprehension relates to training mastery is independent of many organization-specific variables such as the type of organization, its location, and so on. Efficacy evidence provides a rationale for generalization. In contrast, as Huffcutt et al. (1996) note, the meta-analytic validity evidence for interviews is relatively lacking in construct specification. As a result, the primary bases for interview validity generalization to a particular organization are (a) an analysis of the fit between the organization's characteristics and the profile of organizational attributes represented in the aggregated samples, and (b) an analysis of the fit between the elements of the interview's structure and those elements representative of the interviews included in the meta-analysis. In other words, in this case generalization does not depend on the meaning of the interview scores. This is likely to be a more tenuous basis for generalization than, for example, the construct basis available for cognitive tests.

In addition to the distinction between efficacy and effectiveness evidence, the distinction between proximal and distal criteria certainly affects the meaning of a particular validity coefficient. For example, training mastery would be considered a proximal criterion for verbal comprehension because the nomological net of causal linkages between them has relatively few (presumably) other causal factors. In contrast, a supervisor's overall performance rating is likely to be more distal from verbal comprehension in that there is likely a longer chain of causal links between verbal comprehension and the supervisor's overall performance rating, and there are likely many more factors influencing that rating.

I suggest these distinctions between efficacy and effectiveness evidence and between proximal and distal criteria because such distinctions will become more important as validation research looks for ways simultaneously to capture the multiple relationships between many predictors and many criteria. For example, the validity of verbal comprehension is likely to be higher for a proximal criterion such as training mastery than for a distal criterion such as supervisor's overall performance rating. These two validities do not measure the same relationship and their average would have no meaning. Similarly, the efficacy-type validity may well be different from the effectiveness-type validity. Again, it would not be meaningful to average these types of evidence to produce an "overall" validity estimate. Although the modeling of many-to-many predictor-criterion relationships will advance the understanding of selection systems and the usefulness of research for practice, it will also demand that explicit distinctions be made among a wider variety of validity relationships than are commonly discussed in one-to-one selection research literature.

Differential Prediction

A multivariate selection system approach to research will enable a fundamental question to be addressed about how the currently accepted definition of differential prediction should be applied and interpreted in the context of multiple criteria. The question is this: What is the appropriate criterion to choose to evaluate the differential prediction of a predictor? A multivariate selection system approach to selection research will explicitly seek multidimensional criteria appropriate to the dimensions of performance and other work behavior as well as, perhaps, different levels of aggregation of performance. In this multivariate research design, an explicit choice of criterion will be required for differential prediction analyses.

As a simple example, suppose that an analysis of customer service performance includes just two dimensions—information accuracy and interpersonal relationships. Which of these two criteria would be more appropriate for a differential prediction analysis of a composite cognitive ability test that assesses, say, general reasoning, coding speed, and verbal reasoning? Or would an overall performance measure that reflected both be more appropriate? Clearly, if differential prediction analyses are intended to assess predictive bias due to measurement bias, then the information accuracy dimension would be appropriate and the interpersonal relationship dimension would be much less appropriate. In this case, the overall performance composite would also be inappropriate because it would include the inappropriate dimension. But if differential prediction is intended to assess predictive bias due to some form of overall selection system bias—such as the absence of a relevant predictor—then the appropriate criterion would be the overall performance composite. To be sure, differential prediction analyses are simply a methodology that can serve both purposes.

For selection program managers, a critical purpose of differential prediction analyses is to satisfy the regulatory requirement that such analyses be done to demonstrate the absence of predictive bias for *individual* selection procedures, particularly those that result in differences between protected groups. In this situation, the criterion chosen for differential prediction analyses should be the performance measure that is commensurate with or rationally relevant to the predictor or some composite that reflects an appropriate combination of all valued work behaviors. It would be meaningless to assess the predictive bias of the cognitive composite described with respect to the measure of interpersonal relationship performance. One was not intended or chosen to affect the other, so their relationship would not provide evidence of either measurement bias or outcome bias. This analysis suggests that the description of differential prediction analysis should be expanded to include a consideration of criterion appropriateness for the purpose of the analysis. This expansion, or generalization, of the definition of differential prediction would provide the rationale by which the predictive bias of any predictor could be appropriately evaluated. Currently, predictors that produce little or no group score difference are generally not evaluated for predictive bias. For example, personality assessments of service-oriented attributes generally do not yield substantial race group score differences, and as a result, are generally not subject to differential prediction analyses. However, if differential prediction analyses were conducted for such predictors with near-zero group differences and positive validity using performance measures showing the usual magnitude of race group differences, there would likely be evidence of predictive bias.

Research on the effects of predictor combinations on group differences should also evaluate the impact of predictor combinations on differential prediction. However, these analyses should consider the differential prediction of the overall selection system on an overall composite criterion as well as on a criterion composite that is construct relevant to the reweighted predictor composite. In the context of multivariate predictor and criterion models, modifications of the predictor composite have implications for the facets of performance and their weights that are most appropriate to the restructured predictor composite. For example, increasing the weight of personality relative to cognitive ability implies that the reconfigured selection system is placing relatively more importance on the facets of performance that derive from the personality attributes being used in the predictor. This consideration should be important if the purpose of differential prediction analyses is to assess whether prediction bias results from measurement bias. Changing the predictor composite for reasons other than measurement accuracy suggests either that measurement bias can no longer be assessed using differential prediction analyses or that the appropriate criterion should also reflect the same types of weight changes.

Diagnostic Procedures

The work of Raymark et. al (1997) exemplifies the type of research and tools that will have direct application by selection program managers. The need is to have diagnostic tools that can identify appropriate selection criteria based on information about the work. Raymark et al. have developed and validated a job analysis tool that diagnoses personality attributes relevant to performance in that work. Other possible diagnostic tools that would have similar value include tools for assessing the information complexity of work to diagnose the type and relevance of cognitive selection criteria. The important question for selection practitioners is whether such diagnostic job information can be sufficient to establish validity for selection criteria or whether it is only sufficient to narrow the range of possibly valid criteria.

Organizational Focus

Selection program managers value research about organizational factors because it is strategic and relates to their role as human resource managers. Organizational research supports decisions about whether and how to implement selection practices as well as the linkage between selection strategies and other related HR strategies such as performance management and recruiting. Generally, evidence of organization-level impact of selection would not be viewed as validity as much as value. The four topics discussed here all relate to these types of strategic issues.

Impact on Organizational Outcomes

There are two facets to this issue. One is the extent to which performance benefits at the individual level accumulate to produce organization-level results. A few studies in the 1990s have sought to evaluate a broader version of this question. Terpstra and Rozell (1993), Arthur (1994), Huselid (1995), and Welbourne and Andrews (1995) sought to estimate the relationship between HR practices and organizational results. Expressed in terms of variance accounted for, these effects appear quite small and perhaps unreliable. Expressed in absolute terms, however, these effects are possibly substantial. At this point, there appears to be no research that directly assesses the impact of selection on real organization-level results.

The other facet of this issue is more dynamic. To what extent can or do organizations adapt to employee skills and qualities to produce outcomes necessary for organizational success? For example, do organizations that do not select employees based on cognitive ability tend to focus recruiting on sources likely to yield higher-ability candidates or adapt training materials to require lower levels of reading or reasoning ability? Conversely, can or do organizations that adopt highly selective employment strategies design other HR systems to take advantage of the higher levels of abilities or job knowledge or personal qualities to multiply the benefit of being selective?

These questions will be extremely difficult to answer using quasi- or nonexperimental methodology because of the large number and dynamic nature of organizational variables that might influence the outcome measures. This realization creates an interest in what has been described as the "McDonald's experiment" (D. J. McCormick, personal communication, 1998). This experiment requires an organization that has many highly similar "centers" that could be randomly allocated to one of a few selection conditions. The more interesting version of this experiment would allow those centers to adapt other HR processes to the caliber of new hires produced by the experimentally controlled selection practices.

Whether the McDonald's experiment is fanciful or possible, such research would contribute significantly to our understanding of the manner in which selection affects organization-level results and the organizational factors that selection program managers must attend to in order to translate individual gains into organizational results.

Organizational Influences on Selection Practices

The practice choices of selection program managers are virtually always made in an organizational context. Practices are implemented only with organizational support, probably in large part because of the legal risk and costs. This is a research issue that our professional society could help to advance. For example, our knowledge about these issues would be significantly advanced by regular surveys of selection professionals and related HR professionals about their selection practices, the reasons for and barriers to such practices, and the organizational demographics that influence such choices.

Selection and Other HR Systems

An important theme in many of the chapters in this volume is that selection is increasingly viewed and managed as a component of the broader range of HR processes and systems. Although this integration has not been a deliberate focus of the community of I/O psychologists, increasingly common management practices relating to quality in HR and technology-based HR information systems can result in integrated HR planning and strategy. At least two fundamental questions about this linkage between selection and HR are important to selection program managers. First, how does the nature and size of selection's impact on the organization compare with that of other HR processes and systems? Based on a typical range of validity, selectivity, and dollar value of predicted performance, a representative description of the utility of a professionally developed selection system is that it would cause performance to increase in the range of 5 percent to 15 percent over essentially random selection. How does this compare with the impact of other HR systems? For example, is the difference between effective supervision strategies and ineffective strategies as great? To the extent that selection program managers are engaged in broader HR planning and strategy development, this type of research would help inform HR investment decisions that affect selection.

Second, are the people and job attributes that are the foundation of selection programs similar to or different from the attributes that are the basis for other processes, such as compensation, workforce planning, performance management, and training and development? This is a very pragmatic issue, as commercially available HR information management systems (HRIMS) such as PeopleSoft are adopted by increasing numbers of organizations and as locally developed HRIMS are developed to support the implementation of more efficient and more automatic HR processes. To the extent that attributes of people and jobs that support different processes can be supported in a single taxonomy, the integrated processes could be more effectively managed. Certainly, in many organizations the introduction of competency modeling has raised this prospect. Research that seeks to extend and define such taxonomies to satisfy the requirements of diverse HR processes will enhance the actual linkage between selection and other HR processes. My personal experience with local and commercially available HRIMS taxonomies is that considerable improvement is necessary before HR systems can be fully integrated.

Conclusion

In this chapter I have attempted to describe the relationship between selection practice and selection research with an emphasis on the professional and scientific requirements of selection program managers. The key points of this chapter are as follows:

- Research and practice are components of the science of selection psychology.
- Selection research and practice are closely related, especially when it comes to the foundations of measurement and methodology.
- Selection practice would benefit considerably from a more comprehensive research base on selection systems issues and organization-level factors that influence and are influenced by selection practices.

- The governance of selection practice should more effectively acknowledge the primacy of generalization as the basis for conclusions about the validity of local practices.
- Selection research in its current state is capable of making significant advances in the understanding of multifaceted selection systems.
- The organized professional community of I/O psychologists should take a more proactive role in sponsoring and shaping research, communication, and governance to advance the public acknowledgment of professionally and scientifically sound practice.

References

American Education Research Association (AERA), American Psychological Association (APA), & National Council on Measurement in Education (NCME). (1985). *Standards for Educational and Psychological Testing.* Washington, DC: American Psychological Association.

American Psychological Association (APA). (1992). Ethical principles of psychologists and code of conduct. *American Psychologist, 47,* 1597–1611.

Arthur, J. B. (1994). Effects of human resource systems on manufacturing performance and turnover. *Academy of Management Journal, 37,* 670–687.

Barrick, M. R., & Mount, M. K. (1991). The big five personality dimensions and job performance: A meta-analysis. *Personnel Psychology, 41,* 1–26.

Campbell, J. P., Daft, R. L., & Hulin, C. L. (1982). *What to study: Generating and developing research questions.* Thousand Oaks, CA: Sage.

Campion, M. A., Palmer, D. K., & Campion, J. E. (1997). A review of structure in the selection interview. *Personnel Psychology, 50,* 655–702.

Carson, K. P., Becker, J. S., & Henderson, J. A. (1998). Is utility really futile? A failure to replicate and an extension. *Journal of Applied Psychology, 83,* 84–96.

Cascio, W. F., Outtz, J., Zedeck, S., & Goldstein, I. L. (1991). Statistical implications of six methods of test score use in personnel selection. *Human Performance, 4,* 233–264.

Cook, T. D., & Campbell, D. T. (1979). *Quasi-experimentation: Design and analysis issues for field settings.* Skokie, IL: Rand McNally.

Cullen, B. J., Klemp, G. O., Jr., & Rosini, L. A. (1981). *Competencies of organizational effectiveness consultants in the U.S. Army* (Res. Note 83–13).

Alexandria, VA: U.S. Army Research Institute for the Behavioral and Social Sciences.

DeShon, R. P., Smith, M. R., Chan, D., & Schmitt, N. (1998). Can racial differences in cognitive test performance be reduced by presenting problems in a social context? *Journal of Applied Psychology, 83,* 438–451.

Dunnette, M. D. (1990). Blending the science and practice of industrial and organizational psychology: Where are we and where are we going? In M. D. Dunnette & L. M. Hough (Eds.), *Handbook of industrial and organizational psychology* (2nd ed., Vol. 1, pp. 1–27). Palo Alto, CA: Consulting Psychologists Press.

Dunnette, M. D., & Hough, L. M. (1990). *Handbook of industrial and organizational psychology* (2nd ed., Vols. 1–4). Palo Alto: Consulting Psychologists Press.

Guion, R. M. (1988). *Pratfalls in the march of science.* Invited address (upon award for Distinguished Scientific Contributions) presented at the annual meeting of the American Psychological Association, Atlanta.

Hackman, J. R. (1985). Doing research that makes a difference. In E. E. Lawler III, A. M. Mohrman, Jr., S. A. Mohrman, G. E. Ledford, Jr., & T. G. Cummings (Eds.), *Doing research that is useful for theory and practice* (pp. 126–149). San Francisco: Jossey-Bass.

Hakel, M. D., Sorcher, M., Beer, M., & Moses, J. L. (1982). *Making it happen: Designing research with implementation in mind.* Thousand Oaks, CA: Sage.

Hogan, J., & Roberts, B. W. (1996). Issues and nonissues in the fidelity/bandwidth tradeoff. *Journal of Organizational Behavior, 17*(6), 627–637.

Hough, L. M., Eaton, N. K., Dunnette, M. D., Kamp, J. D., & McCloy, R. A. (1990). Criterion-related validities of personality constructs and the effect of response distortion on those validities [Monograph]. *Journal of Applied Psychology, 75,* 581–595.

Huffcutt, A. I., & Roth, P. L. (1998). Racial group differences in employment interview evaluations. *Journal of Applied Psychology, 3,* 179–189.

Huffcutt, A. I., Roth, P. L., & McDaniel, M. A. (1996). A meta-analytic investigation of cognitive ability in employment interview evaluations: Moderating characteristics and implications for incremental validity. *Journal of Applied Psychology, 81,* 459–473.

Hunter, J. E., Schmidt, F. L., & Jackson, G. B. (1982). *Meta-analysis: Cumulative findings across research.* Thousand Oaks, CA: Sage.

Huselid, M. A. (1995). The impact of human resource management practices on turnover, productivity and corporate financial performance. *Academy of Management Journal, 38,* 635–672.

Jackson, S. E., Schuler, R. S., & Rivero, J. C. (1989). Organizational characteristics as predictors of personnel practices. *Personnel Psychology, 42,* 727–786.

James, L. R., Mulaik, S. A., & Brett, J. M. (1982). *Causal analysis: Assumptions, models, and data.* Thousand Oaks, CA: Sage.

Johns, G. (1993). Constraints on the adoption of psychology-based personnel practices: lessons from organization innovation. *Personnel Psychology, 46,* 569–592.

Kehoe, J. F., & Tenopyr, M. L. (1994). Adjustment in assessment scores and their usage: a taxonomy and evaluation of methods. *Psychological Assessment, 6*(4), 291–303.

Latham, G. P., & Whyte, G. (1994). The futility of utility analysis. *Personnel Psychology, 47,* 31–46.

Levy-Leboyer, C. (1988). Success and failure in applying psychology. *American Psychologist, 43,* 779–785.

McDaniel, M. A., Schmidt, F. L., & Hunter, J. E. (1988). Job experience correlates of job performance. *Journal of Applied Psychology, 73,* 327–330.

McDaniel, M. A., Whetzel, D. L., Schmidt, F. L., & Maurer, S. (1994). The validity of employment interviews: a comprehensive review and meta-analysis. *Journal of Applied Psychology, 79,* 599–616.

McGrath, J. E., Martin, J., & Kulka, R. A. (1982). *Judgment calls in research.* Thousand Oaks, CA: Sage.

McHenry, J. J., Hough, L. M., Toquam, J. L., Hanson, M. I., & Ashworth, S. (1990). Project A validity results: The relationship between predictor and criterion domains. *Personnel Psychology, 43,* 335–354.

McIntyre, R. M. (1990). Our science-practice: The ghost of industrial-organizational psychology yet to come. In K. R. Murphy & F. E. Saal (Eds.), *Psychology in organizations: Integrating science and practice* (pp. 27–48). Hillsdale, NJ: Erlbaum.

Murphy, K. R. (1994). Potential effects of banding as a function of test reliability. *Personnel Psychology, 47,* 477–495.

Murphy, K. R., & Saal, F. E. (1990). What should we expect from scientist-practitioners? In K. R. Murphy & F. E. Saal (Eds.), *Psychology in organizations: Integrating science and practice* (pp. 49–66). Hillsdale, NJ: Erlbaum.

Murphy, K. R., & Schiarella, A. H. (1997). Implications of the multi-dimensional nature of job performance for the validity of selection tests: Multivariate frameworks for studying test validity. *Personnel Psychology, 50,* 823–854.

Nathan, P. E. (1998). Practice guidelines: Not yet ideal. *American Psychologist, 53,* 290–299.

Ones, D. S., Viswesvaran, C., & Reiss, A. D. (1996). Role of social desirability in personality testing for personnel selection: The red herring. *Journal of Applied Psychology, 81,* 660–679.

Peterson, D. R. (1991). Connection and disconnection of research and practice in the education of professional psychologists. *American Psychologist, 46,* 422–429.

Raimy, V. (Ed.). (1950). *Training in clinical psychology.* Upper Saddle River, NJ: Prentice Hall.

Raymark, P. H., Schmit, M. J., & Guion, R. M. (1997). Identifying potentially useful personality constructs for employee selection. *Personnel Psychology, 50,* 723–736.

Rice, C. E. (1997). Scenarios: The scientist-practitioner split and the future of psychology. *American Psychologist, 52,* 1173–1181.

Rothstein, H. R., Schmidt, F. L., Erwin, F. W., Owens, W. A., & Sparks, C. P. (1990). Biographical data in employment selection: Can validities be made generalizable? *Journal of Applied Psychology, 75,* 175–184.

Russell, C. J., Colella, A., & Bobko, P. (1993). Expanding the context of utility: The strategic impact of personnel selection. *Personnel Psychology, 46,* 781–801.

Rynes, S. L., Orlitzky, M. O., & Bretz, R. D., Jr. (1997). Experienced hiring versus college recruiting: Practices and emerging trends. *Personnel Psychology, 50,* 309–339.

Sackett, P. R., & Roth, L. (1996). Multi-stage selection strategies: A Monte Carlo investigation of effects on performance and minority hiring. *Personnel Psychology, 49,* 549–572.

Schmitt, N., & Borman, W. C. (Eds.). (1993). *Personnel selection in organizations.* San Francisco: Jossey-Bass.

Schmitt, N., Rogers, W., Chan, D., Sheppard, L., & Jennings, D. (1997). Adverse impact and predictive efficiency of various predictor combinations. *Journal of Applied Psychology, 82,* 719–730.

Seligman, M.E.P. (1995). The effectiveness of psychotherapy: The *Consumer Reports* study. *American Psychologist, 50,* 965–974.

Society for Industrial and Organizational Psychology (SIOP). (1987). *Principles for the validation and use of personnel selection procedures* (3rd ed.). College Park, MD: Author.

Spychalski, A. C., Quinones, M. A., Gaugler, B. B., & Pohley, K. (1997). A survey of assessment center practices in the United States. *Personnel Psychology, 50,* 71–90.

Stricker, G. (1997). Are science and practice commensurable? *American Psychologist, 52,* 442–448.

Stricker, G., & Trierweiler, S. J. (1995). The local clinical scientist: A bridge between science and practice. *American Psychologist, 50,* 995–1002.

Terpstra, D. E., & Rozell, E. J. (1993). The relationship of staffing practices to organizational level measures of performance. *Personnel Psychology, 46,* 27–48.

Tesluk, P. E., & Jacobs, R. R. (1998). Toward an integrated model of work experience. *Personnel Psychology, 51,* 321–355.

Tett, R. P., Jackson, D. N., & Rothstein, M. (1991). Personality measures as predictors of job performance: A meta-analytic review. *Personnel Psychology, 44,* 703–745.

Uniform guidelines on employee selection procedures. (1978). *Federal Register, 43,* 38290–38315.

Van Maanen, J., Dabbs, J. M., Jr., & Faulkner, R. R. (1982). *Varieties of qualitative research.* Thousand Oaks, CA: Sage.

Welbourne, T., & Andrews, A. (1995). *Predicting performance of initial public offering firms: Should HRM be in the equation?* (CAHRS Working Paper 95–02). Ithaca, NY: Cornell University, School of Industrial and Labor Relations.

Name Index

Subject Index

A

"A" levels, 255–256

Ability tests: utility analysis of, 129; validity of, 125. *See also* Cognitive ability tests; Physical ability tests

Academic *versus* nonacademic research settings, 406, 411–412

Acceptance phase, 78, 87

Accessibility, of work environment, 327

Accommodation for persons with disabilities, 319–364; Americans with Disabilities Act requirements for, 320–327, 328–329; application for, 328–333; centralized *versus* decentralized approach to, 348–349; complex, 350–357; "direct threat to health and safety" limitation on, 335–336; duty to make, 333–334, 335–336; evidence requirements for, 331–333; flagging scores for, 349; frequency of requests for, 358; industrial/organizational psychology role in, 388–389; informational resources on, 360–364; initiation of, 328–336, 348–349; innocuous, 350; legal *versus* psychometric issues in, 357–358; levels of, 349–350; limitations on duty to make, 335–336; litigation of failure to make, 328–329, 336–342; on-the-spot, 348–349; organizational approaches to, 348–357; overprediction effect of, 357, 358–359; perspective for, 357–359; psychometric research on, 342–348; psy-chometrically complex, 350–357; reasonable, 320–321, 327–336; reasonable, defined, 334; retesting for, 330–331; selection psychology research on, 403; test content modifications for, 352, 356–357; test waiver for, 335, 352, 356–357; in testing for groups of jobs, 334–335; testing medium modifications for, 350, 351, 353–354; undue hardship limitation on, 335; untimely self-identification and, 330–331. *See also* Americans with Disabilities Act; Americans with Disabilities Act claims

"Accomplishment record" approaches, 57

Accumulative conclusions, 408

Achievement orientation, team member, 221, 222

Achievement-oriented cultures, 251–253

Act quickly, ability to (as worker attribute), 45

Actor-referent-object approach, 230–231

Adams Mark Hotel, 304, 310

Adaptability, 263

Administration cost, 104

Administrative efficiency: for customers of selection, 181, 183; dimensions of, 143; importance of, to human resource constituents, 143–144; metrics of, 143, 147; and value of selection, 142–144

Administrative Office for U.S. Courts, 302